JAY DIAMOND
Professor Emeritus,
Nassau Community College

RETAIL

ADVERTISING

and

PROMOTION

FAIRCHILD BOOKS
NEW YORK

EXECUTIVE EDITOR: Olga T. Kontzias

SENIOR ASSOCIATE ACQUIRING EDITOR: Jaclyn Bergeron

ASSISTANT ACQUISITIONS EDITOR: Amanda Breccia

EDITORIAL DEVELOPMENT DIRECTOR: Jennifer Crane

DEVELOPMENT AND LINE EDIT: Progressive Publishing Alternatives

CREATIVE DIRECTOR: Carolyn Eckert

ASSISTANT ART DIRECTOR: Sarah Silberg

PRODUCTION DIRECTOR: Ginger Hillman

PRODUCTION EDITOR: Jessica Rozler

COPYEDITOR: Susan Hobbs

ANCILLARIES EDITOR: Noah Schwartzberg

PHOTO RESEARCHERS: Linda Sykes Picture Research, Inc., Hilton Head, SC; Lauren Vlassenko

COVER DESIGN: Carolyn Eckert

COVER ART: Photo by Pat Tobin/Courtesy of Getty Images

TEXT DESIGN: Hans Teensma

PAGE COMPOSITION: SR Desktop Services, Ridge, NY

IMAGE CREDITS: page xviii: Courtesy of iStockphoto/Alex Slobodkin; page 2: Image courtesy of The Advertising Archives; page 28: PRNewsFoto/Gap; page 50: Courtesy of iStockphoto/Alex Slobodkin; page 53: Concept and design by 3 Advertising. Illustration by Ted Boonthanakit. ©2010 Seattle Fish Company of New Mexico; page 78: Josh Olins/United Colors of Benetton; page 102: © Cooter/Alamy; page 124: Art Director: Mike Fiorentino/Copy Writer: Chris Kostyal/Agency: Big House Communications, Inc., Vancouver, BC; page 150: Billboard: Geoffrey Holman/iStockphoto; page 152: Photo by Carolyn Eckert; page 176: Courtesy of Elizabeth Arden; page 202: © Kevin Foy/Alamy; page 203: Getty Images/Justin Sullivan; page 258: © TS Corrigan/Alamy; page 278: Courtesy of iStockphoto/Thomas Acop; page 280: Bloomberg via Getty Images; page 310: © Lloyd Sutton/Alamy; page 328: Courtesy of iStockphoto/Alex Slobodkin; page 330: Courtesy of WWD/ David Pruitting; page 354: Courtesy of WWD/ Kyle Ericksen; page 379: Associated Press/Frank Franklin II; page 400: Getty Images/Moises De Pena

Library of Congress Catalog Card Number: 2010925369

ISBN: 978-1-56367-898-1

GST R 133004424

Printed in the United States of America

TP08

RETAIL ADVERTISING *and* PROMOTION

Contents

Extended Contents

311   Broadcast Media

PART FIVE: PROMOTIONAL TOOLS USED BY RETAILERS

331   Special Events

355   Visual Merchandising

PART SIX: PUTTING IT TOGETHER

Preface

One of the ways in which retailers promote their companies and the merchandise that they sell is through advertising. Using a variety of media they are able to contact those who have been regular patrons as well as others who are potential customers. Although increased sales is always the goal of the merchant, and advertising helps to accomplish this goal, it is also the promotional activities in which they are involved that often bring them additional recognition from the consumer. By dovetailing the two, many retailers have come to enjoy success that has separated them from the competition. The art of creating distinguished advertising and promotional devices is no simple matter. It requires a wealth of professionalism to translate the retailer's mission into advertisements and promotions that will capture the attention of the consumers and sufficiently motivate them to respond by satisfying their shopping needs.

Although there are numerous texts in the field that address advertising and promotion in a general manner, the pages of this book are the only ones that exclusively concentrate on the retailing industry and the activities that its participants engage in to capture the attention of the consuming public. Instead of concentrating on the likes of the Fortune 500 business giants, as the vast majority of texts do, *Retail Advertising and Promotion* exclusively explores the promotional endeavors of the marquee retailers like Macy's and Bloomingdale's as well as the small proprietorships such as boutiques that play an important role in satisfying the consumers' merchandise needs. By carefully exploring the pages of this text, those who are considering entering the retail field to impart their promotional expertise or those who are already engaged in retailing, a wealth of tried and true practices await their study.

Like the textbooks that are general in nature, *Retail Advertising and Promotion* explores all of the essential principles and practices in which the world of advertising and promotion is engaged to bring their best efforts to fruition. Topics such as the planning of the advertising program, the exploration of the media available for imparting the company messages, the technical needs used in the production of broadcast and print media, and the promotional tools that are used to generate consumer interest are all addressed in detail. The only difference is that every principle, practice, and application is retail-oriented. Unique to this text is a concluding section titled "Putting It Together." This section is devoted to the manner in which a small independent merchant dovetails the advertising and promotional tools that are available to his company. It requires more ingenuity and comparatively few dollars to carry out a successful campaign.

Whereas the basic principles and practices of advertising and promotion are explored throughout the text, each chapter is augmented with "Focus" sections that feature retailers, trade associations, agencies, and other organizations that in some way provide advertising and promotional expertise to the arena, and "Media Insights" that are reprints of articles from a variety of advertising publications and blogs. By examining these two features, the reader is able to get a first look

at the forecasts and happenings that comprise today's promotional scene. In addition to these two chapter highlights, the book is replete with a wealth of visuals that include advertisements from each of the media and promotions of special events that have distinguished retailers around the country.

Each chapter also features many pedagogical endeavors that help bring the greatest understanding of the material to the reader. Included are learning objectives, summaries of key points, terms of the trade, discussion questions, exercises and projects, and Web sites that can be used to further explore specific areas of advertising and promotion.

An instructor's manual is also available that contains a series of examination questions, as well as a PowerPoint presentation that highlights the major themes of the text.

PART ONE

INTRODUCTION TO ADVERTISING

Pepsi makes the party

Pepsi adds the light touch. This is the *light* refreshment—always refreshing, never filling. Have an ice-cold Pepsi anywhere: at home, at play— or at your favorite soda fountain. GOWNS BY PAULINE TRIGÈRE

"PEPSI-COLA" AND "PEPSI" ARE TRADEMARKS OF PEPSI-COLA COMPANY, REG. U. S. PAT. OFF.

Be Sociable, Have a Pepsi

Refresh without filling

The Impact *of* Advertising *on the* Retail Industry

CHAPTER OBJECTIVES

After you have completed this chapter, you will be able to discuss:

★   How retailing has changed since its introduction early in the history of the United States.

★   The roles of advertising and promotion in the retailer's everyday operation and how the two differ.

★   The historical development of advertising, from its use in ancient Greece and Rome to today, and how the focus of advertising has changed over time.

★   Many of the factors merchants consider before they make advertising commitments.

★   The media choices of the retail community that help them communicate with their regular customers and potential clienteles.

★   How retailing impacts the consumer in both positive and negative terms according to economists.

★   Retailers' expectations of advertising.

★   Why the government regulates advertising despite the industry's involvement in self-regulation.

★   Many of the probable changes and innovations the future holds for retail advertising.

As we entered the twenty-first century, retailers were experiencing challenges they had never encountered in the past. Not only did competition from the traditional on-site sources continue to escalate, but the impact from offsite ventures such as catalogue-only merchants and Internet operations began to significantly impact retailers' abilities to maintain positive sales positions. Products from every classification and price point became available through these outlets in such abundant quantities that consumers no longer needed to shop in stores to buy merchandise. The escalating competitive nature of retailing forced many marquee merchants to hang the GOING OUT OF BUSINESS sign or, in some cases, to be taken over by the giants of the industry. Legends such as Marshall Fields in Chicago, Rich's in Atlanta, and Burdines in Miami, for example, were absorbed into the Federated Department Stores and relabeled Macy's, as were numerous other well-known retail leaders.

Adding the enormous influx of foreign entities to the domestic retail mix further complicated the playing field for American merchants. No longer were the long-established players operating in the environments they once "owned": at this time different operating formats were surfacing, such as H&M, ready to capture some of their market.

Given the complexity of today's business scene, merchants must do everything in their power to meet and beat the challenges that begin with the development of new merchandising approaches. They need to offer unparalleled services, and culminate with creative advertising and promotional endeavors that will gain the attention of their existing clientele and attract new consumer markets. Industry professionals consider advertising a necessity to keep those in business profitable. The concepts of advertising, as well as other promotional endeavors that appear to have credibility in today's retail arena, are fully explored in this textbook to give those already in the field, or those with aspirations to enter it, the ability to professionally and capably apply accepted practices in a meaningful and productive manner.

This chapter discusses the factors that determine retailers' advertising commitments and influence their media selections. We review the benefits that retailers expect to gain from advertising and examine the past and current state of retailing. We also look at the history of advertising to lay the groundwork for the contents of this book.

Rounding out the perspectives of the advertising environment is a consensus of many economists' opinions regarding the impact of advertising on the consumer and industry, the regulations that govern mass communication efforts, and what the future of advertising is expected to reflect.

The first three parts of the book focus on advertising, and Part 4 underscores the role played by promotion in bringing the retailer's efforts to the attention of the consumer.

Retailing in the United States: Yesterday and Today

The avenues used to reach consumers were few in pre-colonial times, when retailing first began in the United States. The only game in town was the **trading post**, where bartering was the main attraction and patronization was merely on a hit-or-miss basis. Eventually, the first permanent shopping venue, the **general store**, appeared on the scene. At the general store, customers could buy everything from food and piece goods for their own needs, as well as feed and agricultural necessities for their livelihoods. Advertising was relegated to signage that was placed in the store's windows. In the late 1800s, when the **limited-line store** joined the fray, the business model was different, but the advertising efforts were basically the same as those used by the general store. Advertising as we know it today was not really a part of the limited-line store's operations, but visual merchandising was the sole promotional tool used to attract shoppers to the stores. Of these early entries, it is the limited-line store that remains a key player in retailing. Now called

a **specialty store**, it remains a significant part of today's retail scene. It was with venture that advertising became an important tool for increasing sales. Small merchants usually placed ads in local newspapers to alert potential shoppers to visit their stores. As these establishments became successful, they expanded into **chain organizations** and often embarked on advertising campaigns that had widespread coverage in newspapers and magazines, with some merchants using direct mail to sell their wares. The chain classification is still one of the more important ventures worldwide. Whether it is toys, household goods, clothing, accessories, electronics, cosmetics, shoes, or other products, chains of more than 1,000 stores are commonplace in retailing. As we explore later in the text, they remain one of the industry's major users of advertising to reach their markets.

Joining those already in business in the late 1800s was the **department store**. This major innovative undertaking led to a new concept that combined the diversity of product mix first offered by the general store with the specialization marketed by limited-line merchants; however, the approach of department stores had an orderliness of presentation not seen in earlier efforts. At the turn of the twentieth century, consumers throughout the United States embraced the department store concept, and its success would soon be realized. In addition to departmental merchandising and offering depth and breadth of product lines, the department store's presence was enhanced by significant consumer awareness, due in large part to consumers' embracing of advertising. Newspapers, magazines, and direct mail spearheaded the advertising explosion; later in the century, radio and television were added tools. Retailers continued to expand their promotional budgets because their advertising investments brought positive results to the department store's coffers.

With the expansion of the specialty stores as chains and the proliferation of the department store concept through **branch** additions, the need to advertise became even more obvious. No longer limited to local campaigns, merchants who were achieving national attention turned their attention to media that covered larger trading areas. **Spin-offs**, which are specialty units belonging to department store organizations, continued to surface as those enormous retail institutions

determined that representation of successful departments was the way to capture market segments. Bloomingdale's opening of several home furnishing centers, for example, necessitated significant advertising investments in addition to those earmarked for its individual department stores (Figure 1.1). Of course, throughout the twentieth century other forms of retailing were introduced with considerable success. **Discounters, off-pricers, manufacturer's outlets, designer boutiques, franchises, warehouse clubs, catalogue operations, cable programming,** and **Internet merchants** each brought a new business methodology, and with that new methodology, a need for more advertising and promotion. Not only were U.S. companies formed and expanded to reach the ever-growing population, but global retailers from almost every corner of the world joined the domestic landscape, making the scene more competitive and the need to advertise even more necessary.

Whatever the road taken by retailers to make their marks in this crowded business arena, be it one specific approach such as **bricks-and-mortar retailers** or a **multichannel approach,** the need to advertise continues to be of paramount importance for success. Table 1.1 lists the top 20 retailers in the United States.

Advertising: A Historical Perspective

Before a retail institution, or any business organization of any size, decides to advertise, it should develop an advertising plan. To be successful, a business should examine the competing businesses from the earliest to the most current ventures, so that executives can make meaningful decisions based on what has transpired, what routes have led others to success or failure,

1.1 Bloomingdale's is expanding through home furnishing spin-off stores. *Tim Boyle/Getty Images.*

TABLE 1.1

Top 20 Retailers in the United States, 2008

RANK	COMPANY	HEADQUARTERS	2008 REVENUE (000)	Y/Y CHANGE (%)	2008 EARNINGS (000)	Y/Y CHANGE	NO. OF STORES	Y/Y CHANGE
1	Wal-Mart	Bentonville, Ark.	$405,607,000	7.2%	$13,400,000	5.3%	7,873	8.4%
2	Kroger	Cincinnati	76,000,000	8.2	1,249,000	5.8	3,654	−0.2
3	Costco Wholesale Corp.	Issaquah, Wash.	72,483,020	12.6	1,282,725	18.5	544	5.0
4	Home Depot Inc.	Atlanta	71,288,000	−7.8	2,260,000	−48.6	2,274	1.8
5	Target Corp	Minneapolis	64,948,000	2.5	2,214,000	−22.3	1,682	5.7
6	Walgreens	Deerfield, Ill.	59,034,000	9.8	2,157,000	5.7	6,934	15.6
7	CVS Caremark Corp.	Woonsocket, R.I.	48,989,900	8.7	N.A.	N.A.	6,981	10.8
8	Lowe's Companies Inc.	Mooresville, N.C.	48,230,000	−0.1	2,195,000	−21.9	1,649	7.5
9	Sears Holdings Corp.	Hoffman Estates, Ill.	46,770,000	−7.8	53,000	−93.6	3,918	1.8
10	Best Buy Co. Inc.	Richfield, Minn.	45,015,000	12.5	1,003,000	−28.7	3,942	200.0
11	SUPERVALU Inc.	Eden Prairie, Minn.	44,564,000	1.2	−2,855,000	N.A.	2,421	−2.1
12	Safeway Inc.	Pleasanton, Calif.	44,104,000	4.3	965,300	8.7	1,739	−0.2
13	Rite Aid Corp.	Camp Hill, Pa.	26,289,268	8.1	−2,915,420	N.A.	4,901	−2.5
14	Macy's Inc.	Cincinnati	24,892,000	−5.4	−4,803,000	N.A.	847	−0.7
15	Publix Super Markets Inc.	Lakeland, Fla.	23,929,064	4.0	1,089,770	−8.0	1,044	7.4
16	McDonald's Corp.	Oak Brook, Ill.	23,522,400	3.2	4,313,200	80.1	31,967	1.9
17	Ahold USA Inc.	Chantilly, Va.	21,830,000	4.0	N.A.	N.A.	711	0.9
18	Delhaize America Inc.	Salisbury, N.C.	19,239,000	5.9	N.A.	N.A.	1,594	1.5
19	Amazon.com Inc.	Seattle	19,166,000	29.2	645,000	35.5	—	N.A.
20	TJX Companies Inc.	Framingham, Mass.	18,999,505	1.9	880,617	14.1	2,652	3.5

N.A., not available or not applicable.

Note: The *STORES* Top 100 Retailers are ranked by annual revenues as reported in SEC filings, public statements by the companies, and, where noted, estimates based on Planet Retail research (planetretail.net).

Source: "STORES Top 100 Retailers 2008," *Stores Magazine*, July 2009.

and what tools seem to best maximize advertising investments. Using this research-oriented approach, dollars that are expended are more likely to bring positive results. A good starting point is a clear understanding of the meaning of advertising and promotion. In many discussions, advertising is considered part of promotion; in

others, it is a separate entity. In either case, these are some of the accepted definitions of each.

Advertising, according to many professionals in the field, is a form of communication that typically attempts to persuade potential customers to purchase or to consume more of a particular brand or service. For retail practitioners, advertising is an attempt to not only persuade consumers to buy a particular brand (except in the case of a **private label**) but also to convince shoppers to patronize their stores, catalogues, and Web sites no matter which brand or label is being promoted. MSN Encarta uses the term *mass communication* to show that advertising is not a one-on-one approach, as in sales, but rather is an all-encompassing effort.

Promotional advertising, which is examined later in the text, is described in many marketing texts as a frequently used tool that encourages purchasing. Susan Ward, in an article for About.com, specifies that promotion is different from advertising in that "promotion is the broader, all-inclusive term. Advertising is just one action you could take to promote your product or service. Promotion, as a general term, includes all of the ways available to make a product and/or service known to and purchased by customers and clients. A store might advertise a big promotion on certain items." Thus, a designer appearance, special sale, or fashion show would be a promotion. Advertising the special event or promotion would, the retailer hopes, increase customer attraction for the occasion.

Pre-Nineteenth-Century Advertising

Although retailing as we have come to know it did not really exist before the nineteenth century (except for the trading post and general store), in ancient Greece and Rome sales messages painted on walls or rocks were commonplace. In Europe during the Middle Ages, when most people were illiterate, cobblers, millers, and other merchants used signs with images (a shoe, a bag of flour) to identify their products.

In the fifteenth and sixteenth centuries, printing was developed, and advertising handbills were commonly used to call attention to the wares being sold. And in England, during the seventeenth century, early print advertisements began to appear in weekly newspapers.

Nineteenth-Century Advertising

As merchants in European countries such as England and France engaged in what was primarily newspaper advertising, American merchants followed suit. In order to assist with their messages, **advertising agencies** opened their doors, and many businesses, retailers included, employed their services. The first of these agencies was N.W. Ayer & Son of Philadelphia; the agency provided not only layouts, copy, and artwork but also assumed responsibility for the ad's contents. N.W. Ayer was the forerunner to the full-service ad agencies abundant in the United States today.

Recognizing that advertising was the route to customer awareness, retailers who were to become giants in the field embraced the concept. In 1826, Lord & Taylor, followed by Macy's in 1858, began its investment in newspaper advertising. Soon after, in 1876, Wannamaker's, a major Philadelphia merchant (eventually absorbed by the Macy's chain), began advertising. Others in the retailing world soon followed suit, and newspaper advertising was on its way to becoming the major tool for mass retail communication.

Twentieth-Century Advertising

As the major retailers spread their wings by opening branches and limited-line stores expanded through increasing numbers of units, advertising commitments became more aggressive. Not only did the budgets include significant increases in newspaper spending but also other media reliance was now in play. Early on, direct marketing pieces were used to attract the attention of regular customers and potential shoppers. These pieces were often one-page fliers that announced everything from new merchandise to special sales. Starting out with these simple mailers in the late 1800s, Sears expanded its direct-mail advertising with catalogues in the early 1900s that served as both advertising vehicles and sales tools. In the 1920s, with 60 percent of American households now having radios in their homes, retailers started using that medium for advertising. In the late 1940s and early 1950s, television offered another medium through which retailers could communicate with the consumer market. Eventually, television became an important outlet for retail advertising.

Today, all of the aforementioned media are still used by merchants for mass communicating with audiences that range from loyal customers to prospective patrons. The list of media has now been expanded to include the Internet, cable television, digital communications, and the like.

TABLE 1.2

Advertising Expenditures

	1993	1994	1995	1996	1997	1998	1999	2000	2001	2002	2003	2004	2005
Newspapers	31,869	34,109	36,092	38,075	41,330	43,925	46,289	48,670	44,305	44,102	44,939	48,244	49,436
Magazines	7,357	7,916	8,710	9,180	9,821	10,518	11,433	12,370	11,095	10,995	11,435	12,247	12,847
Broadcast TV	28,020	31,133	32,885	35,965	36,893	39,173	40,011	44,802	38,881	42,068	41,932	46,264	44,323
Cable TV	2,564	3,034	3,595	4,360	7,237	8,547	12,570	14,429	15,736	16,297	18,814	21,527	23,654
Radio	9,457	10,529	11,320	12,105	13,491	15,073	17,215	19,295	17,861	18,877	19,100	19,581	19,640
Direct Mail	27,266	29,638	32,900	34,840	36,890	39,620	41,403	44,591	44,725	46,067	48,370	52,191	55,218
Yellow Pages	9,517	9,825	10,275	10,845	11,423	11,990	12,652	13,228	13,592	13,776	13,896	14,002	14,229
Miscellaneous	17,281	18,812	20,315	21,820	23,940	25,890	28,490	31,491	28,895	30,730	31,990	34,645	35,692
Business Papers	3,260	3,358	3,525	3,845	4,109	4,232	4,274	4,915	4,468	3,976	4,004	4,072	4,170
Out of Home	1,090	1,167	1,260	1,360	1,455	1,576	4,780**	5,176	5,134	5,175	5,443	5,770	6,232
Internet					600	1,050	2,832	4,333	5,645	4,883	5,650	6,853	7,764
TOTAL ALL MEDIA	137,924	149,783	161,120	172,804	187,200	201,594	221,949	243,300	231,349	236,946	245,573	263,766	271,074

Source: Advertising Association of America.

Table 1.2 traces advertising expenditures from 1993 to 2005 for each type of media. Each is fully explored in later chapters in terms of its importance in today's retail environment, market reach, costs, production techniques, and so forth.

Determinations for Making the Advertising Commitment

When a company, no matter how large or small, has committed itself to remaining a viable retail outlet, a number of different factors must be addressed before the right advertising and promotional approach is put into play. The company must assess areas such as the present size of the company in terms of units and/or sales volume, market size, expansion plans, new merchandising models, ethical initiatives, special promotions, seasonal events, unplanned circumstances, institutional needs, planning and budgetary strate-

gies, and so forth. Each of these considerations is addressed here in a limited manner but is given greater attention throughout the text in the relevant chapters.

Company Size

Without question, one of the major factors that determine the size and scope of an organization's commitment to advertising is its size. Department stores and large specialty chains lead the way in promoting their products, services, and names. Examining both print and broadcast media, immediately a wealth of single ads as well as campaigns that concentrate on either products or **institutional messages** is apparent. Sales volume, or the present number of units or projections, also figures into the size of the expenditures.

Expansion Programs

Retailers that are achieving success often make plans to expand their operations. For the bricks-and-mortar merchant, this expansion might be additional units, entering the Internet market, establishing a catalogue operation, or expanding its present offsite presence. Whatever the approach, success is generally predicated on committing to short-term and long-term advertising programs that will pursue broader markets.

New Merchandising Models

The trap of remaining stagnant in terms of merchandising philosophies sometimes spells defeat for a retailer. The status quo often results in hanging the GOING OUT OF BUSINESS sign. Students of retailing history and industry professionals may recall retail giants such as Abraham & Straus, Montgomery Ward, Wanamaker's, and Marshall Fields, all marquee names that either went out of business or were absorbed into other organizations. Each had its own woes in maintaining a place in retailing, the causes of which are numerous. Many merchants could have faced similar circumstances, but new merchandising models helped them resurrect themselves. A case in point is Banana Republic. Originally a khaki-laden emporium with safari merchandise, Banana Republic reinvented itself with a modern approach, new merchandising techniques, and appeals that captured a new market. Through keen advertising strategies and significant budgetary commitments, it became a "new" successful brand that led to widespread expansion.

Special Promotions

The same old everyday, often monotonous, business approach may lead to a company's downfall. Retailers that lend excitement to their onsite and offsite ventures by promotional campaigns may find that this approach will keep the company alive. Developing promotions is a task that demands creativity and ingenuity. Getting the attention of the consumer is another requirement that can make or break such an event. The use of advertising is one way in which promotions may be highlighted (Figure 1.2).

Ethical Initiatives

Popular buzzwords of the 21st century are **going green**. Retailers, as well as other businesses, governmental agencies, consumer groups, and

1.2 The Macy's Thanksgiving Day Parade is an annual special promotion.
Matthew Peyton/Getty Images.

the like, became involved in numerous ways to do their part in protecting the environment. America's largest retailer, Wal-Mart, broke a national advertising campaign that included print, broadcast, and online ads, along with a 16-page insert in many issues of popular consumer magazines, that addressed **sustainability**. Featured were products that helped the consumer live "greener" in the world. Augmenting the advertising campaign was store signage that offered information on environmental benefits and the impact of sustainable products.

Throughout this text, significant attention focuses on the advertising and promotional aspects of going green.

Seasonal Events

One of the mainstays of retailing is the seasonal event. Season openings for fashion retailers, holidays such as Christmas and Mother's Day, events such as back-to-school sales, and so forth compel merchants to spend large sums on advertising. The Christmas selling season, for example, is the time when retailers spend the major portion of their advertising budgets. The days that precede Black Friday (the first day of the major shopping period immediately after Thanksgiving) are used to motivate shoppers to begin their holiday purchasing. Newspaper inserts and television commercials, in particular, offer boundless promotions for consumers to consider. The hope is that a sufficient number of shoppers will help retailers meet their anticipated sales figures.

Unplanned Circumstances

The famous recession of 2008 saw many merchants' planned sales erode, which left them with unprecedented inventory levels. Most retailers resorted to drastically reducing prices in an attempt to encourage purchasing. This is just one example of how advertising played an important role in alerting shoppers to bargains and helped sellers reduce their unusually large merchandise stock. Such ads are not part of the planned advertising budgets, but the need for inventory reduction or other unplanned circumstances necessitates these actions.

Institutional Needs

Many merchants use advertising to promote goodwill, acknowledge worthy causes, address social issues, raise consciousness, and underscore image. With the use of broadcast and print

1.3 Green initiatives are examples of institutional promotions. *Courtesy of Barneys.*

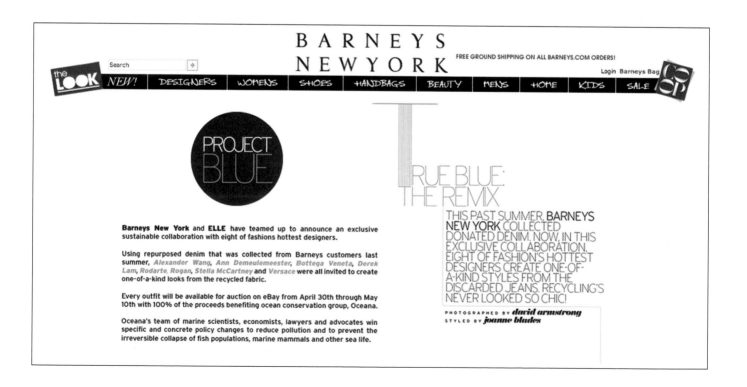

BARNEYS NEW YORK
FREE GROUND SHIPPING ON ALL BARNEYS.COM ORDERS!

Search
Login Barneys Bag

the LOOK | NEW! | DESIGNERS | WOMENS | SHOES | HANDBAGS | BEAUTY | MENS | HOME | KIDS | SALE

PROJECT BLUE

TRUE BLUE: THE REMIX

Barneys New York and **ELLE** have teamed up to announce an exclusive sustainable collaboration with eight of fashions hottest designers.

Using repurposed denim that was collected from Barneys customers last summer, *Alexander Wang, Ann Demeulemeester, Bottega Veneta, Derek Lam, Rodarte, Rogan, Stella McCartney* and *Versace* were all invited to create one-of-a-kind looks from the recycled fabric.

Every outfit will be available for auction on eBay from April 30th through May 10th with 100% of the proceeds benefiting ocean conservation group, Oceana.

Oceana's team of marine scientists, economists, lawyers and advocates win specific and concrete policy changes to reduce pollution and to prevent the irreversible collapse of fish populations, marine mammals and other sea life.

THIS PAST SUMMER, BARNEYS NEW YORK COLLECTED DONATED DENIM. NOW, IN THIS EXCLUSIVE COLLABORATION, EIGHT OF FASHION'S HOTTEST DESIGNERS CREATE ONE-OF-A-KIND STYLES FROM THE DISCARDED JEANS. RECYCLING'S NEVER LOOKED SO CHIC!

PHOTOGRAPHED BY *david armstrong*
STYLED BY *joanne blades*

the like, became involved in numerous ways to do their part in protecting the environment. America's largest retailer, Wal-Mart, broke a national advertising campaign that included print, broadcast, and online ads, along with a 16-page insert in many issues of popular consumer magazines, that addressed **sustainability**. Featured were products that helped the consumer live "greener" in the world. Augmenting the advertising campaign was store signage that offered information on environmental benefits and the impact of sustainable products.

Throughout this text, significant attention focuses on the advertising and promotional aspects of going green.

Seasonal Events

One of the mainstays of retailing is the seasonal event. Season openings for fashion retailers, holidays such as Christmas and Mother's Day, events such as back-to-school sales, and so forth compel merchants to spend large sums on advertising. The Christmas selling season, for example, is the time when retailers spend the major portion of their advertising budgets. The days that precede Black Friday (the first day of the major shopping period immediately after Thanksgiving) are used to motivate shoppers to begin their holiday purchasing. Newspaper inserts and television commercials, in particular, offer boundless promotions for consumers to consider. The hope is that a sufficient number of shoppers will help retailers meet their anticipated sales figures.

Unplanned Circumstances

The famous recession of 2008 saw many merchants' planned sales erode, which left them with unprecedented inventory levels. Most retailers resorted to drastically reducing prices in an attempt to encourage purchasing. This is just one example of how advertising played an important role in alerting shoppers to bargains and helped sellers reduce their unusually large merchandise stock. Such ads are not part of the planned advertising budgets, but the need for inventory reduction or other unplanned circumstances necessitates these actions.

Institutional Needs

Many merchants use advertising to promote goodwill, acknowledge worthy causes, address social issues, raise consciousness, and underscore image. With the use of broadcast and print

1.3 Green initiatives are examples of institutional promotions. *Courtesy of Barneys.*

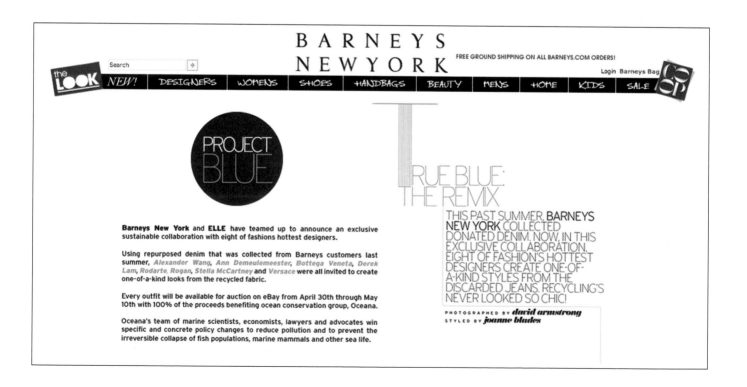

media, they attempt to appeal to the public with messages that will bring future sales to fruition (Figure 1.3). Unlike promotional or product advertising, the results of which are more easily measured, the success of these investments is difficult to measure. Nonetheless, professional advertising executives use institutional formats to reach targeted audiences.

Planning and Budgetary Strategies

Retail organizations plan their advertising strategies using a variety of techniques, such as the percentage-of-sales method and the task method. Whichever approach is used, the organization should make an advertising commitment so that its desired sales will be achieved. Planning and budgeting strategies are so vital to a retailer's success, and Chapter 5 is devoted to these topics.

Putting the Advertising Plan into Action

After the advertising commitment has been made, it is essential to evaluate the available media and to determine how each will best help the merchant reach projected sales goals. The task is generally approached from a historical perspective; that is, past experiences with advertising are evaluated in terms of their successes and failures. This knowledge is coupled with any new approaches in advertising as extolled in professional journals, seminars, and trade association recommendations and with any other meaningful resources.

In terms of past experience with advertising approaches, merchants have used a variety of outlets to communicate with their regular customers and potential shoppers who might consider these stores as viable places to satisfy their product needs. For the small-business entrepreneur, the ideal reach is local in nature because his or her market is generally restricted to a small trading area. For larger retailers, local, national, and perhaps international reach is the goal. With the advent of the Internet, more and more merchants are looking globally to attract shoppers to their companies.

Whatever the ideal targeted market, businesses have numerous media options for reaching them.

Each is briefly addressed here, and broader discussion is offered in later chapters.

Newspapers

Newspapers offer attributes such as timeliness, relatively inexpensive costs, and wide readership. Although television is a more widely used medium for businesses in general, retailers more commonly use display ads. Display ads may be run on occasional, individual basis, or they may be full campaigns that cover broader time periods. Institutional ads, or the image-building variety, are used to a lesser extent. Each retail organization must apportion its budget to decide which route to take in its pursuit of shoppers.

Although the newspaper is still considered the lifeblood of retail advertising by many of the industry's giants, there is a growing concern about the significant decline in the number of newspapers now being published. This problem is discussed in Media Insight 1.1.

Television

The "live" action of television creates excitement with sound and images, but it is often not cost effective for many retailers to use. By and large, it is the major companies that use this outlet, but not as frequently as other media. Airtime costs, production costs, the significant lead time required for production, the inability to focus on narrow markets, and so forth make television impractical for widespread use. When special events such as Black Friday sales are planned and large turnout may be motivated by its usage, television is often used.

Radio

Radio attracts only about 8 percent of U.S. advertising dollars. It is primarily a local tool and is used sparingly by retailers. It is most widely used when special sales or events are scheduled. Radio has seen a small increase in usage with the proliferation of such devices as the Sony SRF-59 FM/AM Walkman and Apple iPod, which enable users to listen when they are performing physical activities in the gym, relaxing on the beach, or taking walks. Radio is a relatively inexpensive way to reach consumers, thus making it a choice for many smaller merchants with limited market size.

Drastic Decrease Predicted in Number of Major U.S. Newspapers: Younger Readers Get Their News from the Internet

Washington—Most U.S. big-city daily newspapers will disappear in the next 20 years to be reinvented through the Internet and other "new media" forms, several journalism experts tell America.gov.

Paul Gillin, a Massachusetts-based writer and media consultant specializing in information technology topics, said he expects the survival of only four or five major newspapers, which include the *Washington Post, New York Times, Wall Street Journal,* and *USA Today.*

Those newspapers will continue to exist, he said, because they all made a wise business decision to invest money for national distribution of their publications to gain more readers.

Gillin, who writes a blog (online journal) called "Newspaper Death Watch," said major U.S. newspapers continue to offer valuable news. "But their business models simply won't survive . . . the economics are all working against them," Gillin said. By this, he means that papers are experiencing huge financial losses because of the high overhead for a large staff of reporters and for those who design, manufacture, and circulate the product.

The financial losses are made worse by demographic studies showing that people under age 30 do not read traditional print newspapers, Gillin said. The younger generation, he said, now gets its news largely on the Internet.

Gillin said he expects an "explosion" in what he called small journalism, involving free community newspapers that can be read for a 25- to 30-minute commute to work. The trend, he said, is typified by a company called Metro International, which publishes free newspapers in Boston, New York, Philadelphia, and other cities around the world aimed at offering news that appeals to young, upwardly mobile professionals.

Gillin also expects corporations to take advantage of the void left by the demise of daily newspapers by using "cheap, online tools to become, in essence, corporate publishers."

"We're already seeing professional journalists move into the capacity of corporate publishers," he said. That means, Gillin said, "the need for professional communicators will continue to be high."

Journalists also will need training in becoming "multimedia" reporters, in which they learn to shoot video "in the field" to complement their story.

In addition, Gillin said, journalists will have to become "aggregators," meaning that a published story will continue to expand by using such new media tools as podcasts and videos.

"We have to get rid of this idea that once a story is published that's the end of it," Gillin said. The journalists will serve as the "funnel" in which updates constantly are being added to stories, the method employed by the online information service called Wikipedia.

Gillin wrote in his February 14 [2008] blog that if Thomas Jefferson (third U.S. president, 1801–1809) were alive today, "he'd be an active blogger." The new forms of media, Gillin said, represent "the most democratic process to hit the publishing industry in 500 years."

Objective Reporting Seen as Outdated

Steve Boriss, associate director of the St. Louis–based Center for the Application of Information Technology at Washington University, sees news becoming part of "one big industry of entertainment, ranging from the very serious to the whimsical."

Boriss, who also writes a blog called "The Future of News," said news reporters will be aggregators and packagers of news stories who add their own opinion and analysis to articles.

He says a "myth" developed over the past 100 years that news stories were to be reported with total objectivity and without the reporter's personal opinion.

But a reporter's selection of what are the relevant facts for an article also represents an opinion, Boriss said. "It's the opinion of what [a reporter] thinks is important."

Boriss said the United States, at its creation, was supposed to be about people expressing themselves freely and debating issues. Offering your opinion was "sacred," he said.

Some 100 years ago, Boriss said, "Attempts were made to turn journalism into a science and journalists into truth-tellers. It's a model that's lasted longer than it should have." The old "model is falling apart," he added.

Boriss said major newspapers such as the *New York Times* and the *Washington Post* traditionally have set the "national conversation," with the TV networks following their lead.

"But now the Internet is allowing many, many conversations and all the news doesn't have to be filtered through a [small] supply chain," he said.

Boriss wrote in his blog that "after a Darwinian struggle, Internet news will be the only news medium to survive."

Former Reporter Would Be Sorry to See Newspapers Go

Not everyone is thrilled by the predicted changes for journalism. Former *New York Times* reporter Charles Kaiser, for instance, says that for him, reading the printed newspaper is a "vastly better experience" than reading it on the Internet.

"There's just no way you can see as many stories in an hour [on the Internet] as you will flipping through the paper version," said Kaiser, also a noted author and former writer for *Newsweek* magazine and the *Wall Street Journal.*

Kaiser, who writes a blog called "Full Court Press," said he worries that the extinction of traditional printed newspapers will have negative unintended consequences.

Having fewer reporters, especially investigative reporters, Kaiser said, means "fewer things are looked at in depth, which is the essential role of the press in keeping democracy vibrant."

Source: U.S. Department of State's Bureau of International Information Programs, America.gov Web site: http://www.america.gov/st/democracy-english/2008/February/20080220114229lxenee rgo.323559.html. February 21, 2008.

Direct Mail

Sent either through the U.S. Postal Service or, increasingly, via e-mail, direct mail has become an extremely important tool for retailers to reach targeted audiences. By contacting regular customers who are on store mailing lists or potential purchasers whose addresses are obtained through the purchase of mailing lists, direct mail is considered a surefire way to communicate product information, special events, storewide sales, and so forth. The wealth of catalogues dispersed by direct mail continues to increase. It is not unusual for the average consumer to receive as many as five single-page mailers or catalogues in a day.

Yellow Pages

Telephone directories that list businesses according to their offerings and classification are augmented with display ads. These are local entries, and they are used by retailers of all sizes. Their costs are nominal, and directory ads are therefore attractive to small operations.

Magazines

Although magazines rank sixth in overall advertising usage in the United States, they are not significantly used by retailers. Cost, preparation time, and difficulty in targeting a narrow market make magazine advertising impractical for most merchants. Generally, it is used by high-end fashion retailers such as Saks Fifth Avenue, whose geographical presence justifies the investment, and other retailers, such as Gap, who benefit from very broad national coverage.

The Internet

With an increase in usage by consumers every year, the Internet has become a medium embraced by retailers. By using **banners**, **pop-ups**, and other devices, more and more merchants are moving vigorously into Internet advertising. As part of their multimedia approaches to reaching shoppers, major retailers, in particular, are using the Internet along with the traditional print and broadcast formats.

Outdoor Advertising

Although sparingly used by retailers, outdoor advertising is a method that some use in their overall advertising schemes. It offers considerable exposure to commuters and other travelers. Its advantage is that it offers the lowest cost per exposure of any major medium.

Miscellaneous Media

Car cards used in buses and trains, signs on buses and taxis, posters placed in subway stations, and taxi-top signage (Figure 1.4) are sparingly used. Retailers such as Gap and Banana Republic, however, make use of these **transit ads** in major cities where they have retail properties.

1.4 Transit ads are used to attract the attention of people on the street.
Fairchild Publications, Inc.

In store point-of-purchase tools such as posters, streamers, and banners offer yet another advertising approach that often promotes impulse buying. Placed in heavy traffic areas of a store, point-of-purchase advertising can help bring a product to the attention of the shopper.

Retailers' Expectations from Advertising

The major reason retailers of all sizes and classifications invest in advertising is because they expect to increase sales and maximize profits. Whether the company is a small entrepreneurship or an industrial giant, the advertising commitment it makes is intended to reach this goal and improve the company's position as a competitor in a very difficult business environment. Of course, the money that companies spend to meet their expectations vary according to the company's size and method of operation. The major players are involved in a multitude of advertising directions, but smaller merchants must narrow their involvement according to budget constraints and practical marketing goals.

Using the appropriate media to achieve market reach requires considerable expertise and judgment on the part of management, as do the approaches that the advertising will take. Some merchants use only product advertising, for example, in their pursuit of shoppers, whereas others might opt for a combination of product and institutional ads and special events to motivate purchasing. Still others might restrict their campaigns to underscore value and follow the route of promotional advertising. Whatever the approach, it is vital to have a definite plan of action that is compatible with the company's method of operation. If a fast turnover rate is the primary driver of the company, as is the case for discounters and off-pricers, then the use of promotional campaigns is probably the appropriate route to follow. On the other hand, if a fashion-first image is a factor that must be conveyed to the potential customers, a combination of institutional and product advertising might be the better direction.

The advertising direction should not be inflexible, but rather should be subject to change.

The annual reexamination and assessment of the company's promotional direction is typical, but changes might be in order earlier if circumstances such as economic downturns necessitate redirection. Whatever the prescribed time frame might be, a periodic evaluation of the company's advertising efforts are generally undertaken so that the expected results may be assessed and redeveloped if the expected goals are not reached.

If the projected sales goals and the anticipated return on the advertising investment are to be achieved, a number of different expectations from the promotional commitments must be realized. Some goals, such as increased sales from specific ads, should be immediately realized, whereas other goals, such as image building, might require longer-term advertising efforts.

Retailers hope to achieve a number of different immediate and future benefits by advertising their companies and products. If these expectations are realized, they will more than likely achieve the goal of profitability. In addition to sales increases and maximization of profits, companies expect from their advertising such benefits as gaining an advantage over their competitors, increasing overall sales and number of units sold, developing their own brands or private labels, selling goods when markups are maximized, and underscoring their commitment to and sponsorship of charitable causes.

To Gain a Competitive Advantage

Whether it is the major retailer who depends on in-store traffic for the bulk of its business, the small independent entrepreneur who relies on regular patronage from loyal customers, the catalogue merchant who relies on direct marketing for sales, the Internet company that gets its orders from online ordering, or the merchant who operates a **multichannel operation**, competition is keen. To capture a fair share of their markets and maintain a competitive edge, companies need to be in the public eye. Bricks-and-mortar retailers who regularly advertise, for example, have a distinct advantage over those who do not advertise but merely wait for passersby to come into their shops. By using motivational devices in their ads to stimulate interest in their products, retailers that advertise can expect a certain number of consumers to follow through with store visits and potential purchases. The regular advertising commitments of continuous media exposure to those who are considered loyal followers of the merchant and to those who have potential to become steady patrons often bring a return on this investment. Using hit-or-miss approaches to advertising—that is, using the media only once in while—does not usually result in the same impact that regular participation does, and those who forego advertising entirely probably will be less competitive.

To Increase Traffic in Bricks-and-Mortar Operations

Whereas some consumers visit stores on a regular basis to satisfy their shopping needs, others need some type of motivation to make a store visit. Before women were common in the workforce, meeting friends and enjoying lunch in the retailer's dining facility, as well as browsing the merchandise counters and racks, was considered entertainment for women of that day. Retailers could count on loyal customers to make these visits frequently. Today, however, with the vast majority of the female population in the workforce, shopping for pleasure is no longer part of their regular routines.

Because of time constraints, many consumers now replace in-store shopping with catalogue and Internet purchasing. These purchasing venues do provide the retailer with sales, but store visits generally result in larger purchases. A great deal of impulse purchasing takes place when consumers simply walk through the store aisles. Products such as cosmetics, in particular, are often bought without any preplanning.

Retailers generally turn to advertising to generate store traffic. By using product and promotional ads, they often motivate consumers to take time from their busy schedules to come to the stores to shop. When in the store, shoppers might purchase not only the advertised items but also products that simply catch their attention through attractive visual presentations.

To Increase Sales of Advertised Items

There is no doubt that merchandise purchases can occur without the use of advertising. Many shoppers stroll through stores and stop to examine merchandise that appeals to them, with

a purchase often the end result. These products are the winners that professional retail buyers have successfully merchandised. Although these items sell without having been advertised, many seasoned merchants believe that these very items when advertised will bring even greater sales results. When this is the case, these products will be reordered and will help the retailer maintain the necessary markup that leads to greater profitability. The number of these units sold at the regular price will also defray some of the losses necessitated by marking down slow sellers.

To maximize the sales potential of the advertised goods, professionals recommend the **cross-media approach**. That is, by using a combination of the media that has proved most successful in previous advertising endeavors, such as newspapers, magazines, television, direct mail, and so forth, the expected success of advertisements will be reached.

To Promote the Store as a Brand

Just as manufacturers try to establish their companies as brands, so do retailers. Many merchants achieve recognition and customer loyalty not merely because of the merchandise mix they offer but also because of the name recognition for their company. Examples of retailers that promote themselves as brands are Gap, Jos. A. Bank, Ann Taylor, and Banana Republic (Figure 1.5). Through their advertising campaigns, they underscore their names rather than the specific products they sell.

The goal of this type of promotion is to motivate shoppers to remember the advertiser's name and not manufacturer brands and labels that are available in a host of outlets.

To Expand the Awareness of Private Brands and Labels

Increasing numbers of retailers are developing private brands and labels in their merchandising plans. Most major traditional retailers create their own products so that they can reduce some of the competitive disadvantages, such as price-cutting, associated with stocking manufacturer's brands. In fact, some of today's more successful merchants, such as Gap and Banana Republic,

exclusively subscribe to the **store-is-the-brand concept**, requiring that only one label be merchandised throughout the company.

Although the potential for success with brand exclusivity is excellent, there is a need to significantly promote these store-produced goods. In the case of manufacturer brands, a great deal of advertising is used by the producers themselves to motivate consumer acceptance. By doing so, the retailer becomes the beneficiary of these campaigns and needs a much smaller outlay of money to encourage consumer purchasing. On the other hand, making the retailer's own products known requires significant spending by the merchant. Macy's, for example, initially spent considerable sums promoting its Charter Club label. The effort paid off, and the brand became a profitable part of the company's overall merchandise mix.

To Encourage Consumer Purchasing at Times That Maximize Profits

Retailers who deal in seasonal or fashion merchandise often have little time in which to sell their goods at profitable margins. They begin the new season at a time when they anticipate customers will be ready to commit to purchasing the new collections. Retailers such as Saks Fifth Avenue, Neiman Marcus, Bloomingdale's, and Bergdorf Goodman advertise early in the season when their markups are at their peaks. In this way, if the ads capture the attention of the shopper, and purchasing follows, the merchants will maximize profits. If, however, consumer purchasing is delayed and markdowns become necessary to motivate buying, profitability is decreased.

Similarly, those selling seasonal products such as ski apparel and swimsuits must also spend advertising dollars to encourage purchasing.

With the selling season window relatively short, those who are successful with their advertising expenditures will reap the benefits of maintaining their initial markups, a factor that leads to greater profitability.

To Assist in Charitable Causes

Many retailers participate in charitable events, and this serves two purposes. First, the retailers benefit by being recognized for their humanity and compassion, and second, they are often the beneficiaries of future purchases made by those who remember their charitable commitments. Neiman Marcus and Bloomingdale's have long been affiliated with charitable causes, presenting fashion shows that donate the proceeds to charity, luncheons that benefit worthy causes, and so forth (Figure 1.6).

When properly advertised, these events often make long-lasting impressions that provide goodwill and the eventual patronage of appreciative consumers.

To Address Ecological Initiatives

With today's headlines focusing on the need to save the environment from irreparable damage and to concentrate efforts on ecological advances, many retailers have initiated advertising campaigns to lend their assistance to these concerns. Their participation in these efforts are many and include refitting their premises with energy-saving installations; replacing packaging supplies such as plastic bags, which cause considerable problems at landfills, with reusable totes; replacing products manufactured from oil-based fibers with organic alternatives; and so forth.

Patagonia, a company that manufactures and retails its merchandise primarily through its catalogues, has been a leader in addressing **ecological initiatives**. In all of its catalogues, Patagonia devotes considerable space to addressing issues that impact conservation, climate change, energy alternatives, and the like. Through substantial advertising, it has successfully raised the consciousness of consumers to the concept of going green.

To Dispose of Slow-Selling Merchandise

Even with the best of intentions, the seasoned retail buyer makes merchandising mistakes. Although careful planning reduces the risk of filling the retailer's shelves with merchandise that does

1.6 Assisting charitable causes helps boost a retailer's image. *Courtesy Neiman Marcus.*

not appeal to prospective customers, it does not guarantee that everything will sell. Wrong colors, ill-fitting apparel, unforeseen circumstances such as inclement weather and economic downturns, and so forth result in quantities of items that must be cleared to make room for new arrivals.

The key to disposing of these unwanted items is generally a promotional sale. Merchandise that does not sell at the original selling price is generally marked down. The best way to make the shopper aware of these discounts is through advertising (Figure 1.7).

Merchants use a variety of media for this purpose. Newspaper ads, television commercials, radio announcements, direct-mail pieces, and Web site banners are some of the communication tools

used to advertise merchandise that needs quick disposal. A relatively new advertising approach used by retailers to divest themselves of sale items is e-mail. Retailers such as Brooks Brothers, Ralph Lauren, Vineyard Vines, Restoration Hardware, Bloomingdale's, and Harry & David use this format to notify their customers of the availability of certain goods at discount prices. The approach has advantages such as cost-effectiveness, quick notification, and targeted consumer reach and is reported to bring immediate positive results.

To Promote Special Events

One of the ways in which retailers promote their names and/or encourage in-store shopping is through the use of special events. These events include such extravaganzas as Macy's annual fireworks display (Figure 1.8) and Thanksgiving parade, designer appearances that introduce new collections, celebrity visits that capture the attention of faithful fans, cooking demonstrations by renowned chefs, and special shopping nights for regular customers.

To ensure that the public is aware of these events, advertising is the tool that generally promises the best results. Because promotions of this nature may be extremely expensive, as in the case of Macy's Thanksgiving Day Parade, the advertising investment is substantial. The company spends enormous sums of money on both print and broadcast media, which, coupled with Internet and digital advertising, costs enormous sums. However, the return on this investment, attested to by the numbers who come to watch the parade and make their way to the stores on Black Friday and by others who buy through the Web site, justifies the monetary commitments.

It should be noted that Macy's expenditure is extreme. Other retailer investments to promote special events may be significantly less. For example, notifying customers of a special sale via e-mail is virtually free.

Commemorate Events of Historical Significance

From time to time, events that are both inspirational as well as troubling become part of America's past. Most horrifically memorable in recent history was the September 11, 2001, attack on the World Trade Center in New York City,

1.7 Slow-selling merchandise is reduced for quick disposal. *Courtesy of DSW Shoe Warehouse.*

LEGENDARY DESIGNER EVENT

UP TO

50% OFF

HURRY... LUXURY ITEMS WON'T LAST!

COVETED ITALIAN LEATHER
HANDBAGS

STARTS BLACK FRIDAY, NOVEMBER 27
DOORS OPEN AT 8 AM

ONLY AT DSW UNION SQUARE AND CARLE PLACE

DSW
SHOE WAREHOUSE®

While supplies last.

1.8 The annual fireworks display calls attention to Macy's. *Wally Santana/ AP Images.*

where thousands of people were killed. Many merchants placed print ads in newspapers to honor their memories. On the brighter side, the election of Barack Obama as the first African-American president of the United States on November 4, 2008, not only made headlines but also was the subject of a multitude of retailers' newspaper advertisements. These ads, and others like them, are institutional in nature. They are used by retailers to underscore that they are not only purveyors of merchandise but also socially conscious–minded organizations.

Impact of Retail Advertising

Advertising offers many pluses to industry and the consumer alike, according to many economists. Whereas there are naysayers who disagree with this concept, those with positive beliefs about the impact of advertising offer the following:

- By making the consumer aware of the products and services that merchants offer, manufacturers often are the beneficiaries of increased sales in retail outlets. The increase in sales can lead to greater employment and thus boost the economy.

- Prices often decline if production increases, resulting in savings for the consumer. Electronics and food products are examples of this concept.

- Because they can review product details through advertisements, consumers benefit by making more educated purchases.

- By examining advertisements, consumers can spend less time looking for specific items, because ads generally tell shoppers where products are available.

Those with negative opinions about advertising offer the following:

- The cost of advertising adds to the ultimate price the consumer will pay.

- Advertising encourages purchasing that often is unnecessary, leading to the potential

for overspending and the inability to pay credit card balances.

- Teens are sometimes "pressured" to purchase items such as cosmetics to make themselves more appealing. The often questionable advertising claims for these products may lead to unrealistic goals and unhappiness.

Advertising Regulation

Some of the different ways in which regulation of advertising is carried out are presented here. In terms of ethics and integrity, a more detailed account is addressed in Chapter 2, "Ethics and Social Responsibility in Today's Advertising Arena."

Governmental Regulation

All levels of government are involved in the regulation of advertising. Federal, state, and local governments have enacted legislation throughout the years that affects the manner in which retailers communicate their offerings to consumers. Although self-regulation is on the rise in the industry, it alone does not sufficiently "police" advertising, thus necessitating government involvement.

THE FEDERAL TRADE COMMISSION

Established in 1914, the most important of the federal regulatory agencies in regard to advertising is the **Federal Trade Commission**, or FTC. Its overall responsibility is to oversee and enforce many different laws that protect the consumer, most importantly laws against misleading advertisements. An ad might contain misrepresentations, words of omission that might prove to be harmful, untruths, unsubstantiated claims, and so forth. Although the protections are in place to prevent misrepresentative ads, retailers are sometimes the culprits.

For the resolution of consumer claims, the Consumer Product Safety Commission, composed of five members appointed by the president and confirmed by the Senate, operates at the federal level. Case referrals come from individual consumers and court referrals by the court, governmental or trade agencies, or even from the attorney general of the United States.

Some of the concerns that arise from potential retail misrepresentation that are brought to the attention of the FTC include the following:

◆ Retail television ads that use substitute materials to make the products seem better than they actually are. In supermarket advertising, prepared foods are sometimes enhanced to give a better impression to the viewer.

◆ Print or broadcast ads that use celebrity endorsements where actual use by the endorser is suspect.

◆ Misusing the term "free," such as when a product advertised as free actually requires the purchase of another item.

More detailed concerns, such as puffery, that sometimes require FTC intervention are examined in Chapter 2.

LOCAL LEGISLATION

FTC regulation applies to advertising in interstate commerce when retailers and other businesses have operations that cross state lines; that is, companies such as Macy's, Bloomingdale's, Gap Stores Inc., and Wal-Mart, which have units in many states, are subject to the rulings of the FTC. In cases in which the organization is limited to intrastate advertising, many local laws have been enacted based on the **Printers Ink Model Law** of 1911, which deals with fraudulent advertising. In essence, the 1911 law specifies the following:

Any person, firm, corporation, or association, who with the intent to sell anything, directly or indirectly, to the public, publishes, disseminates, circulates or places before the public, or causes to be placed before the public, an advertisement of any sort which contains any assertion, representation or statement of fact which is untrue, deceptive or misleading, shall be guilty of a misdemeanor. (*Printers Ink*)

This law, initially intended to cover print media, has been adopted by many localities to include all media.

Industry Regulation

In an ever-increasing attempt to present advertising as having the highest standards for the sake of good business practices and ethical principles, retailers and trade associations continue to police themselves. Many major retailers have their own requirements regarding the appropriateness of advertising, as do such associations as the National Retail Federation (NRF) through its **Retail Advertising and Marketing Association (RAMA)** division, which is the subject of Focus 1.1.

The media establish advertising guidelines to ensure protection of their subscribers in terms of questionable advertising. The American Advertising Federation has long been an advocate of **truth in advertising**, as have the American Association of Advertising Agencies and the Association of National Advertisers. Watchdog agencies such as the Better Business Bureaus also play a role in promoting good advertising.

The Future of Advertising

As in every other aspect of business, changes and innovation in advertising are always on the horizon. Some have been monumental, others more subtle. The invention of television, for example, brought new dimensions to advertising. The Internet and its role as a vehicle for advertising to the masses in a new manner seems to have just scratched the surface in mass communication. Digital advertising is taking its place as yet another means of providing product information to consumers. These are just some of the past and current phenomena that have affected and continue to affect the manner in which retailers make consumers aware of their offerings. Following are a sampling of likely developments that will impact the future of advertising:

◆ Significant evidence shows that the number of major newspapers in the United States will continue to decrease. Declines in readership, especially with young readers, may result in the demise of newspapers or at least the reduction of pages in those that will remain in production. At the time of this writing, for example, the Tribune Company, owner of the *Chicago Tribune* and

Retail Advertising and Marketing Association (RAMA)

The National Retail Federation, or NRF as it is commonly called, is the world's largest retail trade association. Through a multitude of endeavors, it provides members with current information regarding the state of the industry and how their companies might better perform. Represented in its membership are all retail formats, such as department stores, chain organizations, drugstores, and grocers. The NRF represents an industry with more than 1.6 million retail operations in the United States, more than 25 million employees (which accounts for about one in five American workers), and sales of more than $4.5 trillion.

Recognizing that advertising is an integral part of the retailer's success, the NRF has as one of its divisions the Retail Advertising and Marketing Association, known in the trade as RAMA. It has a membership of about 1,600 retail marketing and advertising professionals from every conceivable type of company as well as their counterparts engaged in agency, media, and service-provider sides of the business. Its mission is "to provide visionary leadership that promotes creativity and excellence within all marketing disciplines that strategically elevates members and individuals" (From RAMA Web site: http://www.rama-nrf.org).

RAMA is the sponsor of the Retail Advertising Conference (RAC), the largest and most prestigious annual gathering of retail advertising and marketing professionals in the industry. The RAC is an event at which the retail world meets to promote creativity and inspiration. Retail professionals from global arenas such as Canada, South America, the United Kingdom, Western Europe, the Far East, Australia, New Zealand, and the United States are treated to industrial advertising exhibits featuring the latest in advertising products, services, and innovative technology. Sessions of vital interest to retail advertising professionals are presented by the industry's "stars."

In addition to the invaluable up-to-the-minute information gained by attending RAC, the benefits derived throughout the year from membership include the following:

◆ Consumer research that reports on the marketplace, a vital component in guiding future advertising.

◆ Publications that address industry-wide sales, economic activity, holiday season results, and industry matters on local and national levels.

◆ Quarterly economic reports that provide information on retail sales forecasts that could impact advertising expenditures.

◆ Interfacing with the NRF, which participates in proactive government relations dealing with issues involving advertising.

◆ Invaluable networking opportunities to exchange advertising techniques and strategies with colleagues from all over the world.

◆ Bimonthly newsletters that contain articles written by industry professionals, timely tips on advertising, and advice on a host of different topics that could substantially improve a company's advertising results.

RAMA is the only association of its kind that is globally based, thus providing pertinent information not available from any other group.

the *Los Angeles Times*, is filing Chapter 11 bankruptcy. If this is a sign of the times, newspaper advertising will decline, making the retailer opt for other formats to feature its product offerings. The article featured in Media Insight 1.1 earlier in the chapter presented an analysis of the situation.

◆ Global advertising for retailers will increase as a result of the Internet. Merchants will be able to reach consumer markets all over the world with their products. With the speed and accuracy of ordering online, merchandise unavailable in many parts of the world will now be easy to come by with Web site access. Pop-ups, flash advertisements, banners, and the like, already in use, will expand to bring even greater business. With this expected increase, it is a must for advertisers to be familiar with the cultural differences of people in order to make the right impression and realize sales. The information in Media Insight 1.2 is critical for those retailers who are expanding their global reach.

◆ Product placement and the showing of real stores on television programs and in films will probably be used on a larger scale than ever before.

◆ The use of digital advertising is expected to increase. Walgreens, the nation's largest drugstore chain, uses an ad network in Times Square, New York City, a 17,000-square-foot sign on a building in that heavily trafficked area (Figure 1.9). The sign displays messages from producers of products sold in the drugstores. From moving signs to iPhones and other handheld devices, consumers increasingly will be shown changing messages from retailers and other businesses.

◆ E-mail will continue to be a format that presents retailers' "news" directly to the consumer. Merchants such as Brooks Brothers, L.L. Bean, Vineyard Vine, and others regularly alert their customers of special events such as sales. This format is

designed by **GilmoreGroup**

particularly targeted to those who prefer to use the Internet for their information rather than the newspaper.

◆ The use of direct mail will increase, as evidenced by the large number of merchants who have become multichannel retailers. Mailings will be used not only at traditional time periods, such as during the Christmas selling season, but also throughout the year. Bloomingdale's, Neiman Marcus, and Tiffany & Co., at the high end of the retail ladder, already make significant use of direct mail frequently during the year.

1.9 Digital advertising on buildings helps attract the attention of the passersby. *www.broadcasting cable.com.*

International Advertising: Understanding Cultural Differences

Neil Payne

Culture is a little like dropping an Alka-Seltzer into a glass—you don't see it, but somehow it does something.

—Hans Magnus Enzensberger

Culture affects everything we do. This applies to all areas of human life from personal relationships to conducting business abroad. When interacting within our native culture, culture acts as a framework of understanding. However, when interacting with different cultures, this framework no longer applies due to cross-cultural differences.

Cross-cultural communication aims to help minimize the negative impact of cross-cultural differences through building common frameworks for people of different cultures to interact within. In business, cross-cultural solutions are applied in areas such as HR, team building, foreign trade, negotiations, and Web site design.

Cross-cultural communication solutions are also critical to effective cross-cultural advertising. Services and products are usually designed and marketed at a domestic audience. When a product is then marketed at an international audience, the same domestic advertising campaign abroad will in most cases be ineffective.

The essence of successful advertising is convincing people that a product is meant for them. By purchasing it, they will receive some benefit, whether it be lifestyle, status, convenience, or financial. However, when an advertising campaign is taken abroad, different values and perceptions as to what enhances status or gives convenience exist. These differences make the original advertising campaign defunct.

It is, therefore, critical to any cross-cultural advertising campaign that an understand-ing of a particular culture is acquired. By way of highlighting areas of cross-cultural differences in advertising, a few examples shall be examined.

Language in Cross-Cultural Advertising

It may seem somewhat obvious to state that language is key to effective cross-cultural advertising. However, the fact that companies persistently fail to check linguistic implications of company or product names and slogans demonstrates that such issues are not being properly addressed.

The advertising world is littered with examples of linguistic cross-cultural blunders. Of the more comical was Ford's introduction of the "Pinto" in Brazil. After seeing sales fail, they soon realized that this was due to the fact that Brazilians did not want to be seen driving a car meaning "tiny male genitals."

Language must also be analyzed for its cultural suitability. For example, the slogan employed by the computer games manufacturer EA Sports, "Challenge Every-thing," raises grumbles of disapproval in religious or hierarchical societies where harmonious relationships are maintained through the values of respect and nonconfrontation.

It is imperative, therefore, that language be examined carefully in any cross-cultural advertising campaign.

Communication Style in Cross-Cultural Advertising

Understanding the way in which other cultures communicate allows the advertising campaign to speak to the potential customer in a way they understand and appreciate. For example, communication styles can be explicit or implicit. An explicit communicator (e.g., United States) assumes the listener is unaware of background information or related issues to the topic of discussion and, therefore, provides it themselves. Implicit communicators (e.g., Japan) assume the listener is well informed on the subject and minimizes information relayed on the premise that the listener will understand from implication. An explicit communicator would find an implicit communication style vague, whereas an implicit communicator would find an explicit communication style exaggerated.

Colors, Numbers, and Images in Cross-Cultural Advertising

Even the simplest and most taken-for-granted aspects of advertising need to be inspected under a cross-cultural microscope. Colors, numbers, symbols, and images do not all translate well across cultures.

In some cultures, there are lucky colors, such as red in China, and unlucky colors, such as black in Japan. Some colors have certain significance; green is considered a special color in Islam, and some colors have tribal associations in parts of Africa.

Many hotels in the United States and United Kingdom do not have a room 13 or a 13th floor. Similarly, Nippon Airways planes in Japan do not have the seat numbers 4 or 9. If there are numbers with negative connotations abroad, present-ing or packaging products in those numbers when advertis-ing should be avoided.

Images are also culturally sensitive. Whereas it is common to see pictures of women in bikinis on advertising posters on the streets of London, such images would cause outrage in the Middle East.

Cultural Values in Cross-Cultural Advertising

When advertising abroad, the cultural values underpinning the society must be analyzed carefully. Is there a religion that is practiced by the majority of the people? Is the society collectivist or individualist? Is it family orientated? Is it hierarchical? Is there a dominant political or economic ideology? All of these will impact an advertising campaign if left unexamined.

For example, advertising that focuses on individual success, independence, and stressing the word "I" would be received negatively in countries where teamwork is considered a positive quality. Rebelliousness or lack of respect for authority should always be avoided in family-orientated or hierarchical societies.

By way of conclusion, we can see that the principles of advertising run through to cross-cultural advertising, too. That is—know your market, what is attractive to them, and what their aspirations are. Cross-cultural advertising is simply about using common sense and analyzing how the different elements of an advertising campaign are impacted by culture and modifying them to best speak to the target audience.

Source: Neil Payne, The Sideroad, www.sideroad.com.

- The projected growth of the Hispanic community will motivate retailers to increase their media expenditures. Table 1.3 provides the increased media spending patterns between 2006 and 2008. In addition, many retailers may alter some advertising formats to include dual copy. That is, messages will be in both English and Spanish in order to adequately communicate with multicultural audiences.

- Going green is likely to become more common in advertising campaigns because Americans are becoming increasingly aware of environmental issues and will be motivated to purchase products that are eco-friendly.

Summary of Key Points

- Retailing has evolved from the early forms of trading posts and general stores to a mix of newer entries such as the department and chain stores, as well as discount operations, off-price and manufacturer's outlets, designer boutiques, franchises, warehouse clubs, catalogue operations, cable programming, and Internet merchants. Many merchants use only one type of advertising, whereas others use the multichannel approach to reach their targeted markets.

- Advertising dates back to the ancient civilizations of Greece and Rome and has developed ever since as a major way for

TABLE 1.3 — Media Spending Patterns, 2006–2008

RANK	MEDIUM	U.S. ADVERTISING SPENDING IN HISPANIC MEDIA			
		2008	2007	%CHG	2006
1	Network/national TV	$1,807.3	$1,789.4	1.00%	$1,733.9
2	Local TV	707.4	707.0	0.05	690.1
3	National radio	221.8	221.3	0.20	214.3
4	Local radio	529.2	524.1	0.98	511.7
5	National newspapers (excl. classified)	124.0	123.8	0.19	120.7
6	Local newspapers (excl. classified)	186.2	185.7	0.25	182.0
7	Internet	225.5	179.9	25.40	132.0
8	Magazines	115.4	110.6	4.34	100.2
9	Out-of-home	86.9	86.2	0.79	83.9
	TOTAL	4,003.7	3,927.9	1.93	3,768.7

Source: Hispanic Fact Pact—2009, Advertising Age.

retailers to communicate their offerings to consumers. Today, newspapers remain the leading medium for merchant use, with direct mail making a strong bid to rival them. The Internet, although still a relatively new outlet, is gaining momentum as a medium to reach prospective shoppers.

◆ A retailer's advertising commitment is based on several factors, including the size of the company, its projected plans for expansion, changes in merchandising models, special promotions it undertakes, ethical initiatives, seasonal and institutional needs, and, of paramount consideration, its planning and budgetary strategies.

◆ The impact of advertising includes making the consumer aware of the products merchants have to offer, bringing the facts about the merchandise to the shopper's attention, and reducing the time it takes to complete the satisfying of the shopper's merchandise needs.

◆ Those with negative advertising opinions believe advertising contributes to increasing product costs, motivates unnecessary spending, and pressures consumers to purchase unneeded products.

◆ The regulation of advertising is twofold: it is shared by governmental oversight and by self-regulation by businesses themselves and groups such as trade associations.

◆ The future of advertising includes the potential for a decline in the number of newspapers that will be available to readers, an expansion of global reach, an increase in use of digital technology and e-mail to reach consumers, and the targeting of multicultural markets by tailoring ads to have more individualized messages.

◆ Promotion is a way in which retailers differentiate themselves from the competition. In-store events, such as special sales, demonstrations, fashion shows, and sampling, and off-premises events,

such as holiday parades and charitable functions, are just some of the formats in use today.

For Discussion

1. Differentiate among the numerous classifications of retailing, describing how each differs from the others.

2. Explain how retailers determine the depth and breadth of their advertising commitments by highlighting some of the areas of consideration used in these determinations.

3. Address the different forms of mass communication that merchants employ when they put their advertising plans into action.

4. Comment on the positive and negative impacts of advertising, according to professional economists, and defend each with sound reasoning.

5. If the retail community self-regulates in terms of its advertising outreach, discuss why there is a need for governmental oversight. Describe the different governmental and nongovernmental agencies that help regulate advertising.

6. Explain the reason for the increased attention by retailers to spreading their reach to global markets and identify which medium they will be using most often to achieve this goal.

7. Many merchants are expanding their efforts to attract multicultural population segments to their stores, catalogues, and Web sites. Discuss the reasons for these ambitions and how merchants will target these populations.

8. What are the retailers' expectations from advertising?

Exercises and Projects

1. Explore the different classifications of retailing and how each differs from the other. Make sure to highlight their methods of doing business, the consumer markets on which they focus their marketing efforts, and the multichannel efforts of many. The information may be taken from the Web sites of specific merchants or by accessing search engines such as Google.

2. Using business periodicals such as *Advertising Age* and *Stores Magazine* (available at most college and public libraries) as a resource, research how global advertising is impacting the retail environment. Make certain that you indicate the main populations that American retailers are pursuing and the media being used to capture these markets.

Web Site Exploration for In-Depth Analysis

About Retail
http://www.aboutretail.net/history/retail_history_index.htm
    This site provides a complete history of retailing and addresses many aspects of the industry.

Terms of the Trade

advertising

advertising agencies

banners

branch

bricks-and-mortar retailers

cable programming

catalogue operations

chain organizations

cross-media approach

department store

designer boutiques

discounters

ecological initiatives

Federal Trade Commission (FTC)

franchises

general store

going green

institutional messages

Internet merchants

limited-line store

manufacturer's outlets

multichannel approach

multichannel operation

off-pricers

pop-ups

Printers Ink Model Law

private label

promotional advertising

Retail Advertising and Marketing Association (RAMA)

specialty store

spin-offs

store-is-the-brand concept

sustainability

trading post

transit ads

truth in advertising

warehouse clubs

Ethics *and* Social Responsibility *in* Today's Advertising Arena

CHAPTER OBJECTIVES

After you have completed this chapter, you will be able to discuss:

★ The reasons retailers are embracing ethical standards for their advertising ventures.

★ How ethical advertising benefits retailers in today's business arena.

★ Which principles of ethical advertising are employed by most retailers in the United States.

★ Many of the unethical advertising practices some merchants employ in their ads.

★ How the Better Business Bureaus help regulate advertising.

★ The codes of ethics retailers use in carrying out their advertising responsibilities.

★ The different agencies that provide advertising oversight.

★ Why social responsibility has become an important part of many retailers' operations.

★ "Cause marketing" and its impact on helping charitable organizations.

The headlines that abound in today's newspapers and on television often speak of the unethical practices that have become commonplace in the spheres of business, government, investments, and other areas. Successful professionals have committed immoral deeds to make themselves financially secure at the cost of their companies and the people they serve. Fortunes have been lost and lives ruined due to greed. Although immoral practices have always been part of the fabric of society, today's participants seem to be in greater numbers than ever. Some retailers, for example, resort to many misdeeds in order to improve their bottom lines while short-changing the consumers they serve. Their dishonesty is especially obvious in the advertising nuances that many merchants use to entice shoppers to purchase from them.

It is not unusual to find advertisements that use terms such as "liquidation sale" when in fact prices have not been lowered. Customers find limited availability of advertised discounted items used as teasers only to bring shoppers to the stores. They see terms such as **comparable value**, which does not really mean anything, and they find advertised rebates that are difficult to redeem. Although arguably within the law, in many instances this type of advertising is unethical and often the cause of consumer pain and the eventual demise of many retail operations.

Although ignoring social responsibility is by no means an immoral or unethical action, doing so is considered by many to be a dereliction of duty for retailers. Does the retailer really have a moral obligation to engage in social responsibility at some level, or do its actions in such matters merely translate into a sound business practice? With operational costs spiraling upward, many merchants are foregoing the need to be concerned with anything but the products they sell. Given the uncertainty of today's retail environment, the question of social responsibility is not clear-cut.

This chapter focuses on both ethics and social responsibility. It discusses the need to ethically advertise to regular clientele and potential customers and the benefits both provide; the unethical practices that have become part of the advertising picture; the **codes of ethics** that address ethical advertising; and the industrial and governmental agencies that oversee advertising. A discussion of social responsibility underscores its role in the retailer's business as well as the use of **cause marketing**, in which advertising campaigns significantly influence the effectiveness of socially responsible endeavors.

Ethics

For retail practitioners who want to remain viable entries in an ever-competitive environment, it has become more important than ever to make consumers aware of the moral paths the retailers are taking. Not only are the appropriate merchandising philosophies and service parameters significant to retail success but it is also imperative that ethical standards are portrayed as part of the company's image. Before any retailer places a single advertisement or embarks on a complete campaign, the advertising department and the agencies that represent the retailer must understand that only ethical values can drive the advertising. To achieve the goals of bottom-line excellence and a positive image that meets the highest moral standards, management must consider some of the following factors in steering their operations toward success.

The Benefits of Ethical Advertising

Keeping loyal customers and attracting potential new shoppers often begins with the advertisements that retailers use to motivate purchasing on-site or off-site. Whether through newspapers, magazines, catalogues, direct mail, television, radio, or the Internet, ads must be straightforward, using the necessary ingredients of artwork and copy while avoiding unethical practices to make their selling points. If this approach is faithfully employed, then many benefits are likely to accrue.

For example, maintaining a regular customer base and building a broader clientele are two likely benefits of ethical advertising. Return business is the key to success in retailing, and without

Does Being Ethical Pay?

Companies spend huge amounts of money to be "socially responsible." Do consumers reward them for it? And how much?

Remi Trudel and June Cotte
May 12, 2008

For corporations, social responsibility has become a big business. Companies spend billions of dollars doing good works—everything from boosting diversity in their ranks to developing eco-friendly technology—and then trumpeting those efforts to the public.

But does it pay off?

Many companies hope consumers will pay a premium for products made with higher ethical standards. But most companies plunge in without testing that assumption or some other crucial questions. Will buyers actually reward good corporate behavior by paying more for products—and will they punish irresponsible behavior by paying less? If so, how much? And just how far does a company really need to go to win people over?

To find out, we conducted a series of experiments. We showed consumers the same products—coffee and T-shirts—but told one group the items had been made using high ethical standards and another group that low standards had been used. A control group got no information.

In all of our tests, consumers were willing to pay a slight premium for the ethically made goods. But they went much further in the other direction: They would buy unethically made products only at a steep discount.

What's more, consumer attitudes played a big part in shaping those results. People with high standards for corporate behavior rewarded the ethical companies with bigger premiums and punished the unethical ones with bigger discounts.

Finally, we discovered that companies don't necessarily need to go all out with social responsibility to win over consumers. If a company invests in even a small degree of ethical production, buyers will reward it just as much as a company that goes much further in its efforts.

The following looks at these tests in more detail. But first, a definition—and a caveat.

For our purposes, "ethically produced" goods are those manufactured under three conditions. First, the company is considered to have progressive stakeholder relations, such as a commitment to diversity in hiring and consumer safety. Second, it must follow progressive environmental practices, such as using eco-friendly technology. Finally, it must be seen to demonstrate respect for human rights—no child labor or forced labor in overseas factories, for instance.

Now the warning, which may not come as much of a surprise. Even though we think ethical production can lead to higher sales, not all consumers will be won over by the efforts. Some may prefer a lower price even if they know a product is made unethically.

With that in mind, here's a closer look at our results.

How Much Are Ethics Worth?

Our first experiment asked two questions. How much more will people pay for an ethically produced product? And how much less are they willing to spend for one they think is unethical?

To test these questions, we gathered a random group of 97 adult coffee drinkers and asked them how much they would pay for a pound of beans from a certain company. We used a brand that's not available in North America, so none of the participants would be familiar with it.

But before the people answered, we asked them to read some information about the company's production standards. One group got positive ethical information, and one group negative; the control group got neutral information, similar to what shoppers would typically know in a store.

After reading about the company and its coffee, the people told us the price they were willing to pay on an 11-point scale, from $5 to $15. The results? The mean price for the ethical group ($9.71 per pound) was significantly higher than that of the control group ($8.31) or the unethical group ($5.89).

Meanwhile, as the numbers show, the unethical group was demanding to pay significantly less for the product than the control group. In fact, the unethical group punished the coffee company's bad behavior more than the ethical group rewarded its good behavior. The unethical group's mean price was $2.42 below the control group's, whereas the ethical group's mean price was $1.40

above. So, negative information had almost twice the impact of positive information on the participants' willingness to pay.

For companies, the implications of this study—albeit limited—are apparent. Efforts to move toward ethical production, and promote that behavior, appear to be a wise investment. In other words, if you act in a socially responsible manner and advertise that fact, you may be able to charge slightly more for your products.

On the other hand, it appears to be even more important to stay away from goods that are unethically produced. Consumers may still purchase your products, but only at a substantial discount.

How Ethical Do You Need to Be?

Our next test looked at degrees of ethical behavior. For instance, are consumers willing to pay more for a product that is 100 percent ethically produced versus one that is 50 percent or 25 percent ethically produced?

To find out, we tested consumers' responses to T-shirts from a fictitious manufacturer. We divided 218 people into five groups and presented them with information about the company and its product. One group was told the shirts were 100 percent organic cotton, one group 50 percent, and one group 25 percent. Another group—the "unethical" one—was told there was no organic component. The control group got no information.

In addition, all the groups but the control were shown a short paragraph detailing the detrimental effects of nonor-

ganic cotton production on the environment.

Then the participants were asked how much they were willing to pay for the shirts on a 16-point scale, ranging from $15 to $30. As in the first test, we found that people were willing to pay a premium for all levels of ethical production, and they would discount an unethical product more deeply than they would reward an ethical one.

But consumers didn't reward increasing levels of ethical production with increasing price premiums. The 25 percent organic shirts got a mean price of $20.72—not much different from the 50 percent ($20.44) and 100 percent ($21.21).

It seems that when companies hit a certain ethical threshold, consumers will reward them by paying higher prices for their products. Any ethical acts past that point might reinforce the company's image, but don't make people willing to pay more. (Of course, if 100 percent ethical becomes expected among consumers, anything less may be punished.)

What Effect Do Consumer Attitudes Have?

In our final experiment, we looked at the attitudes people bring to the table. If consumers expect that companies will behave ethically, will that change how much they reward and punish behavior? What if they expect that companies are just in it for the money, maximizing profits and not taking ethics into account?

Once again, we tested coffee drinkers—84 this time—and split them into groups that received positive, negative, and no ethical information about the manufacturer and its methods. But first

we measured the people's attitudes toward corporations and labeled them high-expectation or low-expectation.

Once again we found that—regardless of their expectations—consumers were willing to pay more for ethical goods than unethical ones, or ones about which they had no information. Likewise, negative information had a much bigger bearing on consumer response than positive information. People punished unethical goods with a bigger discount (about $2 below the control group) than they rewarded ethical ones with premiums (about $1 above the control group).

So, what effect did consumer attitudes have? People with high expectations doled out bigger rewards and punishments than those with low expectations. Those with high expectations were willing to pay a mean of $11.59 per pound for the ethical coffee, versus $9.90 for those with low expectations. And the high-expectations group punished the unethical coffee with a price of $6.92, versus $8.44 for low-expectations consumers.

The lessons are clear. Companies should segment their market and make a particular effort to reach out to buyers with high ethical standards, because those are the customers who can deliver the biggest potential profits on ethically produced goods.

Source: Wall Street Journal *Online. Available at http:// online.wsj.com/public/article_ print/SB121018735490274425. html. Copyright 2009 Dow Jones & Company, Inc. All Rights Reserved.*

continued patronage, the merchant will eventually diminish his or her consumer base and possibly fail. It is estimated that one in four people are considered to be **conflicted consumers** who easily change their loyalty from one retailer to another. Clear-cut, straightforward ads that maintain high professional standards are likely to sway conflicted consumers. In the case of The Body Shop, with more than 2,000 stores in 50 countries and one of the most successful companies to market itself using an ethical message, Jon Entine, writer of a monthly column "The Ethical Edge" for the British magazine *Ethical Corporation*, claims, "The Body Shop's only real product is honesty." The benefit of such marketing and advertising is that continuous sales increases result from customer loyalty, leading to the eventual benefit of profitability.

Another benefit of ethical advertising is a reduction in the number of people who resort to a **watchdog agency** such as the Better Business Bureau to air complaints. Occasionally, disgruntled consumers who have been duped by less than straightforward, honest ads use these agencies to voice their grievances. Such unfavorable publicity not only causes unhappiness with the complainant but also usually acts as a deterrent for others who might otherwise make purchases. By avoiding this pitfall, the merchant is likely to be the beneficiary of honest advertising.

Positive image building can be a benefit. At a time when unparalleled competition abounds, a good image often leads to long-term patronage. When a customer can trust the retailer to send a positive message through advertising, allegiance to that merchant can bring greater sales. Avoiding unethical practices such as questionable pricing methods, grandiose statements, and so forth sets a company apart from the rest and imparts an image that is often spread by word of mouth.

Media Insight 2.1 addresses the rewards of practicing sound business ethics.

The Principles of Ethical Advertising

To meet the minimum standards of truth and ethics in their business enterprises, retailers should develop a framework of principles for communicating their sales messages in individual advertisements and campaigns.

The copy, or content, is an integral part of an ad's layout and requires careful preparation. Copy should be honest and should not exploit consumers' possible lack of knowledge or experience. Ambiguous or grandiose words that misrepresent the product advertised should be avoided. Statements should be simple. Instead of using unsubstantiated claims, for example, that may lead to disbelief and potential consumer disputes, copy should contain only "principled facts."

Exaggerated claims and **puffery** should not be used in advertising. The written message should not be subjective, but should contain only objective, pertinent information to guide the consumer in his or her purchasing. The message should include some components of sound advertising, such as the price, delivery options, payment options, benefits of product usage, guarantees, materials, special advantages, and so forth. Each of these should be statements of fact and subject to scrutiny. Superlatives tend to mislead and should be avoided.

Often used in advertisements, comparison terms, such as *comparative value* and *value,* should be avoided unless they are verifiable. When using price reductions as a selling point, the terms *originally*, *usually*, and *formerly* should be authentic and the opinion of the merchant. Akin to the use of comparative terms are other terms such as *factory direct, wholesale prices, at cost, wholesale outlet*, and *factory to you*, each of which are often untrue and merely used to give the impression of unbelievable prices.

Testimonials and **endorsements** (Figure 2.1) have become mainstays in the ads of some companies. Unless they are genuine and not the result of some paid-for sponsorship, they should not be used. In addition to endorsements by individuals, statements such as "the vast majority of homeowners" should not be used because it is not easy to measure the actual number of homeowners represented in the claim, and such statements tend to be seen as a vague.

The layouts, artwork, copy, and format of an ad should be original, not a reproduction of another retailer's presentation. Distinctive campaigns are ultimately associated with the retailer and eventually become recognizable as the company's own. Copying the style of other retailers serves no purpose.

If guarantees or warranties are offered, they must be clearly stated so as not to misrepresent the intentions of the merchant. Where used, the statements of warranty should be complete and not just part of the entire concept. Not only are untruthful guarantees and warranties subject to legal action, but their misuse often results in a loss of consumer patronage.

Avoidance of very fine print exceptions should be avoided, as should the "fast-talking" points sometimes used in broadcast advertising. These tactics are ill-advised because they are rarely read or heard by consumers and could lead to product returns. For example, when an automobile ad features a price that seems too good to be true and uses an asterisk next to the price that references the **fine print**, that fine print usually explains many additional costs that the consumer often neglects to examine. This practice may lead to a bad experience when the consumer visits the dealership, and it rarely results in a purchase.

Only verifiable facts, such as real energy savings, performance, safety, and so forth should be used in ads. Unsubstantiated claims can cause consumer dissatisfaction and lead to lawsuits.

Illustrations and artwork should be accurate and not enhanced. Reliable imagery will eliminate surprises. Shoppers who expect to see the merchandise as advertised, only to find that it was enhanced in the ad, are disappointed, causing them to distrust the company. Similarly, if items purchased through catalogues or online were misrepresented in illustrations, the sellers can expect frequent returns.

Using fine print meant to be overlooked by readers is legal, but it is often an unethical practice. Some retailers advertise extremely low prices as a means of getting shoppers to their premises, but included in these ads, in significantly small font sizes, are statements indicating the extra

2.1 Celebrities are sometimes used to endorse stores or products. *Courtesy of Bloomingdale's.*

costs that must be paid in addition to the highly visible touted sales prices. Automobile agencies, in particular, are typical users of this type of advertising. These advertisements are common, but their use of hard-to-read fine print makes them unethical.

The principles should be in line with other codes of ethics the retailer follows.

Unethical Advertising Practices

In spite of the benefits derived by merchants when ethical considerations are practiced, some continue to reach the consumer through unscrupulous methods such as the following.

The deliberate use of **borderline truths** is evident in some advertisements. One example of a borderline truth is to imply, without substantiation, that the merchandise is actually more valuable than the price being charged. In print, broadcast,

2.2 Sometimes these ads are merely the opinions of the advertiser.
Courtesy of Barneys.

and Internet usage, terms such as *incredible value* and *once-in-a-lifetime opportunity* often are used merely to motivate purchasing.

Retailers sometimes use **mechanically altered photographs** that make merchandise appear to be of better quality than it actually is. As discussed in the previous section, this practice leads to customer disappointment and distrust.

Capitalizing on the **green movement** with the use of such terms as *environmentally sound, ecologically safe, sustainable,* and *going green,* which are excellent catchphrases to attract the attention of environmentally conscious consumers, is often merely a marketing tool. Some advertisers are known to stretch their true involvement in conservation to generate interest in their companies and do not really make significant efforts to go green.

Ambiguous claims, such as by some retailers who advertise their willingness to take returns of unwanted merchandise without any hassles, are often untrue. Such claims often do not specify the time limit for returns or the need for a sales receipt. At the point of purchase, however, customers may be greeted with conditions that prevent the returns.

The use of price reductions on items with **limited availability** sometimes results in the absence of such products. Reduced prices often motivate shoppers to come to a store because it has been implied that an unlimited number of products are for sale and there is no time limit for the purchase. Some retailers avoid this unethical dilemma by offering rain checks that honor sale prices at a future date.

The term **closeout of famous brands** implies that marquee designers' or well-known manufacturer's products are available at reduced prices (Figure 2.2). Whether or not a brand is famous may be the opinion of the merchant and not necessarily accurate; rather, it is a marketing gimmick to motivate visits to the store.

Voluntary Self-Regulation of Advertising

Because advertising is an integral part of doing business, it is important that it is properly used to maximize its effectiveness. Although most companies understand the need to produce ads that are truthful and that assist potential customers in making satisfactory buying decisions, some companies do not follow the rules. Retailers and other business enterprises generally take the high road to truthful advertising and engage in voluntary self-regulation. The Better Business Bureaus, the subject of Focus 2.1, are nonprofit organizations that work to maintain standards in business and advertising.

Codes of Ethics

Increasing numbers of retailers are subscribing to codes of ethics that guide their employees in the right approaches to business practices. By "doing the right thing" in such areas as customer relations, conflicts of interest, price gouging, advertising, and so forth, they are helping themselves not only to remain viable and profitable companies but also to stay on the right moral track.

The codes vary from unwritten understandings to more formalized documents that carefully spell out the ethical standards that govern a company. Some are the workings of in-house departments and apply only to the specific company, whereas others are general procedures and suggestions of outside groups such as the Better Business Bureaus, federal regulatory agencies, and trade associations such as the American Advertising Federation (AAF), which is the subject of Focus 2.2.

In addition to the suggested codes of ethics by the AAF and other professional organizations, in terms of advertising, retailers should be guided by their own concepts of right and wrong and by the mandates of the media that publish advertisements. Many media outlets have their own codes of ethics that pertain to what may be printed or aired.

Governmental Oversight

In addition to self-regulation regarding ethics and the business agencies that participate in this area, the government plays a role in overseeing advertising and how it is used. At all levels of government, agencies are charged with protecting the consumer by focusing on practices that are often unethical and sometimes illegal.

The Better Business Bureaus

The Better Business Bureau system is coordinated by the Council of Better Business Bureaus (CBBB), headquartered in Arlington, Virginia. The CBBB does not have the authority to take legal action against offending companies that are involved in advertising complaints, but it can refer cases to law enforcement agencies as it deems appropriate. It works closely with the Federal Trade Commission, a regulatory agency of the federal government, and consumer protection agencies.

Self-regulation, according to the CBBB, is an integral part of its operation. Its primary purpose is to help resolve complaints lodged by consumers. Businesses are encouraged to help solve a variety of problems, including those that involve advertising. The most widely used service of the CBBB is its inquiry and information service, which is updated on a daily basis. If problems are not settled to the satisfaction of the two parties in the dispute, which is sometimes the case, an arbitration program is available. Its purpose is to avoid litigation. The arbitration process is provided without cost to the consumer and often with no expense to the business.

One of the major areas of problem solving is in the advertising arena. With a detailed code of advertising, retailers are made aware of a host of basic principles that should be understood before any ads are placed. Along with the retailers who have the ultimate responsibility for their advertisements, the CBBB strongly suggests that advertising agencies and the media familiarize themselves with the basic advertising standards the CBBB recommends. The CBBB also recommends that industry members consult its *Do's and Don'ts in Advertising*, a two-volume loose-leaf compendium that is updated as necessary.

Among the many issues that may lead to the need for dispute settlement is the use of *comparative prices*, *list prices*, *imperfects*, *sale*, *credit terms*, *warranties*, *superiority claims*, *puffery testimonials*, and *rebates*.

For those with a broader interest in the CBBB, additional resources are available at its Web site: http://www.bbb.org.

American Advertising Federation

The American Advertising Federation (AAF) is headquartered in Washington, D.C., and, according to its Web site, acts as the "unifying voice for advertising." It is the oldest national trade association in the United States, representing 40,000 professionals in the ad industry. It oversees a national network of 200 ad clubs located across the country. In addition to representation of industry professionals, the AAF has 225 college chapters that provide advertising majors with real case studies for exploration as well as connections to corporate America, which is important to eventual entry into the field of advertising. Among its members are more than 125 blue-chip corporate members that are advertisers, agencies, and media companies. Their general mission is to "protect and promote the well-being of advertising." This mission is accomplished through a nationally coordinated grassroots network of advertisers, agencies, media companies, local advertising clubs, and college chapters. Among its commitments to advertising ethics and principles adopted by the AAF in 1984, and still recommended to its constituents, are the following:

◆ TRUTH Advertising shall tell the truth and reveal significant facts, the omission of which would mislead the public.

◆ SUBSTANTIATION Advertising claims should be substantiated by evidence in possession of the advertiser and advertising agency prior to making such claims.

◆ COMPARISONS Advertising shall refrain from making false, misleading, or unsubstantiated statements or claims about a competitor or his or her products or services.

◆ BAIT ADVERTISING Advertising shall not offer products or services for sale unless such an offer constitutes a bona fide effort to sell the advertised product or services and is not a device to switch consumers to other goods or services, usually higher priced.

◆ GUARANTEES AND WARRANTIES Advertising of guarantees and warranties shall be explicit, with sufficient information to apprise consumers of their principle terms and limitations, or, when space or time restrictions preclude such disclosures, the advertisement should clearly reveal where the full text of the guarantee or warranty can be examined before purchase.

◆ PRICE CLAIMS Advertising shall avoid price claims that are false or misleading or saving claims that do not offer favorable savings.

◆ TESTIMONIALS Advertising containing testimonials shall be limited to those of competent witnesses who are reflecting a real and honest opinion or experience.

◆ TASTE AND DECENCY Advertising shall be free of statements, illustrations, or implications that are offensive to good taste or public decency.

FEDERAL GOVERNMENT

At the national level, regulatory agencies promote awareness of advertising improprieties and the ways in which consumers can protect themselves from unethical and illegal practices. The Federal Trade Commission (FTC) and the Federal Communications Commission (FCC) actively oversee advertising.

Federal Trade Commission An independent regulatory agency of the U.S. government, the FTC was established in 1914. Its mission of consumer protection continues to this day and involves many different areas, including a broad number of laws and guidelines covering advertising. Specifically, in regard to retail practices, the agency oversees advertising and marketing on the Internet, screens advertisements, publishes a guide concerning the use of endorsements, issues warnings about **bait advertising**, alerts users of the word "free" in their ads, and answers a host of frequently asked advertising questions.

Federal Communications Commission Like the FTC, the FCC is a regulatory agency of the U.S. government, established in 1934. Its duties and responsibilities include the regulation of interstate and international communications by radio, television, wire, satellite, and cable. The FCC monitors advertising messages that are seen and heard by consumers and has the right to evaluate the contents of advertisements to make certain they comply with FCC standards.

LOCAL GOVERNMENT

Throughout the country, a variety of agencies handle problems associated with advertising schemes, unethical art and copy usage, and illegality in ads that cause harm to the citizenry of their communities. States, cities, and municipalities enact legislation to eliminate unfair practices. Two such agencies are the New York City Department of Consumer Affairs and the Office of Consumer Protection, Pinellas County, Florida.

New York City Department of Consumer Affairs The law authorizes the New York City Department of Consumer Affairs to adopt rules and regulations that protect the public from all deceptive and unconscionable practices in advertising and other areas involving consumer goods and services. In terms of advertising, the most commonly cited rules in consumer disputes and complaints are the following:

- ◆ Any limitations imposed on a "free" offer must be disclosed in advertising.

- ◆ Limitations or conditions of any nature on advertised offers must be disclosed clearly and conspicuously in print ads and announced on broadcast ads.

- ◆ Items may not be called "limited" unless there is a predetermined maximum quantity available or a reasonably short ordering period.

Office of Consumer Protection, Pinellas County, Florida In protecting its citizenry from advertising fraud and unethical practices, the Office of Consumer Protection offers clear rules regarding advertising practices such as *bait and switch, false price comparison, going-out-of-business sales, buy one get one free offers*, and *misrepresentations*. It also publishes guidelines for purchasing:

- ◆ Do shop around to make your own price comparisons.

- ◆ Do, whenever possible, check out all advertising claims before making purchases.

- ◆ Do ask for a rain check when advertised products are not available for sale.

- ◆ Do ask to see a permit for a going-out-of-business sale before buying at such sales.

- ◆ Do be on your guard when you see advertisements offering anything "free."

- ◆ Don't allow yourself to be "switched" from a low-priced "bait" product to a more expensive alternative.

- ◆ Do report all cases of false advertising to the Department of Consumer Affairs.

Social Responsibility

As an ethical or ideological theory, social responsibility requires that organizations, be they governments, businesses, or corporations, have a responsibility to society to take a proactive stance in its improvement. Retailers of all sizes and classifications, as an example, are focusing on becoming more socially responsible and taking positive approaches to improve the world's social conditions. Many are paying closer attention to such issues as environmental protection, making decisions that positively affect the health of individuals, aiding in charitable causes, raising consumer consciousness regarding worldwide social issues, and other worthy initiatives—in other words, they are looking beyond their own bottom lines at ways to improve the community, both locally and globally. Instead of waiting for government intervention to address societal woes, self-regulation is the key to realizing the benefits of social responsibility. From small, individually owned entrepreneurships to the corporate giants, business participation in socially responsible endeavors is becoming commonplace.

Some cynics maintain that a business's emphasis on social initiatives is purely for the publicity and marketing pluses accrued by such actions, but the benefits to society are real. By going green in any number of ways, for example, retailers are making significant differences in the well-being of the country and its inhabitants. Of course, the positive public relations garnered from many socially responsible activities may ultimately result in a better profit margin for the participants.

Cause marketing, which involves the cooperative efforts of "for-profit" businesses and nonprofits, is a method effectively used to foster social responsibility (see Figure 2.3). Together, these entities account for raising a large percentage of funds for social and other charitable causes.

Advertising is an integral part of cause marketing and is significant to the success of these social programs. Newspapers, magazines, radio, television, direct mail, and other media outlets are used to inform consumers of the socially responsible activities of specific retailers and other businesses. More and more print space and broadcast airtime is being devoted to underscoring specific activities that constitute retailer social responsibility.

Benefits of Retail Participation

The need for retailer participation in fund-raising as well as consciousness for social programs has become more significant than ever. With governments at all levels curtailing their contributions to worthy causes because of the need to exercise fiscal restraint, charitable groups, in particular, have had to use other means to fund their causes. Retailing is one of the major business categories involved in making up for the shortfall that continues to plague nonprofit organizations engaged in social programs and fund-raising. Retailers of all classifications are becoming proactive participants in partnership with the nonprofit organizations to make sure that they are among the socially responsible business enterprises.

AIDING THE LESS FORTUNATE

In a country characterized by success and fortune and the potential for everyone to become self-sufficient, there are vast numbers of people who are unable to fulfill their dreams. Within this collective group are people of all ages, nationalities, religions, ethnicities, and gender. Due to either their inability to prosper and maintain standards of living that afford them the necessities to satisfactorily function or to their having had short-term needs as a result of circumstances not of their own making, many must resort to the assistance provided by socially responsible retailers and other businesses.

Table 2.1 lists a few of the merchant-sponsored charities, such as Ronald McDonald House, Children's Miracle Network, Goodwill Industries, and Salvation Army, along with their programs' emphasis. See Figure 2.4.

THURSDAY THROUGH SATURDAY, MARCH 4-6 AT STEIN MART

give & receive

Receive up to **4** coupons good for **20% OFF** ANY ONE REGULAR PRICE, SALE OR CLEARANCE ITEM when you bring your gently used clothing to Stein Mart during our *give & receive* event.*

*Limit 4 coupons per customer, but you can donate as many items as you'd like. Earn and redeem coupons March 4-6, 2010. Bring your garments to any participating Stein Mart. Tax receipts are available.

All garments received will be donated to

THE SALVATION ARMY · DOING THE MOST GOOD

Stein Mart®

once you **go** you get it

Visit steinmart.com for store locations and to view our Fair Pricing Policy • 1-888-steinmart

2.3 Cause marketing usually involves a retailer and a "cause." *Courtesy Steinmart.*

TABLE 2.1

Major Retailers' Cause Marketing Outreach

COMPANY	CHARITY	PROGRAM EMPHASIS
Neiman Marcus stores	New West Symphony	Outreach programs to schools
Bloomingdale's	United Planet	Fostering cross-cultural understanding and friendship
Macy's Inc.	American Heart Association	Go Red for Women movement
Limited Brands Corp.	Susan G. Komen for the Cure	Eliminating breast cancer
Belk Inc.	Local charities and schools	Various activities
Dillard's Inc.	Ronald McDonald House Charities	Helping children with severe illnesses and their families
Target Corp.	Salvation Army	Providing essential items for families in need
Wal-Mart	Children's Miracle Network	Saving children's lives
Kohl's Corp.	Kids Who Care	Scholarship programs
Banana Republic stores	Goodwill Industries International Inc.	Education and career services for economically challenged individuals

2.4 Major retailers often engage in cause-marketing outreach programs.
Courtesy Nordstrom and Susan G. Koman for the Cure.

RAISING ENVIRONMENTAL CONCERNS

With a great deal of press regarding global warming, damage to the ozone layer, the shortfall of renewable energy, and other factors that some experts warn are damaging our environment, some retailers have joined the effort to raise public awareness of these potentially devastating occurrences. Through numerous advertising initiatives, some of which are addressed later in the chapter, retailers show their commitment to being socially responsible (Figure 2.5).

Some businesses demonstrate their environmental awareness by becoming **LEED certified** through the Leadership in Energy and Environmental Design Green Building Rating System. To qualify for LEED certification, a company's new construction or redeveloped property earns points by complying with standards such as using salvaged or refurbished materials, maximizing use of daylight to reduce energy consumption, using on-site renewable energy, and taking any of a number of other actions set forth in the LEED certification requirements.

IMPROVING THE BOTTOM LINE

When civic-minded individuals are motivated to purchase from retailers who participate in socially responsible programs, retailers benefit with improved profit margins. According to the Cone Cause Survey completed in 2007, sale of brands associated with a good cause have climbed to 87 percent.

POSITIVE PUBLIC RELATIONS

Favorable publicity benefits both nonprofit organizations and the businesses that sponsor them. For nonprofits, positive publicity provides a greater degree of visibility, increases their financial resources, and helps them to reach potential supporters through the businesses that cooperate with them. For the retailer, positive publicity may enhance public relations and increase traffic to their stores and offsite divisions.

Cause Marketing for Retail Organizations

Many businesses participate in joint ventures with nonprofits to promote good causes, and the retail industry is a major participant. Through numerous activities, merchants of all sizes actively interact with nonprofit organizations to raise consciousness and generate funds for their causes. Fund-raising is enhanced through print and broadcast ads as well as the Internet (Figure 2.6).

2.5 Retailers sometimes commit themselves to raising consciousness about environmental issues. *Courtesy of Kohl's.*

2.6 Retailers often sponsor outreach programs.
Courtesy of Kohl's.

Table 2.1 lists some of the major retailers who demonstrate social responsibility through cause marketing.

Given that cause marketing is a practice that seems to be growing at a significant rate for retailers and other businesses, it is important to understand the ways in which this marketing direction can be mastered. Media Insight 2.2 offers steps for mastering the concept.

Advertising Initiatives

Not too long ago, only a handful of retailers expressed interest in becoming socially responsible. Those who did generally limited their participation to one area, such as sponsoring a charity, merchandising their inventories with sustainable design in mind, or altering their premises to improve the environment. Today, many merchants participate in a broad range of socially responsible activities, and they use advertising to let consumers know of their commitment to the community.

ENVIRONMENTAL PROTECTION

By going green, many retailers are doing their share to protect the environment and the individuals who inhabit it. They do so by modifying their facilities to save energy, using renewable resources such as quick-growing bamboo in their store fixtures, and so forth. To raise the consciousness of their consumers and potential patrons, many retailers are committing to advertisements. In different degrees, merchants are setting aside portions of their advertising budgets for this purpose. One such company that has been participating in these activities is Patagonia, an organization that produces and sells its own products primarily through catalogues and the Internet. In addition to displaying the goods it markets, Patagonia's catalogues (Figure 2.7) devote space—including vivid photographs—to such articles as "Patagonia Employees Pull Fences to Restore Habitat," which tells of their concern for such problems as erosion and wetland damage and how Patagonia is contributing to solutions. Patagonia is a leader in spreading the word for social responsibility.

In addition to employing energy-saving devices on their premises and using renewable resources for their fixturing, retailers are making greater attempts to add organic products to their merchandise assortments. From the high-end retailers who feature luxury products in their merchandise mixes to the grocers who increasingly stock organic foods, and many in-between retailers, the movement toward safer, healthier, earth-friendlier products is growing.

Cause Marketing Matters to Consumers

Social responsibility makes consumers take notice. Follow these five steps to create a successful cause-based marketing campaign.

Kim T. Gordon
October 14, 2008

In this new era of social responsibility, what you don't do can cost you. Cause marketing is now the norm, and customers who visit your Web site and see your advertising want to know that you share their desire to make the world a better place by supporting an important cause.

If your business or brand doesn't stand for a cause, consumers may turn to your competitors. The number of consumers who say they would switch from one brand to another if the other brand were associated with a good cause has climbed to 87 percent, a dramatic increase in recent years, according to a Cone Cause Evolution Survey.

Even niche markets, such as the nation's college students, now show a striking preference for brands they believe to be socially responsible. According to a newly released College Explorer study from Alloy Media, nearly 95 percent of students say they are less likely to ignore an ad that promotes a brand's partnership with a cause.

There's a strong connection between entrepreneurship and giving. The challenge is to make your socially responsible efforts a winning proposition for the nonprofit group you support, the community, and your business. You can master this marketing challenge by following these five important steps:

Step 1. Give from the heart.

Cause marketing works best when you and your employees feel great about the help you're providing to a nonprofit group, so work with an organization you and your team believe in, whether this means supporting the fight on behalf of a national health issue or rescuing homeless pets. What matters most to you, your team, and your customers? You'll work hard to make a difference when you give from the heart.

Step 2. Choose a related cause.

A solid cause-marketing campaign often starts with the right affiliation. So as you go through the nonprofit selection process, look for a cause that relates to your company or its products. For example, when Procter & Gamble's Olay brand skin-care line partnered with the American Society for Dermatologic Surgery, its campaign goal was to inspire women to protect their skin from the sun. PR support yielded widespread broadcast, print, and online coverage, helping the program attract more than 9,000 individuals for free skin cancer screenings.

Step 3. Contribute more than dollars.

For many types of businesses, cause marketing involves donating products or services and not simply writing a check. This can help form even stronger consumer associations between what you offer and the good work you do. My own firm, for instance, works hard to support two local groups—a shelter for homeless women and children and an organization that helps cancer patients pay their rent and other bills while undergoing treatment. As a marketing expert, I contribute services that include producing an annual Woman's Hope benefit concert and direct-mail and public relations campaigns that in the past 8 months have netted approximately $250,000 for these nonprofits.

Step 4. Formalize your affiliation.

To make your affiliation a win-win for everyone, work with the nonprofit you choose to define how it will help your business increase its visibility, brand, or company awareness. If the organization has a newsletter or other communications with its constituents, negotiate for opportunities to do joint promotions. Discuss how you will use the organization's logo and name in your marketing campaigns and how it, in turn, will use your company logo and name in its press releases, on the organization's Web site, and in other materials.

Step 5. Mount a marketing campaign.

Success in cause marketing often means motivating an audience to take action, such as making a donation or participating in an event. Using a dedicated marketing campaign, you can reach and persuade the target group while also raising awareness for your business and its commitment to social responsibility. For example, to enhance its relationship with the black community, State Farm created the 50 Million Pound Challenge to educate blacks about the risks associated with being overweight. A special Challenge Web site was created to provide ongoing advice and support and has helped hundreds of thousands of people lose weight.

Source: Entrepreneur. *Available at http://www.entrepreneur. com/marketing/marketingcolumnistkimtgordon/article197820.html.*

we'd like to offer you 15% OFF your next order of $50 or more

15% off does not pertain to wetsuits, footwear or gift cards

mention code M2981297 · offer valid through November 29, 2008 · catalog or internet orders only · cannot be used in conjunction with any other offers

In the apparel retail market, Barneys, the upscale, New York–based operation with stores throughout the country, is offering eco-conscious lines of goods. With organic fabrics and sustainable and environmentally friendly processed goods, which Barneys calls to the attention of the shopper in its ads, Barneys has jumped on the eco-friendly bandwagon (Figure 2.8). At the other end of the fashion price-point spectrum, H&M, the Swedish-based retail giant with stores across the globe, continues to add environmentally appropriate lines to its inventories. In the grocery arena, Whole Foods Market has an enormous inventory of eco-friendly products. Its marketing campaigns regularly extol the virtues of these types of products and have helped build Whole Foods Market's image as a protector of the environment.

SPONSORSHIP OF CHARITABLE EVENTS

Retailers have long been associated with cause marketing by sponsoring events that not only raise awareness about charities but also raise funds that help with charities' goals. Charitable organizations of every type have benefited from retail participation. Large retailers such as Macy's, Bloomingdale's, Neiman Marcus, and Saks Fifth Avenue, as well as small entrepreneurships, sponsor fashion shows, luncheons, formal galas, guest-speaker forums, and other events for the purpose of raising funds. Advertising these

functions in newspapers, on television and radio, and on Web sites has spread the word to their customers. While aiding the charity through its participation, the retailers benefit from defining themselves as being socially responsible and, at the same time, often develop relationships with consumers who become customers.

IMPROVING SOCIETAL PROBLEMS

When catastrophes such as hurricane Katrina strike, not only is the government responsible for helping its citizens but other groups also need to provide aid and comfort. When Katrina left thousands stranded on rooftops and others in makeshift shelters, many retailers banded together to make people across the world aware of the disaster victims' plight. Similarly, when the horrific 9/11 tragedy struck the United States, many merchants used institutional ads to inform the public of how they could help in the aftermath. Through the use of advertising, businesses help raise public consciousness and foster a better understanding of our need to act as a unified society.

DISCONTINUANCE OF SHOCK ADVERTISING

The deliberate use of advertising that is meant to shock people is socially irresponsible and ultimately may cause a negative reaction from

2.7 *(opposite)* Patagonia raises consciousness about the importance of environment protection. *Courtesy of Patagonia.*

2.8 Organic products help to protect the environment. *Courtesy of Barneys.*

would-be purchasers. This form of advertising violates the personal ideals and social values of most people. Most retailers refrain from **shock advertising** because consumers usually find it offensive. It is not considered by most retailers to be a viable means of motivating consumers to buy. The negativity associated with the Benetton ads in the late 1980s caused businesses to take a better look at the tactic and determine that it does not foster the appropriate image.

Benetton came under considerable scrutiny due to its shock campaigns. Although it did achieve recognition from some for its heightening of awareness of social issues, the approach was generally dismissed as unnecessary. Examples of the ads include a priest and a nun leaning to kiss each other, a man dying of AIDS, a newborn with its umbilical cord still attached, and a duck covered in oil to protest oil spillage.

Some retailers still use advertising that many consider offensive, but not sufficiently shocking to cause its discontinuation. The partial nudity used by Victoria's Secret, for example, still gains attention and is considered to be in the realm of decency (Figure 2.9).

RECOGNIZING HISTORICAL ACCOMPLISHMENTS

When Barack Obama won the presidency of the United States, retailers throughout the country celebrated the first African American's ascendancy to the highest office in the land. Immediately, newspaper ads expressed pride and praise as another means of displaying social responsibility.

This was just one of many such recognitions provided by advertising space and time. Nelson Mandela's rise to national attention as the first

2.9 The partial nudity used for Victoria's Secret still gains attention and is considered to be in the realm of decency. *Image courtesy of The Advertising Archives.*

VICTORIA'S SECRET

democratically elected president of South Africa and Martin Luther King Junior's "I Have a Dream Speech" are some other examples that received widespread retail advertising spreads.

Summary of Key Points

◆ Ethical advertising is an extremely important concern for retailers who want to remain profitable entities in today's extremely competitive society. With consumer awareness constantly being heightened by stories that address unethical occurrences in business and government, people are now, more than ever, educated in terms of the adversity that may affect them when dealing with less than candid retail practitioners.

◆ Ethical advertisements benefit the retailer in many ways, including the advantage of maintaining loyal customers as well as attracting newcomers; the avoidance of oversight from watchdog agencies such as the Better Business Bureaus, which can cause considerable damage to their reputations; and potential sales increases.

◆ Some of the principles of ethical advertising include the careful use of copy that relies on honesty and integrity; avoidance of puffery; the appropriate use of comparison terms such as *comparative value* and *value*, which often do not really have any true meaning; and the avoidance of enhancing advertising artwork to make the product appear to be better than it is.

◆ Unethical advertising claims are commonplace, even with all of the negative effects that come with them. Some of the most common unethical claims include advertising bargain-priced merchandise that has insufficient availability, using "closeouts of famous brands" in the copy when the "fame" of the brand may be only the retailer's opinion, using ambiguity regarding return policies, and using fine print that is too small for most people to read.

◆ Codes of ethics are used by retailers as a means of making certain they stay on the right track when advertising their products. They are often written by in-house management, procured from trade associations such as the American Advertising Federation, or supplied by federal government regulatory agencies such as the FTC and FCC and local governments that often provide guidelines on ethics through their departments of consumer affairs and offices of consumer protection.

◆ More and more retailers are becoming socially responsible and are taking positive steps to improve social conditions. Typical of such involvement is the "adoption" of a charitable organization to help raise consciousness and funds, becoming proactive in environmental causes by going green, spreading public messages such as the need for better health care for the uninsured, and so forth. These activities assist the less fortunate in many cases, but naysayers argue that retailers do good deeds only for the positive publicity they may achieve.

◆ Cause marketing is the approach taken by retailers or other businesses to promote worthy causes. It involves the cooperative efforts of for-profit businesses and non-profit organizations and directs them both in a way that betters the causes they want to promote.

For Discussion

1. Why is the concern for ethical advertising more important than ever to retailers of all classifications?

2. List and discuss three benefits the retailer achieves when ethical advertising is used regularly in single ads or campaigns.

3. Discuss some of the principles of ethical advertising for retailers and indicate how their use can help retailers gain their customers' confidence.

4. What are some of the unethical practices still used by some retailers today, and why might they cause retailers adverse publicity?

5. Describe the American Advertising Federation's code of ethics suggested to its constituents, including some of its recommendations.

6. Which two regulatory agencies of the federal government oversee advertising, and how do their areas of responsibility differ?

7. What is social responsibility as it pertains to retail organizations, and what areas of concern does it often address?

8. Discuss some of the benefits derived from retail participation in worthy causes.

9. What is cause marketing?

10. Discuss some of the advertising initiatives of today's retailers.

Terms of the Trade

ambiguous claims

bait advertising

borderline truths

cause marketing

closeout of famous brands

codes of ethics

comparable value

conflicted consumers

endorsements

fine print

green movement

LEED certified

limited availability

mechanically altered photographs

puffery

shock advertising

testimonials

watchdog agency

Exercises and Projects

1. Many retailers have written their own codes of ethics to ensure that those involved in creating their ads are aware of the parameters that have been established for print and broadcast advertising. Contact five major retailers of any classification (department stores, chains, supermarkets, off-pricers, etc.) to learn more about their codes of ethics, specifically as it concerns advertising. The information may be obtained either through direct contact with the retailers or, in some cases, from their Web sites. Use a chart similar to the one below to input the information.

2. Using any search engine, such as www. google.com, search on keywords such as *advertising regulations* or *regulation of advertising* to research the areas of regulations as they pertain to consumer protection. Summarize all of the key elements regarding the various regulations that you uncovered in a two-page, double-spaced paper, citing the resources from which you found your information.

Retailer	Classification	Code Features

3. Contact a major department store's public relations department to learn about the charitable endeavors in which they are involved in connection with a nonprofit organization. The contacts may be made by in-person visits if feasible or by e-mail, letter, or phone call. Produce a paper with attention to the following:

- The name of the company

- The charitable organization that it assists

- The scope of its involvement

- The fund-raising methods it uses

- Its media activity aimed at customer enlightenment

Web Site Exploration for In-Depth Analysis

National Resources Defense Council LEED Certification Information
http://www.nrdc.org/buildinggreen/leed.asp
 This site provides a complete description of LEED certification, a "green" initiative taken by many retail organizations.

http://www.foundationcenter.org/getstarted/faqs/html/cause_marketing.html
 A complete overview of cause-related marketing, also referred to as cause marketing, is presented at this Web site.

Federal Trade Commission
http://www.ftc.gov
 All of the activities of the Federal Trade Commission, in addition to advertising regulation as discussed in this chapter, are available at this site.

Federal Communications Commission
http://www.fcc.gov
 This site provides details of the workings of the Federal Communications Commission.

PLANNING THE ADVERTISING PROGRAM

FISH EATERS OF THE WORLD

NEW ENGLAND CRAB CRUNCHER

A curious species native to the Northeastern United States, they're easily caught with North Atlantic Oysters, Dungeness Crab or Live Lobster.

CORPORATE SHARK

The Corporate Shark can be found primarily in trendy environments. She feeds mainly on Sushi, Swordfish and Oysters on the Half Shell.

LARGEMOUTH YUPPIE

The Largemouth Yuppie congregates in urban areas. Reel him in with Copper River Salmon, Mahi Mahi and Alaskan King Crab.

BACKCOUNTRY TRAILWALKER

The Backcountry Trailwalker avoids populated areas, but congregates in "green" grocery stores and restaurants. Reel him in with MSC certified sustainable products, including Oregon Pink Shrimp, Pacific Halibut and New Zealand Hoki.

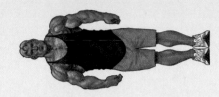

MUSCLES

Muscles can be found in nearly any restaurant environment, usually in close proximity to a gym. Catch and release with Pacific Halibut, Shrimp, Scallops or any other high-protein, low-fat fish.

DESERT DWELLER

The Desert Dweller can be found in traditional Southwestern restaurants. They avoid exotic fish, but are easily caught with grilled Rainbow Trout, Atlantic Salmon and Catfish.

THE SPONGE

Found in schools, the Sponge soaks up knowledge while feeding on brain food. You'll catch them with sustainable omega-3 fish like grilled Salmon, Herring and Mackerel.

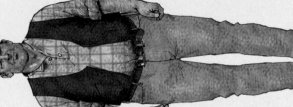

PUB CRAWLER

The Pub Crawler feeds primarily on fried foods. Ideal baits include Catfish, Popcorn Shrimp and Calamari.

TEENAGE GROUPER

The Teenage Grouper travels in groups of similar individuals. They're easy to hook with Gulf Shrimp, Tilapia or any other quick-serve fish.

PACIFIC COAST TRANSPLANT

The Pacific Coast Transplant migrated from large, West Coast cities and is attracted to any trendy, upscale restaurant. Lure her in with Albacore Tuna, Pacific Rockfish and Santa Barbara Prawns.

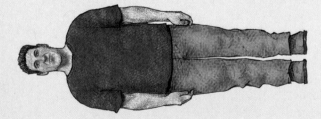

SUNBAKED SAMARITAN

You'll find the Sunbaked Samaritan in environmentally balanced restaurants and stores. Catch him with sustainable MSC seafood like Gulf of Alaska Pacific Cod, US North Pacific Sablefish and Patagonian Scallops.

ENLIGHTENED EPICUREAN

The Enlightened Epicurean can be found in environmentally conscious grocery stores and restaurants. She feeds exclusively on MSC sustainable fish, such as Alaskan Salmon, South Georgia Patagonian Toothfish and Pacific American Albacore Tuna.

GULF COAST SWAMP DWELLER

Native to the Gulf of Mexico, this species has a unique palette. They feed primarily on Cajun Crawfish, Catfish and Wahoo.

FEARLESS GOBBLER

The Fearless Gobbler isn't a picky eater. He'll often eat prey more timid creatures would pass up. Reel him in with Whole Crawfish, Alligator, Monkfish and Conch.

Seattle Fish Company provides the Southwest's largest variety of high-quality fresh and frozen fish.
So no matter what pond you're fishing in, we've got the bait for you.

Catch more customers.

Seattle Fish Company of New Mexico, Inc. 2500 Comanche Rd. NE, Albuquerque, NM 87107 | 505.888.6969 | seattlefishnm.com

Pre-Planning: Researching *the* Target Markets

CHAPTER OBJECTIVES

After you have completed this chapter, you will be able to discuss:

★ The reasons market segmentation is important to retailers' ability to reach the proper consumer base.

★ Why generational age classifications have played a vital role in categorizing consumer markets.

★ The manner in which marketing researchers have classified individuals according to their family life cycles.

★ How psychographics takes demographic analysis to a new level of segmentation.

★ The differences between the classes in terms of their needs and importance to the retailing community.

★ How Maslow's hierarchy of needs addresses the different stages of needs satisfaction.

★ Motivational behavior in terms of emotional, rational, and patronage motives.

★ The necessity for consumer research to be conducted in today's retail arena.

The key to success in retailing is to develop a plan that addresses all of the components necessary to run the business and return a profit for its investors. In terms of advertising commitments and approaches, before a plan is put into action the target markets must be researched so that the expenditures for such endeavors will bring the projected results. One of the essential parts of the planning process is to identify the **market segments** on which the company will focus its efforts. Each market or consumer group must be identified according to specific characteristics or traits to make certain that the appropriate advertising strategies are applied to meet their needs and translate into sales. After **market segmentation** is completed, the retailer can pinpoint those groups that best fit the company's intended "reach."

The educated merchant must conduct market research before opening the doors for business and must continue to do so on a regular basis so that the company's advertising efforts and other decision making is constantly updated as needed due to changes in the retail environment. Early decisions include the company's overall concept (e.g., will it be a traditional, discount, or off-price operation?) and its product mix and price points so that these factors can be incorporated into the advertising messages. When these decisions have been carefully addressed, the plan can be put into action and the company can begin to reach out to its audiences.

The merchant's research must include demographic analysis, family life cycles, psychographics, social class structure, and the study of needs theories and consumer behavior. Such information may come from original research conducted by an in-house staff, outside marketing research organizations, trade associations, and governmental agencies. Often, the investigation involves all of these resources.

Whatever the approach, the research project should be carefully executed and analyzed and should become the framework for the company's method of operation.

Market Segmentation

Using a **one-size-fits-all philosophy** to try to reach consumers is unrealistic. Shoppers' needs differ! For the retailer to identify the market or markets that most closely parallel its offerings, the markets must be studied and separated into homogenous groups according to characteristic similarities. The concept known as *market segmentation* categorizes people and allows the retailer to determine the target market best suited for its needs. Most often, market segmentation begins with demographic analysis.

Demographic Analysis

Using population characteristics, or **demographics**, such as traditional generational age classifications, income, education, geographic location, occupations, ethnicity, and population concentration, helps pinpoint the retailer's targeted markets.

TRADITIONAL AGE CLASSIFICATIONS

The merchandise needs of one age group are unlikely to be identical to that of others. Even in the case of food, there are different requirements for every household. Apparel needs also differ from one group to another, making the focus of advertisements different. It is, therefore, necessary for retailers to study each age classification and make certain that their ads are carefully developed to reach these different age groups.

Age classifications are traditionally segmented, according to the U.S. Department of Commerce, into children, teens, young adults, young middle-aged, older middle-aged, and elderly. By examining these traditional groups, merchants can more scientifically target their advertisements. The Department of Commerce updates age demographics regularly, so the latest information is easy to access.

Children This category includes newborns to children age 13, but there is considerable difference between the needs of newborns and the needs of preteens, as well as the needs of those who fall somewhere in the middle. Although the younger members of this group have no purchasing power, they do influence their parents' buying decisions. By far, it is television advertising that impacts children the most. Toys and games merchants most often make their appeals through this media, as do retailers such as GapKids.

Teenagers Trendy clothing retailers such as The Gap, American Eagle Outfitters, and Old Navy target the teenage market primarily through television commercials. Because teenagers are one of the most important segments of the viewing audience, retailers spend most of their advertising budgets appealing to this group (Figure 3.1).

Although television is still a very important medium for reaching teens and children, digital media, as discussed in Media Insight 3.1, is gaining momentum in reaching these markets.

Young Adults The vast majority of the 20- to 34-year-old age group is interested in fashion merchandise. Whether for career clothing, leisure wear, activewear, or special occasion apparel, they are the targets of the retailers' advertising programs. Companies such as Banana Republic, J. Crew, and Ann Taylor use a variety of media outlets to reach this group, primarily magazine ads and television commercials.

Home furnishings are also of considerable importance to this group. Home furnishings retailers such as IKEA, Restoration Hardware, and Crate & Barrel use television, magazines, radio, and the Internet to reach this market.

Finally, members of this group are major purchasers of computer products. To reach them, companies such as Office Depot, Best Buy, and Staples primarily use newspaper ads, television commercials, and the Internet (Figure 3.2).

Young Middle-Aged The young middle-aged group has considerable spending power and is the main target of the retailing industry. Using just about every media form, retailers regularly bombard this audience with ads that feature everything from fashion apparel and home furnishings to performance automobiles and exotic travel. This

Sweater $29.95

H&M

In select stores February 20th

3.1 Ads of this nature target the teenage population. *Courtesy of H&M.*

Where the Kids Are: They're Doing a Lot More Than Watching TV

Brian Steinberg
February 16, 2009

Any parent knows how hard it is to keep an eye on several children all at once. So imagine how marketers feel having to keep track of a massive group of them.

Beaming an ad for the latest toy, gadget, or tasty treat at a young person between the ages of, oh, 6 and 14 was once an easy task: put it up on any broadcast network during Saturday-morning cartoons. As cable outlets such as Nickelodeon or Cartoon Network gained traction, advertisers had even more opportunity, as those venues broadcast kid-focused programming during even more hours of the day and days of the week.

Now that digital media has emerged from its infancy, reaching kids has gotten harder. About 48 percent of consumers between the ages of 8 and 12 spend 2 hours online every day, according to eMarketer, whereas 24 percent of teens between 13 and 17 spend more than 15 hours online each week. That doesn't mean they aren't watching TV, but it certainly signifies that there are ways to reach them that don't necessarily involve buying the same old pipelines.

A "First Priority"

"I would say that TV continues to be the first-priority media, but you can't just rely on TV like you could in years past," said Ted Ellet, senior VP–group media director at Interpublic Group of Cos. DraftFCB. "Not everybody is watching TV, and they are getting a lot of their entertainment from the Web, replacing in some cases their TV viewership with online video consumption. They are certainly still consuming all of the stuff that is out there, just on different screens."

Media buyers suggest that the Big Three of kids' TV have managed to carve out a stand for themselves in other venues. According to ComScore Media Metrix, Walt Disney Co.'s Disney.com, Viacom's Nick.com, and Time Warner's CartoonNetwork.com were the three most visited sites among kids 2 to 11 in the United States in 2008.

"There are still a limited number of big players out there, but that's not to say there aren't more new-media companies out there catering to the kids which are becoming options now," said Ed Gentner, senior VP–group client director at Publicis Groupe's MediaVest.

Online, those places include sites such as Hasbro.com and Chuckecheese.com, according to ComScore, a clear sign that marketers are luring kids with their own content, not programming made by somebody else. There are also a number of content sites, such as Pearson's Poptropica and Funbrain.com, where kids can play games, communicate with each other, and even learn a thing or two.

Children growing up these days never knew a world in which NBC was a wholly different animal than TBS. For this digital generation, consumers have always been able to zip back and forth between a TV screen and a computer terminal or laptop, and TV aficionados can see whatever content they want at the push of a button or the load-up of a convenient DVD. Marketing experts expect younger viewers' habits to become even more entrenched on the digital side.

"If I were in the business of spending real dollars, I wouldn't be so naive as to say, 'OK, we'll do Nickelodeon, and that'll do it,' or even MTV," said Tom Donohue, professor of mass communications and psychology at Virginia Commonwealth University. "I'd be on Internet places—MySpace, YouTube. Essentially it's working its way down from what was supposed to be a college-student phenomenon and is becoming a preadolescent phenomenon."

An Eroding Base

Academics believe the rise of social-networking sites, online video, and applications for portable media devices will only drum up the number of hours young consumers spend perusing digital applications. TV remains dominant, but its base is eroding. "I really think advertisers need to look more into placing more dollars on the Web, specifically because a lot of TV shows are being repurposed on the Web and a lot of dollars are creating original content for the Web," said Trey Stohlman, an instructor at the School of Broadcasting and Cinematic Arts at Central Michigan University.

Expect the youngest customers to become even more difficult to reach in the months and years ahead, Mr. Stohlman said. "We know they text. We know they use cell phones, but that still doesn't necessarily tell us how saturated the marketing really is with this technology. All of these kids are growing up with cell phones or Nintendos or PSPs in their hands, and I don't think we are really portraying that very well," he said.

In other words, TV works and will continue to do so—but there are a host of emerging venues that are likely to reach smaller groups of consumers in more relevant and immediate ways.

Source: Brian Steinberg. "Where the Kids Are: They're Doing a Lot More Than Watching TV." Advertising Age. February 16, 2009.

3.2 The young adult market is an excellent one for computer sales. *Courtesy of Staples.*

group represents a major portion of online shoppers and is, therefore, regularly targeted in this manner. They also are major purchasers through direct-mail catalogues.

Older Middle-Aged Similar in many ways to their young middle-aged counterparts, this group also enjoys considerable purchasing power. Many are at the peaks of their careers and have a great deal of disposable income. They are often patrons of the luxury retailers and many tend to purchase extravagantly. In addition to product purchases, they are excellent candidates for luxury travel and posh dining. Of course, not everyone in this class is privileged. Those with more modest incomes frequent off-pricers and discounters for their needs. Nearly every type of advertising medium is used to reach this group.

Elderly The **gray heads** are generally cautious spenders. For fashion merchandise, they shop in value stores such as Wal-Mart and Target; but more often, they shop for health products. The elderly are generally targeted through newspaper ads and television commercials.

GENERATIONAL AGE CLASSIFICATIONS

Some researchers use **generational categories** in their segmentation analyses—for example, **generation X** for those born between 1963 and 1978, **generation Y** for those born between 1979 and 1995, and **generation Z** for those born between the end of the 1990s and those expected to be born by 2017. Purchasing characteristics differ among these classifications.

Generation X The group that was first categorized in this manner was generation X. They were often verbally abused in the press as overeducated non-achievers who had little regard for the traditions of religion and social institutions. Eventually, they were heralded as being self-reliant and sufficiently ambitious to create their own businesses. Media Insight 3.2 focuses on generation X.

Generation Y Approximately 35 million strong, generation Y members are the retail merchants' dream. Also known as the Net generation, millennials, echo boomers, and iGeneration, they tend to spend more money than previous generations. Advertisers reach them through a variety of media outlets, with the Internet being the most widely used.

MEDIA INSIGHT 3.2

Gen-X: The Ignored Generation?

M.J. Stephey
April 16, 2008

Jeff Gordinier is tired of being force-fed the Beatles, the Summer of Love, Facebook, and Britney Spears. He says being heard over the media din about boomers and their offspring, generation Y, or "millennials" as they're now known, isn't just a challenge, it's annoying. Being overlooked and underappreciated? It's never-ending for him and his tribe of fellow Gen-Xers.

Clearly Gordinier, 41, has a generational chip on his shoulder the size of the whole faux grunge scene circa 1994. Good thing he's got a decent platform. His new book, *X Saves the World: How Generation X Got the Shaft But Can Still Keep Everything From Sucking*, is a tongue-in-cheek polemic that's inspiring age-based debates in chat rooms, living rooms, and offices across the country.

Gordinier's book began as the essay "Has Generation X Already Peaked?" in *Details* magazine. He composed the rant in 4 days after the birth of his first son. "It grew out of a time when I think Gen-Xers were feeling colossally invisible. All the mass-media oxygen seemed to be sucked up by baby boomers and millennials. The baby boomers were turning 60, and that's all you heard about. How the boomers were turning 60 and they were still sexy and they're hot and they're launching their second acts," he said in an interview with

Time. "And at the same time, there's this media monotony, this bombardment of Lindsay/Paris/Britney . . . Lindsay/Paris/Britney . . . Lindsay/Paris/Britney—the Buddhists have a term called *samsara*, which is this sort of hell-cycle that you can never escape from until you meditate your way out of it. And I thought, my God, we're in some sort of *Us Weekly* samsara."

Where, he wondered, amid all this news about "the mating habits of AARP members" and their offspring's "bloggy, bling-bling birdsong of me-me-me-me-me sounds" were the cover stories about generation X turning 40? How about less Bob Dylan and more Kurt Cobain? "If *Nevermind* changed the world, the world changed back pretty fast," Gordinier writes.

Exile in Nicheville

Sandwiched between 80 million baby boomers and 78 million millennials, generation X—roughly defined as anyone born between 1965 and 1980—has just 46 million members, making it a dark-horse demographic "condemned by numbers alone to nicheville," as Gordinier puts it in the book. "I don't really understand the tyranny of the boomer moment," Gordinier says. "Great, you had a party in Haight-Ashbury in 1967, I'm thrilled for you. Can we hear about the flappers in the 1920s instead? How about the Great Depression? There's other times in history that are interesting."

Gordinier is no more entranced with today's teens and twenty-somethings: "They just love stuff. They love celebrities. They love technology. They love brand names. . . . They're happy to do whatever advertising tells them to do. So what if they can't manage to read anything longer than an instant message?"

It's something like a national case of sibling rivalry, with millennials playing the part of the spoiled, naive baby and boomers acting as the self-righteous firstborn. Gordinier's book, then, is like the earnest ranting of a forgotten middle child.

Gordinier graduated from Princeton in 1988, a year after the stock market crashed and just in time for a recession that left him and many of his peers jobless. He recalls moving back home and using FedEx instead of Gmail to send out his resume. Xers witnessed the rise of the yuppie and the burst of the dot-com bubble. Theirs, he argues, was a bleak inheritance. "Instead of getting free love, we got AIDS," says Douglas Rushkoff, author of 1993's *GenX Reader*. "We didn't believe the same kind of things as boomers. It was much harder to fool us." Just as Xers shunned boomer notions, it seems millennials have similarly turned against the Gen-X ethos. "If the Gen-Xers were like 'No, I'm not in it for the money,' millennials rebelled against that and are completely greedy," Gordinier says in a video he posted to YouTube about the book.

"I think they gave us something to work against,"

says Kate Torgovnick, a 27-year-old writer and former colleague of Gordinier's. And though she agrees that her generation might be more ambitious and self-promoting, she says millennials are far from the noncritical consumers that Gordinier portrays. "We grew up with courses that dissect the media and advertising, so I think we're even more aware of what's going on."

Here We Are Now, Ascertain Us

As with most generation labels, "generation X" is a loaded term, first coined and later disowned by Douglas Coupland, author of the 1991 book *Generation X: Tales for an Accelerated Culture.* For Coupland, the letter "X" was meant to signify the generation's random, ambiguous, contradictory ways. Similarly, Gordinier's book is at times contradictory, ambiguous, and random.

Though his original essay was melancholy and defeatist ("It's over, baby. Gen-X has been crushed. You might as well retire"), Gordinier's book conveys a far different message. Shirking the media myth that Xers are slackers, Gordinier argues that generation X has—to borrow a '60s term—changed the world. Citing Gen-X icons like Quentin Tarantino and Jon Stewart, along with Gen-X triumphs like Google, YouTube, and Amazon, among others, Gordinier argues that not only are Xers far from over, they might be the most unsung and influential generation of all time. "Gen-X stomping grounds of the past—the espresso bar, the record shop, the thrift

store—have been resurrected in digital form. The new bohemia is less a place than it is a headspace. It's flexible enough to bypass all the old binaries. It encompasses mass and class, mainstream and marginal, yuppie and refusenik, gearhead and Luddite. It's everywhere and nowhere in particular," he writes.

In short, "Gen-Xers are doing the quiet work of keeping America from sucking."

Gordinier Pleads His Case on YouTube

And what of the legacy that millennials inherited from generation X? Aren't Gen-X creations like YouTube and MySpace largely responsible for millennial narcissism? Didn't punk rock begat Rock Band? Perhaps. "We've created all these great Web sites that now millennials waste their lives on," Gordinier says with a laugh.

Somewhat ironically, these same technologies have also transformed the very notion of generations. Steve Gillon, author of *Boomer Nations: The Largest and Richest Generation Ever, and How It Changed America*, believes that people born between 1946 and 1964 will be the last to really experience national culture in such a unified way. "If you grew up in the '50s and '60s, you came of age at the same time that national culture first developed. There were three major TV networks. Everyone was watching the same thing. The assassination of J.F.K., for instance, was the first event the nation experienced in real time at the same time."

And of course, broad descriptions of generations are

not always true. A *Washington Post* review, titled "Wild Generalization X," called Gordinier's original essay "big fun . . . but all baloney." Gordinier's stock response? His generalizations "are more along the lines of mortadella, which is that really expensive and delicious baloney they make in Italy."

Gordinier wants to be clear about one thing: *X Saves the World* isn't personal. "A lot of what I'm doing is channeling all these things I would hear about millennials in the office, or boomers forcing their history down our throats," he tells *Time*. "It's more about radar. It's more about antennae. These are signals I'm picking up."

Source: M.L. Stephey. "Gex-X: The Ignored Generation?" Retreived from http://www .time.com/time/arts/ article/0,8599,1731528,00.html.

Generation Z Although still in their formative years, generation Z is expected to become a significant group of purchasers. This group consists of individuals who come from diverse backgrounds with a variety of life experiences. Now interested only in the products that typically appeal to children, they will eventually become the consumers of a multitude of products, making them serious targets for marketers.

INCOME

Although many demographic factors influence consumer buying preferences, income, more than any other factor, dictates what can and cannot be purchased. Retailers quickly come to understand that even though a customer might desire a couture design or a top-of-the-line model, his or her income ultimately determines the purchase decision. Shoppers know this, too. Therefore, advertisements should clearly state product prices so that consumers can plan their shopping efficiently and knowledgeably. Straightforward advertising benefits the merchants, as well, bringing more serious buyers and fewer window-shoppers to their stores.

3.3 Those with advanced education often shop in stores such as Brooks Brothers. *Courtesy of Brooks Brothers.*

EDUCATION

Shopping needs often differ according to educational background. People with higher education generally pursue careers that require "business attire" rather than "work clothes." For example, attorneys and investment bankers usually dress in business suits and are likely to purchase from retailers such as Brooks Brothers, who target them regularly in newspaper and direct-mail advertisements (Figure 3.3). People with less education generally can dress more casually for their jobs but may require, for example, steel-toed boots or cold-weather gear.

Retailers, depending on their product offerings, must carefully select their advertising media to reach the desired audience: the magazine *Vanity Fair*, for example, attracts young, educated, affluent readers, whereas *Entertainment Weekly* attracts a slightly older, slightly less-educated, less-affluent audience.

POPULATION CONCENTRATION

Purchasing behavior is influenced by factors such as social status, household composition, mobility,

ethnicity, and population density—factors that also define "neighborhood"—and can vary greatly from one ZIP code to the next. Because neighborhoods attract people of similar income level, ethnicity, age, and other demographics, it is helpful for advertisers to know the overall makeup of various regions, states, cities, small towns, and neighborhoods so they can concentrate their marketing efforts accordingly. The Nielsen Claritas segmentation system is a useful tool to help the retailer locate and define its markets so that advertising and merchandising efforts may be carefully directed. The essence of the Nielsen Claritas system is the subject of Focus 3.1.

OCCUPATION

Very important to today's purchasing decisions are individuals' occupations and places of employment. The investment banker's clothing, traditionally business suits, is significantly different from clothing worn by health-care workers, who often wear uniforms. People who work at home, a growing phenomenon in today's society, often wear relaxed clothing such as jeans and T-shirts. Even in department stores, dress codes are standardized, with retailers such as Bloomingdale's requiring employees to wear black attire. In addition to career dress, the requirements for after-work apparel differ. Fewer and fewer consumers opt for a more formalized look and tend to "go casual" in their leisure time.

Retailers must be aware of the employment needs of consumers and make certain their inventories and advertisements are properly focused on targeted audiences. They must also stay informed about changes in the workplace that affect the needs of their customers.

GEOGRAPHIC LOCATION AND CLIMATE

Where people live influences the types of products they require. Climate, of course, dictates clothing needs, including footwear. Retailers such as The Gap and Foot Locker, with coast-to-coast market reach in the United States, do not stock their northern stores with the same products as their southern stores. Their advertising must, therefore, be tailored to the inventory specific to each store's geographic location.

Geographic terrain (mountain, desert, seashore, etc.) also influences what people purchase. For

Nielsen Claritas

Conceived in 1961 by Jonathan Robbin, a scientist who understood that the United States was becoming a market of diverse populations and that they reacted and behaved differently, the Claritas concept was born. It was based on a segmentation system called PRIZM (Potential Rating Index ZIP Code Market), which sorted the population into similar groups by behavior and attributes so that businesses could make meaningful decisions based on this information. In 1974 Robbin founded Claritas, which means "brightness" in Latin.

The company became a significant marketing research organization that captured the attention of marketers around the country. Robbin's concept used massive amounts of data taken from the U.S. Census and segmented it according to demographic and behavioral information.

Claritas added significant core competencies that made it what many have called the premier market research company.

Claritas was acquired by VNU Group, a global information and media company that also owns Nielsen Media Research. Today known as Nielsen Claritas, the system has distinguished itself with numerous marketing milestones, including the following:

◆ The introduction of COMPASS, a desktop marketing analysis system

◆ The launching of SiteReports.com, a system of demographics for purchase online

◆ The introduction of iMARK Online, a remotely hosted application that allows users to perform site, market, and segmentation analysis over the Internet

◆ The introduction of ConsumerPoint, a target marketing system that harnesses the collective power of market demographics, consumer segmentation, and behavioral survey data to increase marketing effectiveness

example, someone living in the mountains would be more likely to buy mountain-climbing boots or a ski outfit than someone living in a seaside town, who would be more likely to purchase sandals and a swimsuit.

Geographic location and climate also affect the local economy and industries. A retailer in a predominantly agricultural area will be more likely to carry farming-related products than will a retailer in a large metropolitan area.

ETHNICITY

It is impractical to assume that all consumer segments have the same product needs if their ages, incomes, educational levels, geographic locations, and occupations are the same. Buying motives and habits differ among ethnic groups as well; merchants are paying greater attention to the needs and preferences of these consumers. The rich ethnic diversity of Americans—African Americans, Hispanics, Asian Americans, those of European descent, and others—provides retailers unique opportunities to broaden their inventories and customize their advertising to reach these populations.

Chapter 4, "Targeting the Multicultural Markets," focuses on the ways in which merchants are now tailoring their inventories to motivate these diverse segments to patronize their companies.

Family Life Cycle Classifications

By categorizing their potential customers according to family life cycle, retailers can better focus their advertisements. The concept of **life cycle classifications** is based on the premise that families can be grouped according to the age and family status of the heads of households. In addition to traditional groupings, "unconventional" segments now exist. Each classification has its own special requirements, and an understanding of them can help the retailer address them through advertising.

YOUNG UNMARRIED

Whether living alone or with friends or parents, the members of this group are responsible only for themselves. Except for the usual costs of rent and utilities, most of their **discretionary income** is spent on recreation, entertainment, and clothing. They are especially fashion conscious

and are excellent targets for retailers of in vogue or trendy items. Retailers whose product mixes feature fashion items usually get a good return on their advertising investments if their ads are properly targeted to this group. Very often, Internet and catalogue advertising bring significant responses from the young unmarried individual.

NEWLY MARRIED

Today, this family unit usually has two wage earners, making the newly married excellent targets for retailers. Because they share expenses, their discretionary income is often used to purchase clothing, accessories, electronics, entertainment, and other goods and services. Like the young unmarried group, the newly married frequently use online and catalogue purchasing.

SINGLE PARENTS

One of the fastest-growing segments of the population is the single-parent household. With the divorce rate high, this has become a very large group. Single parents must support themselves and their children, who may or may not live with them. Unless they are affluent, single parents often face considerable stress in stretching their incomes beyond the next paycheck. Women, in particular, find their discretionary purchasing power eroding. Typically earning less than their male counterparts and burdened with rearing children without the benefit of a partner, they find making ends meet a difficult task. Thus, single mothers are value shoppers who are targeted with newspaper ads, direct mail, and online focusing from such value merchants as Wal-Mart, Target, Kmart, Burlington Coat Factory, and Marshalls (Figure 3.4).

Single fathers have similar problems. Although either parent may be required to pay child support, and sometimes spousal support, it most often is the father who does so. They, too, are the frequent targets of value merchants' advertising promotions.

MULTIPLE-MEMBER/SHARED HOUSEHOLDS

Another fast-growing group in the family life cycle is the **multiple-member/shared household** group who live with others with whom there is no marital or family connection. This type of living

arrangement is especially common in big cities where apartment rents are extremely high and continue to soar. Several people sharing a single residence has become commonplace and a new household phenomenon.

Included in these arrangements are singles who live together with marriage as their eventual goal, members of same-sex relationships, members of the opposite sex without any amorous connections, and two or more sets of single parents whose children reside with them.

Although they fall into this diverse category, their purchasing characteristics vary considerably. Singles who live together with the intention of marriage often have considerable buying power, which they use to purchase luxury items. The same is true of same-sex relationships in which dual incomes and no plans for child rearing are typical, making this segment a valued target of high-end retail advertisers.

Of course, spending by those who share residences by necessity is most often limited, which makes them excellent households for value retail establishments.

FULL NESTERS

Full nesters fall into three distinct groups: those with very young children, those with teenagers, and those with older children who still live at home. In the first group, money is often in short supply. Either one parent stays home with the children or, if both are employed, the family must pay for child care. Expenditures are often restricted to the necessities of life, with little left for discretionary spending. Retailers who consider these households as their targets are those who sell baby products, food, home furnishings, toys, and some inexpensive apparel. Merchants such as Target, Kohl's, and Wal-Mart often direct their advertising to this group, especially with direct ads and Internet appeals.

The second group generally consists of two earners with more substantial incomes. Fashion merchandise is within their reach and therefore makes them excellent candidates for department and specialty stores. They are often motivated by newspaper ads as well as those that come from off-site formats, such as catalogues or Web sites. Their willingness and ability to spend more than they once did, when their household incomes were significantly lower, increases. Companies such as Macy's, Bloomingdale's, Dillard's, Belk, and Lord & Taylor often focus their appeals to this group.

In the third group, the children living at home are either older teens or in their twenties. Both parents generally work full-time and have greater disposable income than when their children were young. Their purchases often include better apparel, travel, entertainment, and some luxury items such as jewelry. Department stores such as Saks Fifth Avenue and upscale chains often direct their ads to this group (Figure 3.5).

EMPTY NESTERS

With their children now out on their own, **empty nesters'** financial responsibilities diminish. In this group, both the husband and wife may still work, or the couple may be retired. When both partners are working, their spending increases. Upscale fashion merchandise is often within their reach, as are luxury items, making them excellent targets for retailers who merchandise these

products. For retirees, travel is often a major purchase. Through a great deal of direct mail, they are targeted with brochures that sell cruises and planned tours.

SOLE SURVIVORS

As the lone survivor of a relationship, the remaining partner might still be employed or might be retired. In either case, sole survivors spend considerable amounts of money on travel. Those still interested in socialization spend money on clothing and other products. This group, however, is not targeted on a regular basis by retailers, except for those in the travel industry, who use direct mail to motivate older singles.

Psychographics

Along with the study of demographics, researchers use **psychographic segmentation**. The concept analyzes individuals' lifestyles and behavior in terms of their interests, values, opinions, and so forth. Coupled with the typical demographics, the information culled gives the investigator a better understanding of what motivates people to buy. For retailers in particular, the benefits of this type of research enable them to more accurately spend their advertising dollars.

There are numerous ways in which psychographics segments markets. One of the psychographic classification systems devised by the ad agency Young & Rubicam divides the segments into the following groups:

- *Succeeders:* These are individuals who are successful and self-confident. They do not generally purchase "aspirational" merchandise, and they follow their own ideas of what is a good product.

- *Reformers:* These are creative people who are caring and altruistic and are not usually tempted by brands. They purchase what they believe to be in their best interests.

- *Aspirers:* These are individuals who want to "get on."

- *Mainstreamers:* Most people belong to this group. They tend to buy products that are considered to be without risk, generally those that are nationally branded.

On Wednesday and Thursday there is a Trunk Show of the Judith Ripka collections at our Avondale and San Marco Locations.

Representatives of Judith Ripka will also be on hand with the 18 Karat couture collection and the Silver and Gold Judith Ripka collections.

JUDITH RIPKA

Wednesday, November 18th
Avondale
Hours: Noon - 5:30 P.M.

Thursday, November 19th
San Marco Square
Hours: 10 A.M. - 5:30 P.M.

UNDERWOOD'S

Serving Excellence Since 1928
Member American Gem Society

The Shoppes of Ponte Vedra (904) 280-1202
Avondale 3617 St. John's Ave. (904) 388-5406
San Marco Square
2044 San Marco Boulevard
Jacksonville, Florida 32207
(904) 398-9741
www.underwoodjewelers.com

3.5 Some full nesters have sufficient disposable income to purchase luxury items. *Courtesy Underwood's.*

SRI Consulting-Business Intelligence, now called Strategic Business Insights, maintains the Values and Life Style (VALS) psychographic system, the most widely used psychographic segmentation system in the marketing community. It is regularly updated through surveys that investigate consumer attitudes and motivations. Specifically, the VALS system assists retailers in the following:

- Identifying their target markets

- Uncovering what the target group buys and does in their lives

- Locating the areas in which the largest segments of the target market lives

- Identifying the best ways in which to communicate with their target groups

- Gaining insight into why the target group acts the way it does

Such information enables merchants not only to better pinpoint their target markets but also to more directly address their customers' needs.

VALS classifies consumers into eight profiles: **actualizers**, **fulfilleds**, **achievers**, **experiencers**, **believers**, **strivers**, **makers**, and **strugglers**. Each classification represents a different set of interests, motivations, and habits for those in the group (Figure 3.6).

A more detailed presentation of the concept is available at http://www.strategicbusinessinsights.com/vals/about.shtml.

Social Class Structure

Populations worldwide are divided into **social classes**. These class distinctions are based on some of the factors that were addressed earlier in the chapter, such as income and education, and sometimes on birthright. Being born into significant wealth and high social standing, for example, immediately places the offspring in the upper class.

To effectively appeal to the different social classes, the retailer must understand the groups' merchandising needs. This knowledge helps retailers to select the right merchandise mix and to better prepare their targeted ads.

In the United States, class structure is divided in four groups: upper class, middle class, working class, and lower class. For better targeting, the classes are subcategorized.

UPPER CLASS

The wealthiest people in our society belong to the upper class. It is estimated they represent about 3 percent of the population. Money, in particular, is the primary reason for inclusion in this class. Although this is the factor that separates those in this classification from others, it is also necessary to separate the upper class into two subclasses to better target them as purchasers.

Upper-Upper Class At the very top of the social class ladder are those who were born into families whose wealth has accumulated from one generation to the next. Generally, they are considered to have conservative taste and consider product quality of prime importance. Cost is unimportant to this group. In terms of product preference, they are the buyers of understated elegant fashion and automobiles of distinction. They tend to patronize the purveyors that offer them excellent service. Retailers that cater to this class are located on the most prestigious shopping streets in the United States and advertise their offerings in such newspapers as the *New York Times* and publications such as *Town and Country*, *Vogue*, *Harper's Bazaar*, and *Vanity Fair* (Figure 3.7).

Lower-Upper Class Often wealthier than those in the upper-upper class, the lower-upper class does not have the distinction of "family history." They are often the bankers, financiers, entertainers, and business tycoons who have come to be known as the **nouveau riche** of our society. They tend to be **conspicuous spenders**, generally purchasing luxury automobiles and couture clothing and indulging in lavish entertainment. At the end of 2008, when the stock market tumbled, many of the extravagances of these consumers came to light. Some were bilked of their wealth and lost such enormous sums that they tumbled into lower classes. Affected companies were the likes of jewelers such as Harry Winston as well as the couture boutiques and the restaurants that catered to this group.

3.6 The VALS 2 network.
Courtesy of SRI Consulting.

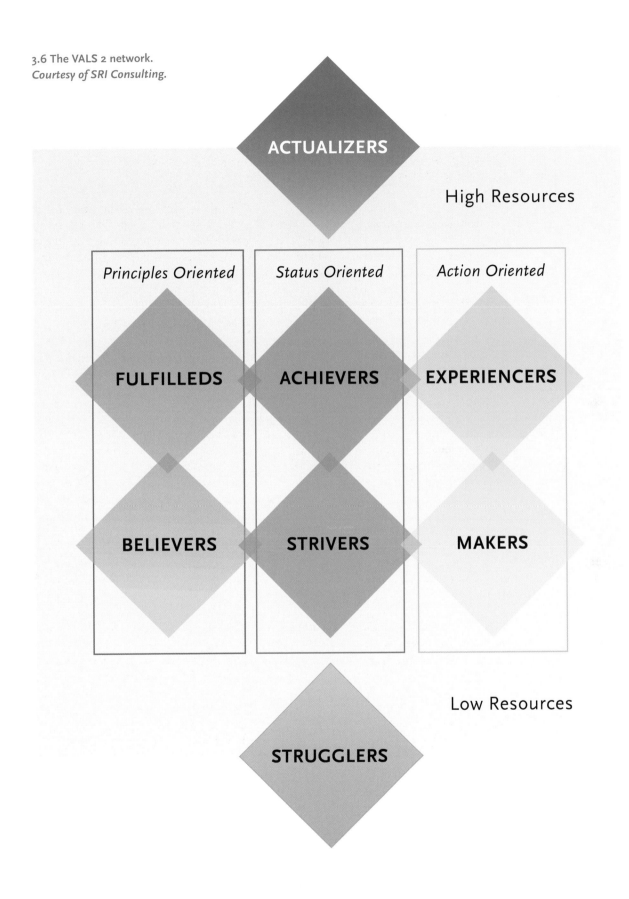

ACTUALIZERS

High Resources

Principles Oriented   *Status Oriented*   *Action Oriented*

FULFILLEDS   ACHIEVERS   EXPERIENCERS

BELIEVERS   STRIVERS   MAKERS

Low Resources

STRUGGLERS

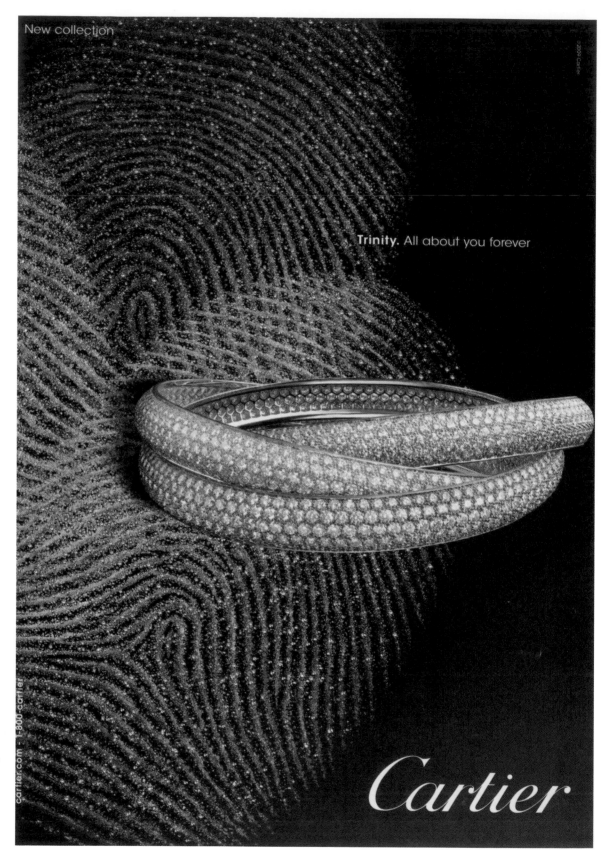

New collection

Trinity. All about you forever

Cartier

cartier.com • 1-800-cartier

3.7 The upper-upper class is often motivated to buy luxury items seen in prestige publications. *Courtesy Cartier.*

MIDDLE CLASS

Grouped together, the upper-middle class and lower-middle class account for approximately 42 percent of the population. Each segment is classified as middle class, but the two are distinctly different.

Upper-Middle Class Although their wealth pales by comparison to those in the upper class, the upper-middle class are considered by retailers to be the best consumer market in the country. Education-minded, they tend to send their children to private schools. They spend a great deal of their income on expensive fashion merchandise, cars of distinction, and extensive travel. They do not necessarily visit the couture boutiques for their fashion merchandise, but they do patronize stores such as Bloomingdale's. With many being savvy shoppers, the off-price venues that carry "bargain-priced" high fashion are the places they frequent (Figure 3.8).

Lower-Middle Class The lower-middle class has significantly less income than their upper-middle-class counterparts. They are cautious spenders and opt for practical merchandise. They frequent such retailers as Target and Wal-Mart, choose economy automobiles, and shop at off-price centers. Many are do-it-yourself enthusiasts. Value is generally what motivates them to buy, and retailers often lure them with advertisements that feature sales and closeouts.

LOWER CLASS

Approximately 55 percent of the U.S. population falls into the lower class. Toward the end of 2008, when the economy tumbled, these shoppers became more price conscious than ever before.

Upper-Lower Class Whether it is apparel, home furnishings, or food, the upper-lower class are first and foremost interested in price. Discounters such as Wal-Mart and Kmart are the retailers they most often frequent. Wholesale clubs such as Costco and Sam's Club are also the beneficiaries of their limited disposable income. Few buy on the Internet or purchase from catalogues but often turn to the home shopping networks for their purchases. Sale advertisements generally motivate them to shop.

Lower-Lower Class These shoppers purchase only what is necessary for survival. They generally shop in secondhand and thrift shops. Often with limited mobility, they are forced to purchase their needs from stores that are convenient to their homes. They are often victims of unscrupulous merchants who take advantage of their inability to go out of their neighborhoods to shop by charging them prices higher than the actual value of the merchandise.

3.8 The upper-middle class is replete with savvy shoppers who love fashion bargains. *Courtesy of Saks Fifth Avenue.*

Maslow's Hierarchy of Needs

American psychologist Abraham Maslow (1908–1970) was born and raised in Brooklyn, New York. Maslow attended the University of Wisconsin, and later, at Columbia University, he was mentored by the notable psychologist Alfred Adler, an early follower of Sigmund Freud. Eventually, he became the leader of the humanistic school of psychology that emerged in the 1950s and 1960s. He visualized human beings' needs arranged like a ladder, with the most basic at the bottom.

The needs process, according to Maslow, is predetermined in order of importance. It is generally depicted in pyramid style, with the most basic of needs at the bottom. These are the physiological needs, such as health, sexual satisfaction, and sleep. Retailers attempt to cash in on these requirements by stocking a host of products to satisfy them and producing ads that will help sell them.

The next level incorporates safety needs, and many products, such as home security systems and medical alert devices, are designed solely to meet this need. The automobile industry points out such safety features as airbags and antilock brakes in their advertisements. Other retailers, particularly of children's products and health-care products, similarly address safety as a key selling point.

Love/belonging comes next in the hierarchy of needs. The benefits of such products as cosmetics and jewelry, for example, are touted both on the selling floor and in ads as items that will make the purchaser more socially appealing.

Next, esteem needs satisfy the individual's concern for achievement, confidence, respect, and so forth. Sellers of prestigious cars such as Porsche sometimes use the notion in their ads that their car will make purchasers the envy of others.

Finally, the pinnacle of the scale addresses self-actualization. Colleges and universities appeal to those who want to maximize their potential.

Figure 3.9 illustrates the five stages of the theory as well as the fundamentals of each stage. It should be noted that as individuals reach each level, the next level in the hierarchy is likely to be fulfilled.

Needs Theories

There are numerous personality and motivation theories, or **needs theories**, the most well known of which is **Maslow's hierarchy of needs** (Figure 3.9). A renowned U.S. psychologist, Abraham Maslow is considered to be the father of humanistic psychology and has served retailers and other businesses, especially in their advertising endeavors, by providing a blueprint for satisfactorily motivating consumers to buy. The essence of his theory is offered in Focus 3.2.

Consumer Behavior

Along with the study of demographics, the family life cycle, social class structures, and psychographics, retailers also try to assess their markets through **consumer behavior** research. By discovering the different motivations and habits that compose the individual's reasons for purchasing, merchants can be better prepared to plan advertisements that will have the greatest appeal. Specifically, they study **buying motives** and **buying habits**.

Buying Motives

Do price and quality motivate a consumer to buy? Does the prestige of a label stimulate purchasing? Does a well-known logo such as the Ralph Lauren polo pony make it a better product or increase its desirability? Does shopping at a particular store provide convenience for the customer? The answers to these questions are used in advertising by the retailer to ensure success. The different responses are categorized as **emotional**, **rational**, or **patronage motives**.

EMOTIONAL MOTIVES

When an Armani suit or a BMW is purchased, it is often for reasons of status and prestige. Both Armani and BMW are impeccable brands in terms of quality and design, but they are often purchased for their prestigious impact as much as for their high-quality design. Many consumers, primarily those in the lower-upper class and the upper-middle class, are motivated to buy because of the pleasure they get from their admirers.

Retailers, when planning print and broadcast ads, understand that there is a marked audience

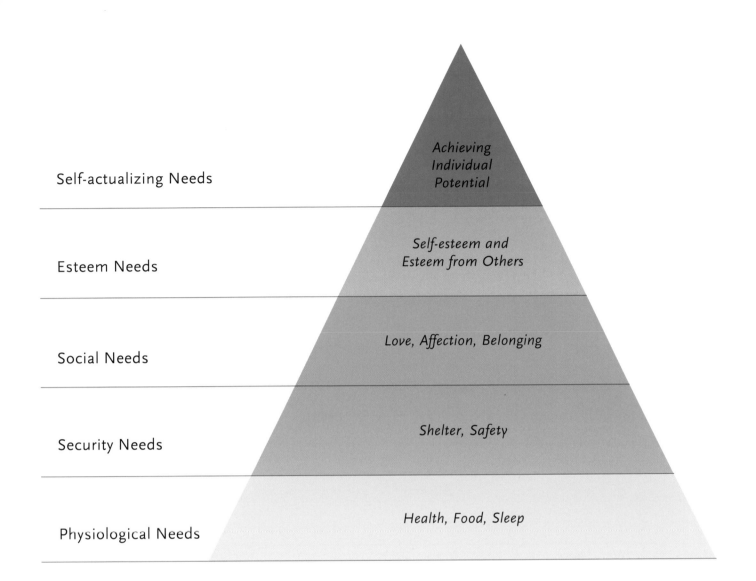

Self-actualizing Needs

Achieving Individual Potential

Esteem Needs

Self-esteem and Esteem from Others

Social Needs

Love, Affection, Belonging

Security Needs

Shelter, Safety

Physiological Needs

Health, Food, Sleep

for whom such an appeal is appropriate. These shoppers are driven by emotional motives. One need only look at the handbag that catapulted Louis Vuitton to fame to understand that emotion rather than rationality encourages the purchase: the bags in the Vuitton line sell for upward of $1,000 and are merely vinyl productions embellished with the LV monogram (Figure 3.10). It is an example of emotional buying at its best!

Merchants all over the world stock their inventories with items that carry the mystique of prestige. They need not extol the virtues of these products; they simply promote them in their stores and catalogues, on their Web sites, and in ads, quickly attracting people who are willing to pay dearly for the emotional comfort they find in such products.

RATIONAL MOTIVES

At the other end of the motivational spectrum is rationality. Goods that deliver quality, price, durability, serviceability, care, adaptability, and warranties are the very essence of value shopping. They attract individuals who strive to purchase the most serviceable products that fill their needs. Especially in times of economic stress, consumers make practical, rational buying decisions.

Retailers such as Marshalls, Wal-Mart, T.J. Maxx, Office Depot, Staples, and Best Buy use rational motivation to attract their markets (Figure 3.11). The increasingly popular off-price centers are the arenas in which rational purchasing is dominant. In both visual displays and advertisements, these retailers emphasize low price and other factors that will attract attention.

3.9 Maslow's hierarchy of needs.

3.10 The purchase of luxury goods is often emotionally motivated. *Courtesy Louis Vuitton.*

It is interesting to note that many people with significant disposable incomes are patronizing the off-price centers to find designer labels at reduced prices. Finding a bargain has become a point of pride for them.

PATRONAGE MOTIVES

In addition to the emotional and rational motives that account for consumer decision making, retailers are concerned with other factors that influence where consumers shop: convenience, services offered, salesperson assistance, price points, exchange policies, assortments, and so forth. With the competitive nature of retailing, it is imperative that merchants let potential customers know what they can expect from the store and the staff. What better way than through advertising to offer this information?

The increase in Internet sales is partly due to the convenience it provides the shopper. When going to the store is impractical because of time constraints and other consumer responsibilities, the retailer's Web site is an ideal alternative: people can shop from home, from work, from the backseat of a taxi cab, or during their child's ballet recital. Catalogue shopping offers similar convenience.

For both on-site and off-site shoppers, merchants must address patronage motives to make the shopping experience as comfortable as possible so that customers keep coming back.

Consumer Research

Today's retailers, more than in the past, are conducting research to make certain they are using the proper tools to motivate consumers to buy: a variety of approaches may be used for this purpose. Outside assistance is one route to use to gain this information, often involving trade

association consultation, governmental resources, and marketing research groups. For the major players, original research is often the answer. Some use marketing research firms to conduct their studies, others maintain in-house teams, and some use a combination of the two.

Research Providers

One or a combination of the following groups provides the information necessary to investigate anything from customer preferences to advertising approaches.

◆ *Trade associations* are generally involved in research that is timely and may help the merchant with data and suggestions that could improve the direction his or her business should take. Membership in such groups as the National Retail Federation (NRF) and the International Mass Retail Association offers access to a wealth of research studies that could help direct decision making.

◆ *Government resources*, especially on the federal level, deliver information without any cost to the retailer. Of particular significance is the U.S. Census Bureau, which provides a wealth of demographic data. Charts, tables, current and projected data, and other reports are easily obtained on the Census Bureau's Web site, http://www.census.gov.

◆ *Market research groups* are numerous, and many specialize in retail research. They offer everything from individual to generic

3.11 People who shop for quality are considered to be rational shoppers. *Courtesy of Best Buy.*

studies. The Nielsen Company is one of the better known organizations that specialize in research for advertising.

- *In-house teams* provide the advantage of studying firsthand the dilemmas that face the retailer, including those that are consumer-behavior oriented. These teams are important components of an organization because they have an ongoing awareness of the direction in which management is taking the company, a plus for any research endeavor.

Areas of Investigation

Studying the consumer helps retailers determine how their businesses can best maximize profitability. Merchants often direct research efforts toward the following:

1. Determining which of the multichannel avenues consumers frequent most for their purchases

2. Assessing the advertisement factors that motivate consumers to buy

3. Assessing whether the company's Web site is easy to maneuver

4. Determining whether their direct-mail pieces generate sufficient excitement to motivate purchasing

5. Assessing the importance of personal service to consumers' merchandise selections

6. Assessing whether the company's price points generally meet consumers' expectations

7. Assessing whether the merchandise assortments are appropriate to consumers' needs

8. Determining whether the shopping hours fit consumers' schedules

9. Assessing which departments best satisfy consumers' shopping experience

10. Determining whether consumers find the Sunday newspaper more important than the daily newspaper

These and other areas of concern are studied using the research tools discussed next.

Research Tools

For consumer research, the most commonly used research tools are focus groups and questionnaires.

FOCUS GROUPS

Focus groups are representative groups of people who are the retailer's customers or who have characteristics that make them potential customers. Typically, the group comprises 10 to 15 people who participate on a one-time or regular basis (Figure 3.12). A moderator notes the participants' various opinions about the topic of study. The information is recorded and generally videotaped. Extremely important to the success of the focus group is the selection of a competent moderator. He or she must be able to record even the smallest subtleties observed in participants' reactions.

Relatively new to the focus group concept of research is the online format. Chat and conferencing technology enabling real-time conversation has in some cases replaced the use of in-person panels. Using online focus groups allows retailers and other business users to save on travel, meeting room rentals, and other costs associated with gathering groups of people in one location. Another advantage, especially for large retail organizations, is the ability to gain insights from audiences who may be scattered around the country or even around the world. Advertising copy research, so important to retailers, can easily be accomplished with online participation.

One of the pioneers of this concept is Brand Amplitude. The use of online focus groups for innovative research and brand strategies is a major component of its investigative business tools. Brand Amplitude's Web site, http://www. brandamplitude.com, reveals the numerous ways in which the company helps businesses.

QUESTIONNAIRES

The standard tool for gathering information about consumers is the questionnaire. Through

a series of questions, retailers can evaluate customers' needs and, of significant importance to satisfying sales goals, the effectiveness of the business's advertisements. Questionnaires are completed through personal interviews, by telephone, through traditional mail, or by e-mail, with the latter becoming the method of choice for many researchers because of its cost-effectiveness and quick response potential. No matter which type of collection procedure is followed, the questionnaire must be carefully prepared to ensure the most helpful response. It should be as brief as possible to gather the necessary information and should use language that can be easily understood by respondents. Questions should be arranged in sequential order and should avoid the use of such words as *generally* and *usually*. Multiple-choice rather than open-ended questions should be used whenever possible for easier recording and processing of data.

After the data have been collected, it is processed and analyzed, then presented in a written report so that management may proceed with its recommendations.

Summary of Key Points

◆ Market segmentation is vital to the success of the retailer because the one-size-fits-all philosophy is no longer applicable to today's diverse population. Segmentation enables the merchant to divide people into groups so that he or she can select those best suited to be targeted.

◆ Demographic analysis is the study of the population in terms of age, income, education, geographic location, occupations, ethnicity, and population concentration.

Terms of the Trade

achievers

actualizers

believers

buying habits

buying motives

conspicuous spenders

consumer behavior

demographics

discretionary income

emotional motives

empty nesters

esteem needs

experiencers

focus groups

fulfilleds

full nesters

generation X

generation Y

generation Z

generational categories

gray heads

life cycle classifications

love/belonging

makers

market segmentation

market segments

Maslow's hierarchy
   of needs

multiple-member/
   shared household

needs theories

nouveau riche

one-size-fits-all
   philosophy

patronage motives

physiological needs

psychographic
   segmentation

rational motives

safety needs

self-actualization

social classes

strivers

strugglers

◆ In addition to the traditional age classifications, researchers use the generational approach and divide the groups into generations X, Y, and Z.

◆ The family life cycle is another tool that helps the retailer learn more about purchasing needs. Each category has its own special requirements, and knowing these requirements helps the merchant better address the needs of potential customers.

◆ Retailers have gone beyond the study of demographics with the use of psychographic segmentation. The concept analyzes lifestyles and behavior in terms of consumers' interests, values, opinions, and so forth.

◆ In the United States, there are three social classes, each of which has different merchandise needs. By studying these classifications, the retailer is better able to pinpoint the methodology that should be used to attract each to his or her company.

◆ The best known of the needs theories is Abraham Maslow's hierarchy of needs. Needs are arranged in five distinct categories, each of which must be satisfied before going on to the next.

◆ Buying motives are categorized into three areas: emotional, rational, and patronage. Each addresses the motives that drive consumer purchasing.

◆ Consumer research is carried out by retailers to make certain they are using the proper business tools to reach their targeted markets. The research providers include trade associations, government resources, market research groups, and in-house teams. The methodology each uses is one and the same.

For Discussion

1. Why is it no longer appropriate for retailers to subscribe to a one-size-fits-all philosophy when trying to reach consumers?

2. Differentiate between the traditional and generational demographic classifications.

3. What is the basis of Claritas's system known as PRIZM?

4. How does categorizing individuals according to family life cycles assist retailers with their advertising appeals?

5. What is meant by the word *psychographics*, and how does psychographics differ from demographics when used to study market segmentation?

6. In what way does the upper-upper class differ from the lower-upper class, and do these differences affect the ways in which each purchase?

7. Discuss the five stages of Maslow's hierarchy of needs.

8. Does the study of rational and emotional buying motives help the retailer make significant adjustments to advertising?

9. Why do some merchants conduct their own research studies if there are numerous studies available from trade organizations and market research organizations?

10. Through what means has the focus group as a research tool reduced its costs to the user?

Exercises and Projects

1. Either through in-person visits to a major retailer's headquarters or by contacting the company by mail, e-mail, or telephone, find out about its approaches to consumer research and prepare a paper outlining the following:

   ◆ How the retailer learns about consumer preferences (e.g., does it use in-house investigation or an outside agency?).

◆ What areas of concern are most important, in terms of consumer research, to the success of the company's advertising approach.

◆ The relative importance of the different multichannel avenues to producing sales.

2. The paper should be two to three pages and double-spaced.

3. Using a search engine such as www.google.com, research "generation Y" to learn more about the group's importance to retailers. Include such information as the types of products they most frequently purchase, the retailers they are most likely to patronize, and channels they prefer in making their purchases. Using the information obtained, prepare a 10-minute talk about generation Y.

4. Prepare a questionnaire that focuses on what consumers look for in advertising. The form should include such pertinent information as age group, sex, income range, level of education, channel(s) preferred when making purchases, and anything else pertinent for a retailer to use in the creation of newspaper ads. The form should be one page in length, present the questions in sequential order, and offer response choices.

Web Site Exploration for In-Depth Analysis

U.S. Census Bureau
http://www.census.gov
This site provides free information, such as charts and graphs of the most recent census, plus projections that are imperative to demographic analysis.

Nielsen Company
http://en-us.nielsen.com/expertise
The site gives a wealth of information about tasks such as measuring market performance, analyzing market dynamics, diagnosing marketing problems, and identifying growth opportunity, all important to researchers.

Journal of Consumer Research
http://www.jcr.wisc.edu/di.htm
This site offers scholarly research on consumer behavior.

UNITED COLORS
OF BENETTON.

Targeting *the* Multicultural Markets

CHAPTER OBJECTIVES

After you have completed this chapter, you will be able to discuss:

★ The purchasing power of the three major ethnicities in the United States—African Americans, Hispanics, and Asian Americans—and why they are important as consumers.

★ Why the Asian-American population is such an important segment of the minority population even though its numbers are far fewer than African Americans, Hispanics, and Caucasians.

★ The significance of the ethnic advertising media to retailers in the United States.

★ Why cable television plays an important role in reaching minority consumers in the United States.

★ The impact of digital advertising on minority consumers.

★ In what ways advertisers tailor their messages to the ethnic minorities.

★ The importance of multicultural ad agencies and how they differ from the traditional agencies.

Not too many years ago, marketers treated the consumer population as a single entity when making their plans to sell products and thus concentrated their advertising efforts with a one-size-fits-all philosophy. That is, whereas market segments were typically fragmented according to such demographics as age, geographic concentration, occupation, population concentration, and so forth, little if any attention was paid to the multicultural nuances that impacted purchasing decisions. Although the assessment of segmentation is still vital to properly address consumer needs, it has become apparent that the concept of **multiculturalism** is important.

In this era of **ethnic diversity**, it behooves marketers to closely inspect the different ethnicities and make certain that their needs are being met. Research initiatives must be broadened to take into account all of the wants and needs of these diverse cultural groups so that retail advertising and promotional endeavors properly reach them. Using appropriate investigative tools and the application of the results from studies, retailers can learn how to best appeal to these ever-growing segments of American culture.

There are a multitude of ethnic minorities in the United States, each with special product needs, but three groups top the list in numbers and buying power: African Americans, Hispanics, and Asian Americans. Often different in terms of needs in such areas as food, clothing, and cosmetics, the significant growth of these ethnic groups in recent years makes analysis of their needs vital to the success of the retailer. Whether it is the department store, specialty chain, supermarket operation, direct-mail merchant, Internet outlet, or any other merchant classification, each retailer must make a significant effort to ensure its advertising programs are being properly coordinated and devised so that these vitally important minority groups are being motivated to purchase its products.

Advertising is not the only aspect of the retailer's operation that must be addressed to best serve a multicultural population. Merchandise offerings, visual merchandising, and staffing are also important in maximizing the sales potential from these population segments.

Media Insight 4.1 succinctly summarizes the importance of the African-American community to merchants and how a great deal of business can be overlooked if the merchant fails to properly target it.

Considerations for Capturing Ethnic Consumer Markets

Given the enormous sales potential that has been predicted by many marketing analysts in regard to minority purchasing, retailers are paying closer attention to the needs of minority groups. With the buying power of the African-American market alone estimated to reach $1.1 trillion by 2012, retail interest in the group has peaked. Of significant interest to upscale merchants is that almost half of that amount will be spent by the affluent African-American segment (Figure 4.1). Those who earn $75,000 or more are extremely interested in fashion apparel and accessories.

Perhaps even more startling are the projected population numbers of the Hispanic community. According to the marketing research organization Packaged Facts Web site, "The Hispanic population will grow much quicker than other population segments, and Hispanic consumers will represent an increasing percentage of the American consumer base."

Although the Asian-American population is significantly lower than the African-American and Hispanic populations, they are the most affluent consumer group in the United States, even when the Caucasian segment is counted. The importance of the Asian-American market is evidenced by the fact that one in three Asian-American households have incomes that exceed $100,000. This is especially important to retailers of upscale merchandise such as luxury automobiles and designer clothing.

Don't Bypass African Americans

Marissa Miley

In 2008, the country's top marketers tapped Barack Obama as Marketer of the Year. Many of those same marketers also cut spending directed at the African-American market.

With advertisers chasing after niche markets such as mommy bloggers on tools such as Twitter, a "niche" worth $913 billion would seem the sort of market companies would be stumbling over each other to get to. Yet the African-American market has to continually make the case that it's a segment worth understanding, and one worth a dedicated portion of the ad budget.

African Americans—and the African-American market—were surpassed in the past five years by the growing Hispanic sector, leading many marketers and the media to focus intently on the "next big thing" in the minority sector. According to Nielson, total spending in Spanish-language media in the first three quarters of 2008 was $4.3 billion, up 2.7 percent from the year before. Total spending on African-American media in that time period was $1.8 billion, down 5.3 percent from the same period in 2007. (Proctor & Gamble was the largest spender in both categories.)

Still, the African-American segment has buying power of $913 billion, according to 2008 data from the Selig Center for Economic Growth at the University of Georgia. That's why African-American marketing experts are flummoxed that there is an implied question floating around the C-suites in the United States:

Why bother targeting the demographic specifically?

Putting aside high-minded issues such as diversity and multiculturalism, the simple answer is: to make money.

"It makes sense to address 40 million people who are African American if you want to capture their consumer behavior," said Alfred Liggins, president and CEO of Radio One, pointing out that marketers frequently target niche consumer segments such as new moms, outdoor enthusiasts, and foodies. "Why is it an issue when you say that Black people are a niche?"

The justifications marketers use are many, particularly in a recession: targeting African Americans costs too much; it takes dollars away from general marketing; it does not add value. On a recent industry panel, Steve Stoute, founder and CEO of consulting/branding firm Translation, suggested some brands do well with African Americans precisely because they don't market to the segment and are therefore seen as aspirational. (Mr. Stoute declined to participate in this story.)

Another justification: "They speak English, don't they?" mocked Pepper Miller, president of Hunter-Miller Group, an African-American market research and consulting firm. She said marketers typically have this reaction because of the significant growth of the Latino market over the past couple of decades.

"That growth has become a catalyst for corporate America to embrace language as a cultural identifier, not race," she said. "It's easier to make the case that a group speaking a different language deserves a unique type of marketing."

African Americans, on the other hand, because they share a common language with White America, are assumed to share the same culture and same interests. Why bother with the research and expense when you can just recycle general-market advertising and maybe throw in a couple Black actors?

"Step one is to recognize both the profitability and buy-ability of these market groups," said Jason Chambers, author of *Madison Avenue and the Color Line*.

Of course, there are some marketers who recognize that. And perhaps it's no coincidence that they are among the most successful brands in the United States.

Najoh Tita-Reid, former director of multicultural marketing at Proctor & Gamble, took the lead on the company's "My Black Is Beautiful" effort before leaving the company last month. She pointed to McDonald's and State Farm Insurance as two large corporations that have invested in the African-American market and met success.

"Do you believe one size fits all?" asked Carol Sagers, director–marketing at McDonald's USA. "Intuitively, you don't."

"African Americans have nuances in lifestyle and nuances in language and culture that should be used to leverage communication," she said. "McDonald's believes in speaking to them directly."

By speaking to African Americans, marketers can enhance their positioning in the general market as well—especially considering how much of mainstream pop culture gets its start in the African-American community.

For example, Ms. Tita-Reid said McDonald's "I'm Lovin' It" campaign was rooted in hip-hop culture but had messaging that transcended race and ethnicity and gained popularity around the world. "It's worth leading with African-American insights," Ms. Miller said. "When companies use these insights to develop their marketing strategies, communication strategies [and] media plans, they have the most effective strategies not only reaching African Americans, but the general market as well."

State Farm has experienced this with its "50 Million Pound Challenge," a sponsored weight loss effort that began in the African-American community. Since the program launched in April 2007, one million Americans have lost 3.5 million pounds.

"It now has a life of its own," said Pamela El, VP-marketing for State Farm. "All races and ethnicities have joined the challenge."

"We know through research . . . that a way to connect to a different customer is to emotionally connect first and help that community."

The Selig Center estimates that Black buying power will rise to $1.2 trillion in 2013—and that this number will translate to nearly 9 percent of the nation's estimated buying power. "Why people continue to question this customer segment continues to baffle me," said Mr. Chambers. "The proof is there."

Of course, treating a market knocking on $1 billion as one cohesive niche is oversimplifying things—similar to making broad generalizations about Hispanics just because they speak Spanish. Yet it's another mistake commonly made when marketers do target African Americans.

"We have never been a homogenous market," Ms. Miller said. "But we have never been as different and segmented as we are today."

Last June, Mr. Liggins's Radio One—the largest African-American broadcasting company, which includes TV One, Interactive One, and *Giant Magazine*—sponsored a Black segmentation study by consumer-research firm Yankelovich. The study, called Black America Today, was the largest of its kind. It surveyed 3,400 African Americans and identified 11 different consumer segments, ranging from "digital networkers" to "broadcast Blacks," each group with its own diverse preferences and needs. Digital networkers tend to be in their 20s and are heavy users of social networking sites, whereas broadcast Blacks are significantly less tech-savvy and rely more on TV and radio.

"I define African Americans as a fast-growing, emerging market inside a mature market in the United States," Mr. Liggins said. "There is still more opportunity in the U.S. market to tap."

Companies need to research the different segments and understand how to efficiently reach each one. Research, though, is neither free nor easy—especially for the ad agencies and research firms who aren't exactly exemplars of racial diversity. "Marketers need to ask questions and listen," said Ms. Miller. "If we are segmented more, and if niche marketing is the new ideal, then why aren't we going after these [segments]?"

One way to tap into these segments is to target Black media. The Black America Today study found that on average, African Americans are more than twice as likely to trust Black media over

mainstream media. Also, 81 percent of all African Americans ages 13 to 74 watch Black-interest TV channels weekly, and 68 percent are online, about the same percentage of Americans as a whole.

But Ms. Sagers cautions against marketing to African Americans exclusively on Black media. "African American media suppliers are very important, but so are all other media suppliers," she said. African Americans consume a lot of different media, and in order to connect with the Black community, "Creative has to touch a nerve," she said.

"There is still money left on the table if [marketers] don't equally invest in the research and insights to obtain market share from this still large, growing, and trendsetting consumer group," Ms. Tita-Reid said.

Many feel that while there have been visible improvements in race-based marketing over the years, a number of challenges that impede further progress stem from a lack of diversity within corporations themselves.

"It's easy to get left out of the dialogue," said Mr. Liggins.

Still, he added that for as many marketers that don't get it, there are those that do. Since the publication of Black America Today, Mr. Liggins has presented to Apple, Unilever, and General Mills, among others, and believes that by educating marketers about his findings, more marketers will see the business value of marketing to the African-American community.

Source: Marissa Miley. "Don't Bypass African Americans." Advertising Age. February 2, 2009.

4.1 According to marketing analysts, affluent African-American women are extremely interested in fashion apparel. *Rolf Bruderer/Blend Images/Alamy.*

Research conducted by ACNielsen using its ScanTrack service evaluates the effectiveness of micromarketing efforts targeted to population segments with specific ethnic characteristics. Unilever and Meredith Integrated Marketing, a communications marketing organization, conclude the following:

◆ By 2012, minorities are expected to constitute more than one-third of the U.S. population.

◆ By 2020, the three major ethnicities are expected to have grown at six times the rate of the **nonethnic population.**

◆ By 2050, one in four workers will be Hispanic. (*Source:* Chiqui Cartagena, *Latino Boom!*, Ballantine Books, 2005; also, personal interview with author.)

Advertisers must carefully evaluate the demographics of minority groups in order to develop effective advertising campaigns that will motivate these groups to buy.

Buying Power

Today's ethnic populations have made inroads in terms of **purchasing power,** once considered improbable by many industry professionals. The increase in buying potential for the three major ethnicities has made them the targets of most U.S. retailers for a wealth of products. The total **disposable personal income** available after taxes for spending on goods and services has prompted advertisers to make considerable adjustments to their advertising focuses and expenditures. Major retailers such as Sears, JCPenney, Wal-Mart, Target, and Kohl's have redirected their advertising and promotional efforts to bring Hispanics, African Americans, and Asian Americans to their premises and off-site ventures.

Table 4.1 shows the dollar changes in buying power, from 1990 through projected 2012 figures, for the major ethnic minorities.

According to Media Trends Track, by 2012 African Americans will spend more on groceries and footwear; Hispanics will spend more on groceries, furniture, and children's clothing; and Asian Americans will spend more on food and children's clothing in comparison to the total population of the United States. Also significant is that African Americans will account for 8.7 percent of all U.S. buying power by 2012, up from 7.4 percent in 1990; Hispanic buying power will be 9.7 percent for the same period, up from 5 percent; and Asian Americans will be 5.2 percent, up from 2.7 percent.

TABLE 4.1 — Buying Power in Billions of Dollars

	1990	2000	2007	2012
African American	318.1	590.2	845.4	1,134.9
Hispanic	211.9	489.5	861.8	1,261.1
Asian American	116.5	268.8	459.3	670.1
Total	4,270.5	7,187.6	10,006.4	12,976.4

Source: Media Trends Track Survey, Television Bureau of Advertising.

Celebrating Over 100 Years

NEW YORK Amsterdam News

Vol. 101 No. 14 April 1-April 7, 2010
© 2010 The Amsterdam News

The new Black view
www.amsterdamnews.com

$1.00 New York City

No budge on budget

By HERB BOYD
Special to the AmNews

On the eve of the state's budget deadline, there was more bad news. Because of critical fiscal problems, Gov. David Paterson announced on Tuesday a delay in the school payment of more than $2 billion.

"The only way our state can put its long-term fiscal house in order is through significant, recurring spending reductions," Paterson explained in a recent statement to the press. "In the short-term, however, plummeting revenue and record deficits have once again forced me to take extraordinary cash-management actions in order to ensure the continued, orderly operation of our government."

Paterson said the school payment may be issued in June, the actual statutory due date, "assuming sufficient cash is available at that time," he said.

This action is certain to put another bump in the road as the governor, the Senate and the Assembly struggle to find common ground on the budget and close the more $9 billion deficit.

There appears to be very little time and wiggle room for the state legislature to find an additional $1 billion in cuts.

On Friday, Sheldon Silver, the Assembly speaker, and John L. Sampson, the Senate Democratic leader, convened a public joint conference but failed to make any headway on revenue and spending.

"There are no changes yet," Silver told the press about the Senate and Assembly budget proposals. "We are now going through a detailed analysis of both with the governor's office, finding where we have joint agreements, both as to cuts and to revenues, and what further cuts or revenues will fit into a fiscal plan for the state."

"Unfortunately, the spending plans
(Continued on Page 29)

The offices of the Amsterdam News will be closed for Good Friday on Friday, April 2, and will reopen for business as usual at 9 a.m. on Monday, April 5.

DUNCES

State misses out on close to $1 billion in federal funds for education

(Bill Moore photo)

By CYRIL JOSH BARKER and MARY ABDUL-ALEEM
Amsterdam News Staff

It appears everyone is pointing the finger at each other as the question arises as to why New York was passed up for millions of federal dollars from the U.S. Department of Education. Between the city, the state and education officials, everyone seems to be a player in the blame game.

According to the U.S. Department of Education, New York ranked 15th out of the 16 finalists for a $770 million grant. Money instead went to Delaware and Tennessee in the first round of Race to the Top grants. A **(Continued on Page 29)**

NAACP says, make it count

By CYRIL JOSH BARKER
Amsterdam News Staff

The NAACP is encouraging the Black community to take part in the 2010 Census. The 10-question sheet used to determine America's population arrived in mailboxes across the nation earlier this month.

The civil rights organization's "Yes We Count" initiative aims to get more Black people to fill out the Census in order to get an accurate count.
(Continued on Page 29)

(Issu Diouf photo)

After Decades of Struggle – A Milestone in Health Care

Urban Agenda by *David R. Jones*
Community Service Society of New York President

See Page 5

TABLE 4.3 — Top 25 Hispanic Newspapers
(by measured advertising revenue, excluding classified)

RANK	NEWSPAPER	GROSS 2008 AD REVENUE ($ IN THOUSANDS)	% CHANGE
1	El Nuevo Herald (Miami)	$72,776	−19.5
2	La Opinion (Los Angeles)	35,193	−23.2
3	El Diario La Prensa (New York)	25,732	0.1
4	El Diario (Juarez, Mexico)	25,308	−24.9
5	Hoy (Chicago)	21,709	8.1
6	El Norte (El Paso, TX/Juarez, Mexico)	12,100	12.5
7	La Raza (Chicago)	10,234	−12.1
8	Hoy (Los Angeles)	10,150	−21.4
9	Washington Hispanic	8,910	−14.3
10	El Sentinel (Miami–Fort Lauderdale)	8,189	33.2
11	La Voz de Phoenix	8,038	27.4
12	Al Dia (Dallas)	6,800	5.8
13	Hoy (New York)	6,460	−39.2
14	Diario Las Americas (Miami)	6,047	1.3
15	La Voz de Houston	4,194	9.6
16	Prensa Hispana (Phoenix)	3,792	−2.1
17	Vida en El Valle (Fresno, CA)	3,568	5.7
18	Al Dia (Philadelphia)	3,534	10.0
19	TV y Mas (Phoenix)	3,512	−48.5
20	Mundo L.A. (Los Angeles)	3,031	N.A.
21	El Latino (San Diego)	2,799	−11.2
22	Lawndale News (Chicago)	2,713	−29.8
23	El Especial (New York)	2,522	−11.1
24	Excelsior (Orange County, CA)	2,185	−3.2
25	El Mensajero (San Francisco)	2,153	−10.5

Source: "2009 Hispanic Fact Pack." Advertising Age, July 27, 2009, Crainn Communications, Inc., p. 22.

Of the 25 newspapers listed in Table 4.3, 14 have experienced declines in advertising revenue. Although the dailies are declining, weeklies are growing in number, as reported by Kirk Whisler, president of the Latino Print Network in Carlsbad, California. An important influence on the Hispanic media is that native-born Hispanics now outnumber Hispanic immigrants in the United States, and most of them are likely to read English, use the Internet, and get more of their news online. According to Whisler,* 60 percent of native-born Hispanics are under the age of 18, and as they age, their impact on the Hispanic publications is likely to grow. Another factor that could affect the viability of the Hispanic newspaper is the slower rate of immigration.

*From Kirk Whisler, "The State of the News Media 2007: Audience." www.journalism.org

4.3 African-American magazines have significant circulation. *Courtesy of Cover Girl.*

A government crackdown on illegal immigration is dramatically slowing immigration to the United States and, therefore, affecting Hispanic newspaper readership.

Asian Americans are targeted through numerous newspapers published in their native languages (e.g., Japanese, Vietnamese, Korean). The most widely read ethnic newspapers in the United

States are published in Chinese. The *Sing Tao Daily*, founded in 1938 in Hong Kong, has grown into one of the largest Chinese-language newspapers in the United States, with editions in San Francisco, New York, Philadelphia, Boston, and Chicago. Its chief rival is the *World Journal*.

Other Asian-American newspaper publications include the *Korea Times*, the *Korea Daily*, and the *Nguoi Viet*, the largest Vietnamese-language paper in the United States.

Magazines

Magazines continue to fare better than newspapers. *Ebony*, *Jet*, and *Black Enterprise*, in particular, have enjoyed monthly circulation gains (Figure 4.3). Each reaches audiences throughout the United States and enjoys a wealth of advertising revenue.

Also showing great staying power is the Hispanic magazine industry. Table 4.4 demonstrates that the top ten Hispanic magazines enjoy considerable advertising revenue.

Rounding out the ethnic minority magazine offerings are the Asian-American publications such as *Jade*, *Hyphen*, *Audrey*, and *Asiance*. As in the case of newspapers, magazines are also published in a variety of major Asian languages.

Television

Cable television is home to three Black networks. Each continues to extend its reach by becoming available to more households. The biggest of these networks is BET, which is available in more than 90 million households. Behind BET is TV ONE, with more than 60 million households enjoying its programming, and the Africa Channel with more than 8 million viewers. Africa Channel, originating from Africa, made its debut in 2008 with outlets in Los Angeles and New York. It features soaps, lifestyle, travel, sports, documentaries, reality shows, music, and news.

For the Hispanic audience, there are two Spanish-speaking networks in the United States, with ratings showing continued demand for Spanish-language television programming (Figure 4.4).

TABLE 4.4

Top 10 Hispanic Magazines
(by measured advertising revenue, excluding classified)

RANK	MAGAZINE	GROSS 2008 AD REVENUE ($ IN THOUSANDS)	% CHANGE
1	People en Español	$53,287	7.2
2	Latina	35,278	−2.1
3	Ser Padres	21,539	NA
4	TV y Novelas	18,934	17.2
5	Vanidades	14,938	18.5
6	Selecciones (ceased publication)	13,155	−14.2
7	Siempre Mujer	12,754	−1.1
8	Mira	8,934	12.5
9	Hispanic Business	7,269	−19.8
10	TV Notas	6,999	11.7

Source: "2009 Hispanic Fact Pack." *Advertising Age*, July 27, 2009, Crain Communications, Inc.

4.4 Many Hispanic households watch Spanish-speaking TV shows.
Ann Johansson/ Corbis.

According to the *Hispanic Fact Pack,* Univision has the greater share with 50 stations and 43 affiliates; Telemundo, owned by NBC, has 15 stations and 35 affiliates. Now that the Hispanic population comprises more U.S.-born Hispanics than immigrants, more original programming, especially at Telemundo, is being focused on second- and third-generation Hispanics. As the Hispanic population continues to grow, these outlets become increasingly important to advertisers.

The diversity of languages among the Asian-American communities makes it extremely difficult for television stations to serve the various Asian communities. The narrow segments of the population leave only a handful of broadcasters to serve these populations. To address the cost factors associated with reaching small markets, some stations use **block programming**, whereby they broadcast in a variety of languages at different times throughout the day.

One of the largest Asian broadcasters is New Tang Dynasty Television, which broadcasts in Chinese. It is a satellite network that broadcasts Western-style news and entertainment 24 hours a day in both Mandarin and Cantonese to Chinese communities in the United States. It is considered to be the Chinese CNN.

The Filipino Channel is the largest television station in the United States targeting Filipino Americans. Other Asian cable and satellite networks in the United States include the Vietnamese-language SBTN and TVK, an aggregate offering that features 19 Korea-based networks and its own programs for Korean Americans 24 hours a day.

Radio

The importance of African-American radio may be best realized with the increase in Black-owned stations from 5 in 2007 to 245 in 2008, a figure released by the National Association of Black-Owned Broadcasters. The largest of these stations is Radio One, which targets African-American and urban listeners. Two other major Black-owned radio companies are Sheridan Broadcasting and American Urban Radio Networks. Cumulatively, they broadcast to more than 300 radio stations and reach an estimated 20 million listeners. With popular talk radio hosts such as Larry Elder, Bev Smith, Joe Madison, Lincoln Ware, and Larry Young, they reach a diverse group of African Americans. One of the reasons for retail and other advertisers to pursue these ethnic-oriented outlets is that their audiences are less likely than their Caucasian counterparts to use the Internet.

Hispanic radio is a key media outlet and, therefore, attracts many retail advertisers. The major stations are Univision Communications and Spanish Broadcasting System. The former has its major listening audiences tuned into KLVE-FM and KSCA-FM, both emanating from Los Angeles; WSKQ-FM and WPAT-FM, originating from New York; and KLAX-FM, based in Los Angeles. It is estimated that 31 percent of Hispanics listen to the radio every week, making it a formidable outlet for advertisers.

Asian-American radio output is particularly strong in Chinese, Korean, and Vietnamese languages. According to Wikipedia, Radio Korea International calls itself "the nation's sole foreign language promotional broadcast of Korea for the broadcast world." Houston has become the center of South Asian–American culture on the radio dial. Little Saigon Radio broadcasts throughout the Houston area and California, both major population concentrations for Vietnamese people.

Internet

In general, African Americans use the Internet less frequently than do Caucasians, but more frequently than Hispanics; however, the African-American community has increased its usage since 2008. Online usage among African Americans increased when Barack Obama's candidacy began to soar, and Web sites such as NewsOne.com and TheRoot.com began to attract significant audiences. African-American newspapers began to offer online editions, many of them attracting significant viewership and offering effective new advertising venues. These news-oriented Web sites, however, remain far less popular than sites such as CNN.com and MSNBC.com

Although the Hispanic population in general uses the Internet less than African Americans, the young, U.S.-born, bilingual, and more educated Hispanics use the Internet at much higher rates than do African Americans. To meet the needs of this fast-growing segment, ImpreMedia, a large conglomerate of Hispanic newspapers, groups all of its publications, which include *La Opinion, El Diario La Prensa*, and the Rumbo newspaper chain, under one umbrella. The site allows users access to multiple channels that feature sports, entertainment, and lifestyle, in addition to news, making it ideal for advertisers to reach this ever-growing market. Telemundo, one of the top Spanish-language broadcasters, also has made moves into the digital media.

Internet usage among Asian Americans is extremely high, making Asian media outlets move aggressively online. Asian Americans use the Internet at higher rates than any other ethnic group in the country, according to the most recent (2008) Current Population Survey conducted by the National Communications and Information administration. About 76 percent of Asian-American households use the Internet (Figure 4.5). Most large Asian-American newspapers continue to improve their Web sites and add new features. Many have added content in English, reflective of the potential market of second-generation Asian Americans. Unique to this market, USAsian, in partnership with Dynasign and Jistar Media, have installed digital screens in Asian American supermarkets at checkout counters and other places where people wait. Much like digital billboards, the digital screens broadcast a combination of news and advertising messages. The approach is used to appeal to people who might not purchase newspapers or read the news online. A Korean–Asian American supermarket chain, H Mart, has 80 percent of its stores outfitted with these screens. In-store digital screens are successful in Korea, Japan, and other Asian countries, and retailers hope to see the same positive results in the United States.

4.5 Internet usage among Asian Americans is extremely high. *Stockbyte/Getty Images RF.*

4.6 *(opposite)* Outdoor advertising is often used to reach different ethnicities. *newscom.*

Direct Mail

More and more retailers are using direct mail as a means of reaching their multicultural markets. Many have found that tailoring mailed advertisements to minority audiences improves their rates of purchasing. With the use of appropriate language, images, and other marketing tools, direct-mail advertising can translate into dollars. Without specifically tapping into these consumer groups, the retailer's market will begin to shrink.

To get the most out of multicultural direct mail, it is important that ads are not merely reworked general-purpose pieces, but rather are carefully considered original ads. Particularly when appealing to foreign-language markets, care must be taken to ensure that the translation is correct. Good copywriters are needed to make certain that taboo words and meanings are avoided. There are cultural differences that must be addressed, and some cultural references often do not translate well to a second language.

Dean Rieck, president of Direct Creative of Westerville, Ohio, cites an account of a particularly poor translation: Pepsi's upbeat slogan "Come alive with the Pepsi Generation" translated into Chinese as "Pepsi brings your ancestors back from the grave."

When targeting the Hispanic market, according to Britt Brouse, associate editor of *Inside Direct Mail,* it is important to bear in mind that "there is no 'typical' Hispanic customer. Marketers must consider immigration status, education, country of origin, and geographic location. It also helps to know where Hispanics are in the product life cycle. Don't assume it's the same as in the general markets—they could be ahead or behind and tend to over-index and under-index in certain areas."

Being inattentive to the differences in multicultural audiences will often waste the money spent to reach them.

Outdoor Advertisements

Although it is considered to be a minor media component, outdoor advertising is used in many cities to reach consumers who are either on foot or are traveling on the major interstates or thoroughfares by means of private automobiles or public transportation. Among the more widely used of this type of media are billboards, posters, and **backlit transparencies**.

To reach the minority segments of the population, retailer billboards depict individuals of particular ethnicities. For example, in areas in which African Americans are the major component of the population, billboards featuring Black individuals are used extensively (Figure 4.6).

Similarly, in Hispanic and Asian-American communities, billboards feature not only people of these minorities but also use second-language written copy.

Posters featuring multicultural ethnicities are also regularly found on the sides and backs of buses to attract the passersby. Another version of the poster that has even more attention-getting potential is the backlit transparency, which features illuminated photographs and copy that can be seen at any time of the day.

Tailoring Advertising Content to Ethnic Markets

To achieve the greatest returns on ethnic advertising investment, retailers and other proponents of using ads that appeal to minority audiences must make certain that the ad content is **minority specific**. Using copy and imagery planned for all audiences and merely making some changes to the copy and artwork does not work. Advertisements used in newspapers, magazines, television, radio, direct mail, digital venues, and so forth must be original and feature components that will catch the attention of their intended ethnic market. An example of a major retailer that tailors some of its ads to maximize its reach to minority markets is JCPenney. Focus 4.1 describes one of JCPenney's campaigns that appeals to its Hispanic customer base.

JCPenney

With 1,200 stores in 50 states and a full-line catalogue operation, JCPenney has become the largest department store organization in the country. Although it has periodically struggled, it has emerged as a success story. Going from a mass-merchandise merchant to one that is now fashion oriented, the transition has been relatively smooth. Together with a host of nationally known labels and private-brand merchandise, JCPenney's merchandise mix has attracted a wide audience.

One of the ways in which the company has expanded its target market is by reaching out to the multicultural population through a number of initiatives, including advertising. By engaging the Vidal Partnership, the largest independent Hispanic marketing agency (further explored in Focus 4.2), JCPenney extended its reach to this minority.

An example of its desire to reach the Hispanic market was the launch of a new Spanish-language Christmas marketing campaign in November 2008. The campaign invited Hispanic customers to celebrate the joy of giving with their company for the upcoming holiday season. Featured was a 30-second broadcast spot, "Joy Cartoons," along with a series of television vignettes designed exclusively with the two top Spanish-language networks in the country—Univision and Telemundo—as well as a television special on Univision in which the company helped make Christmas wishes come true for that season. The 30-second spot focused on a family's joyous emotions as they exchanged Christmas gifts. The commercial aired on all major Spanish-language Hispanic market networks.

With its affiliation with the Vidal Partnership, JCPenney has determined that multicultural marketing is their direction for the coming years.

Source: JCPenney Web site.

Media Insight 4.2 focuses on the importance of the proper language usage in effectively reaching a non-English-speaking audience in advertising.

Some of the essentials of creating ads that will have the greatest impact on the targeted ethnic communities include the following:

- Models in ads should be African American, Hispanic, or Asian American, as appropriate. Minorities will immediately relate to these individuals and be able to visualize themselves using or wearing the advertised products (Figure 4.7).

- The copy must use the language with which these consumers are familiar. Typical English language usage often has different connotations than that which is understood by Hispanics and Asians, in particular.

- Using a layout that was initially intended for the general population and merely inserting minority images in place of White figures is not sufficient.

By contracting with agencies that specialize in ethnic advertising and marketing, retailers are more likely to see better returns on their advertising investments.

Multicultural Agencies

The significant increase in the minority population in the United States has prompted more and more traditional ad agencies and those who specialize in minority advertising to increase in numbers. Because the conventional approaches to appealing to diverse markets does not completely work, agencies that specialize in multicultural advertising are flourishing.

Ad agencies of all sizes and formats that specialize in multicultural advertising are located all over the United States, serving retailers and other businesses to reach the ever-expanding diverse markets.

The Vidal Partnership is a Hispanic agency, and Focus 4.2 discusses how it functions to serve its clients.

4.7 Minorities are attracted to ads that feature models in their own images. *Courtesy of Target.*

The importance of the Hispanic agencies in particular can be verified by the fact that more than 50 agencies are presently in operation in the United States.

Some of the nation's leading African-American advertising agencies belong to the Association of Black-Owned Advertising Agencies, which formed in 2005. It was established to represent members' interests in the field of advertising so that their growth could be realized. The association believed that the time was ripe for such agencies to grow in order to adequately represent the significant African-American segment of the U.S. population. With combined billings of more than $1 billion, the Association of Black-Owned Advertising Agencies represents clients from Fortune 100 corporations as well as major local organizations. Among the founding members are Anderson Communications, E. Morris Communications, Equals Three Communications, Fuse Advertising, and Lattimer Moffitt Communications. Table 4.5 shows the 15 historically Black-owned advertising agencies.

Asian-American advertising agencies are more diverse than those of the other minorities because of the different communities they serve in terms of nationality and language. A large number of Asian Americans are of Chinese descent, but many are of Korean, Vietnamese, Philippine, Japanese, and other ancestries. Although these minorities have settled in most parts of the United States, the vast majority make their homes in Los Angeles, ranked number one in geographic concentration, followed by New York City, San Francisco, Honolulu, and Chicago. With this in mind, the top Asian-American advertising agencies, by U.S. revenue, are located primarily in New York City and in different parts of California (see Table 4.6).

Exploring New Horizons Through Multicultural Marketing Offers Mucho Potential

LuAnne Speeter
February 19, 2008

So you have this store ad you've created. The copy is letter-perfect, cleverly peppered with dry wit and double entendres. The graphics are great, too—a little retro and quirky, but fun. However, now you need to repurpose it for a new location in a Latino neighborhood. *Hmmm. . . .*

Hey, your best friend's girlfriend majored in Spanish. She could translate it, *no problemo!*

But hold on. Although it's true that language can be an impediment to reaching a non-English-speaking audience, a poorly executed translation and irrelevant graphics could be just as ineffective. Cross-cultural marketing may seem at first to be as simple as Spanish 101, but in reality, it is a many-faceted issue that inspires a fresh new way of looking at the so-called "cultural barrier."

The Benefits of Cross-Cultural Marketing

The minority marker represents enormous growth potential for small and large businesses alike. In fact, American minority groups are rapidly becoming the majority population in the United States. Indeed, the dollar power is there—according to Celent Communications, the spending power of minorities exceeds $1.3 trillion.

Additionally, corporations continue to expand their product lines in response to the vast mosaic of culturally based values, preferences, and needs. For companies to better position themselves to attract and win over these markets, it's important to develop a marketing strategy that communicates with certain ethnic segments based on their own cultural framework. By understanding their values and buying patterns, you'll increase the chances of relating your products and services to their interests.

Five Steps to Broadening Your Advertising Horizons

Appealing to the cultural needs of your target audience requires that you do some upfront research to set the stage. Here are a few suggestions:

1. *Learn about your community.* Minority marketing begins with gathering information about your target market's ethnicity and language preferences. Analyze this data to identify pockets of opportunity.

Consider, too, that there is a tapestry of interrelated cultures and subsegments that differ in economic status, lifestyles, and customs. Additionally, within each minority is a broad range of cultural assimilation, varying with an individual's age, length of time in the country, and the level of community unity.

Perhaps the most universally effective method of gathering, tracking, and analyzing information about your market is through Web survey technology. This allows you to pretest everything from your brand perception to creative layout so you can appeal to the broadest percentage of your target market possible.

2. *Increase rapport with your community.* After you've learned their preferences, include variables in your marketing that identify your company with your minority markets. This can include using multicultural faces in campaign photography and incorporating a color palette in publications or on your Web site that are applicable.

If your company has public persona, invite better interaction with your community through minority and bilingual personnel at store locations or in your call center.

3. *Promote in a variety of media.* The Internet can be an extremely cost-effective way to reach minority markets. In fact, according to the Pew Internet and American Life Project, 85 percent of English-speaking Asian Americans, 80 percent of English-speaking Hispanics, and 61 percent of African Americans routinely use the Internet. The comparable figure for Caucasians is 74 percent.

As connectivity has increased and costs have decreased, minorities have migrated to the Internet for e-mail, instant messaging, games, music, voice over Internet protocol (VOIP), job hunting, job training, and more. For education and trust building, consider seminars, webcasts, print ads, pamphlets, direct mail, and magazines or newsletters. Additionally, word-of-mouth advertising is important to reach close-knit minority communities, so referral incentive can prove very effective.

4. *Don't just translate; trans-create.* Ad copy that may seem clever in English runs the risk of being illogical—or worse yet, offensive—when translated. For example, when the Dairy Association's "Got Milk?" campaign was introduced in Mexico, the translated version said, "Are you lactating?" Whenever possible, produce marketing campaign copy in the foreign language initially rather than translating from English. However, if your available resources won't allow an entirely independent campaign, a careful translation is a reasonable approach.

When producing bilingual versions of print marketing, keep your page layout flexible enough to allow for differences in language. Text translated from English into another language can increase space needs by 20 percent or more. Some languages read from right to left; others up and down. English has fewer than 256 characters, whereas some Asian languages have thousands of characters.

Graphics, too, should be relevant to your audience. Choose images that reflect the demographics of the minority group and be consistent with local scenery, housing styles, and climate.

5. *Measure the effectiveness of your campaigns.* As with any other marketing campaign, establish a means to determine the impact your efforts have on your target market. With your initial campaign, however, your primary goal may be to test the minority community's perception of your brand rather than expect a strong return on investment. This can help ensure that you avoid—or at least minimize—cultural missteps in ongoing marketing.

As much as possible, measure your results in real time. Track calls to your call center and clicks to promotions with dedicated pages on your Web site. Include methods to determine immediately which promotions prompted response so you can adjust your methods as needed.

A New Approach for Long-Term Growth

Initiating a multicultural marketing program may seem like a challenge, but take it one step at a time. By researching your target communities and identifying their key motivators, you'll eventually develop a formula for communicating on a personal level with each consumer. And that will help your company grow well into the future.

Source: LuAnne Speeter. February 19, 2008. Advertising Federation Minnesota, www.adfed.org/edgeonline.

Vidal Partnership

The Vidal Partnership is the largest independent Hispanic marketing agency in the United States. It is an integrated full-service marketing communications agency that is 100 percent minority owned and managed. It is headquartered in New York City and has regional offices in Miami, Los Angeles, Dallas, and Nashville. Its staff of 200 bilingual and bicultural professionals gives it a huge edge over other agencies that deal with multicultural communication. It is a founding member of the Association of Hispanic Advertising Agencies (AHAA) and the recipient of more than 100 creative awards, including two Advertising Age Best of Show Awards. The Vidal Partnership's client list includes many of the top business organizations in the United States, including such major retailers as JCPenney, Home Depot, and Wendy's, for whom they provide a wealth of advertising and promotional campaigns.

The mission of the Vidal Partnership is "to be the most effective Hispanic communications agency in the United States dedicated to our core business and clients' success, by achieving unmatched market insight, innovative and flawless execution across a broad range of communications disciplines." Among its goals is to build a national reputation for great work, to be known among future em-ployees for great creativity, to be known among prospective clients as brand builders, and to be known by its peers as winners.

The Vidal Partnership's 200 bilingual language specialists have the ability to use the right words to transform their clients' communication materials into culturally relevant advertisements, direct-marketing pieces, event promotions, and public relations efforts that resonate with their target audiences. Composed of American Translators Association members, writers, and journalists, the company's international staff has an in-depth knowledge of a wide range of subjects, including consumer goods, so that they may develop the most meaningful ads and promotions. Their cultural insight and linguistic experience provide the right nuances to make a difference in advertising appropriateness for the Hispanic community.

To make their efforts even more productive, each marketing communications discipline is headed by an owner with vision, experience, authority, and energy to direct and inspire cutting-edge talent in specific areas of expertise.

Source: Vidal Web site.

TABLE 4.5 — The 15 Historically Black-Owned Advertising Agencies with the Largest Billings, 2007

RANK	AGENCY	FOUNDED	LOCATION	ANNUAL BILLINGS (MILLIONS)	EMPLOYEES
1	GlobalHue	1988	Southfield, MI	$720	300
2	Carol H. Williams Advertising	1986	Oakland, CA	345	155
3	UniWorld Group	1969	New York	243	146
4	Burrell Communications Group	1971	Chicago	205	135
5	Sanders Wingo Advertising	1983	El Paso, TX	90	72
6	Images USA	1989	Atlanta	72	45
7	Prime Access, Inc.	1990	New York	71	44
8	Muse Communications, Inc.	1985	Hollywood	71	45
9	Matlock Advertising	1986	Atlanta	57	35
10	Fuse Advertising	1997	St. Louis	55	23
11	Footsteps Advertising	2000	New York	54	30
12	Equals Three Communications	1984	Bethesda, MD	47	34
13	Anderson Communications	1971	Atlanta	45	15
14	R.J. Dale Advertising	1979	Chicago	44	26
15	E. Morris Communications	1987	Chicago	41	40
Total				$2,160	1,145

Source: Black-owned Advertising Agencies Web site.

TABLE 4.6 — Ten Top Asian-American Advertising Agencies by U.S. Revenue

RANK	AGENCY	LOCATION	GROSS 2008 AD REVENUE	% CHANGE
1	Kang & Lee Advertising [WPP (Y&R)]	New York	$15,500	3.3
2	Admerasia	New York	10,250	−2.4
3	InterTrend Communications	Long Beach, CA	10,245	−15.5
4	IW Group [Interpublic]	West Hollywood	9,085	−10.8
5	AdAsia Communications	New York	7,059	22.3
6	Time Advertising	Millbrae, CA	5,800	−18.3
7	PanCom International	Los Angeles	5,103	−13.5
8	Global Advertising Strategies	New York	5,000	11.1
9	ES Advertising	Los Angeles	4,486	−5.0
10	AAAZA	Los Angeles	3,000	71.4

Source: Advertising Age, April 19, 2004.

Planning *and* Budgeting Strategies

After you have completed this chapter, you will be able to discuss:

★ The number of different marketing considerations that retailers address when budgeting their advertising expenditures.

★ Why the advertising budget plans are approached in different ways by different retailers and those they most often employ.

★ How many advertising classifications merchants use in their budgeting plans and the purposes of each.

★ The various approaches used for budget allocation after the total amount has been determined.

★ Why celebrity endorsements are standard practice for many retailers as an advertising strategy.

★ Why cause marketing has become standard practice for so many retail organizations.

★ How the multicultural phenomenon has impacted advertising.

★ The different media that retailers consider in their ad campaigns.

For retailers to achieve success with their advertising programs, they must carefully strategize their promotional plans. Advance planning is essential so that their budgets are used in a way that carefully addresses the goals the ads are intended to achieve. In this time of significant competition, it is necessary for each merchant to individualize every aspect of the operation, including merchandise assortments, price points, customer service, promotional endeavors, and advertising. The approach to advertising is extremely important because it conveys messages that distinguish one retailer from the other. With product offerings somewhat similar from one merchant to another within a particular price point and merchandise mix, ideas that motivate consumers to opt for a particular store or off-site visit require that a merchant offer something unique.

What better vehicle is there than advertising to advance this message? It reminds loyal customers of what the retailer has to offer and alerts potential customers that the retailer is there to serve them. The manner in which retailers spend their promotional dollars is all important because their ads deliver news about their stores, their merchandise, and their services.

With the economic downturn of the early 2000s, it is more important than ever that retailers wisely budget their advertising expenditures and plan their **budgeting strategies**. When profits are considerably greater and the funds set aside for advertising are more plentiful, some merchants may spend more frivolously. Even in a strong economy, however, planning and budgeting, along with careful advertising strategies, must be professionally addressed so that the desired return on investment is realized.

Before any budgeting and strategizing takes place, a growing number of retailers are using **integrated marketing communications** (IMC) to ensure that their marketing campaigns are properly planned. IMC subscribes to a holistic approach that integrates all of the marketing tools necessary to

it's our
grand
opening

NORDSTROM FASHION ISLAND
OPENS FRIDAY, APRIL 16
AT 10AM

STORE DEPARTMENTS   OPENING DETAILS   STORE SERVICES   CAREERS

5.1 Retailers usually run ads of this nature when expanding their operations. *Courtesy of Nordstrom.*

5.2 *(opposite)* The addition of a private label is usually advertised by the company. *Courtesy of Macy's.*

ADDING MULTICHANNEL COMPONENTS

Today's retail organizations almost always expand their store operations into multichannel operations. Even many small entrepreneurs add Web sites and catalogue components to their on-site businesses. By offering purchasing opportunities through these channels, retailers can increase their market reach to shoppers who are not in the store's general trading area. The addition of off-site divisions usually necessitates the use of print or broadcast advertising, or both, to make these new channels known. With the significant expense of becoming a multichannel company, leaving it to chance for consumers to learn about the Web site and catalogues would be a poor business decision. An advertising campaign, planned by experts, is the only way to get the message out.

PRIVATE BRAND ADDITIONS TO THE MERCHANDISE MIX

One of the ways retailers reduce the problems associated with competition from other merchants is with the addition of private labels or brands to the existing product mix. The reliance on nationally advertised brands, though often excellent sellers, is no longer viable in most large retail organizations. Most retailers have added their own brands and labels to their merchandise mixes so that they can deliver a degree of exclusivity to their clienteles as well as gain the advantage of better profit margins (Figure 5.2).

Even smaller retailers are availing themselves of private brands that have been established by market consulting firms, often called resident buying offices.

LAFAYETTE 148 NEW YORK

DESIGNED BY EDWARD WILKERSON

5.3 The expense of such an ad is often shared by the designer, manufacturer, and retailer. *Courtesy Lafayette 148.*

draw attention to all of their products. Rather than pinpointing monies for specific divisions, departments, or merchandise classifications, as discussed later in this section, the overall budget is meant to bring an increase in company awareness and general sales revenues. Efforts are more likely to be made in terms of media selection, types of promotions, and so forth. Supermarkets, for example, use their advertising dollars most often in newspaper inserts to motivate purchasing by promoting prices across the board.

DIVISIONAL APPORTIONMENT

Most of today's major retailers operate their businesses through on-site and off-site divisions. The merchants who operate multichannel companies generally realize the majority of their sales in their bricks-and-mortar outlets, with the catalogues and Web sites lagging behind in sales. In most of these businesses, the stores, catalogues, and Web sites are managed and merchandised independently of each other. Separate buyers and merchandisers are used to purchase inventories, make marketing decisions, and develop the advertising to promote each division.

In terms of advertising budgeting, each division is generally assigned a dollar amount to be expended. If the in-store units account for the majority of the sales revenues, then they will receive the lion's share of the budget. Similarly, the offsite ventures will be allocated dollars to be used for advertising in accordance with the sales they bring to the company. Most often, the percentage-of-sales method is used to determine how much each will receive. Of course, other factors affect budget distribution. For example, if the Web site shows disproportionate sales increases, it will be allotted more than the amount indicated by the percentage of past sales. Similarly, if the catalogue operation is showing signs of bringing more revenue to the company, its efforts will be rewarded with more money for advertising.

Currently, when **multichannel retailing** is the smart business choice, it is imperative that the objectives of the company are carefully evaluated in terms of sales expectancy, and advertising budgets should be regularly adjusted to conform to sales results realized from each of the company's divisions.

FINAL CLEARANCE

Save up to 50% off regular retail prices*

GOING ON NOW

Brooks Brothers

BROOKSBROTHERS.COM   800 274 1815

*Offer valid only at U.S. and Canadian Brooks Brothers Retail, Brooks Brothers Country Club and Airport Stores, online and by phone. Not valid in Factory or "346" Brooks Brothers Stores. Sale applies only to select items, while supplies last. Not valid on Men's Cordovan Shoes, Made-To-Measure or Special Order Clothing purchases. Discount may not be applied towards taxes, shipping & handling, monogramming & engraving, alterations or personalization. Not valid on previous purchases, or for the purchase of the Gift Card. If you return some or all merchandise, the dollar value of this promotion is not refunded or credited back to your account. Void in states where prohibited by law, no cash value except where prohibited, then the cash value is 1/100 cent.

DEPARTMENTAL APPROPRIATION

Retailers that offer a wide variety of merchandise, such as department stores, often assign an advertising budget according to the sales generated by each department in the past or according to sales forecasts. Some departments within the organization are better sales producers than others. In Bloomingdale's, for example, although home furnishings products make up part of the inventory, fashion apparel brings the most business to the store. The need to carry home furnishings is less

5.4 This is how retailers try to quickly dispose of unwanted goods. *Courtesy of Brooks Brothers.*

Macy's

With all of the press given to Macy's in recent years, it is safe to assume that most Americans are familiar with the Macy's organization. Once merely a traditional department store organization, Macy's has grown into the largest department store group in the United States. Now owning and operating more than 800 units, it has achieved recognition that few retailers enjoy. With its acquisitions of such venerable retailing giants as Marshall Field, Rich's, Filene's, Famous Barr, and Robinsons-May, to mention just a few, it now serves shoppers from coast to coast.

In addition to all of the merchandising strategies that have made Macy's a shopping magnet for a vast number of consumers, it has established itself as a special events guru. Each of its regional flagships uses a number of annual events that make it a place to visit for a multitude of attractions. Macy's flagship in New York City provides the lion's share of special events for the company and the most institutional advertising that promotes these endeavors.

The granddaddy of all the special events is the annual Thanksgiving Day Parade, which draws thousands of spectators to watch the event in person and more than a million viewers who see it on television. Important to the company is that the parade terminates in front of the Herald Square flagship store, where it is seen by the television audience. With the Macy's store always in view on camera, it is a constant reminder of its presence.

The annual Flower Show (Figure 5.5) transforms the entire first floor of the Herald Square store into a colorful arboretum. The main windows of the store are filled with exotic flowers from around the world and attract both passersby and those who were motivated to come by the multitude of advertisements.

The Fourth of July Fireworks Display is yet another special event that draws throngs of visitors to many parts of New York City where it can be observed. It, too, gets considerable attention from the numerous ads in both print publications and on television.

These are but a few of the events that Macy's uses to bring attention to its company. The key to its success is the use of advertising to motivate attendance and, the store hopes, future purchasing.

5.5 Ads of this nature help to bring attention to a retailer. *Courtesy of Macy's.*

important to overall merchandising, but it is a decision that management makes to keep its image as a "general merchandise" retailer, a philosophy it has maintained since Bloomingdale's inception. Bearing this in mind, the company allocates more advertising dollars to fashion apparel than it does to home products. Other retailers follow the same practice: the better-performing departments are rewarded with more money for advertising.

MERCHANDISE CLASSIFICATION ALLOCATION

Just as different departments generate different sales revenues, so do different merchandise classifications. In a company such as Saks Fifth Avenue, where fashion merchandise, including menswear, is essential to the company's overall merchandising offerings, women's apparel accounts for the greatest sales figures (Figure 5.6).

This fact results in more money being spent on advertising women's fashions than on all other merchandise classifications.

MARKETING INITIATIVES

As discussed earlier, retailers often engage in plans or activities beyond their normal operations, such as company expansion, new channels of distribution, additional merchandise categories, and private label introductions (Figure 5.7). The new operations generally require a wealth of advertising dollars to bring them to the attention of the regular clienteles and potential customers. Often, the budget determined by the percentage of past or projected sales or by the number of units sold or projected to sell is sufficient to carry out the company's regular goals, but the new marketing initiatives require expenditures over and above the budget.

5.6 In many department stores it is women's fashion that warrants the largest advertising expenditure. Courtesy of Saks Fifth Avenue.

5.7 Retail expansion often requires advertising initiatives. *Courtesy of Nordstrom.*

In this case, objectives of the company are thoroughly researched and a decision is made concerning the investment needed to meet those objectives. Spending over budget is usually a difficult route to take, not only in terms of merchandising, staff additions, changes in company policy, and so on but also in terms of advertising dollars needed to successfully market the new initiatives. Budget increases for new initiatives are generally planned within a specified time frame: once management is satisfied that the budget has achieved its goals, the extra expenditure is eliminated from the advertising budget.

Media Apportionment

After the advertising budget has been allocated, it is necessary to decide how it will be apportioned to the media. With significant changes sometimes taking place in regard to media effectiveness and returns on investment, budget planning of this nature must be regularly addressed.

Traditionally, department stores invested the largest share of their advertising budgets in newspaper advertising, which regularly proved to be a reliable medium for most merchants. Today, with newspapers facing a grim outlook, retailers are rethinking the large sums they invest here.

Magazines have also been a reliable medium for retail advertising, but they, too, have had their difficulties, and many merchants, except for some of the upscale institutions such as Saks Fifth Avenue, have eliminated or reduced the dollars spent on magazine advertising.

Direct mail has been a mainstay for many retail operations, large and small, and retailers continue to make use of this medium. Catalogues are a major force in retailing and still garner great attention from consumers, justifying the costs for merchants of all sizes.

Today, the Internet has gained a great deal of advertising revenue, and digital media components continue to be important to many retailers. Their use has taken allocations away from the traditional media and has made the new media major recipients of advertising dollars.

5.8 (opposite) **Celebrity endorsements often help sell products.** *Courtesy of NutriSystem.*

The dilemma for most retailers is where to commit their advertising budgets, to what degree, and to which specific outlets to afford them the best return on investment.

In Chapters 7 through 11, each advertising medium available to retailers is addressed. The advantages and disadvantages of each, their importance to today's retailer, the components inherent in each are fully explored.

Advertising Strategies

After the advertising budget is set, it is time to build the advertising campaign strategy. Those in decision-making positions are generally involved in planning the advertising strategy. In addition to in-house management, outside resources may be used to make recommendations as to the best ways in which to spend advertising dollars. Outside resources may include ad agencies and media services (the degree to which they are used is discussed in Chapter 6) and even resident buying offices, which sometimes maintain promotional divisions specializing in advertising. Within the organization, input may come from retail merchandisers, buyers, management personnel, and others, with top management usually making the final decisions regarding strategy.

With an advertising strategy in place, tasks are delegated to move the plan forward. The industry giants usually have advertising and promotion divisions that handle ad creation; in smaller chains, the advertising might be left to an ad manager, and in small retail units such as boutiques and single-specialty stores the proprietor might set the strategy either alone or in consultation with a media expert or freelance specialist.

Advertising strategies employ a variety of approaches, depending on the goals of the campaign, the chosen media venue, and the length of time the campaign is scheduled to run. Some of those approaches are described next.

Celebrity Endorsements

One of the advertising strategies that retailers and other businesses use is **celebrity endorsement**: hiring individuals with "star power" to promote their products. Celebrities, such as stage and movie stars or sports heroes, command a following among different groups of consumers. Selection of the celebrity depends on the objective of the campaign, the target audience, the allotted budgeted, the media used, and so forth (Figure 5.8).

Nutrisystem, Inc.

One of the largest dollar expenditures for consumers involves weight loss. A wide variety of products are sold: diet books, cookbooks, fat-free foods, appetite suppressants, "fat-blocking" pills, "fat-burning" pills, weight-loss supplements, exercise programs and equipment, and many more. Consumers also spend a significant amount of money on diet plans that are generally marketed directly to the consumer. Among the most successful in this direct-marketing category is Nutrisystem.

Nutrisystem has been in business for about 35 years and consistently expands its consumer reach year after year. With an innovative Web site, it has positioned itself as a leader in the weight-loss industry. Its advertising strategy involves the use of successful "losers," ranging from everyday citizens to celebrities who have become company spokespersons. To reach a broad spectrum of consumers, both men and women of all ages, the company employs celebrities from the sports and entertainment industries, each of whom appeals to a specific targeted audience.

For those enamored with sports heroes, Nutrisystem uses football legends such as Don Shula, former coach of

the Miami Dolphins, and Dan Marino, former star quarterback of the same team. Because of their legendary status in football, they appeal not only to overweight men of their age group but also to younger individuals who are familiar with them. The idea is to make men, often uncomfortable with weight-loss programs, comfortable with the Nutrisystem approach because it worked for their heroes.

From the entertainment world, 1970s pop singer Tony Orlando is a Nutrisystem spokesperson. He holds appeal for a middle-aged and older audience—many of whom are battling the "middle-age spread." Another Nutrisystem spokesperson is Marie Osmond. Her fame dates back to her teenage years, and she is still a popular entertainer who appears in Las Vegas, on television, and in theater. She connects with women her age who are troubled by excess weight.

Through a significant television advertising campaign augmented by print advertising, Nutrisystem markets a successful weight-loss program. Its Web site also features a variety of stars, underscoring the importance of celebrity endorsements (Figure 5.8).

One very successful advertising strategy that employs celebrity endorsements is used by Nutrisystem, Inc., a weight-loss system company that is marketed primarily through television commercials and, to a lesser extent, magazine advertising. Focus 5.2 explores how Nutrisystem uses celebrity endorsements to market its concept directly to the consumer.

Cause Marketing

Many retailers sponsor charitable causes to increase their sales. One of the strategies used in these endeavors is to sponsor cause-related events that will bring shoppers to the store. In this way, both the causes and the merchants benefit.

Coldwater Creek, a women's clothing chain, used its Web site to advertise its intention to raise money for various charities. It offered to donate $1 to a particular charity for each consumer who visited one of its stores and tried on an article of clothing. Of course, the hope was that trying on the clothing might encourage the shopper to purchase the item.

Macy's, through e-mail advertisement, invited women to dress in red on National Wear Red Day (supporting the fight against heart disease) and visit its stores, promising discount coupons. The coupons, of course, would be used for store purchases.

Sometimes, the cause-marketing initiative is a collaboration between a vendor and a retailer. One such example is an event that Levi's and JCPenney cosponsored in support of VH1's Save the Music Foundation. Levi's and JCPenney pledged to raise $100,000 for the foundation, which supports music programs in public schools by donating musical instruments. Levi's donated $5 for each purchase of two pairs of jeans at a JCPenney store or online. Customers benefited by receiving a $10 gift card, JCPenney benefited by increased in-store traffic and potential sales, and Levi's benefited by increased sales of its products. Advertising was accomplished through a JCPenney circular and a VH1 e-mail blast.

Media Insight 5.1 focuses on ways to guarantee the success of a cause-marketing plan.

Cause marketing is not limited to industry giants; small businesses can also benefit by showing their commitment to being socially responsible community members.

Use of Multicultural Imagery in Ads

For many years, when planning their print and television advertisement, retailers generally took a traditional approach in their choice of models. Except for merchants who catered primarily to minority groups, most used photographs of Caucasian models in their ads. It was standard practice not to use African Americans, Hispanics, Asian Americans, or other minority images.

Today, discussed in Chapter 4, the growth of ethnic communities in the United States is significant and plays an important role in many retailers' search for business. In addition to carefully merchandising their product lines and hiring diverse populations to work on the selling floor, most retailers are replacing their Caucasian-oriented advertisements with images that represent their multicultural clientele. Today's multicultural customer base is catered to in newspaper and magazine ads, catalogues, television commercials, Web site ads, and direct-mail campaigns. This strategy announces to consumers that people of all cultures are welcome as shoppers and that their individual needs are being considered.

Targeted Discounts

The practice of reducing merchandise prices is typical of all retailers at certain times. Immediately after Christmas, for example, most retailers, except for those in the food business, slash prices as a means of motivating shoppers to buy. It helps make room for new merchandise arrivals and also helps to improve the merchant's turnover rate.

Some retailers use a different form of discounting to increase sales. They target specific groups for a brief period of time in hopes of attracting more of these consumers into their stores. One group that retailers target is senior citizens. Merchants hope to encourage this age group, who typically purchase only necessities, to spend money on products they ordinarily would not buy. For example, Belk, a department store chain, offers promotions directed toward senior citizens: using the one-day sale concept, they extend discounts of 15 percent to all senior citizens who visit their stores. In this way, they not only move merchandise in larger than the usual quantities but also encourage the over-55 set to become customers. These promotions are primarily advertised in newspapers, the major medium that attracts senior citizens (Figure 5.9).

The Ten Commandments of Cause-Related Marketing

Kurt Ascherman

Introduction

Cause-related marketing is a partnership between a for-profit and a nonprofit where each has something to offer the other, and both realize a benefit. When you select a potential partner that has a natural affinity with your nonprofit, the result can be added revenue, increased media exposure, public relations, or all three—for both partners.

To be successful you have to think creatively. In fact, think less about cause marketing and more about partnering—becoming the partner of your corporate collaborator—and you will have more success.

So how about some commandments for becoming a partner of a corporation?

First Commandment: Understand your product and your value.

Not only must we understand what uniqueness we are bringing to the table in a relationship (our unique service proposition, if you will) but we also must understand the value we bring to the table. Your brand is worth something. Make sure you know that and articulate that to your potential partner. It's the value of your brand (and your ability to execute) that are worth something to a corporation.

Second Commandment: Understand business and how it works.

You don't need an MBA, but when a partner talks about "market share," you need to understand the jargon. Our goal in relationships is to have the corporate partner say, "You aren't like other nonprofits." We must demonstrate an understanding of what they are doing—and that we can help.

Third Commandment: Follow classic account management principles.

Classic account management means that one person handles our partner's account and acts as that partner's principal contact within the organization. A management team may be involved—during brainstorming sessions, for example—but when the partners want answers, they know exactly where to turn. Remember, you want each partner to believe it is your only partner. We want each of our partners to think its project is our primary responsibility. Our projects with Microsoft, Major League Baseball, Crest, Circuit City, and Finish Line, just to name a few, each have their own "account manager" as well as a back-up person. When our partners call, they get an answer. Even if their primary contact is out, the call is referred to another team member. There is no lag between call and response.

Fourth Commandment: When first meeting, leave the paper at home.

Some of our best proposals happen without paper. Bringing a written proposal, an actual document, to the first meeting gives your potential partner the option of saying no. At Boys & Girls Clubs (B&GCA), we practice "proposal-less fund-raising," listening to our partners and identifying their needs. Then, we draft a proposal with the partner. This gives the partner a sense of ownership in the project— something to feel good about. Although we do bring public relations kits and other information along on the calls, we don't burden potential partners with too much reading material. At the same time, we make sure our partner knows what Boys & Girls Clubs is all about.

Fifth Commandment: Listen up!

Listening is a lost art. Everyone wants to talk—to get his or her point across. We learn a lot about our potential partners just by listening. This knowledge helps us make intelligent suggestions on how a relationship can work.

Sixth Commandment: Patience is a virtue.

Cause-related marketing takes time. It's like planned giving— requiring an enormous initial effort but perhaps not producing immediate results. It took an entire year before the Coca-Cola partnership came to fruition. Major League Baseball took 4 years. But when you do come up with a plan, patience will be rewarded with a stronger, longer-lasting relationship—because your partner will have helped you create it.

Seventh Commandment: Cause-related marketing is an agencywide effort.

When I took on fund-raising for B&GCA many years ago, I was thrilled to find out that Roxanne Spillett (now our president but then the head of program services) understood the need to identify and solicit funding sources for the programs she wanted to implement. The same now holds true for every department at B&GCA. Everyone thinks about fund-raising here. People constantly refer potential cause-related marketing partners to us.

Eighth Commandment: Cause-related marketing is about relationships.

All these "commandments" are nothing more than good relationship management. As the saying goes, people give money to people. Taking it one step further, people do more for those they like and trust and those who care. Cause-related partnerships—like all good relationships—are about caring for your partner's needs.

Ninth Commandment: Cause-related marketing is about delivering.

The first time you do not deliver what you promised a corporate partner, it's time to find a new line of funding. Corporations are willing to work with you, but only if you do what you said you would do. That means: Can't be sure you can do what they ask? Say no. Tell them the truth. Failure in execution is much worse than telling a partner you can't do something.

Tenth Commandment: Cause-related marketing is about becoming part of the business strategy of a corporation.

Where's the big money in a corporation? Bingo—it's in sales and marketing. The charity side may have some money for you, but the potential is much higher in sales and marketing. That means if you can convince your corporate partners your collaboration will benefit their business, you have a leg up (and the potential for a lot more money!).

Conclusion

Cause-related marketing really isn't that difficult. Just handle the relationship, deliver what you promise, and provide value to your partner. Best of all, cause-related marketing is fun and exciting. The sooner you master it, the sooner everyone will benefit from its incredible potential.

Source: Kurt Ascherman, www.causemarketingforum.com

5.9 Targeting special groups helps sell more merchandise. *Courtesy of Belk.*

Commemorating Historically Significant Events

When important events occur—whether tragic or joyful, local or global—many retailers want consumers to know they care about issues that impact the community. They use institutional advertising to convey their messages. Institutional advertising serves two purposes. One is to acknowledge the event and show that the company cares about issues beyond its bottom line. The other is to generate goodwill that will eventually translate into sales.

When President John F. Kennedy was assassinated, just about every major newspaper in the United States featured retailer advertisements commenting on the tragedy. Many retailers withheld their traditional ads for several days. Also acknowledged through advertising was the shocking devastation caused by the 9/11 terrorist attacks. On a happier note, when the U.S. astronauts landed on the moon, many merchants heralded this accomplishment with ads that conveyed the message. The most recent joyful event was the election victory of Barack Obama, the first African American to become president of the United States.

adding multichannel components, adding private brands to the merchandise mix, and retargeting.

- Advertising budget planning usually follows one of three traditional methods: percentage of sales, units sold, or objective and task.

- Ad classifications that include product advertising, promotional advertising, and institutional advertising should also be considered in the budget's formulation.

- Budget allocation takes several different routes and includes divisional apportionment, the total company concept, departmental appropriation, and merchandise classification allocation.

- Strategies are necessary to ensure that the company's goals are being met. They include the use of celebrity endorsements, cause marketing, multicultural imagery in ads, and targeted discounts.

Summary of Key Points

Integrated marketing communications planning is used by many retailers to better accomplish their goals in increasing sales. By integrating many communications aspects, such as advertising and promotion, their goals are being met more consistently.

- Advertising reminds existing customers and informs potential customers of what retailers have to offer.

- Advertising planning and budgeting, along with advertising strategies, must be professionally addressed so that the desired return on investment will be realized.

- When budgeting for advertising, numerous marketing factors must be considered, such as expansion of the existing company,

For Discussion

1. Discuss the concept of integrated marketing communications, and explain why the retailing industry has started to embrace the concept.

2. Cite some of the marketing considerations that retailers address when budgeting, and describe three of them.

3. Discuss the difference between the percentage-of-sales and the objective-and-task approaches used in budget planning.

4. What purpose does institutional advertising serve if it does not result in immediate sales?

5. Describe the different approaches used by retailers in their budget allocations.

6. In what way does cause marketing effectively bring results as an advertising strategy?

7. Describe how some retailers are addressing their multicultural shoppers through advertising.

8. How does promotional advertising differ from product advertising?

9. Why must the available media be examined before a merchant decides where to spend the budgeted dollars?

Exercises and Projects

1. Select a product ad, a promotional ad, and an institutional ad from a major newspaper in which retail ads are dominant: mount them on foam board and give an oral presentation discussing the major differences among the three ads. In addition, offer a commentary on the effectiveness of the ads.

2. Scan various newspapers, magazines, direct-mail pieces, Web sites, and any other media to discover examples of cause marketing. Affix at least two such advertisements to 8-1/2 × 11-inch paper and evaluate them in terms of their effectiveness.

3. Using any print media, look for ads that depict multicultural models. Write an analysis discussing whether you think the ads truly appeal to many different ethnicities.

Web Site Exploration for In-Depth Analysis

Host Analytics
http://www.HostAnalytics.com
   This is an outstanding demonstration, with sound, on advertising budgeting software.

Terms of the Trade

ad campaign

budget allocation

budgeting strategies

celebrity endorsement

demographics

integrated marketing communications

institutional advertising

merchandise mix

multichannel retailing

multicultural population

objective-and-task method

percentage-of-sales method

price points

product advertising

promotional advertising

retargeting

units-sold method

that operates as a separate entity from its other divisions, may maintain a separate advertising department with dedicated staff, or may assign advertising duties within its **table of organization**. A company's size, merchandise classifications, business methodology, corporate structure, channels of distribution, and so forth, influence how it chooses to manage its advertising.

Magazines have traditionally sold advertising space to clients who supplied camera-ready copy for publication. Today, some magazine publishers, such as Condé Nast Media Group, are offering advertising development services to their advertisers at little or no cost (see Media Insight 6.2 later in this chapter). Publishers gain a competitive advantage by saving their clients money, and clients benefit by having knowledgeable professionals plan their advertising.

Assisting both advertisers and advertising agencies in their quest to be better informed about industry matters and news are two major trade associations, the American Association of Advertising Agencies (AAAA) and the Association of National Advertisers (ANA), both of which are discussed in this chapter.

In-House Advertising Agencies

Many retail operations find that operating their own advertising agency enables them to better control all aspects of advertising and allows them to develop their own unique signature. This approach is beneficial in many ways, but the in-house advertising venture is usually appropriate only for those merchants who operate major retail businesses. Establishing and maintaining a department or division to carry out the company's advertising program is often so expensive that the benefits do not outweigh the cost.

Advantages of the In-House Agency

There are many reasons why some retailers opt for their own staff to develop and design their ad campaigns, including the following:

1. Forty-two percent of companies cite cost efficiency and savings as the reason for keeping their advertising in-house, according to the ANA Web site.

2. The ANA study found that the ability to get the ad quickly from its conception to placement—or improved **turnaround time**—was the second most-cited reason for having an in-house team. An in-house team knows the product well and understands the company's needs and expectations; therefore, it has a time advantage over outside agencies, which need time to learn about the product and company before they can begin to develop effective advertising.

3. The **in-house shop** often reports directly to the company CEO or other top management and therefore has a clear understanding of the goals of the ad campaign.

4. Outside resources are known for high employee turnover rates, often affecting the client relationship, but the in-house staff is generally more stable. According to Forrester Research, the turnover rate of an in-house staff is less than 5 percent.

Disadvantages of the In-House Staff

Not all retailers feel that operating their own advertising staff is appropriate for their companies. Following are some of the disadvantages.

1. **In-house ad staffing** generally results in long-term savings, but the start-up costs, especially in times of economic distress, are too high for some companies to justify. Exorbitant overhead and staffing costs could outweigh the eventual benefits.

2. In-house experts may experience burnout in the effort to continually come up with exciting, new marketing ideas for the same product or type of product.

3. Hiring the industry's best and brightest for an in-house position is often difficult because many professionals prefer the creative challenges of an outside agency that represents a wide variety of clients (and therefore products and services).

4. Unless the in-house staff is dedicated solely to advertising, their other duties may compromise the creativity and focus needed to develop outstanding advertising strategies and products.

In Media Insight 6.1, the discussion of in-house agencies applies to businesses in general and most certainly to the retail industry.

Roles of the In-House Agency

Although the roles of an in-house agency differ from company to company, a study of ANA member companies (found on ANA's Web site) reveals that the following responsibilities, in addition to print ad development, are typically handled by in-house staffs:

◆ Collateral products, such as point-of-sale displays (Figure 6.1), brochures, and other material (97 percent)

◆ Internal and company communications (82 percent)

◆ Internal and company videos (69 percent)

◆ Brand-identity efforts (66 percent)

◆ Direct mail (65 percent)

◆ Web site creation and maintenance (65 percent)

◆ Online banners and other static online creative material (62 percent)

◆ Other services, such as television advertising, packaging, search engine marketing (60 percent)

◆ Media planning (35 percent)

◆ Media buying (24 percent)

6.1 Point-of-sale signage attracts shoppers.
Paul Sakuma/ AP Images.

For a limited time only.
Get 20% off today when you get a GapCard.*

When to Establish an In-House Advertising Agency

Jeffrey Hauser

In my 30 years as an advertising consultant, I ran into many businesses that could have benefited from an in-house advertising agency. Instead, they spent fortunes on various agencies that were more concerned with making money than helping the client. So perhaps it's time to set the record straight and offer some advice to anyone that fits the following criteria. There are several types of businesses that could be better off if they created a small division to handle their marketing needs.

If you have a product you manufacture, you are tops on my list. It's your product, and you should be controlling every aspect of the promotions. That includes product development, packaging, logo design, national media placement, along with trade publications, public relations, press releases, trade show booths, annual report publication, and any supplemental support materials like brochures, spec sheets, and documentation.

It sounds like a daunting task, but any company that requires any or all of these marketing tools should consider doing it in-house. Why? Because of control and self-interest. The business gets to control every aspect of what the public sees regarding the image of the company, and it's in the business's best interest to make the right decisions that will affect them most. In other words, would any advertising agency give them all the time and effort it takes to produce the work they desire? Perhaps they might, but at what cost?

Which brings up another issue: expense. Hiring a marketing director, copywriter, and artist will be cheaper in the long run if the company can support the investment. It will prove more advantageous down the road to build this department and have a say in the personnel that runs it. You will have to provide the technology needed for the department to function, but having the ability to create internal collateral material is a time- and cost-saving luxury even a medium-sized business can appreciate.

Another point raised: business size. At what point in a business's life can it begin to contemplate hiring a staff for an in-house team? Review your current advertising expenses. What would a staff cost in comparison, realizing the control you are achieving? Look at the media costs. Most media allow 15 percent agency commissions that you gain through your own in-house marketing. What is that worth?

But what about the little guy? If you're a small business that places ads on a regular basis, consider a single marketing person with the ability to design and place ads.

It's the beginning of an agency with a much lower cost. It's how I began in the business. I was a designer for a small firm during college. I worked part-time and they used me as they saw fit. The investment doesn't have to be large or long term. But you'll find more loyalty and cost benefits, for the most part.

That's not to say that using a quality advertising agency or consultant on occasion wouldn't pay off. They may still be needed for a special project or second opinion. But consider the value of an in-house person dedicated to your business. You may find that it was the best investment you ever made.

Source: Jeffrey Hauser. "When to Establish an In-House Advertising Agency." Retrieved from http://ezinearticles. com/?When-to-Establish-an-In-House-Advertising-Agency&id=148741.

Despite the benefits offered by an in-house ad agency, some retail organizations have disbanded their in-house staffs. For example, Best Buy, the largest electronics retailer in the United States, decided that with its significant growth and expansion plans, both in the United States and overseas, it needed more expertise and hours than its in-house staff could provide for its ad campaigns. Best Buy hired BBDO for account planning, ad strategy, and media and consumer connection planning.

A unique departure from the in-house agency—and a challenge to traditional ad agencies—is the "miniagency" service offered by Condé Nast Media Group and other publishers (see Media Insight 6.2).

External Advertising Resources

Most retailers in the United States contract with a number of outside sources to develop their advertising strategies, plan their campaigns, design advertising, place ads with the media, and provide a host of other services. In addition to the advertising agencies, which constitute the largest of these resources, other professional groups perform a wide range of services: the media offer a number of services, such as demographic analysis, layout formats, and writing the copy for the ads; market consultants, also known as resident buying offices, assist merchants with their promotional plans; and freelancers work independently on noncontract arrangements and perform

Publishers Creating Their Own In-House Ad Agencies

Louise Story
June 4, 2007

Similar to executives at advertising agencies, Richard D. Beckman and his team talk to managers at consumer brand companies about the customers they want to reach. Four to six weeks later, they present a marketing and advertising plan.

But Mr. Beckman does not run an advertising agency. He is the president of the Condé Nast Media Group, a division of the magazine company that publishes titles such as *Vogue*, *Wired*, and *The New Yorker*. Over the last 5 years, Mr. Beckman has developed an agencylike business within Condé Nast's ad sales unit, generating new revenue by planning events for advertisers and creating advertisements that help sell more magazine pages.

Traditionally, magazine companies have made money by selling ad space in their magazines or, more recently, on their Web sites. Now some of them have set up what amount to internal miniagencies that work with clients to design campaigns for their own pages. Sometimes this work spills out into other forums, such as radio and television ads.

Condé Nast Publications, the Meredith Corporation, Reader's Digest, Hearst [Corporation], and even *Surface* magazine, a small independent title dedicated to fashion and design, are now handling some creative work for their advertisers. The trend poses a challenge to traditional agencies and has created some unusual partnerships (think of *Vogue* designing ads for Wal-Mart stores).

The Condé Nast Media Group has been developing sweepstakes, television specials, radio spots, in-store events, and, of course, magazine ads for brands such as Dillard's, Kohl's, Grey Goose, and Lexus. The unit, which relies on a panel of more than 100,000 consumers to evaluate advertising, generates about $200 million of revenue from these marketing programs.

Mr. Beckman's group has drawn the most attention for *Fashion Rocks*, a television special about music and the fashion industry that goes beyond a typical agency project. The event, now in its fourth year, ties in several large advertisers such as Chevrolet, Citigroup, L'Oréal and Cingular, and was featured last year in a custom magazine sent to Condé Nast subscribers.

The idea behind [this] program is to create a so-called television event, custom magazine and other content that showcases each advertiser. During *Fashion Rocks* last year, for example, Elton John performed a private show the night before that was streamed only onto Cingular Wireless cell phones.

Andrew McLean, president and chief client officer of Mediaedge:cia, the ad-buying agency that represented Cingular Wireless when it worked with *Fashion Rocks*, said that his client's work with Condé Nast had moved from "just buying bits of paper in a magazine to a much more multifaceted relationship." Mediaedge:cia is part of the WPP Group.

Mr. Beckman's unit also has the ability to approach celebrities who do not often work directly with advertisers. For example, Condé Nast arranged for Robert F. Kennedy Jr. to appear in an ad for Lexus that also showcased the Waterkeeper Alliance, a water protection group that Mr. Kennedy heads.

"They have the cachet and the credibility for top-tier celebrities to want to partner with them," said Robin Steinberg, senior vice president and director of print investment and activation for MediaVest, an agency that buys media in the Publicis Groupe.

For Dillard's, Condé Nast has created everything from the store chain's current slogan— "The Style of Your Life"—to fashion shows for local department stores. Condé Nast set up the first national campaign for Dillard's last year, with components such as radio and television ads, online videos, and magazine ads.

Condé Nast's internal agency evolved from within, but Meredith, which publishes such titles as *Family Circle*, *More*, and *Ladies' Home Journal*, took a different approach. Last summer the company established Meredith 360, an advertising consulting group that is a separate business unit from the publishing group. Meredith has purchased three advertising agencies in the last year, allowing it to offer a broad spectrum of services.

"A lot of our different divisions do what a lot of different agencies do," said Nancy Weber, Meredith's chief marketing officer.

Hearst also has a division that does creative work for its largest clients, in formats that include print, online, video, mobile, and outdoor. Hearst has modeled its marketing division after an ad agency, said Jeff Hamill, senior vice president of Hearst Integrated Media, complete with a sales staff that serves as account directors, creative teams, and researchers.

Mr. Hamill said that agencies that buy ads are often involved in the process, but agencies that create ads are not because Hearst can do that work.

Meredith 360 charges for its services, whereas Condé Nast and Hearst charge for costs only when they create custom programs for advertisers, executives at those companies said. (Condé Nast also makes a profit from events such as *Fashion Rocks*.) The rate structure means that Condé Nast can often beat ad agencies on price, Mr. Beckman said.

"We don't have to make money from our creative, because we make money from our media," he said.

Some advertisers think that's the way it should be. Condé Nast [works] with CIT, the financial services company, on a series of interviews with people such as fashion designer Marc Ecko, whose clothing company is called Marc Ecko Enterprises. The interviews are featured online, and Condé Nast [produces] live events and magazine sections . . . for CIT.

Kelley Gipson, director of brand marketing and communications for CIT, said that she does not expect to pay Condé Nast anything more than the cost of the pages her company purchases.

"I look at it as part of the value chain for media," Ms. Gipson said. "We don't charge for it when we're working with our customers. We look at the opportunity to provide sort of intellectual capital as the glue in the relationship, so we challenge our media partners to think about it the same way."

Source: The New York Times, June 4, 2007.

everything from planning the advertisements to final placement in the media.

Advertising Agencies

The lifeblood of the advertising world is the advertising agency. It is responsible for most of the ads placed by organizations worldwide, and retail advertising is just a small part of its business. Agency involvement in producing and placing ads dates back to 1850, when Volney B. Palmer opened the first U.S. advertising agency in Philadelphia. In 1877, James Walter Thompson purchased an agency started by William James Carlton and named it the James Walter Thompson Company. Now known as JWT, it is the oldest U.S. ad agency. Thompson hired artists and writers to develop advertisements, which led to his agency being the first to establish a creative department.

Today, advertising agencies are a huge part of the advertising industry, with agencies operating around the globe to serve the needs of for-profit and nonprofit organizations of every size and magnitude. In the United States alone, according to the most recent figures given by the U.S. Census Bureau, there are more than 13,000 agencies, with staffs ranging in size from as few as 2 employees to as many as 2,500 or more. The smaller agencies are single-location houses, whereas the giants have offices in many parts of the world. Most agencies, approximately 8,000, employ four people or fewer, followed by about 2,000 that employ between five and nine individuals. It is only the major advertising agencies that employ more than 2,500 people.

Larger agencies have as their clients various types of businesses, including retailers. Small agencies, especially those with few staff members, often specialize in servicing a particular segment of the market, such as retailing.

AGENCY HOLDING COMPANIES

An **agency holding company** is a media and advertising conglomerate with subsidiaries based throughout the world. These giant companies, headquartered in international business centers such as London, New York, Paris, and Tokyo, are the major players in the advertising industry. They provide through their subsidiaries a comprehensive range of marketing services, including advertising direction, public relations, media services, and problem solving.

Focus 6.1 features the Omnicom Group, now number two in the field behind the London-based WPP Group.

Table 6.1 lists the world's top 25 agency holding companies by volume of work.

INDIVIDUAL AGENCIES

Agency holding companies consist of individual agencies, most of which are advertising giants in their own rights. Heading the list is BBDO Worldwide, an affiliate of the Omnicom Group. These individual agencies range in size from the very small, with just a few employees, to major organizations, with thousands of people on their staffs. Many are full-service operations that offer services ranging from ad creation and placement to public relations. Others are more specialized, concentrating on specific areas of expertise, such as digital advertising, direct marketing, or multicultural targeting. Digitas, for example, specializes in digital advertising, Carlson Marketing in promotion and event marketing, Interbrand in branding and identity, Clinree Davis & Mann in health care, and Rapp in direct marketing. Some are unaffiliated and operate their own companies, and others are part of the giant holding companies.

Table 6.2 lists the top ten specialty agencies in the United States according to their specialization, headquarters, and 2008 revenue.

Of particular importance in the area of specialization for advertising agencies is the multicultural market. As explored in Chapter 4, the African-American, Hispanic, and Asian-American markets are growing to the point that retailers and other businesses are paying close attention to them and are using advertising as a means of drawing these customers to their companies (see Figure 6.2, page 136). The major agencies that specialize in these ethnic markets are featured in Chapter 4.

Most advertising agencies assist their clients with strategic development before initiating a campaign, develop the concepts to be used in the ads, proceed with the creativity necessary to meet their objectives, place the ads with the media, and offer a host of other services. Because advertising

FOCUS $ 6.1

Omnicom Group

Omnicom Group is a global agency holding company. With a wealth of subsidiaries, it provides its international client list with professional services that include every aspect of advertising, public relations, marketing, and communication solutions. It offers services such as brand consultancy, social responsibility consultation, crisis communications, custom publishing, database management, direct marketing, directory advertising, entertainment marketing, environmental design, experiential and field marketing, business-to-business advertising, graphic arts, event marketing, and a host of other specialties.

The components of the Omnicom Group are as follows:

◆ *Global advertising*, which consists of numerous global networks such as BBDO Worldwide, with 350 offices in 76 countries; DDB Worldwide, centered on the former advertising giant Doyle Dane Bernbach Needham, with more than 206 offices in over 99 countries; and TBWA, with 225 offices in 72 countries.

◆ *National advertising agencies*, which include prestigious firms that are known for strategic and creative excellence, such as Arnell Group; Element 79 Partners; Goodby, Silverstein & Partners; GSD&M; Martin/Williams; Merkley & Partners; and Zimmerman Partners.

◆ *Media services*, known as the Omnicom Media Group (OMG), which consist of OMD Worldwide and PHD Network.

◆ *Media specialist solutions*, which consist of Novus Print Media, Icon International, and Full Circle Entertainment.

◆ *Public relations, lobbying, and marketing services*, the responsibility for which is the purview of Diversified Agency Services (DAS), which includes such major public relations firms as Fleishman-Hillard, Kerchum, and Porter Novelli.

A host of other groups within Omnicom provide all of these services to both for-profit and nonprofit organizations.

Of particular importance to the retail industry, Integrated Merchandising Systems, headquartered in Morton Grove, Illinois, and a member of the Omnicom Group, is a leading merchandising service agency with a fully integrated retail management system designed to deliver strategic management to the retailer. Included in its offerings, and of special interest to merchants involved in catalogue operations, is its expertise in branded merchandise catalogues that the company designs and develops. In this era of off-site retailing, this is an important service that the subsidiary offers its clients.

TABLE 6.1 — World's Top Agency Holding Companies

RANK 2008	RANK 2007	AGENCY COMPANY	HEADQUARTERS	WORLDWIDE REVENUE (IN MILLIONS) 2008	2007	%CHG	U.S. REVENUE (IN MILLIONS) 2008	2007	%CHG	REVENUE FROM OUTSIDE THE U.S. (IN MILLIONS) 2008	2007	%CHG
1	2	WPP	London	$13,598	$12,383	9.8	$4,735	$4,538	4.3	$8,864	$7,846	13.0
2	1	Omnicom Group	New York	13,360	12,694	5.2	6,890	6,704	2.8	6,470	5,990	8.0
3	3	Interpublic Group of Cos.	New York	6,963	6,554	6.2	3,786	3,651	3.7	3,176	2,903	9.4
4	4	Publicis Groupe	Paris	6,900	6,393	7.9	2,946	2,760	6.7	3,954	3,633	8.8
5	5	Dentsu*	Tokyo	3,296	2,932	12.4	111	110	1.1	3,185	2,823	12.8
6	6	Aegis Group*	London	2,490	2.215	12.4	504	512	−1.6	1,986	1,703	16.6
7	7	Havas	Suresnes, France	2,307	2,094	10.2	702	694	1.1	1,605	1,400	14.7
8	8	Hakuhodo DY Holdings*	Tokyo	1,560	1,392	12.1	NA	NA	NA	1,560	1,392	12.1
9	9	MDC Partners	Toronto/ New York	585	534	9.5	485	427	13.6	99	107	−6.9
10	11	Asatsu-DK	Tokyo	503	454	10.8	4	3	38.4	499	451	10.6
11	10	Alliance Data Systems (Epsilon)	Dallas	491	469	4.8	461	440	4.7	31	29	6.6
12	12	Media Consulta	Berlin	427	415	3.1	32	49	−33.9	395	366	8.0
13	13	Microsoft Corp. (Razorfish)	Redmond, WA	409	368	11.1	317	299	6.0	92	69	33.3
14	15	Photon Group*	Sydney	383	314	21.9	NA	NA	NA	383	314	21.9
15	14	Carlson Marketing*	Minneapolis	367	349	5.1	265	253	4.8	102	96	6.0
16	16	Cheil Worldwide	Seoul	340	300	13.4	31	27	14.6	308	272	13.3
17	17	IBM Corp. (IBM Interactive)	Armonk, NY	313	278	12.6	205	188	9.0	108	90	20.0
18	19	Sapient Corp. (Sapient Interactive)	Cambridge, MA	306	241	27.0	211	166	27.0	95	75	27.0
19	26	inventive Health (inventive Communications)	Westerville, OH	280	204	37.1	238	184	29.4	42	21	105.0
20	22	Grupo ABC (ABC Group)	São Paulo, Brazil	280	228	22.6	4	NA	NA	276	228	20.7
21	20	STW Group	St. Leonards, Australia	256	235235	9.0	NA	NA	NA	256	235	9.0
22	25	LBI International	Stockholm, Sweden	241	211	14.2	47	28	68.5	194	183	6.0
23	23	Clemenger Group	Melbourne, Australia	239	220	8.5	NA	NA	NA	239	220	8.5
24	24	Cossette Communications Group	Quebec City	238	218	9.6	20	17	15.1	218	200	9.1
25	18	George P. Johnson Co.	Auburn Hills, MI	238	256	−7.0	162	188	−13.8	76	67	12.1

Source: Advertising Age, April 27, 2009, p. 12.

Ten Top U.S. Agencies According to Specialty
Ranked by 2008 U.S. revenue. Dollars in thousands.

RANK '08	RANK '07	AGENCY	HEADQUARTERS	U.S. REVENUE 2008	% CHG
DIGITAL					
1	1	Digitas [Publicis (Digitas)]	Boston	$377,000	9.3
2	2	Razorfish [Microsoft Corp.]	Seattle	317,000	6.0
3	5	Sapient Interactive (Sapient Corp.)	Cambridge, MA	211,140	27.0
4	3	Ogilvyinteractive [WPP (Olgilvy (OgilvyOne))]	New York	207,500	7.0
5	4	IBM Interactive [IBM Corp.]	Chicago	205,000	9.0
6	7	Wunderman [WPP (Y&R (Wunderman))]	New York	160,800	16.9
8	9	Rapp [Omnicom (DDB (Rapp))]	New York	149,400	27.7
9	13	Rosetta	Hamilton, NJ	129,600	35.1
10	8	Organic [Omnicom (BBDO)]	San Francisco	129,100	3.0
SEARCH MARKETING					
1	1	iCrossing	Scottsdale, AZ	$79,000	16.2
2	2	360i	New York	50,000	19.0
3	7	Rapp [Omnicom(DDB (Rapp))]	New York	36,500	40.4
4	3	Performics [Publicis (VivaKi)]	Chicago	33,600	−1.2
5	4	iProspect [Aegis Group (Isobar)]	Watertown, MA	33,000	16.2
6	5	Razorfish [Microsoft Corp.]	Seattle	33,000	17.9
7	6	Web.com	Jacksonville, FL	20,600	9.7
8	8	Efficient Frontier	Sunnyvale, CA	30,000	16.3
9	9	Group M Search [WPP (Group M)]	St. Louis	29,100	42.0
10	12	Acronym Media	New York	25,000	54.3
DIRECT MARKETING					
1	1	Epsilon/Purple@Epsilon [Alliance Data Systems]	Irving, TX	$460,500	4.7
2	2	Rapp [Omnicom (DDB (Rapp))]	New York	364,500	12.2
3	3	DraftFCB [Interpublic (DraftFCB)]	Chicago/New York	306,000	8.8
4	4	Wunderman [WPP (Y&R)]	New York	268,000	7.2
5	5	Aspen Marketing Services	West Chicago, IL	212,600	−8.8
6	7	Merkle	Columbia, MD	211,100	16.8
7	6	Harte-Hanks Direct	Yardley, PA	177,664	−2.3
8	9	OgilvyOne Worldwide [WPP (Ogilvy (OgilvyOne))]	New York	115,800	−3.1
9	10	Ketchum Directory Advertising [Omnicom (OMG)]	Overland Park, KS	101,200	−8.0
10	13	Digitas [Publicis (Digitas)]	Boston	94,250	NA
PROMOTION AND EVENT MARKETING					
1	2	Carlson Marketing	Minneapolis	$172,250	4.8
2	1	George P. Johnson Co.	Auburn Hills, MI	162,484	−13.8
3	4	Integer Group [Omnicom (TBWA)]	Lakewood, CO	136,200	3.5
4	7	Momentum Worldwide [Interpublic (McCann)]	New York	135,000	17.4
5	6	Mosaic Sales Solutions	Irving, TX	127,933	5.5
6	8	G2 [WPP (Grey)]	New York	122,040	7.5
7	3	BBDO Worldwide [Omnicom (BBDO)]	New York	117,000	−25.0
8	5	Jack Morton Worldwide [Interpublic]	Boston	116,900	−9.0
9	9	Derse	Milwaukee	116,626	9.8
10	10	GMR Marketing [Omnicom (Radiate)]	New Berlin, WI	106,500	6.5

TABLE 6.2

TABLE 6.2 (CONT'D)

RANK				U.S. REVENUE	
'08	'07	AGENCY	HEADQUARTERS	2008	% CHG
BRANDING AND IDENTITY					
1	1	Interbrand [Omnicom (DDB)]	New York	$120,300	4.6
2	2	Landor Associates [WPP (Y&R)]	San Francisco	88,000	3.5
3	4	Rapp [Omnicom (DDB)]	New York	40,100	75.9
4	3	FutureBrand [Interpublic (aligned with McCann)]	New York	30,000	0.0
5	5	Siegel & Gale [Omnicom]	New York	19,400	7.8
6	6	iCrossing	Scottsdale, AZ	15,000	15.4
7	7	Beanstalk Group [Omnicom]	New York	12,400	0.8
8	8	Addison Whitney [inVentiv Health (inVentiv Communications)]	Charlotte, NC	11,345	10.2
9	9	Bernstein-Rein Advertising	Kansas City, MO	8,522	−12.6
10	15	Periscope	Minneapolis	5,526	52.2
MEDIA					
1	1	OMD Worldwide [Omnicrom (OMG)]	New York	$216,700	3.0
2	3	Starcom USA [Publicis (SMG)]	Chicago	179,300	3.2
3	2	Mindshare Worldwide [WPP (Group M)]	New York	176,200	0.6
4	4	Mediaedge:cia [WPP (Group M)]	New York	175,400	19.0
5	5	MediaVest USA [Publicis (SMG)]	New York	134,600	2.8
6	6	Zenith Media USA [Publicis (ZOG)]	New York	129,600	2.4
7	8	MediaCom [WPP (Group M)]	New York	121,900	10.3
8	7	Carat [Aegis Group (Aegis Media)]	New York	109,600	−6.9
9	9	Universal McCann [Interpublic (Mediabrands)]	New York	102,100	13.3
10	10	Initiative [Interpublic (Mediabrands)]	New York	78,900	19.4
HEALTHCARE					
1	1	CommonHealth [WPP]	Parsippany, NJ	$141,800	5.0
2	2	Cline Davis & Mann [Omnicom]	New York	129,500	2.0
3	4	Lowe Healthcare Worldwide [Interpublic (Lowe)]	Parsippany, NJ	108,600	4.4
4	5	Euro RSCG Life [Havas (Euro)]	New York	108,500	6.4
5	6	TBWA/WorldHealth [Omnicom (TBWA)]	New York	101,000	0.0
6	7	McCann Healthcare Worldwide [Interpublic (McCann)]	Parsippany, NJ	99,500	2.2
7	3	Sudler & Hennessey [WPP (Y&R)]	New York	92,000	−12.4
8	8	GSW Worldwide [inVentiv Health (inVentiv Communications)]	Westerville, OH	89,318	5.8
9	9	Saatchi & Saatchi Healthcare Comms. [Publicis (PHCG)]	New York	85,000	1.0
10	11	DraftFCB Healthcare [Interpublic (DraftFCB)]	New York	77,800	6.6
HISPANIC-AMERICAN					
1	1	Dieste [Omnicom]	Dallas	$44,900	11.1
2	2	Vidal Partnership	New York	35,000	12.9
3	3	Bravo Group [WPP (Y&R)]	Miami	31,500	5.0
4	7	GlobalHue	Southfield, MI	28,178	37.2
5	4	Lopez Negrete Communications	Houston	24,150	1.6

TABLE 6.2 (CONT'D)

| RANK | | | | U.S. REVENUE | |
'08	'07	AGENCY	HEADQUARTERS	2008	% CHG
6	8	Zubi Advertising Services	Coral Gables, FL	21,500	9.7
7	5	Brombley Communications [Publicis]	San Antonio, TX	21,100	−6.6
8	6	Conill [Publicis (Saatchi)]	Miami	19,900	−3.9
9	9	LatinWorks [Omnicom]	Austin, TX	17,440	1.5
10	12	Alma DDB [Omnicom (DDB)]	Coral Gables, FL	14,800	13.0
AFRICAN-AMERICAN					
1	4	GlobalHue	Southfield, MI	$25,900	31.6
2	1	UniWorld Grooup [WPP]	New York	25,668	−4.0
3	2	Carol H. Williams Advertising	Oakland, CA	23,900	−5.9
4	3	Burrell Communications Group [Publicis]	Chicago	22,000	−4.3
5	5	Sanders/Wingo	El Paso, TX	14,340	21.5
6	8	Fuse	St. Louis	9,351	14.5
7	9	Images USA	Atlanta	9,253	47.9
8	7	Footsteps [Omnicom]	New York	7,000	−14.6
9	6	Matlock Advertising & Public Relations	Atlanta	5,107	6.4
10	11	Moroch Partners	Dallas	5,000	6.4
ASIAN-AMERICAN					
1	1	Kang & Lee Advertising [WPP (Y&R)]	New York	$15,500	3.3
2	3	Admerasia	New York	10,250	−2.4
3	2	InterTrend Communications	Long Beach, CA	10,245	−15.5
4	2	IW Group [Interpublic]	West Hollywood, CA	9,085	−10.8
5	7	AdAsia Communications	New York	7,059	22.3
6	5	Time Advertising	Millbrae, CA	5,800	−18.3
7	6	PanCom International	Los Angeles	5,103	−13.5
8	9	Global Advertising Strategies	New York	5,000	11.1
9	8	ES Advertising	Los Angeles	4,487	−5.0
10	17	Aaaza	Los Angeles	3,000	71.4

Source: Advertising Age, April 27, 2009, p. 16.

6.2 Many advertising agencies are multi-culturally oriented. *Courtesy of Macy's.*

is a very sensitive area of marketing, the usual rule for an agency is to avoid conflicts of interest by limiting their representation to **noncompeting companies**.

Clients and agencies typically enter into contracts for specified periods of time. This enables the

agency to become more familiar with the client's needs and to adapt the advertising plan as needed to best serve the client's interests.

Table 6.3 lists the top 25 agencies in the United States.

Top 25 U.S. Agencies from All Disciplines

RANK		AGENCY	HEADQUARTERS	U.S. REVENUE (IN MILLIONS)			REVENUE FROM OUTSIDE THE U.S. (IN MILLIONS)			WORLDWIDE REVENUE (IN MILLIONS)		
2008	2007			2008	2007	%CHG	2008	2007	%CHG	2008	2007	%CHG
1	1	BBDO Worldwide Omnicom (BBDO)]	New York	$636	4628	1.2	$1,350	41,271	6.3	$1,986	$1,899	4.6
2	2	McCann Erickson Worldwide [Interpublic (McCann)]	New York	530	490	8.2	1,211	1,175	3.1	1,741	1,665	4.6
3	3	DraftFCB [Interpublic (DraftFCB)]	Chicago/New York	510	485	5.2	445	440	1.1	955	925	3.2
4	4	Epsilon/Purple@ Epsilon [Alliance Data Systems]	Irving, TX	461	440	4.7	31	29	6.6	491	469	4.8
5	5	Digitas [Publicis (Digitas)]	Boston	377	345	9.3	90	19	371.1	467	364	28.2
6	6	Rapp [Omnicom (DDB (Rapp))]	New York	365	325	12.2	275	250	10.0	640	575	11.2
7	7	Euro RSCG Worldwide [Havas (Euro)]	New York	343	325	5.5	827	782	5.7	1,170	1,107	5.7
8	8	Y&R [WPP (Y&R)]	New York	340	307	10.7	760	712	6.7	1,100	1,019	7.9
9	9	JWT [WPP (JWT)]	New York	332	302	9.8	826	800	3.2	1,157	1,102	5.0
10	10	Razorfish [Microsoft Corp.]	Seattle	317	299	6.0	92	69	33.3	409	368	11.1
11	11	DDB Worldwide [Omnicom (DDB)]	New York	300	291	3.0	1,210	1,141	6.0	1,509	1,432	5.4
12	13	Wunderman [WPP (Y&R Wunderman))]	New York	268	250	7.2	451	410	9.9	719	660	8.9
13	12	Carlson Marketing	Minneapolis	265	253	4.8	102	96	6.0	367	349	5.1
14	16	Saatchi & Saatchi [Publicis (Saatchi)]	New York	236	230	2.6	554	560	-1.0	790	790	0.1
15	19	Leo Burnett Worldwide [Publicis (Saatchi)]	Chicago	229	215	6.5	566	526	7.5	795	741	7.2
16	17	Oglivy & Mather Worldwide [WPP (Oglivy)]	New York	221	226	-2.1	550	553	-0.5	771	779	-1.0
17	21	TBWA Worldwide [Omnicom (TBWA)]	New York	219	208	5.4	1,138	1,084	5.0	1,357	1,292	5.1
18	20	OMD Worldwide [Omnicom (OMG)]	New York	217	210	3.0	690	648	6.5	907	859	5.6
19	18	Grey [WPP (Grey)]	New York	215	221	-3.0	400	392	2.0	614	613	0.2
20	15	Aspen Marketing Services	West Chicago, IL	213	233	-8.8	NA	NA	NA	213	233	-8.8
21	31	Sapient Interactive [Sapient Corp.]	Cambridge, MA	211	166	27.0	95	75	27.0	306	241	27.0
22	27	Merkle	Columbia, MD	211	181	16.8	NA	NA	NA	211	181	16.8
23	14	Campbell-Ewald [Interpublic]	Warren, MI	210	239	-12.0	NA	NA	NA	210	239	-12.0
24	22	OglivyInteractive [WPP (Oglivy (OglivyOne))]	New York	208	194	7.0	166	151	10.0	374	345	8.3
25	25	IBM Interactive [IBM Corp.]	Chicago	205	188	9.0	108	90	20.0	313	278	12.6

Source: Advertising Age, April 27, 2009, p. 13.

AGENCY REMUNERATION

Numerous methods are employed in **agency remuneration**. They range from the traditional commission methods to value-based principles.

Commission-Based Compensation Traditionally, advertising agencies receive compensation from the media in which they placed their client's ads, usually a 15 percent commission to cover all of their services: creating the ads, helping to plan strategies, selecting the appropriate media and the choices within them, and so forth. Fifteen percent is still the norm for **commission-based compensation** in some agency–client relationships, most often for small accounts. Major advertisers are generally charged a smaller commission, typically 10 percent, but the actual rate depends on the ability of the advertiser to negotiate terms and on the number of ads placed.

Annual Fees Many agencies negotiate a fee for the services they provide to their clients. The more services expected, the greater the fee. The fee might be a general amount for all of the services rendered, an amount based on projected staff hours required to service the account, or a sliding fee based on service and actual dollars spent by the advertiser. Some agencies receive an annual fee plus additional payment if special services are required for a particular campaign.

Performance-Based Fees Some agencies negotiate fees based on the expected outcomes of the agency's efforts on behalf of a client. Objectives and goals are established by the advertiser, with a fee to be paid for achievement of these expectations. **Performance-based fees** are usually in the form of a pre-established percentage, with incentives (e.g., a bonus payment or an increased percentage) built in if the expected goals are surpassed.

Project Billing Some agencies base the remuneration plan on a specific project for an organization. Often, the advertiser might have an in-house staff or agency that performs its routine advertising functions but requires outside assistance for a special campaign. Retailers, for example, might want to promote a major anniversary celebration, a store opening in a new market, or expansion into a multichannel venture. For this sort of one-time service, the agency generally uses **project billing** (Figure 6.3).

Monthly Retainer Some of the smaller agencies permit advertisers to reserve their services on a retainer basis. Each month, the client pays an agreed-upon fee that ensures the agency will be available at any time the client needs its services. The amount of a **monthly retainer** is usually minimal.

Hourly Rate Basis Smaller agencies sometimes charge **hourly fees**, particularly when the client requires only one function, such as creating an ad or researching which media will best serve the client's needs. It is usually the infrequent advertiser who opts for this payment method.

Cost-Based Fees Some ad agencies base their fees on the costs incurred for specific services performed. **Cost-based fees** must take into account copywriting, original artwork, layout, media selection, media placement, and so forth.

SERVICES OF THE AD AGENCY

Ad agencies provide a wide range of services, some of which are described in the following sections.

Strategic Planning At the heart of a company's advertising is **strategic planning**, which ensures the greatest return on the company's investment. The plan should define the company's objectives and how advertising will help achieve those goals. Whatever the objective—to increase overall sales, expand market reach, better define the merchandising philosophy, or build brand acceptance—a strategic plan must be developed to meet it.

Creating the Advertisement The creative department is charged with designing the layout that will be used in any of the media the client will require. Included are the copywriting and artwork components (Figure 6.4), which are the basis of the advertisement, media selection, print production, and so on. All of this is detailed fully in Part 4, "Creating the Advertising."

Media Planning Not only is it necessary to choose the appropriate media for the client but also to determine which media outlets are most appropriate to carry the message to the consumer. If the newspaper is the best choice, it is necessary to research which publication has the best demographics for the client's company,

Our Polo Ralph Lauren Factory Stores
are proud to offer you merchandise of the
highest quality at generous everyday savings.
In appreciation of your ongoing patronage,
we are pleased to present you
with this special gift.

Best wishes to you and your family
this holiday season.

Susie McCabe
President, Polo Ralph Lauren Factory Stores

FIND THE PERFECT GIFTS
FOR EVERYONE ON YOUR LIST!

POLO RALPH LAUREN
FACTORY STORE

YOU'RE INVITED TO RECEIVE
20% Off
YOUR PURCHASE OF $200 OR MORE*
NOVEMBER 30–DECEMBER 24, 2009

6.3 Major special events are often billed as separate projects. *Courtesy of Ralph Lauren.*

whether the message should be in a daily edition or Sunday edition, where in the paper the ad should be located to bring the best results, the size of the ad needed for success, and so on. If television is the choice, the appropriate programs, the best times for exposure, the time needed for each commercial airing, and so forth must be considered. Whichever outlet is planned, careful investigation is necessary to plan the best presentation.

Media Buying In all of the agency holding companies, the purchase of media is done by either a separate entity that is owned by the conglomerate or by a department within the organization. For individual major agencies, a department within the company typically handles media buying. In each case, having the creative division and media buying division under one roof enables them to interact and often to produce

a better ad at a better price. In all of these situations, the advantage is better pricing. Agencies are able to better negotiate with the media because of the significant business they bring to them from their clients.

Even smaller agencies offer media buying, which is one of the reasons advertisers choose to have them as advertising representatives.

Web Design For multichannel retailers, it is important that their ad agencies have the ability to design and manage Web sites (Figure 6.5). Today, nearly every retailer has a Web site. One of the trends in the world of retailing is to use both on-site and off-site components to reach the consumer. Web sites require continuous updating to reflect any changes in the merchant's operation, and having an agency to handle this chore simplifies the effort.

6.4 *(opposite)* Ad agencies offer
expertise in ad design and layout.
Superstock/Fotosearch.

6.5 Agencies design Web sites
for retailers.
Courtesy of Old Navy.

Chapter 10, "Direct Marketing Options: The Internet, Social Networking, and Direct Mail," offers a closer look at Web site retailing.

Public Relations Any major retail operation, or any major business for that matter, is concerned with the image the company portrays to its customers and potential patrons. Fostering a positive "face" for the public to see is a necessity in today's competitive environment. It is also important for businesses to correct any misperceptions and address any misgivings customers may have about their companies. To achieve these goals, public relations must be handled in a meaningful and timely manner. Advertising agencies that provide public relations services often have a competitive advantage over those that do not. Chapter 16, "Public Relations: Promoting and Advancing the Retailer's Image," explores the concept of public relations and the benefit it offers to companies.

Research The key to developing advertising that is motivational and informative and that reaches the most productive markets is to use meaningful **research methodology**. Most major companies have their own research departments but also use outside sources such as advertising agencies to augment their efforts. The depth and breadth of the research offered by agencies depends on the advertising tasks to be addressed as well as the size of the project. The studies undertaken include such areas as demographic analysis, media exploration, market segmentation, advertising concepts, and consumer habits and motivations. Chapter 3, "Preplanning: Researching the Target Markets," examines the nature of research and the purposes it serves.

Mailing List Management For companies that use direct mail, as do many retailers, using the appropriate mailing list is a significant factor in reaching consumers. Many **full-service ad agencies** offer their clients the opportunity to have their lists kept up to date so that their direct-mail efforts will be maximized. With the mailing expense continuously rising, it is imperative that mailed catalogues, brochures, pamphlets, and other direct-mail pieces reach their intended targets. In addition to list maintenance service, agencies provide mailing lists that have been carefully fine-tuned to include potential new prospects who have the right characteristics to become purchasers. Chapter 10 further explores mailing lists.

Advertising Media Assistance

Although the advertising agency is by far the most important outside organization to help businesses with their advertising plans, others, such as the media, offer assistance to advertisers in their quest for effective advertising. Media assistance offers a particularly efficient, cost-effective way for a single ad or a complete campaign to be prepared and placed. Retailers, particularly those with limited budgets, often bypass the agency and go directly to the media for help.

An excellent example of media help in creating and placing ads is evident at nytadvertising.com. The Web site offers simple instructions that lead the user through the various stages of ad preparation and ultimately to ad placement using a self-service advertising platform.

The user begins by choosing from among many ad templates. After the type of ad is chosen, the user clicks the "customize" button inside the ad template, which opens the customization tool that enables the user to add text, images, colors, and a logo. The final ad is then stored in a private library for repeated use, as often as desired, and it can be edited as needed. Customization also includes replication in various ad sizes as desired by the advertiser. Most important to the advertiser with a limited budget is that there is no cost to set up an account or customize an ad. The only charge is for the actual space that it takes in the newspaper.

Other media feature self-placement or personal assistance at little or no cost except for the space or time the ad occupies.

Freelancers

Many advertisers use freelancers to perform one or more services, including writing ad copy, creating original artwork, and developing layout designs. Some specialize in specific media ads such as direct mail or outdoor advertisements, and others perform their duties for every media component. Companies both small and large might use freelancers for a fast turnaround time or a unique presentation (Figure 6.6).

The cost of freelance work varies. Some charge an hourly rate; others charge by the project. Some even use method arrangements. Clients generally prefer the per project arrangement because the cost is fixed up front.

Selection of a freelancer is generally based on cost and specialty as well as a review of the work the freelancer has performed for others in a similar business. By studying a selection of previous work and contacting some of the noncompeting companies that have used the freelancer's services, the retailer can judge whether the freelancer is likely to meet expectations in terms of design outcome and return on the investment.

Advertising Trade Associations

In order for the two collaborative partners involved in the advertising experience to properly interface with each other, major independent organizations oversee the activities. Each trade association offers a wealth of services, expertise, and information regarding the advertising industry and how membership can help lead to better, more productive handling of the rigors and challenges of advertising.

American Association of Advertising Agencies

Founded in 1917, the **American Association of Advertising Agencies** (AAAA) was formed to represent the agency side of the advertising industry in the United States. It is a management-oriented organization that offers its members a broad range of services, expertise, and information to help improve their own companies as well as make their clients' advertising programs more effective. According to their Web site, AAAA's ultimate goal is to help an agency "become a more effective, productive, and profitable marketing communications business."

6.6 Retailers of all sizes use freelance artists to create ad designs. *Comstock/Getty Images.*

Membership in the association is not automatic and can be achieved only through application review. Agencies that have been successful in their applications number less than 10 percent of the more than 13,000 agencies in the United States. The average agency has held membership for more than 20 years, with 111 of the agencies affiliated with the AAAA since its founding in 1917.

Among the numerous services offered to the membership are the following:

- *Research services* that are handled by a staff of information specialists and include virtually every aspect of advertising

- *Management services* that help principals make sound financial, management, and administrative decisions

- *Media services* such as establishing discounts with advertising vendors and assistance with media-related problems

- *Training and development* at regular conferences and special events

By belonging to the organization, members are able to interact with noncompeting agencies and discuss common problems and issues.

Association of National Advertisers

The clients of marketing organizations may be members of the **Association of National Advertisers** (ANA). It is a corporate-based, not an individual-based, association. The association's membership includes 400 companies—with 9,000 brands—that collectively spend over $100 billion in marketing communications and advertising. The ANA's mission is to provide professional leadership that drives marketing excellence and champions and promotes the interests of the marketing community.

All types of businesses are represented in the ANA membership, including a number of high-profile retailers such as Banana Republic, Home Depot (Figure 6.7), Lord & Taylor, Publix Super Markets, Radio Shack, Sears Holding Corp. (Sears and Kmart), TJX Companies (T.J. Maxx and Marshalls), Wal-Mart, and Zappos.com.

Retail Advertising and Marketing Association

A trade association of retail marketing and advertising professionals and their counterparts on the agency, media, and self-provider sides of the business, the **Retail Advertising and Marketing Association** (RAMA) is a division of the National Retail Federation (NRF), the world's largest retail trade organization. RAMA produces the globally famous Retail Advertising Conference, the largest single meeting of retail marketing and advertising executives in the industry. It sponsors the RAC Awards Competition, the industry's most prestigious creative contest for broadcast and print advertising.

The organization provides "visionary leadership that promotes creativity, innovation, and excellence within all marketing disciplines." RAMA is specifically dedicated to strategy that differentiates customers who advocate brands, messages that are creatively meaningful, and results that drive business outcome. RAMA has as its members a significant number of the major retailers in the United States.

Association of Hispanic Advertising Agencies

Unlike the aforementioned trade organizations, the **Association of Hispanic Advertising Agencies** (AHAA) is more specialized in that it represents only those with Hispanic affiliation. It was the first organization of its kind, and since its inception it has attracted numerous agencies that address the needs of agencies trying to reach the Hispanic communities in the United States.

Focus 6.2 discusses the association and its goals and objectives.

Similar minority agencies include the Association of Black-Owned Advertising Agencies (ABAA) and the Association of Asian American Advertising Agencies (Figure 6.8).

6.7 Retailers such as Home Depot are members of the Association of National Advertisers.
newscom.

Association of Hispanic Advertising Agencies

The mission of the AHAA is "to grow, strengthen, and protect the Hispanic marketing and advertising industry by providing leadership in raising awareness of the value of the Hispanic market opportunities and enhancing professionalism in the industry."

The first organization of its kind to concentrate solely on the Hispanic advertising market, the AHAA offers a wide range of benefits for its members. Full membership is reserved for agencies throughout the United States that restrict their services to the Hispanic communities; associate membership is offered to public relations firms, radio and television stations, cable networks, media planning and buying service companies, and event planning companies, all of which have an interest in Hispanic advertising.

The AHAA's goals are:

◆ To raise awareness of the value of advertising to the Hispanic market.

◆ To conduct research that will better target Hispanic audiences.

◆ To promote and encourage high standards and ethics.

◆ To cooperate with educational institutions regarding matters of interest to the Hispanic community.

The association hopes to achieve a better image for advertisers by promulgating standards of practice that include ensuring truthfulness of the messages in ads, substantiating claims made by advertisers, limiting testimonials to those that are truly honest in nature, and avoiding false and misleading price claims.

The organization regularly holds meetings at conventions throughout the country. These are most often creative and account-planning conferences at which attendees obtain the latest information on the industry, meet with others to exchange ideas, and learn about new technology in advertising from the vendors who attend.

Research studies are also an important service offered by AHAA. One significant research undertaking was the Latino Cultural Identity study in 2008, which provided information to members about the cultural differences within the Hispanic communities.

EILEEN
FISHER

Color theory for everyday practice.

6.8 Minority agencies
produce ads representing
specific ethnicities.
Courtesy Eileen Fisher.

Terms of the Trade

advertising agency

agency holding company

agency remuneration

American Association of Advertising Agencies

Association of Hispanic Advertising Agencies

Association of National Advertisers

commission-based compensation

cost-based fees

freelance advertising consultant

full-service ad agencies

hourly fees

in-house ad staffing

in-house operation

in-house shop

monthly retainer

noncompeting companies

performance-based fees

project billing

research methodology

Retail Advertising and Marketing Association

strategic planning

table of organization

turnaround time

Summary of Key Points

◆ Advertising must be approached in a professional manner and requires the services of those who understand the best ways to produce meaningful ads, such as advertising agency specialists, media consultants, and freelancers.

◆ In-house agencies are those that are part of a merchant's organization. Benefits of an in-house agency include cost efficiency for advertising, quick turnaround time from conception to placement of ads, and direct contact with top management of the company.

◆ External advertising resources include ad agencies, the media, and freelancers, all offering a host of services to advertisers. The advertising agencies, which make up the major part of the external resources, are either owned by agency holding companies or are independently owned and operated.

◆ Ad agencies may be full-service operations that offer an abundance of services to their clients or specialty entities that may perform only a limited number of duties.

◆ Agencies are remunerated for their services by a number of different means. Commission-based compensation is the most common. Others include annual fees, performance-based fees, project billing, monthly retainers, hourly rates, and cost-based fees.

◆ The services of an ad agency include strategic planning, creating the ad, media planning, media buying, Web design, public relations, research, and mailing list management.

◆ Independent organizations, such as the American Association of Advertising Agencies, the Association of National Advertisers, the Retail Advertising Marketing Association, and the Association of Hispanic Advertising Agencies, represent both agencies and advertisers.

For Discussion

1. Why do retailers use professionals such as ad agencies or the media to develop their campaigns instead of attempting to do so without experienced help?

2. What are the benefits of establishing an in-house agency or a separate advertising division within the retail organization?

3. Describe the organizations of agency holding companies and the components that make up one of the leaders in the industry, the Omnicom Group.

4. Differentiate between the full-service advertising agency and those that are more specialized in their functions.

5. What is the standard practice for agency remuneration? What other methods of compensation are used by some agencies?

6. Why is it generally more beneficial for retailers to have an agency purchase media space and time rather than doing it on their own?

7. What is the role of the freelancer in advertising?

8. How does an advertising trade association benefit its members?

Exercises and Projects

1. Select one of the agency holding companies from Table 6.1 other than the Omnicon Group. Using either the Internet or direct communication with the agency's public relations office, prepare a research paper highlighting the following:

   ◆ History of the company

   ◆ Member advertising agencies

- Services offered

- Specialized offerings

- Retailers who use the services of the agency

2. Using the list of agencies in Table 6.3, research ten of them to learn about their methods of remuneration. Construct a chart such as the one to the right.

3. Through Internet research, investigate the different multicultural advertising trade associations, other than the AHAA, to study their goals and objectives. Write a two-page, typewritten paper on one of these agencies.

Name of Agency	Remuneration Methods

Web Site Exploration for In-Depth Analysis

Advertising Age
http://www.adage.com

This major advertising periodical, also available in hard copy, provides a wealth of information about the advertising agency business. It updates the information every year with complete agency listings of all classifications.

THE ADVERTISING MEDIA

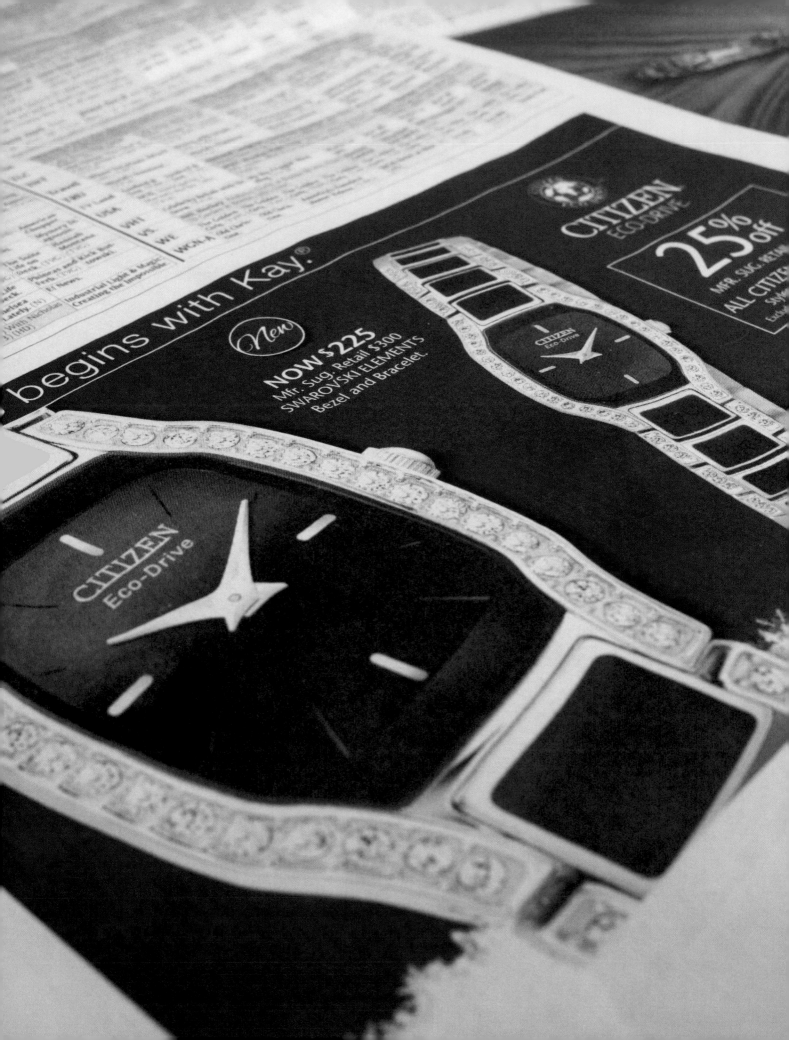

Newspapers

Since its beginnings, the newspaper has been the primary medium in which retailers advertise their offerings to consumers. Although early newspapers were focused mainly on news and were merely the bare bones of what they would eventually become, they did set aside space for merchants who wished to advertise their products and services.

Newspapers grew in both size and importance and eventually became the main source of news for the consumer. It became evident to retailers that they would benefit from running ads in newspapers to capture readers' attention. Even when television gained the attention of the public, and many people began getting their news from this medium, the newspaper still was the primary vehicle for retail advertisements.

It wasn't until early in the twenty-first century that the newspaper industry began to show signs of losing its importance. By 2009, many household names in the newspaper industry had ceased their publishing operations. Even those that remain are still in jeopardy. The Tribune Company, publisher of the *Los Angeles Times* and the *Chicago Tribune,* has filed for bankruptcy, as has the *Star Tribune* of Minneapolis and the *Philadelphia Inquirer.* This, coupled with an economic downturn in 2008, resulted in retailers reducing their budgeted allocations for advertising and eventually caused a decrease in newspaper advertising. According to the Newspaper Association of America, the first quarter of 2009 showed that newspaper sales ads plunged by an unprecedented 28.28 percent.

Despite the doom and gloom, the newspaper remains a medium that benefits retailers, and it still has the potential to recover from the downturn. Of course, given the success of such social networking sites as Facebook and the increase in Internet advertising, it is unlikely that the newspaper will return to the glory days it experienced as the retailers' major advertising medium.

A comprehensive overview of the newspaper as an advertising tool for retailers is addressed in this chapter.

A Historical Perspective

In 1690, Benjamin Harris published what was considered the first American newspaper, *Publick Occurrences Both Foreign and Domestick*, in Boston. It was suppressed by the government after one issue, and not until 1704 did another newspaper appear: the *Boston News-Letter*, which served the colonies. In 1783, the first weekly appeared on the scene and was titled the *Pennsylvania Evening Post*. Little by little, others joined the fray with daily editions that expanded in size and scope and eventually became treasure troves for readers who sought their favorite columns, national and international news coverage, and advertisements from their favorite stores.

By the late 1990s, the newspaper was significantly affected by the advent of the 24-hour news channels as well as the Internet. Consumers' acceptance of these new venues greatly impacted the newspaper industry, resulting in its decline.

Classifications

Some newspapers are aimed at a broad, national audience, whereas others are more clearly targeted to readers in specific locations. Some newspapers offer general topics such as news, entertainment, sports, social events, and so forth. Others are more restrictive in nature and concentrate on a specific area of interest such as finance and business. The former tend to be offered on a daily basis and the latter as weekly publications. Some are even tailored to a specific group, such as the gay community. More and more newspapers are directed at the multicultural community, offering papers in foreign languages.

Dailies

With some exceptions, most **daily newspapers** are published every day (Figure 7.1). There are some, however, that have no Saturday and Sunday editions, as is the case with *USA Today*. For those newspapers that offer the Sunday newspaper, its size is significantly larger than weekday and Saturday editions. With a multitude of special sections and advertising inserts, the Sunday editions are sometimes kept for more than 1 day, making it an excellent outlet for retail ads.

The majority of the **dailies** are directed toward a particular trading area, making the daily an important way for retailers within the area to reach their customers. Some papers, such as the *New York Times*, which is targeted to the New York City region, have such national exposure in addition to that in the local area that retailers can reach consumers anywhere in the country through the subscriptions that are sold to the out-of-towners. Thus, retailers such as Macy's, Saks Fifth Avenue, Barneys, Tiffany & Co., and Bergdorf Goodman, all regular advertisers in the *Times*, do so because they are known nationally and can often generate telephone orders through their ads (Figure 7.2).

Zoned Editions

Many newspapers use **zoned editions** to reach specific markets within their trading area. If the overall area covers several thousand square miles, the interests of one section might not be entirely the same as others in that region. Even though some of the news stories and retailer ads might serve the entire market, some advertisements and social events might be appropriate for a only subset of that area.

Newsday, with the eighth-largest circulation numbers in the United States, is published on Long Island in New York. Its trading area comprises Nassau, Suffolk, and Queens Counties, each somewhat different in terms of demographics. Many of the retailers who advertise in *Newsday* opt for a regional edition because it serves their needs and reduces the costs of the ads.

The *Florida Times-Union*, Jacksonville's only daily, also offers zoned editions of a different type. With the city geographically spread out into many communities, the paper offers a regular "main" section to all of its readers but different inserts a few times a week that cover only a portion of the trading area. Beach residents receive supplements that cover the interests of that community

PELOSI STRUGGLE: TO CORRAL VOTES FOR HEALTH BILL

SWING DEMOCRATS KEY

Fiscal Conservatives and Abortion Opponents Express Concerns

By SHERYL GAY STOLBERG and ROBERT PEAR

WASHINGTON. — The future of President Obama's health care overhaul now rests largely with two blocs of swing Democrats in the House of Representatives — abortion opponents and fiscal conservatives — whose indecision signals the difficulties Speaker Nancy Pelosi faces in securing the votes necessary to pass the bill.

With Republicans unified in their opposition, Democrats are drafting plans to try on their own to pass a bill based on one Mr. Obama unveiled before his bipartisan health forum last week. His measure hews closely to the one passed by the Senate in December, but differs markedly from the one passed by the House.

That leaves Ms. Pelosi in the tough spot of trying to keep wavering members of her caucus on board, while persuading some who voted no to switch their votes to yes — all at a time when Democrats are worried about their prospects for re-election.

Representative Dennis Cardoza, Democrat of California, typifies the speaker's challenge. The husband of a family practice doctor, he is intimately familiar with the failings of the American health care system. His wife "comes home every night," he said, "angry and frustrated at insurance companies denying people coverage they have paid for."

But as a member of the centrist Blue Dog Coalition, Mr. Cardoza is not convinced that Mr. Obama's bill offers the right prescription. It lacks anti-abortion lan-

Devastating Quake Jolts Chile, Setting Off Tsunami Alerts

Worries Rippling Far Across Sea to Hawaii

By ALEXEI BARRIONUEVO and LIZ ROBBINS

RIO DE JANEIRO — A deadly, 8.8-magnitude earthquake struck central Chile early Saturday, collapsing buildings, shattering major bridges and highways across a long swath of the country, and sending tsunami warnings along the entire Pacific basin.

Chile's TVN cable news channel reported 122 deaths less than 12 hours after the quake struck. The death toll was expected to rise, particularly around Concepción, Chile's second-largest metropolitan area, which is roughly 70 miles from the quake's center.

There, cars were overturned, rubble fell into the cracked streets and a 15-story building collapsed, wire services and Chilean news media reported. In the capital of Santiago, about five hours to the north and about 200 miles from the epicenter, frightened residents felt the city shake for nearly 90 seconds.

As more than two dozen significant aftershocks struck the region, President Michelle Bachelet declared a "state of catastrophe." Major airports and seaports were reported out of operation across the central region, Chilean officials said.

The Associated Press quoted Mrs. Bachelet as saying that a huge wave had swept into a populated area in the Robinson Crusoe Island, 410 miles off the Chilean coast, but there were no immediate reports of major damage there. Those reports bore out early fears that a major tsunami was on its way across the Pacific, and the first hemisphere-wide tsunami warning since 1964 was issued all along the basin, according to monitors in Hawaii.

In Hawaii, officials were preparing to evacuate low-lying tourism areas and scheduled a statewide tsunami alert hours

The quake in Chile on Saturday caused severe damage, including in Talca, above. The epicenter was about 70 miles from Concepción, Chile's second-largest city, but Santiago, the capital, also shook for nearly 90 seconds. More photos are at nytimes.com.   SEBASTIAN MARTINEZ/ASSOCIATED PRESS

Generation of Frustrated Strivers Wages Jihad on Pakistan

By SABRINA TAVERNISE and WAQAR GILLANI

LAHORE, Pakistan — Umar Kundi was his parents' pride, an ambitious young man from a small town who made it to medical school in the big city. It seemed like a story of working-class success, living proof in this unequal society that a telephone operator's son could become a doctor.

But things went wrong along the way. On campus Mr. Kundi fell in with a hardline Islamic group. His degree did not get him a job, and he drifted in the urban crush of young people looking for work.

network that carried out some of the boldest attacks against the Pakistani state and its people last year, the police here say. Months of hunting him ended on Feb. 19, when he was killed in a shootout with the police at the age of 29.

Mr. Kundi and members of his circle — educated strivers who come from the lower middle class — are part of a new generation that has made militant networks in Pakistan more sophisticated and deadly. Al Qaeda has harnessed

Umar Kundi

better than our national police academy."

Like Mr. Kundi, many came of age in the 1990s, when jihad was state policy — aimed at challenging Indian control in Kashmir — and jihadi groups recruited openly in universities. Under the influence of Al Qaeda, their energies have been redirected and turned inward, against Pakistan's own government and people.

That shift has fractured long-established militant networks, which were once supported by the state, producing a patchwork of new associations that are fluid and defy easy categorization.

"The situation now is quite confusing," said Tariq Parvez, director of the National

---

as well as ads that feature retailers in their trading area. Similarly, other communities are provided with special sections that are of interest to their communities.

National Newspapers

Some newspapers are produced to reach people across the United States. The *Wall Street Journal* and *USA Today*, first and second in terms of

circulation, respectively, are **national newspapers**. Although their reach is significant, their retail advertising space is insignificant. Retailers opt to place their ads in dailies and other advertising media.

Table 7.1 features the top 25 newspapers, by paid circulation, in the United States, along with their changes from 1990 to 2008.

7.1 Most daily newspapers are targeted to a specific market. *Courtesy of the* New York Times.

SALE

Fall-Winter 2009 Collection

Selected Merchandise

Starting December 4th

CHANEL

NEW YORK · BEVERLY HILLS · SOUTH COAST PLAZA · SAN FRANCISCO
CHICAGO · DALLAS · HOUSTON · LAS VEGAS · HONOLULU · BOSTON
PALM BEACH · BAL HARBOUR · ORLANDO · WASHINGTON, D.C.

800.550.0005 · CHANEL.COM

7.2 Retailers such as Chanel or Gucci are well known past their regular trading areas. *Courtesy of Chanel.*

Weeklies

Weeklies are generally smaller than daily papers. Their readership is restricted to a narrow market, unlike the national publications, which have broader markets. Of the several thousand that are published, most weeklies are marketed to either suburban locales or metropolitan areas within a city. News information is generally local in nature, as are the advertisements that appear in these newspapers. Because the costs of advertising are comparatively low, local merchants use them as a means of attracting shoppers within their trading areas.

Multicultural Newspapers

A large number of newspapers target the minority populations in the United States, and the number in recent years has significantly increased due to the growth of the **multiethnic population**. As we learned in Chapter 4, "Targeting the Multicultural Markets," the African-American, Hispanic, and Asian-American populations, in particular, have caused retailers to rethink their one-size-fits-all advertising policies.

Newspapers that appeal to these ethnicities are expanding rapidly to take advantage of these ever-growing groups of consumers. Their numbers, coupled with positive buying power, have contributed to the importance of multicultural publications. Projected growth of these market segments means that retailers must address these groups' needs with the proper advertising.

Online Editions

Many newspapers provide **online editions** without any cost to the reader. Online news has adversely affected newspaper sales. Young people, in particular, opt to read online editions. Unlike the hard-copy formats, these editions are often void of the advertising that brings much of the revenue to the papers.

International Newspapers

Some newspapers are targeted toward international audiences. The *International Herald Tribune* is one such publication. Although it does bring the news to those who are traveling or who live in other parts of the world, the international newspaper does not help retailers.

Focus 7.1 examines the Gannett Company, Inc., the world's largest newspaper publisher.

Supplements and Inserts

In addition to newspapers, a number of print products are used to offer advertisers a way to

TABLE 7.1

Paid Circulation: Then and Now

1990 RANK	NEWSPAPER	PAID CIRCULATION (1990–2008)	% CHANGE
1	Wall Street Journal	1,857,131 2,011,999	↑ 8.34
2	USA Today	1,427,604 2,293,310	↑ 60.64
3	Los Angeles Times	1,196,323 739,147	↓ 38.22
4	New York Times	1,108,447 1,000,665	↓ 9.72
5	New York Daily News	1,097,693 632,595	↓ 42.37
6	Washington Post	780,582 622,714	↓ 20.22
7	Chicago Tribune	721,067 516,032	↓ 28.43
8	Newsday (Long Island, NY)	714,128 377,517	↓ 47.14
9	Detroit Free Press	636,182 298,243	↓ 53.12
10	San Francisco Chronicle	562,887 339,430	↓ 39.7
11	Chicago Sun-Times	527,238 313,176	↓ 40.6
12	Boston Globe	521,354 323,983	↓ 37.86
13	New York Post	510,219 625,421	↑ 22.58
14	Detroit News	500,980 178,280	↓ 64.4
15	Newark Star-Ledger	476,257 316,280	↓ 33.59
16	Houston Chronicle	442,044 448,271	↑ 1.41
17	Cleveland Plain Dealer	428,012 305,529	↓ 28.62
18	Miami Herald	414,646 210,884	↓ 49.14
19	Minneapolis Star-Tribune	407,441 322,360	↓ 20.88
20	Dallas Morning News	397,555 338,933	↓ 14.75
21	St. Louis Post-Dispatch	382,381 240,794	↓ 37.03
22	Boston Herald	358,925 167,506	↓ 53.33
23	Orange County Register	353,637 236,270	↓ 33.19
24	Rocky Mountain News	351,996 210,282	↓ 40.26
25	Arizona Republic	330,706 361,333	↑ 9.26

Source: Ives, Nat. "Where 1990's Top Papers Are Now." *Advertising Age*, May 9, 2009, p. 4.

Gannett Company

Recognized as the world's premier information company, Gannett has achieved a unique place in global newspaper publishing. Today, it is one of the most diverse news, information, and communications companies in the United States. Beginning in 1906, with a $3,000 investment, loans of $7,000, and notes of $10,000, the company has grown into a multibillion-dollar enterprise. The initiatives of Frank Gannett, its founder, as an innovator in technology in the newspaper industry led the company to unprecedented heights. It is the nation's largest newspaper publisher, with a combined circulation of approximately 7.2 million in the United States and 626,000 in the United Kingdom.

The jewel in the crown of the Gannett Company is *USA Today*. Its humble beginnings were in a cottage in Cocoa Beach, Florida, conceived under the code name Project NN. After 2 years of research to determine what readers wanted, what advertisers needed, and what technology permitted, on September 15, 1982, *USA Today* was born. By the end of 1983, the newspaper was selling 1.3 million copies a day across the United States. It soon achieved a circulation of approximately 2.3 million, making it the largest-selling daily newspaper in the United States.

Gannett employs more than 41,000 full-time and part-time employees worldwide and publishes 84 daily newspapers in the United States and 18 dailies in the United Kingdom. It also publishes more than 1,000 non-

daily publications globally, and *USA Weekend*, a magazine supplement carried by many newspapers. It owns and operates 23 television stations in the United States and a national group of printing facilities and subsidiaries that are involved in survey research, direct marketing, and news media development. Honors that Gannett has received include the following:

♦ Recognition as the best-managed publishing company in the United States, according to a poll of Wall Street analysts that was conducted by the Investment Decisions company in 1986

♦ More than 1,100 professional awards in 2006

♦ Forty-five Pulitzer Prizes

♦ Placement on *Black Enterprise* magazine's list, "25 Best Places for Blacks to Work"

♦ Inclusion in *The Best Companies for Women* (Baila Zeitz and Lorraine Dusky, New York: Simon and Shuster, 1988)

Today, Gannett serves readers through its operations in 38 states and the District of Columbia, Guam, the United Kingdom, Canada, Belgium, Germany, and Hong Kong.

reach readers with their offerings. The major products are supplements and inserts.

Supplements

Most major daily newspapers offer a special section in their Sunday editions known as **supplements**, or magazines (Figure 7.3). They contain a variety of fiction and general-interest nonfiction articles. These publications are either locally written and produced or are edited nationally. The supplement is provided for the newspapers by independent organizations that are responsible for their content. In addition to the informational columns, advertisements make up the remainder of the issue.

Supplements, according to many newspapers, provide retailers with many benefits, including boosting circulation by about 7 percent. Some retailers even report that the use of a supplement has widened their customer bases.

The two most important supplements are *Family Weekly* and *Parade*. They are sold to newspapers throughout the country for insertion in Sunday editions. To make these supplements identifiable as each newspaper's "own," the supplements are imprinted with the dailies' mastheads.

One advantage to advertisers is that the life of the ad is often longer than that of regular newspaper

7.3 Supplements are inserted in Sunday newspaper editions. USA Weekend.

ads because many consumers keep the supplements for later reading.

Inserts

A host of different **preprinted inserts** or **freestanding inserts** are used by retailers as alternatives to their regular newspaper advertisements. Circulars that range from one-page affairs to multipage offerings have become increasingly popular with merchants such as Home Depot and Best Buy. By using specific trading areas or zones for these ads, retailers can reach the market segments that best serve their needs and save advertising dollars. With **four-color reproduction** and better stock quality, the **inserts** are more exciting than the standard black and white used in the body of the paper.

An important advantage to the advertiser that uses **newspaper inserts** (Figure 7.4) is the savings it accrues in comparison to direct mail costs. According to Jim Turner of *ABA Bank Marketing* magazine (Sept 2009 issue), a direct mailing piece may cost about $425 per thousand for a basic flier that goes into the mail. For approximately $50 per thousand, depending on circulation, a newspaper will insert the piece. Thus, a distribution to 20,000 households would cost only $1,000, excluding printing costs. For printing and distributing 20,000 inserts in the newspaper, the total cost would be $3,000. To send the identical flier through the mail would cost about $10,000.

Of course, the insert will be one of many, making it less valuable in terms of competition. The same piece that is mailed directly to home will have the reader's undivided attention.

Inserts are beneficial to advertisers, and their designs are especially important to maximize positive results. According to Karen Taylor, senior account executive, print media, Plus Media (Plusmedia.net), "Creative execution is critical to the success of an FSI [freestanding insert]. Ads should feature visually simplistic designs and copy that clearly communicates the value of the offer. Headlines must immediately convey benefits to the consumer[s] and entice them to read on for additional details, leading them to take action. Offering multiple reply devices (mail, phone, or Internet) is equally as important and

7.4 (opposite) Insert usage is a comparatively inexpensive way to distribute retailer ads. *Courtesy of Bealls.*

will help to increase response, especially for direct response-focused advertisements."

If the insert is carefully designed and strategically placed, it can be a profitable component of a full-scale advertising campaign.

It should be noted that although freestanding inserts are primarily used in major newspapers, they are becoming increasingly important in both suburban and community newspapers because they guarantee a heavy penetration in a specific target area.

Media Insight 7.2 (page 168) discusses some of the positive statistics regarding inserts.

Types of Newspaper Advertisements

Retailers make use of the two classifications of newspaper advertising: **classified ads** and **display ads**. Less important is the classified format, but it nevertheless serves some purposes. Its primary function is to attract the attention of individuals who are seeking employment. Although the Internet has taken much of the employment search from the newspapers through such Web sites as www.monster.com, the classified section is still an option for merchants to use. It is especially successful when midmanagement and senior positions are advertised in special sections, such as that offered by the *New York Times* in its Sunday editions.

Sometimes manufacturers look to dispose of distress merchandise by using small classified ads. Retailers who deal in closeouts, off-price merchandise, and bargain goods often scan the papers for these offerings. This method of advertising, too, has become less important since the advent of the Internet, which regularly features such notices.

Most newspaper advertising is called *display advertising*. These are the ads that try to sell the retailer's products or to promote services and foster a positive image. They are further categorized as product, promotional, institutional, and combination advertisements.

Fall in Newspaper Sales Accelerates to Pass 7 Percent

Tim Arango
April 27, 2009

The rate of decline in print circulation at the nation's newspapers has accelerated since last fall, as industry figures released [in April 2009] show a more than 7 percent drop compared with the previous year, whereas another analysis showed that newspaper Web site audiences had increased 10.5 percent in the first quarter. Of the top 25 newspapers in the United States, all posted declines in circulation except for the *Wall Street Journal*, which eked out a 0.6 percent gain, according to figures released by the Audit Bureau of Circulations. For the others, the declines ranged from 20.6 percent for the *New York Post* to a slight 0.4 percent drop for the *Chicago Sun-Times*.

Both the *Post* and the *Journal* are owned by the News Corporation, the media conglomerate controlled by Rupert Murdoch.

The new circulation numbers are "not very good, and probably a little worse than expected," said Rick Edmonds, media business analyst at the Poynter Institute, a nonprofit organization that owns the *St. Petersburg Times* in Florida. Mr. Edmonds said he had expected an overall drop of roughly 5.5 percent.

The figures, which are based on reports filed by the individual papers, illustrated the continued migration of readers to the Internet and, in some cases, the effort by papers to shed unprofitable circulation.

"One shouldn't be in denial that this represents people quitting newspapers to get news from the Web," Mr. Edmonds said. "But there are many other factors."

Among those factors, he said, are newspapers making reductions in what is known in the industry as "junk circulation"—such as free newspapers distributed at trade shows or in schools. At the same time, he said, some papers have increased prices in an effort to wring more revenue from their core readers while doing away with cheap introductory offers to attract new readers.

"To that extent, it's voluntary," Mr. Edmonds said.

That was one explanation offered by Alan Fisco, the vice president of circulation and marketing for the *Seattle Times*, in a memorandum to his staff about a decline of roughly 8 percent in circulation.

"Most of these losses are due to budget decisions we made throughout 2008 and earlier this year in response to the economic recession," he wrote. "We made these decisions as strategically as possible, with the goal of minimizing the impact to our readership and audience while preserving our core home delivery and single copy strength."

At 395 daily newspapers, weekday circulation declined 7.1 percent for the 6 months that ended March 31 [2009], compared with the previous year. Sunday circulation for 557 daily newspapers was down 5.37 percent.

The *New York Times* reported a smaller decline than the industry average, as weekday circulation fell 3.6 percent to 1,039,031, compared with the previous year. The *Times*, which last week reported a quarterly loss of $74 million, said that circulation revenue was up slightly, reflecting increased prices.

Although newspaper circulation has long been in decline, the latest figures show the drop is accelerating. In the two previous 6-month periods, weekday circulation fell 4.6 percent and 3.6 percent, respectively.

USA Today, which has long bucked industry circulation trends, reported a 7.5 percent drop, partly because some hotels cut back on free newspapers delivered to rooms. *USA Today* is still the nation's largest newspaper by circulation at slightly more than two million. The *Wall Street Journal* and the *New York Times* are the next largest papers.

Both of New York City's major tabloids, which in recent years have fought circulation battles, reported steep drops in weekday circulation. Circulation fell more than 20 percent at the *New York Post* and 14.3 percent at the *Daily News*.

A press release from the *Post* attributed the decline to an increase in the price of the tabloid to 50 cents from 25 cents.

Robert Leonard, a spokesman for the *Daily News*, said 90 percent of its drop in circulation resulted from ending bulk distribution in places like schools.

Meanwhile, the audience for newspaper Web sites continues to grow. In the first quarter of 2009, newspaper Web sites attracted more than 73 million unique visitors each month, on average, according to an analysis by Nielsen Online for the Newspaper Association of America. That is a 10.5 percent increase from the first quarter of 2008.

Source: The New York Times, June 2, 2007.

Product Advertisements

By advertising specific products, the merchant hopes to get immediate attention from the consumer with telephone or mail orders and to entice shoppers to visit the store or Web site to purchase additional merchandise. Product advertisements typically feature the company's better-selling items in the hope that the ads will help them sell even better. Fashion retailers are the major users of newspaper product advertising and generally feature national manufacturer's products or designer merchandise in their ads. Many retailers receive an advertising allowance (money) from the manufacturer or designer whose merchandise the retailer features in its ads. These allowances are **cooperative advertising agreements** in which the retailer and producer share the cost of the ad, usually 50 percent each (Figure 7.5). Some manufacturers are willing to pay a greater percentage of the cost for a marquee merchant to promote their merchandise. Manufacturers are often motivated by this arrangement because it guarantees them a space in a newspaper that promotes their brands and may result in reorders from the retailer.

Promotional Advertisements

Special situations often necessitate that a traditional retailer use promotional advertising to dispose of slow-selling merchandise. It may be the end of a season for fashion items, economic conditions that affect sales, the desire to reduce prices for a limited time, or a host of other reasons.

Some merchants are *value retailers* who offer low prices to draw customers. These merchants use promotional advertising to let consumers know that bargains are available at their stores and Web sites.

7.5 The expense of a cooperative ad is shared by the retailer and the designer or manufacturer. *Courtesy of Macy's.*

estée lauder color spectacular

Only $55, a $340 value

With any Estée Lauder fragrance purchase.
Includes 4 Pure Color Lipsticks in Candy, Rose Tea, Fig and Tiger Eye, a Makeup Brush Set, Gentle Eye Makeup Remover, a Deluxe Eyeshadow Compact, Deluxe Face Compact, 3 Artist's Eye Pencils in Slate Writer, SoftSmudge Brown and SoftSmudge Black, Lash Primer Plus, Projectionist Mascara in Black, a Stand Up Mirror, a Look Book and a traincase with a companion makeup case.

For your purchase, choose from 28 unforgettable Estée Lauder fragrances, including: Estée Lauder Sensuous: 29.50-$75.
Estée Lauder pleasures: 29.50-$72. Beautiful: 29.50-$80.

the magic of ★ macy's
macys.com

Same day delivery in all 5 boroughs! Order by 6pm today. Get it today. We'll deliver to Manhattan, Bronx, Staten Island, Queens and Brooklyn. Service available at Herald Square for in-store purchases in all departments except jewelry and furniture. $18-$50 fee applies; for single area rugs, the fee is $60-$85.

Advertised items may not be at your local Macy's. For store locations and hours, log on to macys.com

Others, such as supermarkets, use promotional ads on a regular basis to alert shoppers that bargains are available for a specific time period.

Promotional advertisements are replete with words such as *closeout* and *clearance* so that value-oriented shoppers will visit the companies' on-site and off-site stores (Figure 7.6).

Institutional Advertisements

Many upscale retailers, especially fashion merchants, reserve a portion of their advertising budgets for institutional advertising. These ads are generally void of specific merchandise, focusing instead on topics that will foster a positive image for their organizations. Institutional ads address social issues, services, prestigious collections that are exclusive to the company, and current events.

When the Yankees won the World Series in 2009, for example, the victory prompted many newspapers in the New York City area to acknowledge it (Figure 7.7).

7.6 *(opposite)* Promotional ads are used to sell merchandise more quickly. *Courtesy of Belk's.*

7.7 Recognizing unusual achievements are common in institutional advertising. *Courtesy of Bloomingdale's.*

Institutional advertising does not result in immediate sales, as might be the case with product or promotional advertising. It is a commitment that hopes to produce long-term, positive relationships with customers or motivate newcomers to become part of the retailer's clientele.

Combination Advertisements

On some occasions, the retailer might choose to combine two types of ads. These are known as **combination advertisements** and might, for example, use a single ad to promote the availability of a specific designer's exclusive collection and a single item from the line (Figure 7.8). The institutional part of the message is the prestige the designer conveys to the public, and the single item is the product component.

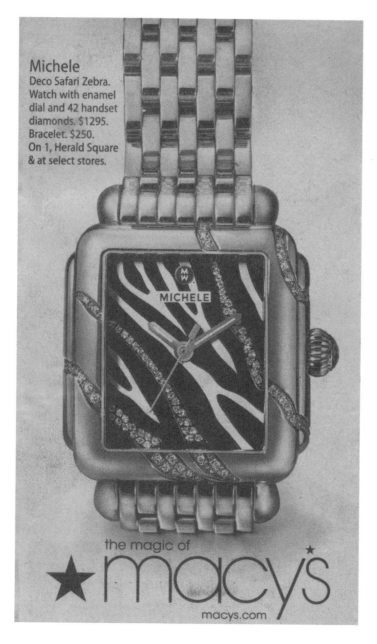

7.8 Ads of this nature promote a product and give prestige to the retailer. *Courtesy of Macy's.*

Michele
Deco Safari Zebra. Watch with enamel dial and 42 handset diamonds. $1295. Bracelet. $250. On 1, Herald Square & at select stores.

the magic of
★macy's
macys.com

Advantages and Disadvantages of Newspapers

Retailers use newspapers to advertise their merchandise and promote their images for a number of reasons, including comparative low cost, diversity of appeal, little time needed to place ads, and so forth. The following is a more extensive list of the reasons newspapers remain an important medium for the world of retailing.

1. The newspaper offers something for every member of the family. It keeps people abreast of local and global news and informs them about sports, entertainment, editorial opinions, and more. Perusal of the newspaper leads the reader to the many ads that fill the pages, making it an excellent place for the merchant to communicate with regular customers and motivate new ones to buy.

2. Although the cost of advertising might seem significant, its potential to reach vast numbers of people makes the cost per consumer reached relatively inexpensive, especially when compared to magazine and television advertising.

3. The **lead time** needed for ad placements is relatively short compared with magazines and television, which require lead times of 2 or 3 months. Retailers can adjust their advertising schedules and modify their ads on very short notice when they use newspaper advertising.

4. The newspaper's subscriber base and the people who purchase the paper at the newsstands, **targeted customers**, are reached with ease.

5. The local paper is especially useful for reaching a specific area. For the small merchant, appealing to distant markets is often unnecessary because the consumers are often too far from the points of purchase. By concentrating on the smaller trading areas, retailers are likely to save money on their advertisements.

6. In a newspaper, the life of the advertising message is longer than it is on television or radio. Newspapers may be examined closely and retained until the next edition is available.

7. Unusual circumstances may warrant last-minute placement of ads. In the case of an impending snowstorm, for example, a retailer who sells snow boots may want to run an ad that would have immediate positive effects.

8. When continuous exposure is necessary to impact the consumer, the newspaper is a very good tool to use. Published on a daily basis, it affords the retailer the opportunity to hammer home the company's message. Magazines, published less frequently, do not offer this advantage.

9. The availability of the preprinted insert used in abundance in many Sunday editions enables the retailer to present color advertisements that are usually more appealing than the standard black-and-white ads found in the body of the paper.

As advantageous as the newspaper is for retailers, there are some negatives associated with its use.

1. If the newspaper's reach is too far from the advertiser's location, then an ad in that paper could have little impact on many of the readers. If, however, the retailer offers telephone or Web site ordering, then placement of the ad is justified.

2. Although the life of a message is greater in a newspaper than on radio and television, it is not as long as the life of direct mail ads, Internet ads, and social networking site ads.

3. Some newspapers are so full of ads that the competition may be severe. It is especially chancy if the same product is advertised by different retailers at different prices.

4. Selecting the right readership is becoming increasingly difficult because of the demise of many newspapers. As newspapers experience declines in sales and circulation, and in many cases are forced to fold, some areas are left without any local newspaper at all, and retailers must find alternative ways to reach consumers. Media Insight 7.1 (page 162) examines the serious challenges newspapers face in today's wired world.

5. The reproduction quality of newsprint does not allow for high-quality imaging. Color is also a problem because it is rarely used, and when it is, it does not reproduce with great clarity. In the case of high-fashion merchandise, where color and clean reproduction are necessary to accurately show the products, the magazine is a better option.

Advertising Rate Structures

The cost of advertising space varies among newspapers. The purchase of space in a local paper is usually a straightforward process because the rates are generally standard and there are usually only one or two local newspapers in a given area. When the retailer chooses to use national newspapers, the challenge is more difficult. Retailers can assess the different rates using the **Standard Rate and Data Service (SRDS)**. This organization is a leading provider of media rates and data for the advertising industry. In addition to listing advertising rates for newspapers across the country, it provides information on editorial or programming content, circulation, and other information about various advertising media. Important to the newspaper advertiser, the SRDS provides instruction for those unfamiliar with rate specifications and placement. Because there are a host of different price structures available to the advertiser, including discounts, ad placement differentials, color costs, zone prices, and combination rates,

Vertis Survey: Newspaper Inserts Grab More Attention Than TV

Karlene Lukovitz
February 25, 2008

Newspaper inserts and circulars are more attention-grabbing than TV advertising, according to the latest Customer Focus survey from Vertis Communications. Vertis, which supplies print advertising and direct marketing vehicles for retailers and consumer services companies, has been conducting the annual telephone survey since 1998.

In this year's survey, conducted on a representative sample of 3,000 adult U.S. consumers, 47 percent said that inserts/circulars best capture their attention, 43 percent cited television ads, and 38 percent cited newspaper display ads.

That represented a 9 percent increase for inserts, a 10 percent decrease for TV ads, and a 7 percent decrease for newspaper ads since the 2003 survey.

Other findings:

• Twenty-seven percent said that inserts/circulars are the ad vehicles most likely to directly impact buying decisions, versus 19 percent for TV ads, 12 percent for newspaper display ads, 9 percent for the Internet, 6 percent for catalogues, 5 percent for direct mail, 4 percent for magazines, 2 percent for radio, and just 1 percent for e-mail promotions.

• Ninety-three percent of insert readers use them for purposes in addition to price comparisons. Over half (55 percent) say they use them to help determine the products they buy; 51 percent to help compile shopping lists; 50 percent to browse for new product styles; and 45 percent to look for new projects/meal ideas/recipes. About a third (37 percent) say they take circulars to the store to help them shop, and the same percentage claim that they use the inserts to make same-day shopping lists.

• Consumers age 50 and older are most likely to use inserts: 63 percent do so (up 8 percent since 2004).

• Fifty-four percent of those between the ages of 18 and 34 report using inserts to help select which items end up in their shopping cart, up from 47 percent in 2004.

• Fifty-five percent of insert readers who earn between $50,000 and $75,000 per year, and 51 percent of those earning more than $75,000, clip coupons.

• Fifty-nine percent of suburbanites clip coupons, versus 51 percent of rural adult residents and 55 percent of adults overall.

• The number of insert readers using the vehicles to help decide which groceries to buy has risen from 52 percent to 59 percent over the past 4 years.

• About half of insert readers say the promotions influence clothing and home electronics purchasing decisions, whereas 43 percent and 36 percent, respectively, say they influence home improvement products and major appliances decisions.

Source: Karlene Lukovitz. "Vertis Survey: Newspaper Inserts Grab More Attention Than TV." Marketing Daily, Feb. 25, 2008.

an understanding of the rates will help maximize the dollars spent on advertising.

A rate card is a document provided by the newspaper that itemizes the various rates available to the advertiser. The following sections explain the many aspects of rate structuring.

Standard Rates

Most newspapers measure ad space using the **standard advertising unit (SAU)**, which is one column (2 1/16 inches) wide by 1 inch deep, called a **column inch**. The cost is figured on a **per column inch** basis. Note that rates vary according to the type of ad and the number of times it is run.

Rate Cards

Newspapers and other publications provide a **rate card** that lists their advertising rates. Many rate cards include other important details concerning ad placement, such as the closing deadlines for placement, demographic compositions of their targeted areas, special policies of the publication, extra fees for special placement, available discounts, and so forth. Some have different rate cards for different types of ads (e.g., different rates for display ads and classifieds). Advertisers must fully understand the rates in order to determine the right price and any terms and conditions that apply.

A sample rate card is shown in Table 7.2.

TABLE 7.2 — Sample Rate Card

ADVERTISING RATES

	Per Column Inch
National Rate	$7.50
Local Open Rate	$7.00

CONTRACT RATES

	Per Column Inch
4 Consecutive Weeks	$6.50
13 Consecutive Weeks	$6.00
Every Other Week—13 weeks or more	$5.50
52 Consecutive Weeks	$5.00
52 Consecutive Weeks—1/4 page or larger	Call for price
Color Charge	$75.00

CLASSIFIED RATES

Display	$7.00 per column inch
Words—25 or less	1st week, $6.00. Subsequent weeks, $4.00
Additional words	Each 25¢

TABLE 7.3 — Mechanical Measurements

DISPLAY ADVERTISING

Printing Method: Goss offset press using photo composition engraved aluminum plates.
Standard PCW ROP sizes: (Six columns) size of printed area 11.625" (wide) × 21.5" (deep).

COLUMNS	INCHES WIDE	PICAS WIDE
1	1.833	11.0
2	3.792	22.9
3	5.75	34.6
4	7.708	46.3
5	9.667	58.0
6	11.625	69.9

Tabloid Advertising
Standard Tabloid Sizes: (Five columns) size of printed area 10.025" (wide) × 11.5" (deep).

COLUMNS	INCHES WIDE	PICAS WIDE
1	1.917	11.6
2	4.000	24.0
3	6.083	36.6

Note: A pica is a unit of measure: 1 pica = 1/6 inch; 6 picas = 1 inch.

Source: Adapted from Waters, Shari. "Understanding Advertising Rate Cards." About.com Retailing. http://retail.about.com/od/marketingsalespromotion/ss/ad_rate_card_6.htm?p=1 (accessed June 16, 2009).

New advertisers often receive special incentives to entice them to advertise on a regular basis. Frequency discounts, or *contract rates*, are also offered to promote repeat business. For example, if a paper's standard rate for a onetime ad is $7.50 per column inch, it might offer a contract rate of $6.50 for a 4-week run, $5.50 for a 13-week (or more) run, and $5.00 for a 52-week run.

In determining the actual cost of the ad, it is necessary to understand the measurements that are used in the industry, particularly the **pica**. Table 7.3 is a mechanical measurement chart typically used in advertising.

In addition to offering rates based on column inches, many newspapers offer precalculated rates based on advertisement size. Ad sizes generally range from a sixteenth of a page to a full page. Figure 7.9 lists the typical sizes offered.

Position Rates

The least expensive newspaper advertising rate is **run of paper (ROP)**. It guarantees that the ad will run in the designated issue but does not specify where in the paper the ad will be placed. Although ROP is less costly than having placement guaranteed in a specific location, it often does not provide the same results as ads that are purposefully positioned.

In every newspaper, some positions have greater appeal to the readership than others. For example, the *Style* section of the *New York Times* is read regularly by fashion enthusiasts, so fashion retailers want their ads in the *Style* section. Other top choices include placement near a popular column or in the first few pages of a newspaper, which generally are read by more people than are the middle pages. Those who desire such advertising locations are charged **preferred position** rates,

7.9 Typical ad sizes.
Illustration by
Vanessa Han.

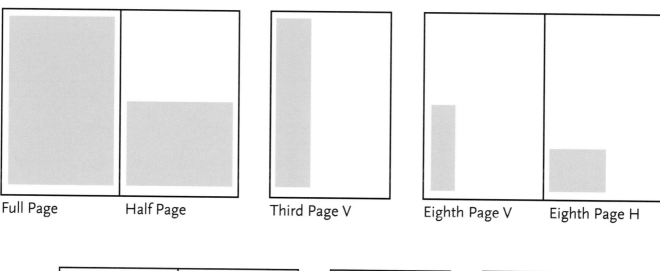

Full Page   Half Page   Third Page V   Eighth Page V   Eighth Page H

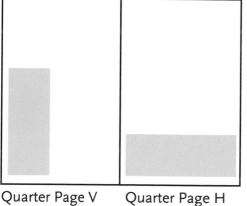      

Quarter Page V   Quarter Page H   Sixth Page V   Sixteenth Page

which are higher than ROP charges. Those who further specify placement at the top of a desirable column, for example, or directly alongside news matter, are charged a **full-position rate**.

Sometimes retailers are even willing to pay more for special space on a regular basis so that their clientele will know exactly where to find the store's advertisements. This is known as **regular preferred position** and is exemplified by the Tiffany ads in the Sunday *New York Times*, which are always featured on page two (Figure 7.10).

Combination Rates

Combination rates can significantly reduce advertising costs. For example, advertisers receive a discount if they run their ad in both the morning and afternoon editions of a paper. They can also receive discounts by contracting for space in several national newspapers.

Discount Rates

Most newspapers offer **discount rates** based on number of column inches and frequency of run. If the space and/or frequency criteria are met in a specified period, such as a year, quarter, or week, a discount may be offered. Samples of some discount options are shown in Table 7.4.

Selecting the Best Newspaper for Advertising

The retailer often must choose from a number of newspapers in which to advertise. Certain factors must be considered in making that selection.

Circulation

An essential factor to consider in deciding where to place an advertisement is the paid **circulation** of the newspaper. The circulation gives the advertiser a picture of the number of regular readers who will see the ad. These are reliable readers who do not have to make the trek to a newspaper stand for a copy.

How accurate are the circulation figures reported by newspapers? The Audit Bureau of Circulations, featured in Focus 7.2, is a watchdog organization that independently verifies circulation.

Demographics

Another element in the decision-making process regarding advertisement placement is the demographics of the trading area under consideration. Although circulation numbers are vital, the raw figures do not suggest the makeup of the readership. If retailers such as Marshalls want to reach an appropriate audience for their products, they will advertise in papers such as the *Daily News*

7.10 Some retailers maintain the same space each week as a "preferred position." *Courtesy of Tiffany & Co.*

TABLE 7.4 — Discount Rates by Advertising Agreement

LOCAL DISPLAY FREQUENCY RATES

Four-inch minimum per week to qualify for frequency contract rates. Copy changes are allowed. Cancelled or unfulfilled contract will be rebilled to open rate.

Frequency Rates

13 Weeks	$13.30	39 Weeks	$11.80
26 Weeks	$12.35	52 Weeks	$9.25

4" minimum per week. Consecutive or every other week.

Pick-up Rates. Multiple Insertions.

Weekly discount plans. All ads must run within 6 publishing days of the first ad. No copy changes on discounted ads. The first ad is full price, and the repeat discounts are as follows.

2nd ad 15 percent	4th ad 35 percent
3rd ad 25 percent	5th–6th ad 50 percent

COLOR RATES

One color & black $115	Two colors & black $190

---

in New York City for which the demographics fit with their merchandise and merchandising direction. Similarly, merchants such as Cartier will use the *New York Times* to advertise their upscale products because the *Times* readership has the appropriate incomes necessary to allow purchasing (Figure 7.11).

A careful assessment of the ages, incomes, types of employment, levels of education, and so forth will make the selection of the newspaper in which to advertise a more meaningful one.

Trading Area

The geographic area that a newspaper reaches is of paramount concern for the retail advertiser. It must reach those who will be able to visit the store effortlessly, especially if on-site purchasing is the only way the merchandise can be bought. Of course, if the merchant offers Internet and catalogue options, the convenience in travel to the store is less important. Small- and medium-

sized merchants rely most heavily on foot traffic as their primary source of purchasing and must make certain that the newspaper ads will reach these shoppers. Even if the circulation figures of one newspaper are significantly lower than that of others that are available, the choice of the latter will not be beneficial if the stores are out of reach.

CPM Analysis

It is essential to compare two or more newspapers in terms of the **cost per thousand impressions (CPM)**. By using this formula, advertisers can compare the real value of the ads. Using the following formula, the results will tell which is a better choice for the retailer.

PROBLEM

If one newspaper has a rate of $5,000 for a full page with a circulation of 250,000, and another has a rate of $4,200 for a full page with a circulation of 195,000, which one will have the more beneficial CPM rate?

The Audit Bureau of Circulations

The Audit Bureau of Circulations (ABC), founded in 1914, came into existence primarily to govern and police the advertising industry that was negligent in reporting true circulation figures. Until that time, the industry was notorious for publishing false and misleading circulation figures, and advertisers had no way to be sure that the reported figures were correct. The purchase of advertising space was often based on unreliable and unrealistic circulation information. In its first year of operation, the ABC, with a group of advertisers, ad agencies, and some responsible publishers, established a watchdog organization that independently verified circulation. Funded by dues and service fees paid for by its constituents, it has become the most reliable source for accurate circulation information and other research tools necessary to make sound advertising decisions.

The ABC approached verification of circulation figures through the voluntary audits of the advertising media, then made its findings available to advertisers and ad agencies. The audits quickly separated the legitimate from the false claims.

The ABC is an independent operation that provides third-party circulation audits of print circulation, readership, and Web site activity. The data culled from its research is disseminated into reports and made available in various formats. With more than 4,000 members in North America, it is a forum in which all components of the world of advertising comingle to provide the most verifiable information regarding circulation, subscriber demographics, and online activity data. Advertisers and agencies of all sizes use the ABC's reports as the basis of their media buying decisions.

In addition to circulation data, the ABC offers a wide range of other reports that help with advanced analysis and trending tools of the industry:

◆ *eStatements:* Through this tool, users can access, view, and print electronic versions of current and historical ABC member reports' such as publisher's statements and audit reports.

◆ *ePeriodical Analysis Tools:* This in-depth offering is updated daily and provides a wealth of verified circulation data for multiple periodicals.

◆ *eNewspapers Analysis Tools:* Data for all ABC-audited newspapers, such as dailies, weeklies, and nonpaid newspapers, may be compared using this tool.

◆ *eFas-FAX:* The user can quickly access and analyze important data for more than 1,100 periodicals and 1,400 newspapers, gleaning information that is essential to decision making.

This is just a glimpse of the ABC. For an overall view of how it completely serves the advertising industry, a visit to its Web site (http://www.accessabc.com) is most enlightening.

Creation of the Advertisement

Most major retailers either have their own in-house staff or use outside agencies to create their ads, but most small merchants have neither. Small companies can turn to the newspaper and other media for ad development without cost. Newspapers and other media provide assistance with **copywriting**, art selection, layout, and anything else that is important in the design of an ad. The advertiser pays only for the space the advertisement occupies.

Demographic Analysis

Occupation, age, educational levels, and so forth play an important part in the retailer's decision regarding use of specific media. By offering these vital statistics, the newspaper helps the merchant judge if the paper is best suited for his or her advertising needs. With so many papers publishing regional or zoned editions, the advertiser can determine if all or just some of the editions serve the company's needs. This service eliminates the necessity of using a marketing research firm to learn about demographic characteristics.

Planning and Budgeting

Many small retailers lack the necessary experience in determining an advertising budget, and they lack the expertise to properly plan their promotional campaigns. Maximizing the benefits derived from advertising will help spread their promotional dollars further. Too often, inexperienced retailers spend on ads that are larger than necessary to attract attention and too infrequently to prove meaningful. Some newspapers guide smaller retailers without the necessary planning and budgeting expertise in this area of decision-making.

SOLUTION

Newspaper 1

$$\frac{5,000 \times 1,000}{250,000} = \$20 \text{ CPM}$$

Newspaper 2

$$\frac{4,200 \times 1,000}{195,000} = \$21.53 \text{ CPM}$$

Newspaper 1 is the better choice even though the actual cost per page is greater.

Newspaper Services Provided to Advertisers

In addition to offering advertisers a place in which to market their goods, the newspaper provides a host of services that benefit them.

Summary of Key Points

- Newspapers come in different classifications: dailies, zoned editions, national publications, weeklies, multicultural editions, online formats, and international editions.

- Many newspapers are part of large organizations that publish a variety of dailies, national editions, and so forth. The largest is the Gannett Company, a diverse news, information, and communication organization.

- Supplements or magazines are often distributed with the newspaper. They are either locally or nationally written and produced and provide an effective medium for advertising.

- Newspaper inserts are important to retailers because they offer a departure from the typical black-and-white format found in the body of most papers.

- Newspaper advertisements come in a variety of types, such as product, promotional, institutional, and combination formats. Each enables the retailer to deliver a different type of advertising message.

- Newspaper advertising is both advantageous and disadvantageous to its advertisers. Each category must be carefully considered before ads are run.

- All media, including newspapers, offer a wide variety of rate structures. The actual costs for newspaper space are based on position of the ad, discounts, and other incentives.

- Selection of the best newspaper by a retailer or any other advertiser is based on circulation, demographics, trading area coverage, and CPM analysis.

For Discussion

1. What are zoned editions of newspapers, and why do some dailies publish them?

2. For what reasons are multicultural newspapers making such an impact on the publishing scene?

3. Describe the difference between regular newspaper publications and the supplements that many feature.

4. What place do newspaper inserts play in the retailer's quest for attention from the consumer?

5. Discuss the differences between product and promotional advertisements.

6. If institutional advertising success is difficult to measure, why do some retailers use this type of advertisement?

7. List and discuss some of the advantages of newspaper advertising for the retail community.

8. Why do newspapers publish rate cards, and what are some of their components?

9. In what way does the run of paper (ROP) rate differ from the preferred position rate?

10. What are some of the services that newspapers offer their advertisers without additional cost?

Exercises and Projects

1. Examine the contents of a daily newspaper to find ads that exemplify product, promotional, and institutional advertisements. Using two of each classification, remove them from the paper, affix them to a foam board, and describe the characteristics of each.

2. Examine a supplement or magazine from a major newspaper. Write a two-page paper describing the content of the supplement and the types of retail advertisements featured within its pages.

3. Contact a newspaper for the purpose of obtaining its advertising rate card. Prepare an oral report outlining the various details of the card and assessing its ease of use or its difficulty for the novice advertiser.

Web Site Exploration for In-Depth Analysis

Audit Bureau of Circulations
http://www.accessabc.com
   This excellent site features all of the roles played by the Audit Bureau of Circulations.

Rate Cards
http://www.ratecards.net
   This online service offers an abundance of information on rate cards.

Advertising Age
http://www.adage.com
   The Web site for *Advertising Age* features a wealth of current articles on the media, including newspapers.

Terms of the Trade

circulation

classified ads

column inch

combination advertisements

combination rates

cooperative advertising agreements

copywriting

cost per thousand impressions (CPM)

dailies

daily newspapers

discount rates

display ads

four-color reproduction

freestanding inserts

full-position rate

inserts

lead time

multiethnic population

national newspapers

newspaper inserts

online editions

per column inch

pica

preferred position

preprinted inserts

rate card

regular preferred position

run-of-paper (ROP)

standard advertising unit (SAU)

Standard Rate and Data Service (SRDS)

supplements

targeted customers

weeklies

zoned editions

Magazines

Magazines had a meager beginning in London in 1731, where the first general-interest magazine was published as *The Gentleman's Magazine*, followed by *The Scots Magazine*, which is still in print today. The current variety of magazines available to consumers seems to be limitless, covering every topic from art to travel, automobiles to fashion, fitness to home decor. Magazines aim their editorial and other content to targeted audiences: hobbyists, professionals, homemakers, naturalists, collectors, sellers, children, retirees—and everyone in between.

Although the magazine is an important media outlet for advertisers, with approximately 160,000 magazines being published annually around the world in about 30 languages, it is not as important to retailers as the newspaper. Other businesses, however, such as manufacturers and fashion design companies, make considerable use of magazines to bring attention to their products.

The economic downturn of 2009 and 2010 has significantly affected magazine publishing and advertising; however, the overall numbers reported by the Audit Bureau of Circulations (ABC) indicate that the medium is still a leader in advertising directed toward the consumer. With the current wealth of entries that grace the newsstands, bookstore shelves, and homes via direct delivery, it is safe to assume that, with some expected changes, magazines will remain a viable medium that attracts consumers all over the world.

Classifications

Several magazine categories are targeted to consumers and business enterprises. Each is aimed at a different segment of the consumer and business communities and disseminates a host of information and advertisements that are expected to generate interest and sales.

Consumer Magazines

The wealth of magazines available to consumers around the world is greater today than at any time in history. Even with the economic downturn, the number of publications in print is significant. Table 8.1 lists the top 25 ABC magazines according to their 2007 and 2008 verified circulation figures.

Although the figures in Table 8.1 show that circulation has remained nearly steady for 2008 compared to 2007, the present situation, as described in Media Insight 8.1, offers a different picture.

TABLE 8.1

The 25 Top Magazines by Paid Circulation

2008 RANK	2007 RANK	PUBLICATION NAME	2008 TOTAL PAID & VERIFIED	2007 TOTAL PAID & VERIFIED	% CHANGE
1	2	AARP Bulletin	24,374,121	23,567,607	3.4%
2	1	AARP The Magazine	24,121,461	24,204,313	−0.3%
3	3	Reader's Digest	8,307,292	9,684,759	−14.2%
4	4	Better Homes and Gardens	7,655,501	7,681,722	−0.3%
5	5	National Geographic	5,060,712	5,051,999	0.2%
6	6	Good Housekeeping	4,676,815	4,686,152	−0.2%
7	7	Family Circle	3,906,135	3,967,065	−1.5%
8	8	Woman's Day	3,897,370	3,924,195	−0.7%
9	9	Ladies' Home Journal	3,842,434	3,918,472	−1.9%
10	10	AAA Westways	3,831,553	3,764,966	1.8%
Total Top 10			89,673,392	90,451,249	-0.9%
11	11	People	3,746,426	3,676,499	1.9%
12	16	Game Informer Magazine	3,508,267	3,189,779	10.0%
13	13	Time: The Weekly Newsmagazine	3,374,366	3,374,505	0.0%
14	12	Prevention	3,335,348	3,390,084	−1.6%
15	14	TV Guide	3,266,323	3,276,474	−0.3%
16	15	Sports Illustrated	3,239,968	3,231,969	0.2%
17	17	Taste of Home	3,200,261	3,188,229	0.4%
18	19	Cosmopolitan	2,932,272	2,909,332	0.8%
19	21	Southern Living	2,818,517	2,807,269	0.4%
20	20	AAA Via	2,816,146	2,832,721	−0.6%
21	18	Newsweek	2,720,034	3,124,059	−12.9%
22	22	Playboy	2,658,885	2,790,300	−4.7%
23	24	AAA Going Places	2,554,147	2,551,164	0.1%
24	23	Maxim	2,528,797	2,558,475	−1.2%
25	25	American Legion Magazine	2,472,955	2,550,056	−3.0%
Total Top 25			134,846.101	135,902,161	−0%

Source: Magazine Publishers of America, www.magazine.org.

Magazine Circulation: Cycles, Trends, and Wobbles

Jim Bilton
April 13, 2009

The consumer magazine business is currently grim—but not necessarily for obvious reasons. The underlying fundamentals of the industry started to weaken well before the recession, and the worsening economy is only one part of a complex mix of cycles, trends, and wobbles.

• *Cycles* are relatively easy to spot because they keep on recurring. Since the late 1980s, the industry has seen two launch booms, the last one in 2003–2005. In 2006, the number and size of launches fell dramatically, and they have continued to drop ever since—the market appears to have lost much of its creative "fizz." Past experience suggests it will return eventually.

• *Trends*—long-term and irreversible changes in the structure of the industry—are less simple to identify. The shift from big-circulation, mass-market magazines to niche titles is a clear trend, as is the move from print to digital—although its speed and scale are sometimes exaggerated.

• *Wobbles* are the really perplexing events. They can still be major and market changing, but they are largely unpredictable and potentially reversible.

Take publishing frequency as an example. The decline of weekly magazines and the rise of monthlies could be observed for decades in the circulation figures and apparently went hand in hand with the shift from mass market to niche. It appeared to be an irreversible shift rather than a temporary change of direction.

Then, around the year 2000, this trend started to reverse, driven by the time-sensitive celebrity market and accelerated by changing shopping patterns. Weekly is now thought to be the perfect print frequency—reflecting a faster pace of life but balancing the frenetic urgency and editorial "skinniness" of the Internet. And weeklies have increased their share of sales, helping to destabilize the monthly market. This volatility hit magazine sales long before the recession started to bite.

So, where does magazine cover pricing fit in? First, price has clear cycles. In recessions, many publishers compensate for falling volumes by jacking up their cover prices. It smacks of panic, but there is a logic to it, and it shows a clear and repeated cycle at work.

Second, stand back from the short-term cycle—we need to examine if there is a long-term structural change taking place in magazine pricing. Some commentators argue that we are moving inexorably to a place where all media content will be at what Chris Anderson, the influential editor-in-chief of *US Wired* magazine, calls "the radical price point of zero." Free magazines follow on from free newspapers, which seem to follow on inevitably from free online information. Others believe that there is still a valid, paid-content model that works for at least part of the media business and that all we are doing currently is sorting out where the new paywalls fall.

So far, it is still not clear whether we are observing a trend in pricing or just a wobble. Yet the answer to this question shapes the future for the entire magazine industry.

Source: The Guardian, *April 13, 2009.*

For the retailing community's advertising endeavors, the **consumer magazines** comprise an abundance of titles. Upscale fashion retailers often advertise in *Elle, Glamour, Vogue, Harper's Bazaar,* and *InStyle* (Figure 8.1); middle-of-the road fashion merchandisers often choose *Good Housekeeping, Woman's Day,* and *Southern Living.* Ten of the **global magazine publications** that provide fashion retailers with excellent media exposure are listed in Table 8.2.

Although fashion merchandise is a primary product classification that retailers promote in magazines, a wide assortment of other merchandise is marketed in this manner. For example, *Ladies' Home Journal* features products for the home in addition to clothing, *Better Homes and Gardens* often runs ads featuring furniture, and *Family Circle* often has food retailer advertisements.

Business-to-Business Magazines

Although the **business-to-business magazine** category is not an important one from an advertising perspective, retailers sometimes do advertise in magazines to reach other businesses. For example, *W* sometimes features ads from apparel manufacturers that are directed to retailers. *Visual Merchandise and Store Design* is a business publication that features display products earmarked for retailer use.

City Magazines

One important category for retailers is the **city magazine**. These magazines are marketed to specific cities and feature a wide variety of news items, editorials, local interest stories, entertainment venues and schedules, dining options, and advertisements that feature the retailers in that magazine's geographic area. In addition to focusing on the population of the particular city, the city magazine also serves as an excellent offering for tourists. Visitors to a city are often in a buying mood and like to learn where they can shop.

New York Magazine is extremely successful. It is read predominantly by upscale residents who have significant purchasing power. An examination of its content shows that it is designed to appeal to this segment of the New York City population. Other cities, such as Chicago, Atlanta, and Los Angeles, also publish city magazines (Figure 8.2).

TABLE 8.2	Major Fashion Magazines	
PUBLICATION	**COUNTRY OF DISTRIBUTION**	**YEAR INTRODUCED**
Harper's Bazaar	United States	1867
Elle	26 countries	1945
InStyle	United States	1993
LOVE	United Kingdom	2009
Vogue	14 countries	1892
L'Officiel	France	1921
Fashion	Canada	1977
PINKY	Japan	2004
British Vogue	United Kingdom	1916
Teen Vogue	United States	2003

Complimentary Magazines

Unlike most magazines, which are distributed via subscriptions or individual purchases at newsstands, **complimentary magazines** (Figure 8.3) are distributed without cost to the consumer. These magazines are given to patrons in theaters, in hotels, on airplanes, and other similar public places. They are targeted to people who are enjoying vacation time or who are away from home on business—markets that often spend more money than they would at home.

AIRLINE PUBLICATIONS

With an audience that is captive for many hours, the airplane has become an excellent venue for advertisers to attract people to their products. Today, with airline meals generally a thing of the past, passengers have even more idle time during a flight.

The airline industry takes advantage of this free time by offering **airline publications**. One publication produced by United Airlines is a monthly magazine that features information about different destinations and other timely stories. With so many frequent fliers, the airlines realize that new editions are necessary. In addition to articles and news, the magazine features advertisements offering products such as luggage and other items that appeal to the leisure traveler and businessperson. The other magazine found at every seat is *SkyMall*, a catalogue of merchandise such as luggage, watches, computers, travel accessories, and so forth. Many travelers take advantage of the convenience of shopping during their forced idle time.

HOTEL MAGAZINES

Most major hotels and resorts place copies of **regional magazines** in visitors' rooms. In addition to articles about the local area, regional magazines contain ads for restaurants and attractions as well as for local stores and businesses. The regional magazine is an excellent place for retailers to display their merchandise because many visitors to an area are often motivated to purchase items while on vacation or business. One of the major **hotel publications** is *Guest Informant*, which publishes regional editions throughout the United States. These types of magazines generally feature upscale fashion apparel and accessories (Figure 8.4).

Vogue Magazine

Introduced in the United States in 1892, *Vogue* has become, according to many professionals' opinions, the "bible" of luxury fashion. Not only does it bring a wealth of fashion news to its readers, it also discusses politics, art, and cultural trends. Its popularity in the United States has prompted its publisher, Condé Nast, to offer international editions in the United Kingdom, France, Germany, and 18 other countries.

The magazine throughout the years has helped to ignite the careers of fashion designers, catapulting many into the limelight, and has dashed the collections of others. Editors, designers, and fashion models have risen to celebrity heights through the pages of *Vogue*. In the 1960s, Diana Vreeland, then editor-in-chief of *Vogue*, became a household name due to her departure from fashion-only editorials to stories that included discussions on sexuality. This openly frank treatment of the topic soon attracted the youth of America as readers. Models who were not often as popular as the designers of the fashions they trotted out on the runways soon became international celebrities themselves. Models such as Suzy Parker and Twiggy became stars in their own rights.

It was not until 1988, however, that editorial leadership at the magazine took on an international flavor. British fashion editor Anna Wintour, *Vogue*'s editor-in-chief at the time, quickly became a marquee celebrity. With Wintour's attention to new fashion ideas and focus on broader audiences for the designs, *Vogue* reached new levels of circulation. One of her departures from the traditional fare at the magazine was to promote the idea of coordinating jeans with haute couture fashion, a trend that quickly caught the attention of the fashion world. In her role as editor-in-chief of *Vogue*, she had great influence on America's taste in fashion.

Wintour's star has not always shone brightly. In 2003, a novel titled *The Devil Wears Prada*, which centered on a character who closely resembled Anna Wintour, became a bestseller. As written by an assistant to Wintour, Lauren Weisberger, the main character in the book had many of the personal and unpleasant characteristics thought to be those of Wintour. It depicted her as a woman who was full of herself, without any regard for people in her employ or anyone else who dared to challenge her ideas. Although the book was extremely unflattering to Wintour, the attention that it and the film based on it received brought new attention to *Vogue* and its power as a leading fashion publication.

The publication and Wintour herself remain leaders in fashion publishing today.

shop at emporioarmani.com

EMPORIO ARMANI

8.1 Fashion magazines feature
a wealth of high-fashion ads.
Courtesy of Emporio Armani.

8.2 City magazines lead shoppers
to stores in that area. Here is an
ad from *New York Magazine*.
Courtesy of Bloomingdale's.

8.3 Magazines of this type are given away without cost.
Courtesy of Where Magazine.

8.4 People on vacation or traveling for business learn about area shops. Here is an ad from *Traditions*, the exclusive publication for The Breakers resort in Palm Beach, Florida. *Courtesy of* Traditions, The Magazine of the Breakers.

Because tourists often need some time for relaxation, complimentary magazines are read with considerable frequency. For newcomers to an area, they are often the only source of shopping information they will see.

ENTERTAINMENT PROGRAMS

Many theatrical productions provide attendees with programs containing information about the upcoming show, stories about other theatrical productions, and advertisements featuring area retailers. With some time before an event begins, audience members may scan the pages and come upon retail ads that pique their interest.

One of the better known of these publications is *Playbill*, a magazine of approximately 50 pages (Figure 8.5). A mainstay at Broadway theaters, it often features advertisements of Macy's, Lord & Taylor, and Bloomingdale's, all merchants with clienteles that frequent the theater. Most often, the retailers use institutional advertising to inform theater patrons of the stores and their proximity to the theater.

An additional advantage of entertainment programs is that they are often kept as a memento, providing the advertiser extra exposure to the reader.

Advantages and Disadvantages of Magazines

Although the magazine is a very important medium for advertising, most retailers opt for newspaper advertising or some other media choice. Those who do spend a portion of their promotional budgets on magazine advertising are the major fashion retailers such as Saks Fifth Avenue and Macy's, both establishments with national exposure and appeal to specific population segments, and general merchandise companies such as JCPenney and Sears, which also have broad audiences because of their many locations across the country.

Some of the advantages of magazines are as follows:

1. *Targeting consumers:* Magazines target specific audiences and enable the retailer to reach a defined market through a publication whose editorial content focuses on delineated topics. Thus, the retailer who sells high-fashion, upscale apparel and accessories will usually have positive responses from magazines such as *Town & Country, Elle,* and *Harper's Bazaar* (Figure 8.6).

2. *Message life:* Television offers the advantage of live action, but the brevity of the message is a disadvantage. Viewers often walk away from the television during commercial breaks. Now, with the advent of television recording systems, viewers can record the program and bypass the commercials altogether. Newspapers offer longer message lives, but often only until the next edition arrives. Magazines, on the other hand, offer a very long **message life**. Most people keep their magazines at least until the next issue arrives, and sometimes longer, making it a long-lived medium. Some people pass magazines on to other households, offering still another advantage to the advertiser. An ad has the potential to be seen by those who are not the original recipients of the magazine.

3. *Reproductive quality:* Better quality stock allows for clarity and excitement not obtainable in newspaper advertising. The use of color and the sharpness of the text and images increases the power of magazine ads. Research indicates that color ads are at least 30 percent more effective than black-and-white ads.

4. *Geographical editions:* With the trading areas of some retailers often limited, magazine advertising might be too expensive to use because the audiences reached may be too distant from the store to warrant the cost, except in cases where mail, Internet, or phone-order services are offered. Advertising in zoned editions could be a better alternative. Many magazines offer this option at costs that are less than that for full circulation.

1.800.365.7989 NEIMANMARCUS.COM

THE
ART
OF
FASHION®

Neiman Marcus

NM EXCLUSIVE
BLUMARINE

8.6 High-fashion magazines
target upscale audiences.
Courtesy of Neiman Marcus.

5. *Editorial commentary:* Magazines generally feature editorial commentary that motivates individuals to purchase a particular publication. Fashion retailers, for example, often advertise in particular fashion magazines because of the relationships that some editors have established with their readership. Those wanting to be informed about style forecasts and trends often choose a particular publication to read. Retailers understand that these readers are potential viewers of their ads and might be motivated to purchase their products.

Although the advantages for advertising are many, as in the case of the other media, the magazine nonetheless has its disadvantages. These include the following:

1. *Lead time:* Unlike newspapers, in which ads can be placed as late as the day before the paper goes to press, magazines require that ad space be reserved weeks to months in advance of the publication date. For retailers who need to place an ad on very short notice, the magazine is out of the question. Some magazines offer "last-minute" placement, but that does not really mean the last minute. It merely suggests that there is a little leeway in the magazine's published deadline for placement. As we know, various situations require immediate attention to ads that must be placed on very short notice. When a snowstorm is reported by the weather bureau, for example, or a heat wave is in the forecast, some retailers run ads that feature apparel or accessories for those weather events. Magazines cannot offer the immediacy required for such ads.

2. *Cost:* The cost per thousand (CPM), as discussed in Chapter 7, "Newspapers," is considerably higher for magazine advertising than for newspaper advertising. Although the costs are justified because of the quality of the final output, it is still beyond many retailers' promotional budgets. A look at most magazines reveals that only the major retail operations can afford the luxury of magazine advertising.

Costs of Magazine Space

Standard rates are the norm for many magazine ad placements, but magazines also offer lower rates based on a number of conditions, such as partial runs and zoned or regional editions.

- A **partial run** is an advertisement that does not appear in every distributed issue.

- A zoned edition is one that reaches a limited region of the magazine's circulation.

A typical magazine rate card, along with the ad specifications, is shown in Table 8.3. Ad dimensions are depicted in Figure 8.7.

Discounted Rates

In addition to the standard, or **open rate**, a price for a onetime, full-page insertion, the publisher offers discounts. Some advertisers receive special discounts when the edition is about to go to press and not all of the advertising space has been sold. Publishers sometimes give last-minute, money-saving considerations to help fill the otherwise blank pages. To avail themselves of such situations, companies must have their advertisements ready for immediate insertion. The copy, artwork, and complete layout must be in hand and ready for publication.

The space for these last-minute deals is known as **remnant space** and may be purchased through agencies that specialize in such placement. One such company is ADBUYS. Table 8.4 features an example of the special rates offered through ADBUYS and some details of the publications it represents. The names of the magazines that offer these special rates are omitted, and only a description of their publications is featured because the publishers do not allow their names to be featured. Also, the full description of each publication is available only by logging on to the ADBUYS Web site, http://www.printadbuys.com.

TABLE 8.3 — Rate Card

	GROSS	1X	3X	6X	9X	12X	18X	24X	36X
4/color	Page	19,260	18,300	17,335	16,370	15,410	14,445	13,485	12,520
	2/3 Page	13,100	12,445	11,790	11,135	10,475	9,825	9,165	8,515
	1/2 Page	10,595	10,065	9,535	9,005	8,475	7,945	7,415	6,885
	1/3 Page	6,740	6,405	6,070	5,730	5,395	5,055	4,720	4,380
	1/4 Page	5,010	4,760	4,510	4,255	4,010	3,755	3,505	3,255
	Spread	29,855	28,365	26,870	25,375	23,885	22,395	20,900	19,405
	GROSS	1X	3X	6X	9X	12X	18X	24X	36X
Black & White	Page	14,635	13,955	13,220	12,485	11,750	11,015	10,285	9,550
	2/3 Page	9,985	9,490	8,990	8,490	7,990	7,455	6,990	6,495
	1/2 Page	8,080	7,675	7,270	6,870	6,465	6,060	5,655	5,250
	1/3 Page	5,140	4,885	4,625	4,370	4,115	3,855	3,600	3,340
	1/4 Page	3,820	3,630	3,440	3,245	3,055	2,865	2,675	2,485
	Spread	22,765	21,630	20,490	19,355	18,215	17,075	15,935	14,795

TABLE 8.4 — Last-Minute Ad Rates

MISCELLANEOUS AVAILABILITY

This listing represents "last-minute" magazine print advertising deals. We have a special agreement with our magazine to give us access to deeply discounted rates, but they won't allow us to publish their magazine names alongside the discounted rates on our Web site.

DESCRIPTION	PAGE SIZE	ISSUE DATE	RESERVE DATE	CIRCULATION	HOUSEHOLD INCOME	% MALE	AVG. AGE	FREQ.	OPEN 4C RATE
This magazine is published for families ...	Full	7/01/2009	5/24/2009	0–500K	$157,000	70%	57	12x	$86,629
Presents a comprehensive look into the p...	Full	10/01/2009	6/15/2009	0–500K	$70,000	99%	52	6x	$3,497
National magazine that reaches an afflue...	Full	9/01/2009	7/01/2009	500K–1MM	$130,695	44%	50	10x	$55,800
Geared toward the tween and teen girls ...	Full	8/01/2009	5/11/2009	0–500K	$60,003	10%	14	12x	$13,300
This magazine is edited for automotive e...	Full	8/01/2009	5/13/2009	500–1MM	$85,700	78%	38	12x	$89,415
Scholarship Monthly magazine is a newly ...	Full	7/01/2009	5/16/2009	0–500K	$0	0%	0	12x	$1,000
Edited for cross-stitch enthusiasts, fea...	Full	9/01/2009	5/28/2009	0–500K	$58,500	0%	55	6x	$4,285
Enlightens, inspires, and entertains read...	Full	9/01/2009	5/28/2009	0–500K	$88,000	0%	58	6x	$2,835
Celebrates the human achievement of flig...	Full	8/01/2009	6/11/2009	0-500K	$71,240	85%	47	6x	$20,695
This magazine is edited for American Jew...	Full	8/01/2009	6/15/2009	0–500K	$82,700	0%	67	10x	$9,900
Each issue informs reader on such firea...	Full	9/01/2009	6/15/2009	0–500K	$60,000	81%	50	12x	$13,405
Geared toward agriculture and a rural w...	Full	8/01/2009	6/23/2009	0–500K	$49,000	52%	57	12x	$55,800

Source: www.printadbuy.com.

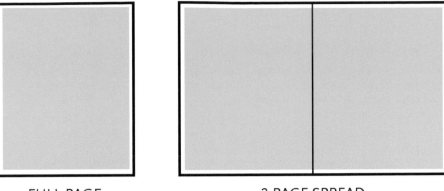

FULL PAGE

2 PAGE SPREAD

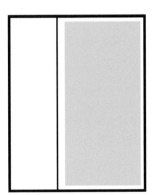

2/3 PAGE VERTICAL

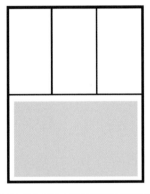

1/2 PAGE HORIZONTAL

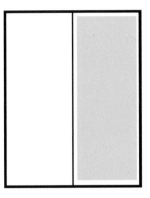

1/2 PAGE VERTICAL

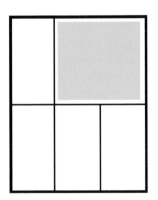

1/3 PAGE

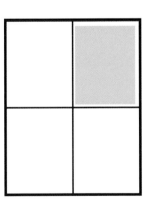

1/4 PAGE SPREAD

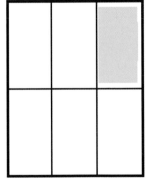

1/6 PAGE

8.7 Ad space illustrations.
Illustration by Vanessa Han.

Negotiated Rate Reductions

As advertising revenues decrease, many magazines depart from their standard and discounted rates to offer **off-the-card rates**. It is becoming commonplace for advertisers to negotiate with the publisher for cost reductions beyond those published on the rate card—hence the term *off-the-card rate*.

There are no rules governing off-the-card rates. In the competitive climate of the magazine industry, with more and more magazines entering the market, publishers are willing to make advertising costs in their pages more attractive. The reduced costs might be based on insertion of a minimum number of pages in a particular issue or an increase in contracted space from the previous year. Better terms are often achieved through the use of advertising agencies because they have more clout with the media than does the individual user.

Short Rates

In trying to cut costs, some advertisers enter into contractual agreements that guarantee they will place a certain number of advertisements of a specified size within a specified time. This arrangement initially benefits both the magazine and the advertiser, but occasionally the requirements of the contract are not fulfilled. Retailers, or other advertisers, might find it necessary to cut back on their original promotional plans, perhaps because of an economic downturn or a sales shortfall. Under these circumstances, the publisher has the right to make adjustments in the rates agreed to in the contract.

Either at the end of the contractual period or when it is decided that fewer ads than originally agreed to will be run, an adjustment, at a higher rate, is determined. This new rate is known as the **short rate**.

Sometimes an advertiser uses more space than initially contracted for, and in such cases, the advertising rate may be lowered.

Position Preference

If an advertiser wants to have his or her ad in a particular place in the magazine, an additional charge is added to the cost of the advertisement.

The most desired places are the back and inside front covers. These positions are more likely to be seen than any other places in the publication. If the advertiser stipulates that the ad must be placed in the first few pages of an issue, this also requires an extra fee.

Foldouts

One way to make an ad more powerful is to use a **foldout ad**. This type of ad is larger than the magazine page (the size of two or more pages) and is folded into the magazine. The impact of a foldout is significantly greater than that of a full-page insertion, but it costs considerably more. When foldouts are placed on the inside front cover (known as the *second cover* in the industry), the costs are even greater.

Bleeds

A dramatic way to call attention to an ad is to have it cover the entire page without a border or margin; that is, the ad image flows, or **bleeds**, right off the edges of the page. Such ads cost approximately 15 percent more than the standard rate. Figure 8.8 shows an ad that bleeds.

Classification of Magazine Advertisements

As discussed in Chapter 7, advertisers use different types of ads for different purposes. In magazines, many of the same types of ads are used, but some have more visibility than others. Promotional advertising, for example, is widely used in newspapers but rarely used in magazines. Most retailers who use promotional advertising do so to dispose of unwanted inventory or to react to slow-selling periods. These conditions are not usually predictable and, therefore, require quick action. The newspaper is an excellent medium because of the short lead time necessary for advertisement insertion. Magazines, on the other hand, although a visually superior medium, require significant lead time, which doesn't work for last-minute retailer use.

The retail ads most often placed in magazines include product, designer-oriented, image or

8.8 (opposite) Bleeds provide a dramatic element to an advertisement. *Courtesy of Bulgari.*

BVLGARI

ATLANTA • BAL HARBOUR • BEVERLY HILLS • BOCA RATON • CHEVY CHASE
CHICAGO • DALLAS • HONOLULU • HOUSTON • LAS VEGAS • NEW YORK
SAN FRANCISCO • SCOTTSDALE • SHORT HILLS • SOUTH COAST PLAZA • BULGARI.COM

prestige, combination, indirect, and institutional advertising.

Product Advertising

Items such as home furnishings, apparel, accessories, gourmet foods, computers, electronics, and so forth, make up the product offerings that retailers promote in the pages of a magazine. A merchant's best sellers or new items are often advertised to motivate the shopper to visit his or her stores or to purchase through mail order and the Internet. The products are highlighted in these ads, but so are the names of the retailers who advertise them.

Designer-Oriented Advertising

Many fashion designers' offerings are promoted through magazine advertising. Their collections are featured in ads to give the reader a taste of what awaits them when they visit the store's premises. Usually, these ads are dramatically rendered using stylized impressions and drawings that distinguish them from other ads. High-fashion retailers such as Neiman Marcus, Saks Fifth Avenue, Bergdorf Goodman, and Bloomingdales use designer-oriented magazine ads (Figure 8.9).

Image or Prestige Advertising

Some retailers use marquee label merchandise in their magazine ads to give the reader the impression of prestige. Many upper- and upper-middle-class shoppers are motivated to purchase from retailers by the mere "snob appeal" of the experience, and **image advertising** often motivates them to visit the stores. In these ads, the image— the impression it leaves in the shoppers' minds— is more important than promoting particular products.

Combination Advertising

Instead of trying to sell a particular item, as in the case of product advertising, the combination ad combines elements to appeal to the reader. It might be a product and an institutional concept, such as prestige afforded the purchaser because of the nature of the product. The retailer might also combine products with messages of exclusivity, increasing the desirability of a product by announcing it is available only from this particular retailer.

Indirect Advertising

In some advertisements, the manufacturer pays for and places the ad, promoting the product and often listing the retail locations where it may be purchased. The retailer that is mentioned is the **indirect advertiser**. Sometimes merchants contribute to the costs of these ads, but often retailers who purchase significant amounts of product from the manufacturer are rewarded with free mention of their names.

Institutional Advertising

As in the case of newspaper advertising, retailers sometimes wish to convey a message to the readership that is not product oriented. It might be the acknowledgment of collection exclusivity, a special service available only at this retailer, unique services such as personal shopping, and so forth. Although not likely to produce immediate sales response, these ads foster positive relationships with the retailers' clienteles.

Some merchants use institutional ads (Figure 8.10) to focus attention on their community mindedness.

Understanding Magazine Circulation

Before a retailer or any other organization places a magazine advertisement, they must learn the details of circulation in order to get the most from the advertising dollars. One of the more important aspects of circulation is to make certain that the figures generated by the publication are true. Before the ABC was established (see Focus 7.2 in Chapter 7), there was considerable evidence of magazines and other media misrepresenting their circulation figures.

It is essential that a magazine's circulation figures are verified by the ABC. It is also important for the inexperienced advertiser, which is often the case for small retailers, to understand the factors and nomenclature associated with advertising.

Circulation refers to the number of copies of a publication that are distributed. These include the

Z SPOKE by Zac Posen
*e*xclusive

TH!NK
ABOUT...

creating your
own alter ego
with the daring
exclusive
collections at
Saks—where
modern
superheroines
get their powers.

Shop the collection in WEAR, on Four in New York

Saks
Fifth
Avenue

saks.com

8.9 Many upscale
magazines feature
designer products
in retail stores.
*Courtesy of Saks
Fifth Avenue.*

Nonpaid circulation includes copies that are distributed to places such as waiting rooms in hospitals, health clubs, or other places where consumers might congregate.

Distribution is not always a constant number. There are often variations due to factors such as changes in demand by the readership, competition from online media, and economic conditions.

Promoting the Magazine Industry's Image

Most publishers try to improve their images with both readership and advertisers by maintaining high standards for their publications. This is accomplished through individual public relations efforts, affiliation with organizations such as the ABC, and involvement with trade associations such as the **Magazine Publishers of America**, the subject of Focus 8.2.

Summary of Key Points

- There are more consumer magazines in publication around the world today than at any other time in history. Leading the list are the Association of American Retired Persons (AARP) publications *AARP Bulletin* and *AARP The Magazine*, followed by *Reader's Digest*.

- *Vogue*, the second oldest in publication in the United States, has maintained its position as the "bible" of luxury, according to many professionals in the fashion industry.

- The number of complimentary magazines is significant. They come in many formats and include those that are published for distribution on airplanes, in hotels, and in theaters.

- Among the advantages of magazine advertising is the magazine's comparatively long message life, its ability to present ads at

8.10 Institutional ads help retailers promote special messages. *Courtesy of Macy's.*

copies that are sold as well as those that are given away. Estimates of these figures are reported by the publishers in a document called a **pink sheet**. The figures are analyzed by independent agencies such as the ABC, then verified and issued in a **white paper**, which is an audit report. Included in the white paper are the average paid and nonpaid circulations.

The paid circulation includes the number of copies that are sold piecemeal at newsstands and retail outlets such as bookstores, supermarkets, airport terminal shops, and so forth. The remainder are sold through subscriptions to individuals and businesses. Media Insight 8.2 looks at the decline in newsstand sales.

high resolutions as a quality offering to advertisers, and the geographical editions that may enable advertisers to better pinpoint their target markets.

- The two main disadvantages of magazine advertising are the considerable cost for ad insertion and the lead time necessary to have an ad published.

- Magazine rates are published on rate cards, which feature a wide variety of options to the advertiser.

- There are rates other than the standard rates, which include negotiated (off-the-card) rates, short rates, and rates for position preference.

- Advertising classifications include product, designer-oriented, image or prestige, combination, indirect, and institutional ads. Each offers the advertiser a different concept for reaching readership.

- The Magazine Publishers of America is a trade association that fosters the image of magazine advertising and offers a variety of advantages to the membership.

For Discussion

1. Who is the present editor-in-chief of *Vogue*, and what major event led to the exposé of her past and recent background?

2. Why are city magazines so important to the retailing industry in particular?

3. Why do airlines publish complimentary magazines, and why are they important to retailers in the markets served by the airlines?

4. Discuss the message life of a magazine and contrast it to that of a newspaper and television program.

5. In what way does the lead time and cost of magazine advertisements differ from those of the newspaper?

FOCUS $___ 8.2

Magazine Publishers of America

The Magazine Publishers of America (MPA) was established in 1919 as an association for consumer magazines. It was organized to advance the interests of magazine publishers with the advertising community, including ad agencies and advertisers, as well as the government, the press, and the consumer. Today, it represents approximately 225 domestic publishing companies with more than 1,000 titles, about 50 international companies, and more than 100 associate members. Its domestic members are publishers whose primary objective is to distribute their publications in the United States, and their international counterparts are based abroad and include single-country and multinational publishers. Associate membership includes non-publishing suppliers, vendors, and private equity firms affiliated with the magazine industry, deriving at least 20 percent annual revenue from the magazine industry.

The MPA's mission is to support its members by encouraging editorial excellence and expanding the market for magazine brands; promoting the value and benefits of advertising; championing the rights of editors and publishers before Congress, the courts, and state governments; and informing and educating members about changes in technology, law, and industry practices.

The association consists of magazine industry specialists and is headquartered in New York City with an office of government affairs in Washington, DC.

Among the many services offered by the MPA are the following:

- Conducting research on advertising and consumer marketing

- Providing educational seminars and "webinars"

- Holding networking events for the industry

- Promoting diversity in publishing

- Sponsoring and conducting surveys

- Protecting membership interests in Washington, DC, and all of the states

Magazine Circulation Falls in Half

Irin Carmon, with contributions from Stephanie D. Smith and Amy Wicks
August 8, 2008

The phrase "flat is the new up" became a mantra in recent years when it came to assessing newsstand sales. Well, as core fashion titles, women's service books, and men's magazines have almost universally posted declines in their single-copy sales in the first half of 2008, how does "less down is the new up" sound?

To wit, Hachette Filipacchi Media's Tom Masterson, senior vice president for consumer marketing and manufacturing, pointed out that although *Elle*'s newsstand was down 6.3 percent in the first 6 months, "many of *Elle*'s competitors decreased more."

That's true—*Vogue* was down nearly 15 percent, though it still outsells *Elle* on the newsstand by an average of about 50,000 copies monthly; *Harper's Bazaar* fell 8.3 percent, and *W*, which gets the vast majority of sales through subscription, was down 10 percent.

Or take *Shape*, which was down about 10 percent overall on the newsstand in the first half but still averaged higher total sales than the troubled fitness category in general. (*Self* had the dubious honor of being less down, but is still smaller; *Shape* has beefed up its distribution at checkout and added 17,000 pockets nationwide.)

Growing market share might be the last remaining competi-tive advantage in an environment where nearly every editor-in-chief is seeing the kind of declines that once would have gotten them fired. The long-standing expectation that a healthy magazine is one that sees successive growth on the newsstand is in question—you can't exactly fire everyone.

Whether the change is cyclical (uncertain economic times that include high gas prices, fewer supermarket trips, and less disposable income) or secular (consumer behavior is undergoing a fundamental change away from newsstand, or from print magazines themselves) depends on whom you ask. Editors and publishers would have it be the former.

"I don't think newsstand softness is systemic to magazines, but rather systemic to the economy," said *O, The Oprah Magazine* publisher Jill Seelig.

But some advertisers and observers are beginning to wonder whether the second diagnosis is upon us. As consumers' attention fractures, spoiled by choice and easy digital access, the culture and entertainment industries already have adjusted their expectations, counting smaller sales numbers than ever as blockbusters. The magazine industry might be falling prey to the same tectonic shift.

Several magazines, such as *Glamour* and *Marie Claire*, have seen disappointing sales for several periods in a row, even when the economy was flush, suggesting more of an overall move away from big women's titles. (Perhaps in reaction, *Glamour* unveiled a redesign this month.) Even newsstand stalwart *Cosmopoli-tan* dropped 6 percent in this period, a difference of more than 100,000 copies, after essentially flat newsstand sales since 2004.

The only source of growth across the board has been in total circulation, which, given the newsstand declines, usually means that publishers are spending more than ever to build and maintain their subscriber bases. And advertisers are traditionally more skeptical of that kind of audience building, given publishers' past practices of steeply discounting subscrip-tions.

That *Men's Vogue*'s newsstand is down 39.1 percent, for example, even as it's raising its rate base to 400,000, can be explained several ways: first, that it suffers from an apples-and-oranges comparison between five issues published in the first half of 2008 and three in the first half of 2007 and second, and more significantly, that it's growing its audience the expensive way, through subscriptions, and not wowing on the newsstand.

The title also has seen its verified circulation (bulk copies in public places) drop by 14 percent since last year. A spokeswoman said, "*Men's Vogue* continues to take risks on covers to recognize accomplishment over celebrity." Case in point [is] the model-free Bugatti cover in May, which sold 45,000 copies, according to *Rapid Report*. (That was still better than the worst cover to date, April with Alex Rodriguez, at 41,000.)

As such, given the flood of negative newsstand figures in the first half, the few examples of uptick in sales should be particularly celebratory— among them, *InStyle*, which, whether you consider it a core fashion title or a peer of *Glamour* and *Marie Claire*, was the only one in either group to see any rise in newsstand, by 4 percent to 783,254. That's before the recently unveiled redesign was even tested on the newsstand.

And Rodale's David Zinczenko showed once again that he can put his money where his mouth is, maintain-ing *Men's Health*'s position as the number one newsstand seller in the men's category with a 2 percent growth and having a hand in two newer magazines, which also have seen good news: *Women's Health*, with its 12 percent rise, and *Best Life*, up almost 20 percent. Maybe that's why *Men's Health Living* has been given a go-ahead in a tough environment for shelter magazines.

So, do the steep declines serve as a harbinger of equally sharp falls in advertising revenue as firms seek other media? Well, for now, media buyers seem to be seeing the big picture. "I don't think we would have seen these types of declines if the economy had been in a different place," said Robin Steinberg, senior vice president and director of print investment and activation at MediaVest. "We would have seen some declines, but not deep declines." That said, she added, "The future of magazines is not going to have the same distribution exposure as in years past," as the business model shifts from emphasizing the number of eyeballs to assessing quality of audience.

And media companies are experimenting with new distribution tools such as Maghound, the so-called Netflix for magazines launching in September. A subsidiary of Time Inc., Maghound will allow consumers to switch in and out titles for a flat monthly fee, and around 300 titles have signed up so far.

Magazine publishers also are trying to figure out how to leverage their Web sites to build a subscription base—a potentially more efficient, or at least cheaper, way to add subscribers than direct mail or verified circulation. Hearst magazines in particular—many of which tend to be big, single-copy-heavy titles in an age of grim newsstand—have suggested this as a winning strategy. In the face of a newsstand decline of 17.3 percent, for example, *Oprah*'s Seelig pointed to the fact that the magazine hasn't had to resort to verified circulation and that subscriptions were up 7 percent, in part because "we played around with the subscription offers on Oprah. com."

She added, "The simple truth is consumers are not going to the places where our magazines are sold as frequently as they were" (i.e., airports, supermarkets, drugstores, and other retailers).

That said, the magazine recently saw the exit of editor-in-chief Amy Gross, billed as voluntary, and new editor of former *Golf for Women* Susan Reed will have to figure out how and if the newsstand can be turned around. George Janson, managing partner/ director of print at Mediaedge:cia, said, "Some magazines have reached a natural level of circulation," pointing to *Oprah* in particular.

"Magazines are also coming off a period where [advertising] spending and circulation have, for the most part, been flat to up," added Janson—meaning that what goes up sometimes has to come down.

But if the latest newsstand numbers prove to be long-term indicators, publishers could be faced with hard choices, such as cutting rate bases or rethinking their distribution models. "As content becomes free on the Internet, I question whether or not the future of magazines will be opt-in and nonpaid," said Steinberg.

FIRST-HALF 2008 CIRCULATION FIGURES					
FASHION	NEWSSTAND 1H08	NEWSSTAND 1H07	% CHANGE	TOTAL PAID AND VERIFIED CIRC 2008	TOTAL PAID AND VERIFIED CIRC 2007	% CHANGE
Allure	228,667	253,056	−9.6%	1,091,147	1,062,147	2.7%
Cosmopolitan	1,753,700	1,867,481	−6.1%	2,937,800	2,915,867	0.8%
Elle	332,167	354,333	−6.3%	1,082,278	1,072,729	0.9%
Essence	233,265	254,698	−8.4%	1,051,130	1,089,495	−3.5%
Glamour	685,633	755,289	−9.2%	2,354,973	2,262,242	4.1%
Harper's Bazaar	167,300	182,506	−8.3%	716,800	722,058	−0.7%
InStyle	783,254	753,358	4.0%	1,827,644	1,780,681	2.6%
Lucky	237,750	250,240	−5.0%	1,156,306	1,167,020	−0.9%
Marie Claire	289,700	329,473	−12.1%	979,500	971,348	0.8%
Self	331,183	360,229	−8.1%	1,495,033	1,486,992	0.5%
Shape	338,607	376,684	−10.0%	1,703,421	1,747,569	−2.5%
Town & Country	44,400	50,293	−11.7%	461,100	461,571	−0.1%
Vanity Fair	376,500	355,190	6.0%	1,144,001	1,153,517	−00.8%
Vogue	385,500	452,207	−14.8%	1,224,131	1,301,575	−6.0%
W	34,917	38,974	−10.4%	458,867	457,996	0.2%
Women's Health	306,864	275,284	11.5%	1,140,068	786,892	44.9%
TEEN						
Cosmogirl	302,800	369,238	−18.0%	1,426,300	1,446,836	−1.4%
Seventeen	328,400	355,480	−7.6%	2,024,100	2,052,666	−1.4%
Teen Vogue	201,200	238,713	−15.7%	1,017,125	973,172	4.5%
LIFESTYLE/SERVICE						
Martha Stewart Living	271,500	307,320	−11.7%	2,037,630	2,005,980	1.6%
More	156,200	186,400	−16.2%	1,266,980	1,254,273	1.0%
O, The Oprah Magazine	734,000	887,836	−17.3%	2,394,300	2,436,703	−1.7%
Real Simple	389,016	398,137	−2.3%	2,026,466	1,973,306	2.7%
Redbook	202,200	244,537	−17.3%	2,228,000	2,374,237	−6.2%
MEN						
Best Life	80,378	67,333	19.4%	518,763	468,777	10.7%
Details	72,680	75,365	−3.6%	458,536	457,186	0.3%
Esquire	112,900	108,480	4.1%	726,400	721,133	0.7%
GQ	211,700	223,452	−5.3%	915,173	931,694	−1.8%
Maxim	426,673	483,281	−11.7%	2,535,884	2,568,339	−1.3%
Men's Health	559,136	547,958	2.0%	1,868,500	1,816,671	2.9%
Men's Journal	72,792	75,323	−3.4%	710,255	707,808	0.3%
Men's Vogue	53,600	87,977	−39.1%	368,898	307,501	20.0%

Source: Publishers' estimates provided to Audit Bureau of Calculations.

6. What is meant by *remnant space*, and how does its use benefit the retailer and other advertisers?

7. What is meant by *short rate*, and how might it be adjusted to the disadvantage of the advertiser?

8. Discuss image or prestige advertising and the benefits it affords its users.

9. Define the terms *pink sheet* and *white paper*, and explain how they are used in publishing.

10. What are the advantages of membership in the Magazine Publishers of America trade association?

Exercise and Projects

1. Obtain a copy of any of the top 25 magazines listed in Table 8.1. Carefully examine the issue you have selected and remove five different types of retail ads that are featured. Affix each ad on foam board or any other display board and indicate the following for each:

   a. Type of ad (product, combination, institutional, etc.)

   b. Name of retailer

   c. Position in publication

   d. Special characteristics (bleed, foldout, etc.)

2. Contact any magazine publication for the purpose of determining the following:

   a. The number of issues published annually

   b. The demographics of the readership

   c. Variable editions (zoned, regional, etc.)

   d. Lead time necessary for ad insertion

   e. Rates

3. Using this information, prepare a typewritten paper that will be delivered orally to the class.

4. Using any search engine, learn more about business-to-business magazines and how retailers may use them for the purposes of advertising. The information obtained should be the basis of a two-page written report.

Terms of the Trade

airline publications

business-to-business magazine

bleeds

city magazine

complimentary magazines

consumer magazines

foldout ad

global magazine publications

hotel publications

image advertising

indirect advertiser

Magazine Publishers of America

message life

off-the-card rates

open rate

partial run

pink sheet

regional magazine

remnant space

short rate

white paper

Web Site Exploration for In-Depth Analysis

Citymagazine.com
http://www.citymagazine.com
   This site shows the major city magazine publications in the United States.

Mediamark Research & Intelligence
http://www.mediamark.com
   Mediamark Research & Intelligence is an excellent site for research on syndicated magazines.

Nielsen Business Media
http://www.vnuemedia.com
   This is an excellent site to learn more about 47 of the major business publications in the United States.

Television *and* Radio

Radio surfaced in the early 1900s as a medium that spoke to the people. It was a new concept for reaching households that heretofore relied on print media for news of the times. Radio was the rage for many years as the only broadcast medium to come into the listeners' homes. With news shows and the "soaps" leading the way, it was an excellent medium for the promotion of a variety of products. By 1928, another broadcast venture came onto the scene in the form of television, but it wasn't until 1947 that the country was treated to one of the first regular television programs, *The Howdy Doody Show*, which captured the attention of children all across the United States. The next year saw what amounted to a blockbuster presentation, the *Texaco Theater* starring Milton Berle, a comedian credited by many as the father of television. The show was so popular that on Tuesday evenings at eight o'clock, the masses literally stopped what they were doing to watch Milton Berle. It was to become the first regular prime-time program to define television viewing. Its popularity was so pervasive that retailers chose to close their doors for business while the show was on because there were too few shoppers to warrant staying opening. Rounding out those early days in television was *The Ed Sullivan Show*, a mainstay on Sunday evenings from 1948 through 1971. It featured legendary performers such as the Jackson Five, Aretha Franklin, Elvis Presley, and the Beatles.

Television soon became the medium of choice for major sponsorship. The *Kraft Television Theater* became a regular offering and helped build sales for that company, as did the *Hallmark Hall of Fame*, which is still on the air today, albeit at infrequent intervals.

Throughout the years, many merchants climbed on the television bandwagon by sponsoring shows. Giants in the industry such as Sears and JCPenney bankrolled entire shows during the medium's early days. As time went on, however, sole sponsorship of television programming became too costly for retailers and other businesses, as discussed later in the chapter.

Neither television nor radio has been widely used, compared to print media and other advertising outlets, to promote retail merchandise offerings. Although television and radio provide voice and live action, many factors, all of which are addressed in this chapter, have played a role in reducing their importance as prime advertising outlets.

Television

Many studies indicate that television remains the dominant medium in most households in the United States, but it does not hold that place in retail advertising. Manufacturers of food products, soft drinks, automobiles, electronics, beer, as well as service organizations, account for most television commercials. Super Bowl 2009, for example, with its $3 million price for a 30-second ad, attracted industrial giants such as The Coca Cola Co., PepsiCo, Audi of America Inc., Hyundai, Bridgestone Americas Inc., and Anheuser-Busch Co., who sponsored the event even with the country's economic downturn. It is an example of the faith they have in the returns on their investments that advertising on television will bring. The Super Bowl is the premium television show each year, but advertising on the medium for regular national programming is comparably expensive as well. Thus, retailers, except for the national giants, opt for other media in which to invest their advertising dollars. Many, however, do use **local television spots** for promotion of their goods, a concept that is examined later in the chapter.

Although television remains a viable media outlet, its future is still unclear. With the announcement by Oprah Winfrey that her show will end its run after 25 years, many believe that network television, as we now know it, will not be in the forefront for advertisers. In Media Insight 9.1, television's future is examined.

The Facets of Television

As consumers, we tend to regard television as just one medium, when in fact, as the professionals in the industry know, it is anything but. It consists of networks, spots, syndicated formats, and cable. Each has different characteristics and offers different benefits to advertisers.

Unsteady Future for Broadcast: A New Economic Model Gives Cable Firmer Footing

Tim Arango and Bill Carter

Oprah Winfrey is fleeing broadcast television for cable. NBC, once arguably the biggest cultural tastemaker in the United States, is being shopped to Comcast, the country's largest cable company.

Have we finally reached a tipping point that suggests a remarkable decline in the fortunes of broadcast television in America?

In the NBC Universal deal, in which General Electric is negotiating to sell a majority stake of its media business to Comcast, it is the cable channels—USA, Bravo, SyFy, MSNBC, and CNBC—that are seen as the most valuable, not the NBC broadcast network, which is mired in fourth place in the ratings among the four major networks.

Most analysts and many executives agree that the economic model of broadcast television—which relies much more heavily on advertising than does cable—is severely fractured. What they are wondering now is if it is irreparably broken.

"It's in a period of huge transformation," said Horace Newcomb, a professor of telecommunications at the University of Georgia and the director of the Peabody Awards, which are awarded annually for excellence in radio and television broadcasting. "It's in a state of confusion."

The business model of the big three networks—which became four when Fox began prime-time programming in 1987—has for decades relied on a simple formula: spend millions on original programming that will attract advertiser dollars and later live on as lucrative reruns in syndication.

But ratings are going down. In the 1952–53 television season, more than 30 percent of American households that owned televisions tuned in to NBC during prime time, according to Nielsen. In the 2007–8 season, that figure was just 5.2 percent.

The mass audience—the bread and butter of broadcast networks—has splintered into niches as viewers flock to alternative entertainment choices on the Internet, to video games, and to cable channels dedicated to individual tastes, like Ms. Winfrey's forthcoming OWN, the Oprah Winfrey Network.

And yet, programming remains expensive—a network drama costs about $3 million for 1 hour—and advertisers are becoming reluctant to pay ever-rising premiums for prime-time shows. All the networks have tried to adjust, putting on more reality programming, for example, that is cheaper to produce.

NBC made perhaps the biggest bet of all—moving Jay Leno to prime time each night at 10, saving the millions it would have cost to develop a scripted show in that time slot. The *Leno* move has been the subject of intense scrutiny by the media because Mr. Leno's ratings have lately fallen on several nights well below even the modest guarantees NBC made to advertisers, requiring them to make yet another change.

Nicholas P. Heymann, an analyst at Sterne, Agee & Leach who follows G.E. (General Electric), said that the consistently ineffective efforts to rebuild the prime-time portion of the NBC network might have led G.E. to begin thinking it was time to exit the entertainment business. And this one particular decision may have pushed G.E. over the edge, he said.

"I think the *Leno* move was the last straw," Mr. Heymann said, "the last roll of the dice for G.E."

Mr. Heymann acknowledged that it seemed unlikely on its face that such a huge deal could hinge on one decision in one slice of an enormous company. But he said, "It's the domino effect of the move, on the shows in front of *Leno* and the late-night shows after it. I think G.E. decided, 'We can't go on doing this.'"

Whereas networks have found it difficult to charge ever-higher advertising rates in the face of declining ratings, big cable channels—like USA, TNT, and TBS—have flourished with the millions of dollars in subscription fees from cable operators that they receive, on top of advertising.

"The cable players have a robust affiliate fee stream that allows them to better finance

original programming," said Anthony DiClemente, a media analyst at Barclays Capital. "The main structural issue right now with broadcast [networks] is that the vast majority of revenues are from advertising."

Profit margins for cable networks are also much better than broadcast networks'. Derek Baine, a senior analyst at SNL Kagan, said big cable networks earned profit margins of 40 to 60 percent, while a good year for a broadcast network is a 10 percent profit margin.

Illustrative of this is a comparison of NBC to ESPN, one of the most popular cable channels. Last year, revenue for the two networks was roughly equal. NBC, according to SNL Kagan, generated about $5.6 billion in advertising dollars; ESPN generated a total of about $6 billion in revenue—$1.6 billion from advertising and $4.4 billion in subscriber fees. But ESPN was vastly more profitable. Its cash flow was about $1.4 billion, whereas NBC's was $304 million.

"The viewership continues to migrate from broadcast to cable," Mr. Baine said. "Over time, advertisers have continued to pay premium prices for prime time, but over time the audiences continue to go down. Eventually you are going to hit an inflection point."

Perhaps the most steadfast defender of the broadcast model is Leslie Moonves, the chief executive of CBS. He says he believes broadcasters can survive without the additional subscription fee revenue that goes to cable networks. He frequently points to the power of broadcasters both to reach mass audiences and to create

assets unmatched by anything on the cable side of the business.

Though he declined to comment for this article, Mr. Moonves, in an appearance at the Paley Center for Media in Manhattan earlier this week, said he had recently closed a deal for a new CBS drama, *NCIS: Los Angeles*, to sell its repeats for the impressive price of $2.35 million an episode. The buyer? USA network, which happens to be owned by NBC.

The original *NCIS* is the most successful program on USA—in repeat episodes.

Mr. Moonves noted that the two NCIS editions taken together "are a billion-dollar property." No show created on any cable network has been able to approach that level of revenue. "My model isn't broken," he said.

CBS executives have pointed out recently that the advertising market has started to show signs of revival. The so-called scatter market, where advertisers buy time on an individual commercial basis, is up about 25 percent, the CBS executives said.

But the cultural implications of the decline of broadcast television may be as profound as the business forces at play. Gone are the days when the nation gathered around television sets in the evening to watch, say, *The Cosby Show* or *All in the Family* and then chat about it the next day at work.

Broadcast television was "a place, an arena, where ideas were presented in a fashion in which people could become attached to or explore," said Mr. Newcomb, the professor.

"Issues with civil rights and the women's movement were

embedded into entertainment programs, and people would see them and either accept it or reject it," he said. "Today, you can watch TV and not have to be challenged."

Source: New York Times, *November 20, 2009.*

NETWORK TELEVISION

A television network comprises two or more stations that broadcast from one location. In the United States, there are four major networks—CBS, NBC, ABC, and Fox—each of which has more than 200 stations or affiliates, most often local television outlets. The exceptions are those stations that are owned and operated by the network, such as WNBC and WABC in New York City.

The compensation accrued from advertising is shared by the networks with their affiliates for the rights to air the messages on the local stations. This arrangement enables the advertiser to pay a specified amount for a commercial to be shown on every affiliated station in the network. Major companies such as automobile manufacturers and food-producing giants benefit from such widespread advertising, but most retailers have neither the need for such widespread advertising nor the willingness to expend the millions of dollars annually for this type of advertising. Except for the few giants such as JCPenney, Sears, Target, Macy's, and Wal-Mart, with outlets all across the country, such advertising is cost-prohibitive unless the advertiser is convinced the commercial will significantly increase sales. Table 9.1 features the top ten broadcast television programs for the week of June 29, 2009, the majority of which attract major advertisers.

TABLE 9.1

	Top 10 Broadcast Television Programs, Week of June 29, 2009 (Live + SD)			
RANK*	PROGRAM	NETWORK	RATING**	VIEWERS***
1	America's Got Talent (Tue.)	NBC	7.6	13.145
2	America's Got Talent (Wed. 9 PM)	NBC	6.9	11.44
3	NCIS	CBS	6.8	10.827
4	The Mentalist (Tue.)	CBS	6.7	10.545
5	The Mentalist	CBS	6.5	9.788
6	Two and a Half Men	CBS	5.9	9.28
7	CSI	CBS	5.5	8.288
7	CSI: NY	CBS	5.5	8.207
8	48 Hours Mystery	CBS	5.4	8.02
8	60 Minutes	CBS	5.4	8.392
9	Criminal Minds	CBS	5.4	8.043
9	CSI: Miami	CBS	5.4	8.011

Live + SD, viewing estimates that include DVR playback on the same day, defined as 3 AM to 3 AM.

*Rank is based on U.S. Household Rating percentage from Nielsen Media's National People Meter Sample.

**A household rating is the estimate of the size of a television audience relative to the total universe expressed as a percentage. As of September 1, 2008, there are an estimated 114,500,000 television households in the United States. A single national household rating represents 1,145,000 households.

***Measured in millions, this includes all persons over the age of 2 years.

Source: Data from Nielsen Media Research.

SPOT TELEVISION

Spot television is a concept whereby national advertisers purchase time in specific locations to air their advertising messages. They forego the use of blanket coverage offered by the networks in order to target their commercials to more clearly defined trading areas that fit their needs. Spot television is especially beneficial to retailers with limited trading areas. Blanket coverage for these merchants would be wasteful because the potential purchasers are not within reach of their stores. Companies such as SteinMart Inc., an off-price chain whose units are geographically limited to certain areas of the country and who do not offer online or catalogue purchasing, pinpoint the spots where they would like their commercials to air.

Use of these spot buys is somewhat more difficult than the purchase of overall network usage. Each spot must be carefully assessed to make certain the demographics of the stations coincide with the retailer's consumer profile and that the choices will result in a positive return on investment.

SYNDICATION

In the world of the broadcast media, the right to run television and radio shows without going to a network is known as **syndication**. Many shows that have gone off the air in their regular network formats retain life as syndicated shows. They are usually reruns of shows, some extremely successful and others marginally so, that still attract audiences. The shows are sold by a **syndicator** to one station in each media area or market. Unlike network television that runs the shows on all of its affiliates in the same time slot (of course, varying by time zones) and on the same day of the week, syndications are aired in different time slots. The purchases are outright sales and allow each station to insert the ads they choose.

The myriad of shows in syndication range from those that first aired as early as the 1950s and run the gamut from game shows to situation comedies, such as *I Love Lucy* and *The Beverly Hillbillies* (Figure 9.1). Many of today's successful television programs are syndicated. Those with more of a blockbuster appeal, such as *Wheel of Fortune*, cost

9.1 Syndication allows for the sale of different shows to different markets. © *Bettman/Corbis.*

AUDIENCE PENETRATION

With a single showing, a television commercial can reach untold numbers of viewers. Since 99 percent of the households in the United States have at least one television, and many have more, the consumer is easily reached. **Audience penetration** is even greater today with the advent of high-definition television (HDTV) receivers featured at sports bars and other restaurants. Unlike newspapers and magazines, which must be purchased, television advertising automatically reaches the masses.

AUDIENCE SEGMENTATION

In addition to the vast numbers of viewers, television advertising may be focused on particular groups. By promoting their merchandise on local television, which uses **audience segmentation**, retailers can be assured that their messages will reach those within easy access to their stores. Local news programs, for example, are excellent outlets for retail commercials.

COST PER VIEWER

Although the initial investment for television advertising is significant for most retailers, the costs per viewer are relatively modest. With repeated use of the same commercial, the costs per viewer are also minimized, and rerunning the same ad tends to make a better impression on television viewers than if new ads were aired at each showing.

LACK OF COMPETITION

When a commercial comes on the screen, it is the only one that can be seen. Unlike newspapers and magazines, where the turn of a page brings new ads into focus, the viewing audience sees only one commercial at a time. Even when watchers move from channel to channel during commercial time, it is likely that they will see the same commercial on other stations. Many advertisers use more than one channel with the same ad at the same time to maximize exposure.

MULTIPLE SIMULTANEOUS VIEWING

Television viewing is often a family affair, so it is likely that more than one person will view a program together. The advertiser can thereby reach many people at one time. Televised sporting events are often seen by a host of individuals with the same interests. In this case, the advertisement gets more attention than does an ad in a newspaper or magazine, which is read only by individuals. General-interest shows are also excellent outlets for television commercials with family appeal. If companies such as Marshalls, with a wealth of men's, women's, and children's merchandise, advertise on these television shows, someone in the family is likely to be motivated to visit the store.

DRAMATIC MESSAGING

With the aid of visuals, sound, motion, and color, a television commercial can capture the viewer's attention like no other advertising media. The excitement generated by commercials, especially those that are repeated frequently, is without competition from newspapers, magazines, or direct mail.

Despite the benefits of television advertising, it has some disadvantages that those considering purchasing airtime should consider.

OVERALL COST

Television advertising is expensive. The costs of production and airtime for repeated runs (key to a commercial's success) are usually beyond the budgets of all but the retail giants. Even the lower rates of local spots at off hours and of cable television airtime can be cost prohibitive for merchants. And although the cost of changing a print ad is minimal, making a change to a television commercial requires new scriptwriting and reshooting—and more money.

BREVITY OF MESSAGE LIFE

In comparison with the print media, the television message is extremely brief. Adding to the problem is the advent of recording devices such as **Comcast on Demand** and **TIVO**, which enable the viewer to bypass commercials. Even though the newspaper's message generally lasts only until the next day's edition arrives, that is still much longer than a television commercial.

CLUTTER

In addition to being able to watch their favorite shows, viewers are bombarded with numerous messages during the showing period. Some programs show as many as eight different advertisements during a commercial break.

Known as **clutter**, this nonprogram material is ever increasing. Industry watchdogs report that as much as 15 minutes in an hour-long presentation is filled with clutter. In an industry in which one or two companies once sponsored an entire television show, the trend now is for numerous advertisers to fill the commercial space of each show.

Evaluating Media Efficiency

Before an advertiser makes his or her advertising decisions, two different formulas are considered: **cost per thousand (CPM)** and **cost prepoint (CPP)** measurements. CPM is a ratio based on the amount it will cost to reach 1,000 people, and CPP indicates how much it will cost to purchase one point, or 1 percent, of the population in the area that is being evaluated. Each measure is independent of the other, and when used jointly, they help advertisers make the soundest decisions regarding the potential for advertising effectiveness.

Another measurement is the rating-point system, which is used for television viewing analysis. It is a system that tells the advertiser the potential reach based on the percentage of television households in a defined market.

Television Rating Systems

When advertisers decide where they are going to spend the dollars they have allocated for television advertising, they want to know where they will get the biggest bang for their buck. They are not interested in qualitative evaluation; instead, they base their decision on quantitative analysis. The viewership characteristics and size of the viewing audience count most in their decision making. By being able to predetermine which programs provide the most appropriate viewers as potential purchasers of their products, they can more effectively use their promotional budgets.

Before making any decisions in terms of where and when to advertise on television, it is essential to know some basic terms:

- *Ratings:* **Ratings** are expressed in points. Each point is 1 percent of the total viewing audience in a particular market. Thus, the more rating points, the more people will see the show and its commercials.

- *Share:* **Share** is a measurement of proportion of all of the viewers who are watching television at a particular time. If the program's share is 20, then approximately one-fifth of the viewers are watching this offering.

- *Frequency:* **Frequency** is the number of times an individual is exposed to a scheduled spot. The more frequent the airings, the more likely the commercial will be remembered. Most professionals agree that it takes a minimum of five airings for a message to be recalled by the viewer.

- *Reach:* **Reach** is the number of households or individuals who were exposed to the media schedule. If the targeted audience is 300,000 women between the ages of 30 to 45, and 100,000 were exposed to the commercial, the reach is then 33.33 percent.

There are different systems and companies involved in determining the ratings.

THE DIARY METHOD

During the formative years of the industry, the **diary method** was the mainstay of television ratings. The system required that a member of a household record which programs were being watched. It also addressed beneficial characteristics of the family. Today, with the increased number of receivers in a single household and the trend toward individual viewing, the diary system no longer plays a role in television ratings. Diary-only markets have been converted to electronic measurement.

ELECTRONIC METERS

Electronic meters allow for more accurate viewing estimates every day of the year, and they provide key demographics. Nielsen Media Research uses the **Local People Meter (LPM)** (Figure 9.3) for accurate measurement. Its LPMs currently measure more than 30 percent of both U.S. households and individuals. By the time the process of increasing the number of its participating households is completed, samples representing 50 percent of local households will be measured by LPMs.

Network Price Chart

TABLE 9.3

SUNDAY	7 PM	8 PM	9 PM	10 PM
ABC	America's Funniest Videos $122,000	Extreme Makeover: Home Ed. $293,000	Desperate Housewives $394,000	Brothers & Sisters $242,000
CBS	60 Minutes $118,000	The Amazing Race $136,000	Cold Case $136,000	Without a Trace $181,000
NBC	Football Night in America $75,000	Sunday Night Football/America's Got Talent/Apprentice/Medium $342,000/$116,000/$168,000/$125,000		
FOX	Comedy Repeat $160,000	The Simpsons/American Dad $293,000/$222,000	Family Guy/War at Home $163,000/169,000	No Fox Programming
CW	Chris/All of Us $82,000/$59,000	Girlfriends/The Game $64,000/$51,000	America's Top Model (Encore) $40,000	No CW Programming

MONDAY	7 PM	8 PM	9 PM	10 PM
ABC		Wife Swap $99,000	Bachelor: Rome $170,000	What About Brian $131,000
CBS		The Class/Met Your Mother $157,000/$173,000	Two & Half Men/Christine $275,000/$211,000	CSI: Miami $259,000
NBC		Deal or No Deal $167,000	Heroes $171,000	Studio 60 $210,000
FOX		Prison Break $193,000	Vanished/24 $140,000/$364,000	No Fox Programming
CW		7th Heaven $72,000	Runaway $56,000	No CW Programming

TUESDAY	7 PM	8 PM	9 PM	10 PM
ABC		Dancing with Stars $229,000	Knights/Help Me $131,000/$140,000	Boston Legal $140,000
CBS		NCIS $137,000	The Unit $159,000	Smith $117,000
NBC		Friday Night Lights $116,000	Law & Order: Criminal Intent $151,000	Law & Order: SVU $204,000
FOX		Standoff/American Idol $110,000/$594,000	House $284,000	No Fox Programming
CW		Gilmore Girls $93,000	Veronica Mars $52,000	No CW Programming

WEDNESDAY	7 PM	8 PM	9 PM	10 PM
ABC		Dancing with Stars $265,000	Lost $328,000	The Nine $224,000
CBS		Jericho $98,000	Criminal Minds $143,000	CSI: New York $182,000
NBC		30 Rock/20 Good Years $176,000/$120,000	The Biggest Loser $136,000	Kidnapped $180,000
FOX		Bones $131,000	Justice/Idol Results/Loop $113,000/$620,000/$310,000	No Fox Programming
CW		America's Next Top Model $135,000	One Tree Hill $70,500	No CW Programming

THURSDAY	7 PM	8 PM	9 PM	10 PM
ABC		Ugly Betty $93,000	Grey's Anatomy $344,000	Six Degrees $172,000
CBS		Survivor: Cook's Island $296,000	CSI: Crime Scene Investigation $347,000	Shark $196,000
NBC		Earl/Office $212,000/$219,000	Deal or No Deal $141,000	ER/Black Donnellys' $282,000/$200,000
FOX		Til Death/Happy Hour $127,000/95,000	The O.C. $128,000	No Fox Programming
CW		Smallville $84,000	Supernatural $66,000	No CW Programming

FRIDAY	7 PM	8 PM	9 PM	10 PM
ABC		America's Favorite Videos NR	Men in Trees $114,000	20/20 $120,000
CBS		Ghost Whisperer $106,000	Close to Home $110,000	Numbers $124,000
NBC		Crossing Jordan $80,000	Las Vegas $99,000	Law & Order $119,000
FOX		Nanny 911 $58,000	Trading Spouses $50,000	No Fox Programming
CW		WWE Smackdown $25,000		No CW Programming

SATURDAY	7 PM	8 PM	9 PM	10 PM
ABC		ABC Saturday Night College Football $135,000		
CBS		Crimetime Saturday $100,000	Crimetime Saturday $82,000	48 Hours Mystery $77,000
NBC		Dateline $45,000		Drama Encores $50,000
FOX		Cops/Cops $53,000/64,000	America's Most Wanted $66,000	No Fox Programming
CW		No CW Programming		

Averages compiled from the estimates of media-buying agencies as reported by *Ad Age*, 2006–2007.

9.4 Cable TV ads are comparatively inexpensive.
TV courtesy of iStockphoto/Philip Prinz; television ad:
Image courtesy of The Advertising Archives.

9.5 The Sony Walkman innovation led to an increase of radio listenership.
© Ocean/Corbis.

radio listeners) for online radio listening measured close to 8.5 million on a weekly, Monday to Sunday, 6 AM to midnight daypart. From every indication, the numbers are likely to increase. Table 9.6, as reported by Arbitron, features seven of the online radio services, along with important breakdowns of the listening audience.

Although less important than the print media and television in terms of retail advertising, radio is still used by some merchants, most notably the large chains, to reach their customers and to motivate others to become customers.

Today's Radio Environment

Today, there are many different radio programming formats on the air for the listener to enjoy. Some of them come without any cost to the audience, and others require a fee for listening. Once the domain of individual ownership, the business of radio changed when the **Telecommunications Act** was passed in 1966. Until that time, the Federal Communications Commission (FCC) restricted ownership to seven AM and FM stations. Today, radio ownership is a different story. The vast majority of the stations are owned by major conglomerates such as Clear Channel and Infinity Broadcasting, the leaders, with the former owning approximately 1,200 stations. The magnitude of these empires has helped return radio to a healthy position as an advertising outlet, although for the retailer, its use still pales by comparison with television, newspapers, magazines, Internet advertising, and direct mail.

Satellite radio and online radio services have transformed radio into a more popular medium. Satellite radio, whose listenership is growing, is different from conventional radio in that the consumer is charged a fee for the service. **XM** and **Sirius**, once competitors in the satellite radio race, have now joined forces as one organization. Consumers subscribe to both XM and Sirius for a combined rate. Although the satellite concept has increased listening audiences, it is not as important to advertisers as traditional radio because many of the programs have no commercials (Figure 9.6).

All important to online radio is the number of Americans who are using this medium. According to Arbitron, 42 million people listen to online radio today, up 27 percent from 33 million in 2008 and more than double the number of listeners in 2005. Also reported is that 17 percent of

9.6 Satellite radio has transformed radio into a more popular medium.
Justin Sullivan/Getty News Images.

IMMEDIATE, PERSONAL COMMUNICATION

Radio listeners can hear their favorite music, news commentators, and sports programs anytime of the day or night and often can communicate with the program hosts. Calling in is often invited by the program hosts so that a two-way dialogue may take place that adds interest to the show. The popularity of Rush Limbaugh, Joe Scarborough, Ed Shultz, and others has increased because of the dialogues that take place between them and their audience while they are on the air. Music stations often invite callers to ask for their favorite songs or performers, and personal advice experts welcome questions from the listening audience.

AUDIENCE SELECTIVITY

The diversity of radio programming makes it possible for advertisers to reach carefully selected markets. Fashion retailers might advertise during a program that deals with women's issues. Golf attire retailers might choose programs that deal with sporting events. Given the enormous number of shows that deal with a variety of topics, retailers may select the ones most likely to be of interest to their potential purchasers.

COSTS PER LISTENER

When it comes to broadcast advertising, radio is considerably less costly than television. Not only is airtime less expensive but so are the production costs. When compared to the other media, the CPM is considerably less. The exception is outdoor advertising.

AUDIENCE REACH

Local radio in particular is an excellent outlet for pinpointing an audience. Magazines and newspapers, unless they are regional editions, reach too far from the point of purchase for the average retailer to take advantage of the readers unless their ads feature online and catalogue shopping.

LATE INSERTIONS

Unlike television and magazines, which require long lead times to place an ad, radio commercials may be inserted in a relatively short period of time. This is especially useful when last-minute sales are being offered.

Despite the advantages of radio advertising, it has some limitations that must be considered, as discussed next.

LACK OF THE VISUAL ELEMENT

Although radio offers the benefit of being able to motivate shoppers with spoken messages, it does not offer the visual image of the merchandise being offered for sale. "A picture is worth a thousand words" is a cliché, but it adequately describes one of the distinct drawbacks of radio. All of the other media offer visuals that immediately reveal the merchandise's appeal. Fashion retailers rely on drawings and photographs to motivate consumer interest in their newspaper and magazine ads and on colorful, live action in their television advertising. Radio offers only a spoken message to stimulate interest. It is, therefore, beneficial to retailers only for sales announcements and promotional endeavors.

LISTENER CONCENTRATION

Often, radio listeners do not pay strict attention to what is on the air. An individual might tune into a music station and tend to other activities, such as homework, household chores, conversation with others, and so forth. Unlike newspaper and magazine reading and television viewing, radio does not require strict focus on words or images.

MESSAGE LIFE

The radio **message life** is just a few seconds and might easily be missed by the listener if strict attention is not paid to the program. Unlike the print media, where the ad may be seen repeatedly, once a radio commercial is missed, it is gone forever. Only when radio messages are run again and again is there hope that they will be heard.

RETENTION OF PERTINENT INFORMATION

Prints ads sometimes feature coupons, telephone numbers, or Web site information that require close inspection if they are to be used. On the radio, however, information such as numbers to call or Web sites to log on to quickly disappear without giving the listener a chance to keep them in mind. The motorist, for example, without the benefit of paper and pen, is unlikely to remember important information, which makes the commercial less beneficial.

Buying Airtime

Each station determines the rates they charge for advertising. The costs are based on the time of day the ad runs, the length of the commercial, and the number of times per week the commercial is aired. Many stations price peak driving times at the highest levels. Conversely, the less important the airtime in terms of potential listenership, the lower the costs. The exact costs are available on rate cards provided by the station.

The rate cards give the advertisers the exact costs of running their radio commercials; however, there are other factors that should be considered before any contractual arrangement is completed. Among the considerations are the demographics of the audience reached by the station and the production costs of the ad.

Demographic analysis should include a breakdown of listeners by age, listeners by gender, areas served by the station, per capita income of the listening audience, median household income, percentage of household by income, and so forth. After these figures have been carefully examined, and they fit the needs of the advertisers, the actual advertising rates should be evaluated. A sample rate card is featured in Table 9.8.

TABLE 9.8 Sample Rate Card: WKRK, North Carolina

DAYPART	SHOW	15 SECS	30 SECS	45 SECS	60 SECS	1 MIN 15 SECS	1 MIN 30 SECS	1 MIN 45 SECS	2 MINS
6 AM–9 AM	Young & Verna Show	$7.50	$11.25	$13.50	$15.00	$18.00	$19.50	$21.00	$22.50
9 AM–2 PM	PartyLine & Midday Report	$7.50	$11.25	$13.50	$15.00	$18.00	$19.50	$21.00	$22.50
2 AM–7 PM	Afternoon Drive Time	$7.00	$10.50	$12.60	$14.00	$16.80	$18.20	$19.60	$21.00
6 AM–7 PM	Run of Station	$6.00	$9.00	$10.80	$12.00	$14.40	$15.60	$16.80	$18.00
12 AM–11:59 PM	Best Times Available	$3.50	$5.25	$6.30	$7.00	$8.40	$9.10	$9.80	$10.50
Production Fee:	$19 per produced radio commercial (includes written script and recorded commercial by a professional production company)								
Live Commercials	Commercials called in live on-the-air or read live on-the-air by our announcers are billed at a minimum 60 second rate and are excluded from our "Buy One, Get One Free" Promotion.								
Buy One Get One Free	For Every Produced Commercial you purchase on WKRK, you will receive one FREE BONUS commercial that will air in our "Best Time Available" period. "Best Times Available" means that we search for the HIGHEST RATED SHOWS to place your free commercial. If all those breaks are sold out, then we search for the NEXT BEST TIME that we have available to place your commercial so that you get the best bang for your buck. We want to get the best possible results that we can. Advertising on WKRK doesn't COST you money . . . It MAKES you money!								
AT NO EXTRA CHARGE	You are purchasing advertising on WKRK Radio (1320AM) in Murphy, NC. At no extra charge to you, your advertising message will air on WKRK's WeatherCenter (Cable TV Channel 25). Your message also is heard around the world via the Internet. WKRK broadcasts our radio signal on our very popular Web site. People all over the world tune into WKRK at www.country.am.								

Courtesy of WKRK.

Arbitron

Founded in Washington, DC, in 1949, and now headquartered in Columbia, Maryland, Arbitron is the premier radio audience research company in the United States. The major purpose of the company is to collect listening audience data and provide its findings to advertisers, ad agencies, and radio stations, all of whom have a keen interest in radio advertising.

Arbitron uses two methods of data collection. For many years, the company has relied on diaries. Each participating household is given a diary for each family member who is 12 years or older. Each diary is for 1 week of radio listening; it is completed and returned to the company for analysis. Arbitron uses a 12-week rating period for each market it analyzes. The magnitude of this research can be best understood by the fact that more than 2.5 million diaries are distributed in a single year.

In an attempt to more accurately record radio listening, Arbitron introduced the Portable People Meter (PPM). The device is similar to a cell phone and is worn by recruited listeners, who are paid for their services. The PPM electronically gathers the information, which is coded to identify the source of each broadcast and radio station. Currently, PPMs are used in limited markets, but Arbitron expects to expand their use to a broader market. The advantage of using the PPM is that it can record data no matter where the participant is listening to the radio. With the increase in automobile listenership, for example, where diary recording is difficult, the meter offers an obvious advantage in accurate data collection.

In addition to the diary and PPM data collection methods, Arbitron offers a service for national network radio. Known as RADAR, the reports generated are based on information gathered in 7-day diaries.

Arbitron offers customized research projects for every facet of the radio industry.

The Future of Radio

Brad Saul
January 8, 2009

The radio industry is clearly under siege. It is being attacked on multiple fronts. Certainly, the economy is the biggest culprit. With Detroit's automakers in severe economic distress and cutting ad budgets dramatically, the impact on radio is dramatic. Almost 25 percent of local radio revenue is derived from auto manufacturers, auto dealers, or related services.

The next barrier to radio's future is the continued growth of new media, specifically online advertising. After several years of little to no growth, radio revenues began to fall [in] 2007 and then more precipitously in 2008. Although Internet advertising growth for 2009 was projected to slow, its continued rise directly affects dollars that would normally be spent on radio advertising.

The third issue radio faces is one of its own making: consolidation. Since the Telecommunications Act of 1996 was put into effect, the consolidation of the industry has created a homogeneous, far less creative industry. Innovation and new talent simply are not being drawn to the industry.

In part, the reason for this begins with younger people. I am 48 years old. I was bitten by the radio bug when I was 13. All I wanted to ever do was be in radio. Today's teenagers have no such love affair with our industry. They are consumed with texting, social networking, television, and cellular telephones. There is no up-and-coming group of people for our industry.

My alma mater, Northwestern University, offers a degree in Radio, Television and Film in its School of Communications. Yet, it does not offer a single course in radio. The dean of the school says, "It is because students are not interested in radio." If students are not interested in radio, where is the next generation of our industry going to come from?

Consolidation also took away what radio always had that no other medium did: a farm system. If you wanted to be in radio, you would go to work for a station in a small town somewhere in the middle of nowhere, and work your way up to the major markets. Today, those small market radio stations are laying off employees, getting rid of most if not all of their local programming, thus eliminating the farm system altogether.

Yet, radio does have some very positive stories to tell. More than 230 million people listen to the radio for an hour or more each day. That listening takes place in the car. Do not be worried about satellite radio. It is a business that is on life support and was doomed from its very beginning. Every pay radio service since the first was created in 1940, radio for 5 cents per day, has failed.

XM/Sirius have done a wonderful job of accumulating billions of dollars in net. The car manufacturers embrace them. Why? They had real estate to sell them inside their car. The satellite companies paid to have satellite radios installed as factory built. With car sales at record lows, new listeners to satellite radio have dramatically dropped. Retail sales of satellite radios are [at a] near standstill. For those receiving satellite radio in the car when they purchase a new vehicle, most receive a free subscription for at least 1 year. The conversion rate, that is, the number of people who turn into paid subscribers after their free trial period expires, is less than 25 percent. There are people who are true audiophiles who love the service: certainly long-haul truck drivers and people who spend an inordinate amount of time in their cars benefit from it. Yet, it is a business that likely will be out of business within the next 2 to 4 years.

The reason for that is simple. That is the growth of Internet radio. As WiFi and Wi-Max get built out, and Internet radios are installed in automobiles, people will have access to thousands of radio stations at no cost. That eliminates any reason for anyone to pay to receive a radio service. Internet radio today is more or less where cable television was circa 1980. It took 10 or so years for the infrastructure to get built out, but here we sit today in 2009, and 80 percent of all television viewing, be it over-the-air television or cable networks, takes place either via cable or satellite. Only 20 percent of television viewing takes place over the air. Television stations have preserved their values because of "must carry." Local cable systems are required by law to carry all of the local television stations on their cable systems. Radio has no such equivalent. That means that when wireless broadband is built out, radio stations will face challenges from anyone who chooses to go into the broadcast business and the value of the radio station "sticks" will plummet. Wall Street has already seen this writing on the wall. In part, that is why there is no pure play radio stock that is above $1.00.

What that means for the radio industry is [that] it needs to use the power of the brands that they have today, when only 78 million people are listening to Internet radio each day, to stake out beachfront property on the Internet now. If stations fail to embrace this opportunity, they will be swallowed up in the next 6 to 8 years and overtaken by Internet radio services such as Pandora, Accu-Radio, and others.

Internet radio is already being made available as a factory-installed option in many automobiles. Chrysler, General Motors, Saab, BMW, and Mercedes-Benz already offer Internet radio receivers as factory-installed options. It is simply a matter of time before the infrastructure takes hold.

So how does all of this relate to the precipitous drop in radio revenues? It's a perfect storm. The economy, the growth of the Internet and other new media, the loss of automotive advertising and related industries, as well as radio having lost its "coolness" along with the lack of a new generation coming into the industry, have resulted in radio being in the place that it is in.

Radio is not going away. It will find a way to redefine itself. There are enough forward-thinking minds in our industry that will creatively take advantage of the opportunities I have described to reinvent this industry. It will not come without a great deal of pain. Industry revenues will likely drop again in 2010. My belief is that radio will end up somewhere around $13 to $14 billion a year in ad revenue. Profit margins, which are already being preserved through layoffs of talent and staff, will continue to allow radio to sign off significant free cash flow of 30 to 40 percent. However, the local flavor of the industry will be dramatically reduced. I have been involved in the radio industry for 35 years. I love it dearly. This past November, I attended the Radio Hall of Fame ceremony and broadcast in Chicago. I found myself with my peers following the event asking this question: "Will this event still be here 10 years from now?" The answer is, I am not sure.

This is a defining moment for our industry. Creativity, hard work, and innovation have to be employed to keep this industry vital. If radio sits on the sidelines and does not try to reinvent itself, its future will be rather cloudy.

Terms of the Trade

audience penetration

audience segmentation

cable television

clutter

cost per thousand (CPM)

Comcast on Demand

cost prepoint (CPP)

cume

dayparts

diary method

electronic meters

frequency

Local People Meter (LPM)

local television

local television spots

message life

metered devices

network television

online radio services

package pricing

Portable People Meter

RADAR

ratings

reach

satellite radio

share

Sirius

spot television

syndication

syndicator

TIVO

Telecommunications Act

XM

Summary of Key Points

◆ Although television remains the dominant medium in most households in the United States, it does not hold that place for retail advertising.

◆ There are many facets of television today, including network television, spot television, syndication, and cable.

◆ One of the major reasons for the use of television advertising is its significant audience penetration.

◆ Some of the major advantages of television advertising include the low cost per viewer, multiple simultaneous viewing, and dramatic messaging.

◆ Despite its advantages as an advertising medium, television also has such disadvantages as overall cost, brevity of the message life, and clutter.

◆ Understanding television rating systems begins with knowledge of such words as *ratings*, *share*, *frequency*, and *reach*. When these are mastered, the comprehension of the rating systems will help advertisers select particular shows on which to air their commercials.

◆ Ratings are derived from the data collected via the diary method or the electronic meter. The latter enables the researcher to collect more accurate viewing estimates.

◆ Airtime costs vary according to the television outlets used, whether the program is for network coverage or local use, and the daypart when the commercial is aired.

◆ Satellite and online radio services have expanded the impact of commercial delivery.

◆ With a wealth of mobility opportunity, the radio has the advantage of reaching more listeners than ever.

◆ One of the drawbacks of radio advertising is the lack of the visual element. This is extremely important to merchants who must show their products in order to motivate purchasing.

◆ Radio airtime costs are listed on rate cards that are supplied by the station. Some offer additional rate cards that feature special package pricing.

◆ In an attempt to gather more accurate data, Arbitron introduced the Portable People Meter, which electronically gathers information from individuals no matter where they are as they listen to the radio.

For Discussion

1. Why do most retail operations shy away from using national network television programming and choose local television instead if the former is considered the premium medium?

2. What television concept has saved programs from going off the air and instead remaining as viable shows?

3. Why was cable television initially introduced in the United States, and how has programming changed since its inception?

4. If television is considered to be the most expensive advertising medium, how can the costs be defended?

5. What is meant by the word *clutter* as it relates to television programming?

6. How does the diary method of data collection differ from the electronic meter?

7. What are some of the options offered to those who wish to advertise but consider network costs too high to warrant advertising on television?

8. Discuss the term *dayparts* as it relates to television and radio advertising.

9. How has today's radio been transformed to make the medium more appealing to listeners?

10. Discuss how radio has moved from the home to other venues to become a more important player in advertising.

11. List and briefly describe the four major disadvantages of radio as an advertising tool.

12. What is a rate card, and what are some of its features?

13. How does the diary method for collecting data differ from the Portable People Meter introduced by Arbitron?

2. Make certain that the contact understands that the information will be used to complete a college course project.

3. Visit an electronics retailer for the purpose of preparing a report on the different types of radios it offers for sale. Every category should be included, such as AM/FM radios, satellite radios, and so forth. With the information gathered, prepare a report that addresses the following:

   a. The number of different brands in each category.

   b. The price ranges for each type of radio.

   c. The capabilities of each radio.

Exercises and Projects

1. Either by writing, e-mailing, telephoning, or personally visiting a major retailer such as Macy's, Best Buy, Marshalls, Jos. A. Banks, or Men's Wearhouse, arrange to interview someone in the advertising department for the purpose of discussing the company's television advertising commitments. The information that should be obtained for use in a research paper should include the following:

   a. The size of the company in terms of units.

   b. The trading areas it reaches.

   c. The demographics of its market.

   d. The type of television advertising it uses.

   e. The expected sales increase after a commercial has been aired.

Web Site Exploration for In-Depth Analysis

E-Poll Market Research
http://www.epollresearch.com
   This company is a major resource for television ratings and trends.

Arbitron
http://www.arbitron.com
   This major radio rating organization offers much more than ratings.

Syndicated Network Television Association
http://www.snta.com
   Syndicated Network Television Association answers all questions relating to syndication.

Nielsen Media Practice
http://www.nielsenmedia.com
   The Nielsen site offers information about television ratings, services, and how Nielsen families are selected.

CHAPTER OBJECTIVES

After you have completed this chapter, you will be able to discuss:

★ The significant increase in Internet advertising by the retailing community and the demographics of the audiences to whom it is directed.

★ The major adult Internet population and which age segment is experiencing the greatest growth.

★ The characteristics of the retail Web sites in existence today.

★ How merchants are using e-mail as an advertising tool and the different motivational concepts they use in e-mail headlines.

★ Many of the do's and don'ts of Internet e-mail messaging.

★ The advantages and disadvantages of Internet advertising.

★ The focus of some of the major social networking sites, special considerations for membership, and the demographics of the people who become members.

★ The pluses and minuses of social networking advertising.

★ The direct-mail pieces retailers use to bring business to their companies.

★ How a company such as Patagonia uses the catalogue differently from most other retail operations.

★ How mailing lists are obtained in addition to those that are constructed by the merchants themselves.

★ The ways in which retailers can maximize the effectiveness of direct mail usage.

Direct Marketing: The Internet, Social Networking, *and* Direct Mail

One of the ways in which retailers are successfully reaching their consumers is through the use of numerous direct-marketing options. Newspaper and magazine advertising has declined, and the use of television has proved too costly for all but the giant retailers in the industry, but the use of the Internet, social networking, and direct mail continues to become more appealing than ever to retailers of all sizes and classifications. Whether it is the upscale fashion emporiums wanting to introduce their latest collections to the marketplace, the merchants who are trying to reduce their inventories by way of bargain pricing, or the retailers who want to reach regular clienteles or motivate newcomers to examine their merchandise offerings, **direct marketing** is an effective tool.

With the explosion of the computer industry that resulted in the vast majority of households having at least one computer in the home, the enormous increase in the sale of laptop computers for transport to every conceivable venue, and the availability of computers in the workplace where individuals often use them for personal use, online interaction has become the norm for retailers to interface with consumers. An examination of most e-mail accounts reveals that a host of merchants are using this communication device to reach potential purchasers. Retailers such as Bloomingdales, Neiman Marcus, Brooks Brothers, Wal-Mart, and others regularly use e-mail to reach targeted audiences.

Social networking, a relative newcomer to the communications scene, has become an overwhelming success as a tool for individuals to reach others. Sites such as Facebook and Twitter continue to grow and offer retailers an inexpensive way to advertise their wares.

Along with the comparatively new direct-marketing formats, the old standby of **direct mail** continues to serve retailers of every merchandise classification. A daily trip to the mailbox quickly emphasizes the significance of catalogue use by merchants. The regular delivery of these pieces indicates that retailers are getting significant returns from their use. Along with the catalogues, merchants are also using direct mail with statement enclosures that feature **hot items**, which are items that sell continuously, specially priced offerings, and letters that make special offers to regular and potential customers.

Each of the direct-marketing tools is fully explored in this chapter.

The Internet

Because computer usage has become a household and business staple, its applications for users have increased significantly. For the retailer, the Internet has been a boon to sales that have seen in-store shopping lag in some markets. With so many women in the workforce, with less time for on-site shopping, the Internet has proven to be an excellent alternative.

The popularity of the medium for retailers has been twofold. One is the Web site, which merchants of all sizes and classifications have

established to advertise their product offerings, services they offer to the purchaser, company policies regarding merchandise returns, practices concerning ethics, and so forth. Consumers are able to easily connect with a retailer's Web site in a matter of seconds and quickly browse the merchandise offerings. The other option is e-mail communication in which direct contact with regular customers and prospects can be accomplished. A relative newcomer on the Internet is the **social networking site**. Its importance as an advertising option for retailers and other businesses has grown so significantly that it is addressed in a separate section of this chapter.

Internet Demographics

An overview of the demographics of Internet users is essential in the evaluation of the medium as an advertising tool. With the facts in hand, retailers can justify its use as a means of spreading the word about their operations and merchandise offerings.

POPULATION OVERVIEW

The fact that the Internet has become a very important promotional tool is evident by the numbers of individuals with access. In 2009, nearly

TABLE 10.1 U.S. Internet Users and Penetration, 2008–2013

YEAR	USERS (MILLIONS)	PENETRATION (%)
2008	192.8	63.4
2009	199.2	64.8
2010	205.3	66.2
2011	210.9	67.3
2012	216.0	68.3
2013	221.1	69.2

Note: An Internet user is a person of any age who uses the Internet at any location at least once per month.

Source: Adapted from eMarketer, February 2009. http://www.emarketer.com/Reports/All/Emarketer_2000561.aspx (accessed Aug. 19, 2009).

TABLE 10.2 — Internet Users in North America (June 2008)

COUNTRY	USERS (MILLIONS)
North America (total)	248.2
United States	220.1
Canada	28.0
Greenland	0.05
Saint Pierre et Michelon	0

Note: 248,241,969 estimated Internet users in North America in June 2008.

Source: Adapted from Internet World Stats. http://www.internetworldstats.com (accessed March 16, 2010). Copyright © 2007, Miniwatts Marketing Group.

TABLE 10.3 — Internet Users in the World by Geographic Regions

REGION	USERS (MILLIONS)
Asia	657.2
Europe	393.4
North America	251.3
Latin America/Caribbean	173.6
Africa	54.2
Middle East	45.9
Oceania/Australia	20.8

Note: Estimated Internet users are 1,596,270,108 for March 31, 2009.

Source: Adapted from Internet World Stats.

200 million users, or 65 percent of the American population, had Internet access. Table 10.1 shows the increase in usage beginning in 2008 and the anticipated access through 2013.

Given the positive numbers in Table 10.1, it seems appropriate to predict that this medium will grow in terms of advertising usage. In Media Insight 10.1, Daniel Indiviglio projects that the Internet will be a vital part of the world of advertising.

A breakdown of Internet users in North America is featured in Table 10.2. Because the purchasing power by way of the Internet comes from places away from the United States, these figures are important to American merchants.

Some major retailers have expanded their operations offshore. Countries all over the globe account for sales at such operations as Gap, Wal-Mart, and many chain organizations. For these merchants and those wanting to encourage shopping from abroad, the figures regarding world-wide Internet usage is essential (see Table 10.3).

USER CHARACTERISTICS

Those who use the Internet for a variety of reasons, including shopping, are represented by all age groups, occupations, levels of education, and income. Some of the more pertinent observations in terms of user behavior and characteristics that should be examined by retailers include the following:

- The major adult Internet population is between 18 and 44 years of age, but the most significant age factor in terms of growth is the 70- to 75-year-old segment. The gray market is the fastest-growing group of Internet users (Figure 10.1).

- Higher-income families shop the Internet more than lower-income households. This is one of the reasons e-mail advertising by retailers is regularly used by such merchants as Bloomingdale's and Neiman Marcus (Figure 10.2).

- Retailers who look to online classified advertisements to fill positions, according to Pew Internet, are more likely to attract college graduates and higher-income earners than nongraduates and lower-income individuals. Table 10.4 shows the demographics of online classified users.

Get Used to Those Internet Ads

Daniel Indiviglio
August 5, 2009

It's no secret that the current recession has hit media companies hard. It's not only consumer demand for their product that suffers—advertisers are also cutting budgets. Although this has affected some types of media more than others, advertising's contraction has been felt across the broad spectrum. But after the recession ends, where will advertisers go?

Print

Of all the types of media, newspapers and magazines have probably been hurt the most. Their turmoil has been caused not only by the recession but also by fewer subscribers who increasingly prefer to do their reading for free online. A prime example of the industry's troubles comes through Condé Nast. The *New York Post* today reports particularly bad times at the company:

Nast is reeling from what is expected to be a loss of 5,000 ad pages this year, translating into a revenue shortfall of between $275 million and $350 million— and very likely pushing the publishing giant into the red.

After Condé Nast's ad-page tally last year fell 10.5 percent to 34,966 from the previous year, according to *Media Industry Newsletter*, the company behind mags like *Vogue* and *Vanity*

Fair is expected to see the ad-page count fall more than 20 percent this year.

Through these numbers, that 5,000-page ad loss would be a decrease of an additional 15 percent this year, after last year's 10.5 percent decrease. The firm has even hired an outside management-consulting firm, McKinsey & Co., to help. . . .

TV

Things aren't much better in television. A recent *Wall Street Journal* article provides an example of TV's troubles through its report on Disney's earnings. They own several TV networks, including the popular sports channel ESPN. *WSJ* says:

At ESPN, a drop in ad sales, higher programming costs, and the absence of money that was deferred into last year's third quarter combined to diminish revenue in the latest quarter. Currently, ad sales are about 10% lower than they were at the same time in 2008, Disney said.

So while TV might not be hurting quite as badly as print media, it's still feeling the pain.

DVR

A part of TV's troubles come through the digital video recording systems like TIVO. They're gaining in popularity, allowing viewers to fast-forward through commercials. Although that's great for viewers, it's terrible for the TV shows and networks that rely on revenue from the advertisements that can now be fast-forwarded through. From the ESPN example, the network should feel this effect even less than most stations. Of all the types of TV you can record, sports is among the least desirable because people like watching sports live. And yet, ESPN's advertising is still suffering.

DVR should continue to gain popularity in the near term. A recent Supreme Court decision cleared the way for getting rid of the boxes altogether, allowing cable subscribers to store their recorded TV shows remotely.

The Internet

The biggest threat to DVR in the long term, however, is the Internet. As new televisions continue to become more compatible with the Internet, DVR will become less necessary because people can simply enjoy the TV shows they missed online instead. TV station Web sites and others such as Hulu have already begun streaming some shows.

An article from Multichannel News characterizes CBS's chief research officer David Pollack as having exactly that belief. The article says:

Poltrack presented data from a variety of sources and studies indicating that Web video streaming is hitting critical mass, that older viewers are increasingly plugged in and watching video online, and that young viewers are increasingly consuming TV programming through a combination of

free over-the-air and broadband service. Overall, consumers overwhelmingly say they would choose to watch ads rather than pay for content.

He further posited that the DVR is poised to go the way of the VCR as near-term technology advancements will make it simpler for consumers to hook their computer directly to their TV screens, allowing online video streams to be played on the biggest tubes at home. DVR will essentially be replaced by computers.

The Future

So what does it all mean? The Internet is the future of advertising. I have always found it odd that advertisers are willing to pay so much more for ad space in a magazine than they do online. I can flip a page just as quickly as I can scroll past a banner. And the Internet has a huge advantage over print because you don't have to be a subscriber to see the advertisement—anyone casually surfing might stumble upon it.

The same can be said for TV versus the Internet. I can fast-forward through TV shows with a DVR or VCR. But most streaming content I've watched has short video clips that you can't fast-forward through. As viewing of online content continues to grow, so that online audiences come closer in number to TV audiences, I will be shocked if online advertising revenue does not also increase dramatically.

The challenge, of course, is preventing the proliferation of software designed to avoid that online advertising, like the DVR does for TV. That's a techno-logical barrier that media Web sites must overcome. I don't think that task is necessarily impossible, but I worry that, for every smart programmer the media industry hires to prevent such software, there will be a smarter hacker who can write more code to undo those preventative measures.

Still, the idea that such niche software can become wide-spread enough that the media industry's advertising efforts can be mostly neutralized seems doubtful. The majority of Americans are not computer savvy enough to visit hacker Web sites to download and install software to block legitimate ads. If I'm wrong, and most people do find a way to systematically eliminate commercials from online content, then advertising in entertainment will cease to exist. The only alternative that media will have under that circumstance will be subscriber fees or some other mechanism forcing users to pay for content.

As David Pollack is said to have asserted above, consum-ers overwhelmingly prefer ads over paying for content. So we might be better off just letting those commercials run, unless we'd rather pay for all the media we consume. As much as I love my DVR, I still find myself pausing recordings to run to the bathroom or grab a snack. Such errands could continue to occur in the future

just like they did in the past—during commercials. But now they'll be online instead of on TV.

Source: Daniel Indiviglio. "Get Used to Those Internet Ads." The Atlantic, August 5, 2009.

10.1 *(right)* The "gray market" is the fastest-growing Internet user segment.
Darius Ramazani/ Corbis.

10.2 *(below)* Higher-income families are regular shoppers at Neiman Marcus.
Courtesy Neiman Marcus.

Demographics of Online Classifieds Users

	% WHO HAVE *EVER* USED CLASSIFIED ADS SITES	% WHO USE THESE SITES ON A *TYPICAL DAY*
All Internet Users	49	9
Gender		
Men	51	12**
Women	47	7
Race		
Whites	49	10
Blacks	44	8
Hispanics	49*	10*
Education		
Less than high school	40*	7*
High school grad	45	8
Some college	49	12
College grad+	54**	9
Household Income		
Less than $30,000	42	6
$30,000–$49,999	47	9
$50,000–$74,000	56**	13**
$75,000 or more	56**	12**
Community Type		
Urban	47**	10**
Suburban	47**	10
Rural	32	4

Note: For all adult Internet users, *n* = 1,687, and the margin of error is ±3%. Sample sizes and margins of error vary by demographic group.

*Due to the relatively small sample sizes for these subgroups, please interpret the data with some caution. N = 110 for English-speaking Hispanics, and *n* = 85 for adults with less than a high school education.

**These demographic groups are significantly more likely than other groups to use online classified ads or to use them on a typical day.

Source: Pew Internet & American Life Project survey conducted from March 26–April 29, 2009. Available at http://www.pewinternet.org/ Reports/2009/7--Online-Classifieds. Accessed on March 30, 2010.

- Internet users who make household incomes of $25,000 or less, according to Pew Research, are reluctant to purchase online because of their fears regarding financial security and giving out credit card information.

- Those with college degrees are more likely to shop online than those with less education.

Online Utilization

Going online provides quick access for shoppers to enter a retailer's Web site or open an e-mail sent from the retailer. In the case of Web site shopping, consumers can go either directly to the Web site or log onto a search engine such as Google, enter the name of the merchant, and be directed to it. Retailers of all sizes use Internet Web sites in addition to on-site selling and have become multichannel merchants. In today's retail environment, use of the Internet has helped many merchants increase overall sales volume and has helped others to compensate for the lag in in-store patronage. It should be noted that one of the advantages of online purchasing is that the shipping costs are often absorbed by the seller, making it an attractive purchase.

10.3 Amazon.com is a Web site–only retailer. *Courtesy Amazon.com.*

RETAIL WEB SITES

Logging on to retail Web sites provides the consumer with a catalogue of merchandise that is available for purchase. The Web site phenomenon not only offers bricks-and-mortar operations yet another opportunity to reach shoppers but also provides a venue for **Web site–only** retailers (those who operate solely on the Internet) to capture the consumer's attention. An example of this type of merchant is Amazon.com (Figure 10.3).

eBay is an untraditional, but still a retail, Web site outlet. Originally designed to be a bidding operation, it has since added fixed pricing to its business model. Fixed pricing enables both individuals and businesses to buy and sell new and used products. eBay is the subject of Focus 10.1.

The characteristics of retail Web sites include the following:

- The merchandise displayed sometimes differs from the inventories that are featured in the stores. Occasionally, the display is a representation of the retailer's overall merchandise inventory, and sometimes it features more products than are available

in the store. Merchandise that is considered out of season, for example, might be found on the Web site and not in the store.

- The Web sites are constantly changing to bring the latest of the retailer's products to the consumer, as is the case of the merchandise offerings in the stores. They frequently offer special sales, closeouts, and other incentives in addition to their regular product lines.

- Retail Web sites vary in terms of what they are trying to accomplish. Most advertise merchandise and make the products available for sale. Few, however, as in the case of off-price merchants, merely use their sites to advertise their stores without making purchasing possible. SteinMart, a chain of more than 250 units, for example, uses its site to tell about the company and the advantages of shopping in its stores.

For merchants who use their sites to advertise and sell their merchandise, it is essential that they make the shopping experience simple. One of the most important factors for a retailer to consider is to make site "navigation" simple. If it is complicated, as some are, the user may elect to abort the action.

Merchants and other businesses attract attention from people who are **surfing the Net** through the use of **banner ads**, **pop-ups**, and **pop-under advertisements**. These ads appear on a variety of Web pages that are accessed by the Internet user. Banners are usually small, rectangularly shaped ads that simply indicate the name of a retailer, a product for sale, and so forth (Figure 10.4). Pop-ups are devices that obscure parts of the Web page, and pop-unders, less intrusive in nature, appear under the body of the content that is being presented. All of these, when clicked on, take the user to the advertiser's site. Sites such as aol.com, yahoo.com, and amazon.com are replete with such devices.

With the ability to quickly alter the Web site, retailers can provide up-to-the-minute product diversity to their online shoppers as well as correct any deterrents to the user from making speedy and accurate purchasing.

FOCUS $ 10.1

eBay

eBay's origin as a company is as unique as the setting for its beginning. Founded in Pierre Omidyar's living room in San Jose, California, in September 1995, eBay has become a premier Web site institution. Initially, it was designed to be a marketplace in which individuals could "retail" goods, but it has evolved into a place where those wanting to dispose of larger quantities of merchandise may also participate. In 1998 the company expanded and recruited professionals from PepsiCo and Disney to take the venture to a higher level. It was at this time that an image change was made to abandon its original concept of auctioning collectibles and move into an arena in which other products would be the focus.

The format that made the company famous allowed sellers to list items for sale and have buyers browse through all of the merchandise and bid on those items in which they were interested. The listing takes but a matter of seconds, making the purchase opportunity almost immediately available. The browsing and bidding are free of charge, but sellers are charged in two ways. First, they must pay an insertion fee, which ranges between $0.30 and $3.30, depending on the seller's opening bid on the item. An additional fee is levied for such listing options as highlighting or boldfacing the listing. Finally, a fee is charged at the end of the auction, which generally ranges from 1.25 percent to 5 percent of the final sale price.

eBay has expanded its business model to include a fixed-price option. Instead of having to wait for an auction to end, the new option allows buyers to sell items at the price they want without having to wait until the bidding has been completed and allows buyers to immediately satisfy their needs. Although the auction format is still the dominant method of buying and selling, the fixed-price concept accounts for 35 percent of all sales and is growing. It has proved to be very successful with those who sell multiple quantities of the same item.

Today, eBay has become a multibillion-dollar player in Web site retailing with many millions of registered users.

10.4 Banner ads help draw attention to retailers.
Courtesy New York Magazine.

E-MAIL COMMUNICATION

In addition to relying on shoppers to enter their Web sites to make their purchases, more and more merchants are directly contacting their customers or potential buyers via e-mail. When individuals log on to the Internet, their first daily ritual is generally to examine e-mail messages. The AOL message "You've got mail," for example, motivates Internet users to open their e-mail.

More and more e-mails feature messages from retailers. These communications generally are special offerings, sales announcements, inducements to buy, hot-item notifications, and so forth. This methodology is exceptionally cost-effective and results in sales that would otherwise not take place.

Some of the typical "headlines" that retailers use to motivate the opening of the messages are listed in Table 10.5.

Internet E-mail Messaging Do's and Don'ts

If a retailer is to gain a significant sales increase by using e-mail, then certain principles must be followed:

◆ An e-mail should have an eye-catching headline if the viewer is to be motivated to open the message. It cannot merely state the name of the merchant to foster curiosity but must also feature a clear and concise phrase. With all of the competition from the host of e-mails that individuals receive, an eye-catcher is most likely to be opened and read.

◆ Unsolicited messages known as **spam** should not be used to elicit business. Advertising sent en masse to people who have not in some way shown interest in a specific retail operation generally reduces the popularity of the company. People usually delete spam.

◆ The number of e-mail messages sent should be carefully considered by the sender. Too many in a brief time period is unlikely to translate into sales. Too few, on the other hand, is insufficient to boost sales. Typically, once a week is a good practice to keep the company in the mind of the consumer yet avoid being an annoyance. If special messages are used in an e-mail, such as limited time offers, they may be offered whenever the need arises.

◆ In every e-mail message, the retailer should provide an option for the recipient to unsubscribe. Offering the ability for the recipient to opt out of receiving future messages gives the sender more credibility, often establishing trust and perhaps bringing the prospective customer back again.

◆ The use of misleading terminology such as *comparable value* should be avoided. Honesty in the message will more than likely bring better sales results and reduce the rate of returned merchandise.

◆ Brevity is an important ingredient in e-mail selling. Often, Internet users receive so many pieces of e-mail that they are unlikely

TABLE 10.5 — Retailer Headlines and Motivations

RETAILER	HEADLINE	MOTIVATIONAL CONCEPT
Lands' End	Save $10 on the Sweaters You Love + Free Shipping	Offer of a bargain
Barneys New York	VENA CAVA fever	A hot label is available at this retailer
Restoration Hardware	Introducing the Fall Collection	New collection arrival
Barnes & Noble	15% Limited-Time Coupon Inside	Time-limited price offer
Tiffany & Company	Introducing Elsa Peretti's Color by the Yard in Sterling Silver	Designer's new product
Brooks Brothers	How Do You Wear Your Jeans?	Arouse curiosity

to read lengthy messages. By getting to the point and using a limited number of product illustrations, e-mail advertisers are more likely to motivate sales.

◆ E-mail messages should dovetail with other advertising offered by the retailer. By using the same messages that have been used in print and broadcast advertising, the e-mail reinforces the other media forms.

Advantages and Disadvantages of Internet Advertising

As in the case of all other media, the Internet offers retail advertisers many advantages and disadvantages. The merchant must consider each and make decisions in terms of the proportion of their advertising budgets to be used for online advertising. Among the positive aspects of Internet promotion are the following:

1. The Internet provides a comparatively inexpensive method for retailers to reach their clienteles and to attract new shoppers to their companies. With this cost advantage, even the smallest retail entrepreneurs can avail themselves of Web site usage.

2. A Web site is relatively simple to construct and does not necessarily require accomplished professionals. This is especially appealing to small merchants who have limited operational funds.

3. Messaging can be easily changed to fit any circumstance the retailer wants to promote. Last-minute sales offerings may be quickly included on a Web site as well as in e-mail. Especially by using e-mail, retailers may quickly and easily construct messages that reach the consumer quickly. If a sudden impending snowstorm is forecasted, the merchant stocked with winter footwear can quickly notify the consumer market of their availability.

4. Expanding the retailer's market is a plus with Internet promotion. Because this communication tool can reach people all over the globe, it significantly expands the market of consumer purchasers.

5. In addition to the still images of the materials presented, the Internet allows for audio and video presentation. It also enables interaction between the seller and buyer.

6. Reaching consumers who are unable to visit the stores because of time constraints, disability, lack of transportation, and so on is a means of expanding the consumer base.

As advantageous as the Internet is, it also presents some disadvantages:

1. The overwhelming use of the Internet by businesses often overloads the medium with offerings so that busy consumers may not even notice individual Web site and e-mail messages.

2. The fear factor of purchasing over the Internet is a reality. Many people do not feel comfortable divulging personal credit card information needed to make a purchase. Even though most businesses offer **secure sites**, which are tamper-proof, many users are reluctant to make Internet transactions.

3. Difficulty in navigating some Web sites sometimes leads to shopper frustration and results in shoppers aborting the sale.

4. Consumers shopping for a particular item may find the item on different Web sites, putting retailers at a disadvantage. Sometimes the product price varies significantly among sites, resulting in a negative image of the retailer with the higher price.

5. Some retailers still use puffery on their Web site, leading to discredited advertisements. Hyperbolic claims often result in customer returns.

6. Retailers who use spam present a negative impression of their companies.

7. Retailers who do not offer an unsubscribe option, but who continue to pursue consumers who do not want their messages, make a poor impression on recipients.

8. Use of automated systems that generate e-mail addresses often results in sending messages to consumers who do not want to receive them.

10.5 Social networks help retailers reach shoppers. *Courtesy of Facebook.*

Social Networking Sites

One of the fastest-growing methods of online communication is social networking. Not only has it created a means for people with common interests to communicate, it also has become an excellent vehicle for retailers and other advertisers to reach significant numbers of individuals and businesses. With its global access, it broadens the opportunity for sellers to market their products and services. With free registration and only a few age restrictions, social networking has become a very broadly used tool for people of all ages.

Although just a few of the social networking sites, such as Facebook, MySpace, and Twitter, seem to gain significant attention, there are literally hundreds of these sites that are active (Figure 10.5). Statistical information about them is available from Alexa Internet, a company that has built an unparalleled database of information about Internet sites (Table 10.6). Information may be obtained by logging onto http://www.alexa.com/company. Detailed information is accessed by typing the URL of any site into the search box on Alexa's Web site.

Some sites are specifically targeted to certain ethnicities, countries, interests, political parties, and so forth. The advertisers must carefully examine the demographics of each site and use those that are specific to the merchandise they sell.

Social Networking Demographics

With the enormous reach of social networking sites, retailers and other businesses are using them as vehicles for their advertising. All important in the use of these outlets is the right mix of demographic characteristics of the different sites' registered users. It is unacceptable to delve into social network advertising, as it is with any of the media, before examining its demographics.

With these sites affording companies the advertising equivalents of newspaper, magazine, television, and radio, blind usage will not provide the return on investment that careful study will more than likely ensure. Advertisers can determine the demographic characteristics of a site's

SITE	FOCUS	REGISTRANTS*	REQUIREMENTS
Facebook	General	250,000,000	Open to ages 13 and older
MySpace	General	263,920,000	Open to ages 13 and older
Twitter	General, microblogging	44,500,000	Open to all
Classmates.com	School, college	50,000,000	Open to all
MyLife	Locating friends and family	51,000,000	Open to all
Tagged.com	General	70,000,000	Open to all
Window Live Spaces	Blogging	120,000,000	Open to all
WAYN	Travel and lifestyle	10,000,000	Open to people 18 older
Adult FriendFinder	Dating	33,000,000	Adults
Bebo	General	40,000,000	Open to ages 13 and older

TABLE 10.6 Selected Social Networking Web Sites

*As of 2009.

users by visiting and exploring the site. One-size-fits-all does not hold true when determining the appropriate use of social network ad campaigns. Each site must be explored to achieve the greatest sales results.

The more than 200,000,000 (as of this writing) registered Facebook users have similar demographics in common, including age, gender, and educational distribution.

AGE DISTRIBUTION

Eighty-four percent of the registered users are between the ages of 14 and 26 (Figure 10.6), although the overall distribution ranges from 13 to 61. With this in mind, retailers such as Gap and Old Navy would benefit from using the site for advertising.

GENDER DISTRIBUTION

Although more females (55 percent) than males (45 percent) are Facebook users, there is not enough difference to warrant any advertising decisions in terms of merchandise offerings.

EDUCATIONAL DISTRIBUTION

The statistics reveal that 47 percent of the membership are high school students or are enrolled in college, whereas the remainder have completed their studies. Most have some level of college education. Based on these figures, retailers with higher price points should use the site to advertise their products because college students and graduates are likely to have higher incomes than those who are less educated.

For advertisers to target the market best suited for their products, it is essential to analyze the users of the various social networking sites. An article that appeared in *Advertising Age*, and the subject of Media Insight 10.2, explores some of the attributes and habits of these outlets that may be used to pinpoint the most likely product purchasers.

10.6 Eighty-four percent of registered social network users are between the ages of 14 and 26. *istockphoto.*

Advantages and Disadvantages of Social Networking Advertising

As has been stressed about all advertising media, each medium offers particular pros and cons. Among the advantages to advertisers on social networking sites are the following:

1. As is the case in general for Internet advertising, the costs are minimal compared to the cost of traditional print and broadcast media. This is especially important to small-business retailers who generally lack the necessary advertising budgets to promote their companies and sell products.

2. The enormous number of registered users on sites such as Facebook, MySpace, and Twitter, in particular, enables the advertiser to reach significant numbers of purchasers.

3. Some sites focus on specific audiences and lend themselves to more targeted consumer markets. Examples include Care2, a site that focuses on green living and would offer green-oriented retailers a market for their products; Flickr, with an audience comprising individuals with photography interests, would be an ideal place for photo retailers to offer their products; imeem, with a membership interested in music and videos, would be a natural place for retailers of those goods to feature their products; and Library Thing, with its book-lovers base, would be an ideal site on which retailers such as Barnes & Noble would benefit from advertising.

4. Ethnicity and nationality are also population components that are easily reached by this form of advertising. African Americans, for example, are easy to locate on BlackPlanet, as are Muslims on the Muxlim site.

5. Construction of an ad is relatively simple and can be accomplished without the expense of a professional team. The Facebook Web site, for example, features an advertising section that takes the potential advertiser through a series of steps that are easy to navigate and complete. It offers suggestions on ad designs, features demographic and psychographic filters that target users 18 and older, makes suggestions regarding the different components of audience targeting, discusses pricing in terms of **clicks** and **viewings**, and finally reviews the impending ads.

6. Social networking sites are available at any time of the day or night, at home or away, making them a potential sales producer whenever the site user deems it appropriate.

On the other hand, there are some potential drawbacks to advertising on social networking sites.

1. With so many of these sites operational, the competition for the viewer is keen.

2. Some people might find the advertising features of these sites interruptive and could resent purchasing products that are advertised in these places.

3. Some site registrants are uneasy about giving personal credit information to the advertisers.

Although the sites are considered to eventually produce sales for their advertisers, it must be understood that use of this tool as the only means of promotion for their advertising needs is insufficient. It should be an advertising component to be used along with the other media.

Direct Mail

Although the Internet has grown considerably as a means of reaching consumers, and cable shopping networks account for some degree of selling to the consumer, traditional print and broadcast media still reign in the world of advertising. Direct mail is still an important way for retailers to reach their clienteles and motivate other shoppers to become regular customers.

The mailbox in most consumer homes is regularly filled with a variety of mailers from merchants that announce special sales, offer limited-time-only inducements to buy, feature exclusive lines of merchandise, and so forth. A wealth of catalogues, brochures, pamphlets, and other pieces regularly make their way into the homes of consumers.

What Your Favorite Social Net Says About You

Beth Snyder Bulik
July 13, 2009

Do you Twitter? Then you are more interested in sex than the average Facebook, MySpace, or LinkedIn user. Like LinkedIn? You're more likely to watch soap operas. Favor MySpace? You're probably not into exercise.

The social network you favor says a lot about you—and you might be surprised by just what it says. A new study by Anderson Analytics is helping identify for marketers your likely interests, buying habits, media consumption, and more. The survey studied the demographics and psychographics of both social networkers and nonusers and found that "there are definite data-driven segments in the social-networking site market, both for nonusers and users," said Tom Anderson, founder and managing partner.

Today, 110 million Americans, or 60 percent of the online population, use social networks, and that number is fairly conservative because instead of counting unique users or everyone who has an account, as many estimates do, the Anderson study counted only people who [had] used a social network at least once in the [previous] month.

Users tend to spend a lot of time on social networks. The average social networker goes to social sites 5 days a week and checks in about four times a day for a total of an hour each day. A super-connected 9 percent stay logged in all day and are "constantly checking out what's new."

Social networkers' feelings about brands online in general are more positive than the researchers thought they would be. Some 52 percent of social networkers had friended or become a fan of at least one brand. When asked if seeing a brand on a social network makes them feel positive or negative about that brand, an almost equal 17 percent said positive and 19 percent said negative. The other 64 percent were neutral or didn't care. When asked if they would like more communications from brands, 45 percent were neutral, whereas 20 percent said yes and 35 percent said no.

Anderson conducted the study online in June [2009] with 5,000 demographically representative respondents, and then went in depth with 1,250 of them. With the help of Mr. Anderson and his team, *Ad Age* dug into the reams of stats to create the mini profiles of three different social-networking groups below.

Facebookers

There are 100 million Facebook users, according to the study, and Facebook users were almost completely average in their level of interest in most areas when compared with users of Twitter, MySpace, and LinkedIn. Out of 45 categories, only national news, sports, exercise, travel, and home and garden skewed even slightly higher than average, and then by only one or two percentage points.

"Facebook is average because it has the most users. When stat testing, anything near the average is less likely to be significant," Mr. Anderson said. "They are also capturing a wider range of users for various reasons, from high school and college fun, leisure user to business and parents and grandparents."

They are more likely to be married (40 percent), white (80 percent), and retired (6 percent) than users of the other social networks. They have the second-highest average income, at $61,000, and an average of 121 connections.

Facebook users skew a bit older and are more likely to be late adopters of social media. They are extremely loyal: 75 percent say Facebook is their favorite site, and another 59 percent say they have increased their use of the site in the past 6 months.

Twitterers

This is the super-user group. Twitterers are more interested than the others in many subjects but skew particularly high in all news categories, restaurants, sports, politics, personal finance, and religion. They also especially like pop culture, with music, movies, TV, and reading ranking higher than average. And their buying habits mirror that. They're more likely to buy books, movies, shoes, and cosmetics online than the other groups.

Twitterers are also entrepreneurial. They are more likely than others to use the service to promote their blogs or businesses. How do they keep going? Coffee, apparently. Some 31 percent buy coffee online, far above the average 21 percent of other social networkers.

They're more likely to be employed part-time (16 percent vs. 11 percent average), have an average income of $58,000, and average 28 followers and 32 other Twitterers they're following. They're not particularly attached to the site, though—43 percent said they could live without Twitter.

MySpacers

They are the young, the fun, and the fleeing. Although MySpace users skew younger, they also said they'd used the site much less in the past 6 months.

The 67 million who are still there are into having a good time. They're more likely to have joined MySpace for fun and more likely to be interested in entertaining friends, humor and comedy, and video games. They're less into exercise than any other social group but seek out parenting information more than any other.

The content MySpace users put up is most often about specific hobbies [and] pictures of family and friends. Their average income is the lowest at $44,000, and they have an average of 131 connections.

They're more likely to be black (9 percent) or Hispanic (7 percent) than users of the other social sites. They are also more likely to be single (60 percent) and students (23 percent).

LinkedIn

It's probably no surprise these guys are all about business. We say guys because LinkedIn has the only user group with more males than females (57 percent to 43 percent). They have the highest average income, at $89,000, and are more likely to have joined the site for business or work, citing keeping in touch with business networks, job searching, business development, and recruiting as the top reasons for signing up.

Their interests reflect that. They like all kinds of news, employment information, sports, and politics. They also are more likely to be into the gym, spas, yoga, golf, and tennis.

Excluding video-game systems, they own more electronic gadgets than the other social networkers, including digital cameras, high-definition TVs, DVRs, and Blu-ray players.

Two surprising things they're more interested in than the others: gambling and soap operas. Some 12 percent seek gambling information online (vs. an average of 7 percent), whereas 10 percent go online for soap-opera content (vs. an average of 5 percent).

Source: Beth Snyder Bulik. "What Your Favorite Social Net Says About You." Advertising Age, July 13, 2009.

Classification of Direct Mail Pieces

Retailers use different types of direct mail to advertise to their regular clientele and prospective customers. Each format is designed to bring the ultimate result of selling merchandise.

CATALOGUES

The catalogue is the form of direct mail most widely used by the retail industry (Figure 10.7). Even though such catalogues as the voluminous Sears editions are no longer in use, and the Spiegel catalogue is just one of a very few sales books that still feature extremely broad merchandise offerings, smaller, specialized types now dominate the direct-marketing scene.

Today's catalogues are generally slick offerings that feature color layouts that rival the most sophisticated magazines. In addition to the merchandise being offered for sale, editorial features appear in some catalogues to underscore the nature of the company. One such direct-mail publication is the Patagonia catalogue, which is actually a sales booklet, advertising compilation, and magazine all rolled into one. Along with the advertised products, it features stories about the fibers it uses in its products, ecologically oriented articles, and other copy that reveals the company's philosophy. Focus 10.2 looks at Patagonia and its catalogue.

Catalogues are sometimes (though not often) used for institutional advertising. The aim is not to immediately sell products, as is the case with most catalogue advertising, but instead it is to impart a positive image of the retailer. One retailer who employs institutional advertising in its catalogues is Brooks Brothers, the perennial purveyor of classic, fine men's clothing. Every so often, it produces a direct-mail piece that covers such topics as the Brooks Brothers "Ages of Style," which traces men's fashion from 1818 to 2003; articles on "fit"; appropriate accessorizing; and so forth. It is the hope of the company, and others that use this direct-mail approach, to generate devotees of the Brooks Brothers label (Figure 10.8).

More prevalent, however, are the catalogues from such retailers as Bloomingdale's, Neiman Marcus, Tiffany, and other major retailers who make the merchandise the centerpiece of the mailers. In addition to the product artwork, the booklets

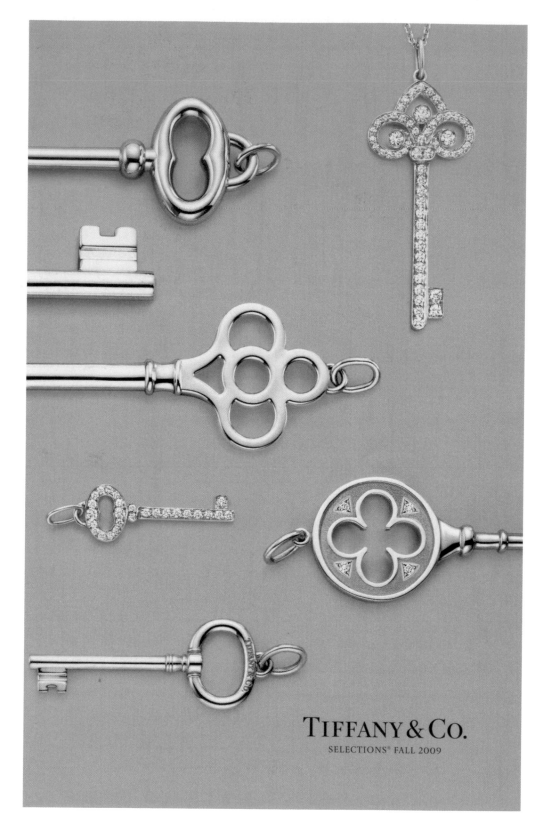

10.7 The catalogue is the most widely used form of retailer direct mail. *Courtesy of Tiffany & Co.*

Patagonia, Inc.

One of the more unique retail operations, Patagonia, Inc., was founded in 1972 as the brainchild of mountain climber Yvon Chouinard. Its focus then, as it is now, was primarily on outdoor apparel and accessories that embraced the essence of environmentally sound materials. Patagonia has grown to be a company that features its collections in its own stores, in outlets of other merchants, on a Web site, and in a most unusual catalogue. Eloquently stated as the company mission are these words that sum up their existence:

> Our Reason For Being: Build the best product, cause no unnecessary harm, use business to inspire, and implement solutions to the environment crisis.

Patagonia's commitment to protecting the environment is quite evident in its catalogue. Not only are the pages replete with a host of different products used by climbers, skiers, snowboarders, surfers, fly fishermen, paddlers, and trail runners but also exhibited are a number of stories that concentrate on environmental topics. The art used in the catalogue is masterfully photographed to impart unusual visual images.

With the essence of a magazine, the Patagonia catalogue draws attention to its merchandise and features a wealth of well-written articles and company traditions that motivate more than a passing glance. Many notable endeavors are also highlighted in the catalogue's pages. These include Patagonia's commitment to environmental grants; up-to-date figures regarding The Conservative Alliance, which the company cofounded in 1989; its "1% For the Planet" appeal that asks for 1 percent donations of annual revenues of businesses; news regarding Grist.org, a source for environmental news; and information about the Wild & Scientific Film Festival in which Patagonia is involved.

It is truly a unique catalogue that contributes not only to the company's bottom line but also to its role as an environmental activist.

Ages of STYLE

BROOKS BROTHERS

1818

Brooks establishes his emporium April 7, and earns early recognition for fine custom tailoring, such as gentlemen's tailcoats and other day and evening wear. In addition, he soon gains praise as a pioneer in the ready-made clothing business. Brooks promises (according to an advertisement in the Morning Courier) "to have on hand a very large stock of ready-made clothing just manufactured with a due regard to fashion, and embracing all the various styles of the day." The important phrase "stock of ready-made clothing" signals the beginning of the modern store.

1832

The growing popularity of Brooks Brothers' ready-to-wear clothing firmly establishes Brooks as one of the country's most important and influential innovators in the clothing trade. As well as catering to the carriage trade, Brooks now represents an upper middle class clientele. Men are now beginning to wear frock coats for day wear, replacing the tail coat, which is reserved for evening wear.

1849

Brooks Brothers advertises ready-to-wear clothing for "the California trade." Elias Howe patents a sewing machine in 1846, which marks the beginning of the Industrial Revolution in the American clothing industry. In 1857, Brooks Brothers opens a large emporium at Broadway and Grand Streets. Short jackets and capes are now being worn for daywear, particularly in the summer.

1861

Brooks Brothers makes uniforms for the Union Army. Manufacturing time is cut in half by the use of machines, and Brooks can now make a first-rate overcoat in three days instead of the six required by manual labor. The Broadway and Grand store becomes the principal place of business for the company during the Civil War years, and it was from this store that Abraham Lincoln ordered his frock coats— one of which he was wearing when he is assassinated in April 1865.

1900

By 1915 the clothing trade will be the country's third largest industry, outranked only by steel and oil. More Americans now have leisure time to enjoy entertainment and summer holidays become common for a growing middle-class. Brooks begins to offer complete lines of leisure and sporting apparel, adopting the fabrics and stylings of golfers and sportsmen in Great Britain. For the businessman, Brooks introduces its "natural look" sack suit. The store soon introduces its button-down collar "Polo Shirt" in several fabrics. This innovative oxford cloth button-down shirt, like the sack suit, becomes part of Brooks' heritage.

1918

The ideal American male is youthful, stylish and casual. During the week he wears two and three-piece natural shouldered suits. Weekends call for tennis flannels and a blazer or bright sweater. Earlier in the century, Brooks introduces the English "wait" coat, a long belted coat originally worn between chukkars at polo matches. This sporty camel hair garment—soon to be known as the "polo coat"—becomes the rage on college campuses during the Roaring Twenties. The Brooks' catalogue now includes casual, sporty items that become classics: white buckskin oxfords and canvas tennis shoes, driving and golf gloves, Panama hats, Shetland sweaters, tweed hacking jackets and corduroy shooting coats.

10.8 Atypical of catalogue advertising is this two-page spread in a Brooks Brothers catalogue. *Courtesy of Brooks Brothers.*

1930

The economic free-fall that began in September 1929 continues to engulf the nation and the world. By 1934, Esquire magazine is promoting new spring fashions with the explanation that, "Since a good appearance is about all that is left to the capitalist anyway, why not go ahead and enjoy it?" Brooks introduces lightweight tailoring in cotton seersucker, tropical worsteds, and rayon (the first of the synthetic fibers). These new fabrics weigh a mere 8 ounces per yard or less, compared to previous summer fabrics weighing up to 13 ounces, thus reducing the weight of a summer suit from over four pounds to less than three.

1950

The gray flannel suit becomes the uniform of choice for businessmen. American writers Mary McCarthy, John Cheever and John O'Hara familiarize the world with the image of the Eastern Establishment Brooks Brothers man. The fifties become the decade of new synthetic "miracle" fabrics that are lightweight, wrinkle resistant, and easily laundered. The "Brooks Brothers Look"—a natural-shouldered gray flannel suit, oxford button-down shirt, and repp-striped tie—rises to major fashion importance on Madison Avenue and college campuses. DuPont chooses Brooks Brothers to develop a wash-and-wear shirting fabric utilizing its trademarked Dacron polyester fiber. Brooks introduces the Brooksweave "wash-and-wear shirt" in 1953.

1961

A new style of casual, conservative dress defines the country: khakis, Shetland crewnecks, and button-down shirts set the tone. A new era of youthful elegance arrives when 43-year-old John Fitzgerald Kennedy is inaugurated President. Campus style predominates, with the corporate "Man in the Gray Flannel Suit" now being replaced by the more casual dress: penny loafers, Argyle socks, and tartan plaid sport coats and shirts. The following year, Brooks opens its "University Shop" for the younger man just beginning his career and in need of less expensive but still classic clothing.

1972

The Age of the Menswear Designer is in full throttle, with a new sartorial flamboyance following in the wake of the London Mod look, Nehru suits, brocaded Edwardian jackets, Chelsea boots, flowered shirts, bell bottomed trousers, and other exuberances. Brooks responds by introducing its new "Brooksgate" line for the entry-level customer. Brooksgate offers a slimmer silhouette, a slightly suppressed waist on its two-button coat suits, wider lapels, and a subdued flare to its trousers. These suits are introduced in a new all-worsted stretch fabric, called BrooksEase, and a new knitted suiting fabric called Brooksknit, a polyester-worsted blend.

1976

Italian designers enter the US market with a loose, flowing silhouette using unisex fabrics for tailored clothing. Brooks introduces a Women's Department in 1975, aimed at the emerging professional woman. The range of clothing includes tailored business wear and sportswear for the contemporary woman, who will no longer have to shop in the Boy's Department for button-downs, Bermuda shorts, Shetland crewnecks, and ribbon belts.

1979

The Disco Era of pastel polyester suits is a trend with the young, but baby boomers go off to work in traditionally tailored clothes. The United States is now an international marketplace where men dress in a variety of American, British, and Italian silhouettes. Brooks Brothers opens its first international store in Tokyo. The Ivy League look becomes the biggest fashion trend in Japan. A year later the Brooks Look becomes a literary phenomenon with the publication of "The Preppy Handbook."

1987

A stock market tumble doesn't impede the new breed of "Young Urban Professionals" from experimenting with expensive, wide-shouldered suits from Europe. Europe soon grows tired of this over-sized silhouette and begins to manufacture a garment modeled on the original Brooks Sack Suit Number One. Italian shirtmakers become enamored with the button-down collar, introduced by Brooks Brothers almost 100 years earlier. Brooks continues to sell its Sack Suit Number One with its soft chest and natural shoulders, and its softly rolled "Polo" button-down shirt. Thought too nonchalant for international acceptance just a few years prior, the Brooks Brothers approach to business dress—propriety, understated elegance and comfort—is fast becoming a global fashion statement, and the most imitated look in the world.

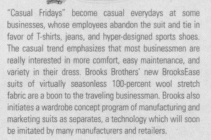

1992

"Casual Fridays" become casual everydays at some businesses, whose employees abandon the suit and tie in favor of T-shirts, jeans, and hyper-designed sports shoes. The casual trend emphasizes that most businessmen are really interested in more comfort, easy maintenance, and variety in their dress. Brooks Brothers' new BrooksEase suits of virtually seasonless 100-percent wool stretch fabric are a boon to the traveling businessman. Brooks also initiates a wardrobe concept program of manufacturing and marketing suits as separates, a technology which will soon be imitated by many manufacturers and retailers.

2003

The "dot.bomb" of the late Nineties, followed by a sustained economic downturn and a worldwide war on terrorism prompt a drastic change in the mood of America. Businesses adopt a more serious demeanor and presentation. "Casual Fridays" are tempered by this new reality, and more organizations return to a more traditional dress code. The "new" is no longer awarded automatic respect as America's attention refocuses on durable values and heritage. Brooks Brothers is purchased by Retail Brand Alliance in late 2001. The 185-year-old merchant immediately begins a return to its heritage in classic American clothing and customers find high-quality suits, shirts and ties back at the core of the business.

BrooksBrothers.com **7**

10.9 Most retailer catalogues offer merchandise that is for sale by the company. *Courtesy of Pottery Barn.*

feature mail-order forms, telephone numbers, Internet ordering information, and general instructions regarding delivery options, merchandise returns, and so forth.

Although catalogue sales continue to be an important adjunct for bricks-and-mortar retailers, trends indicate that the number of catalogues delivered in the future will decline, and some retailers will reduce the size of their offerings. Williams-Sonoma, parent company of Pottery Barn and West Elm, plans to reduce the number of pages in its catalogues by 2011. J. Crew already cut its catalogue circulation by 27 percent in 2009, and Crate & Barrel and Victoria's Secret are beginning to tweak their mail strategies. Although catalogues remain among the least expensive and most effective means of sales marketing, the Internet has started to cut into that direct-mail route. Catalogues generate approximately $7 for every dollar spent, but the Internet returns about $45 for every dollar spent. The saving grace of the catalogue investment is that it results in more new business than does the Internet. Although these indicators are a reality, many people still prefer catalogue purchasing to Internet shopping. Even with the fall in catalogue distribution, it still remains an important advertising and sales tool (Figure 10.9).

BROCHURES

From one-page designs or extravagant foldouts called **broadsheets**, which are sometimes larger than double-spread newspaper and magazine advertisements, the brochure is a direct-mail piece used by the retailer to announce special promotions, exclusive design collections, and so forth (Figure 10.10).

One of the more common uses of brochures by the retail industry is as inserts along with their monthly billing statements to charge account customers. The inserts are usually small, one-page documents that offer savings on such items as hosiery, cosmetics, and fragrances. Because they do not increase mailing costs, statement enclosures often produce high-volume sales results.

10.10 Brochures are used to announce special promotions or exclusive designer arrangements. *Courtesy of Bloomingdale's.*

LETTERS

The simplest and least expensive form of direct-mail advertising available is the letter or invitation. It may be, for example, an offering to open a charge account; an opportunity to take advantage of an unadvertised sale; an invitation to attend a private sale; a chance to attend a **trunk show**, an event at which the designer or company representative brings a "trunk" full of new designs to a store for customers to examine; or an announcement of a charity fashion show.

Reaching the Appropriate Consumer Market

Imperative to the success of direct mail is the ability to deliver the pieces to individuals who are most likely to respond positively to the retailer's offering. If the recipients have no need for the merchant's products or are not at least curious enough to examine the catalogue, brochure, or letter, the monies spent will be wasted. With so many direct-mail pieces arriving at a consumer's home each day, there is a chance that some will be discarded without ever being opened. Traditional print and broadcast media advertising is targeted to a more general audience, but direct mail must be narrowly targeted in order to be effective. Targeting is accomplished using lists, which include **house lists**, **compiled lists**, and **response lists**.

One of the more important sources of names for use in direct-mail advertising comes from the retailer's own customers by way of house lists. In this highly competitive retailing environment, merchants understand the benefits derived from a loyal customer base. Through the use of credit card sales, where the names and addresses of purchasers are automatically recorded, and from the names that are recorded on cash purchases, the retailer has a viable compilation that can be incorporated into a mailing list for direct-mail advertising. Names also come from catalogue purchasers and Internet buyers. If these records are regularly updated, they are certain to offer the names and addresses of consumers most likely to purchase via direct mail.

For retailers wanting to go beyond their own lists and expand their marketing reach, the compiled list is an excellent option. Compiled lists are purchased from direct-mail list brokers who are able to supply names and addresses of individuals with specific criteria, such as age, occupation, educational level, geographic location, and so forth. An Internet search on the keywords *mailing lists* leads to numerous companies that specialize in these lists. The retailer pays a fee each time the list is used. One of the benefits of using list suppliers is that they provide the labels and mail the pieces directly to those on the lists.

Response lists are yet another means of reaching potential new customers. A newspaper advertisement, for example, might feature a section that offers the inquirer a discount for a limited time. Web sites sometimes request the name, mailing address, and e-mail address of an individual for the receipt of regular information about the merchant and its products. These methods of collecting consumer names and addresses often result in well-targeted lists that generate a healthy return on advertising investment.

Maximizing the Effectiveness of Direct Mail

To increase sales through direct mail, there are a number of specifics that should be used by the retailer.

DOVETAILING THE CATALOGUE OR BROCHURE WITH OTHER MEDIA

When the direct-mail piece is part of an overall campaign, it is more than likely the effort will produce greater sales. It is especially beneficial if the company's Web site uses the same merchandise offerings to motivate purchasing. Using the two media together reaches those who prefer off-site shopping to in-store purchasing and often tempts them to buy.

SELECTING THE RIGHT PRODUCTS

As in the case of the best advertising for retailers, it is better to promote items that sell well so that they will sell even better than it is to advertise untested goods. Except in cases where a new collection is being introduced or the start of the new season is at hand, tried-and-true merchandise is best suited for the catalogue or brochure.

CONTINUITY OF THE OFFERINGS

Positive results often require showing the same items repeatedly in direct-mail pieces. The shopper who sees the same product numerous times is more likely to consider purchasing it.

DELIVERING THE QUALITY THAT IS ADVERTISED

All too often, the product as shown in the direct-mail piece is enhanced to make it seem more appealing and does not match what the purchaser receives. This ploy often leads to merchandise returns and causes ill will on the part of the purchaser. Retailers should faithfully represent the merchandise in order to protect their credibility and encourage repeat business.

CHOOSING THE RIGHT MARKET

Catalogue production and delivery costs may be substantial, so it is essential that the right audience is targeted to receive the mailers. By using their own customer base and working with a reputable mailing list provider, retailers increase the likelihood that the direct-mail piece will generate sales.

DESIGNING AN ATTRACTIVE CATALOGUE OR BROCHURE

The essence of success in direct mail is the production of pieces that are unlike those of other retailers and sufficiently attractive to warrant further investigation. The run-of-the-mill catalogue or brochure is often overshadowed by the more exciting piece (Figure 10.11). Busy consumers will choose the most visually appealing pieces to browse through, and they are more likely to discard those that do not catch their eye.

Advantages and Disadvantages of Direct Mail

Direct mail, like other advertising media, has its pluses and minuses. The advantages are as follows:

1. The medium offers both small and large retailers the opportunity to target their merchandise to clearly defined markets. This can be accomplished by using a merchant's own in-house list or one that has been purchased from an outside organization that tailors its lists to specific demographic characteristics.

2. Production costs of brochures and other print products are comparatively inexpensive, which makes direct mail a cost-effective way to reach large audiences. Newspaper, magazine, and particularly television advertising are often too expensive for the small entrepreneur.

3. Devices such as coupons, when incorporated into direct mail, often bring positive results in terms of sales. It is particularly beneficial for a retailer to track the number of coupons returned by consumers whose names were purchased from a list supplier; this information can help in future advertising planning.

4. Mailing costs can be minimized with the use of bulk-mail rates, making direct mail even more cost effective.

5. Turnaround time for production is relatively short, which enables the user to act quickly when necessary.

On the negative side, the following are some considerations:

1. Often, direct mail is considered to be junk mail and is disposed of in the trash bin without being opened.

2. Consumers receive a significant amount of direct mail and, therefore, may not even look at some or any of it. Professionally designed, visually appealing pieces, printed on quality stock, are more likely to be read than poorly designed pieces printed on standard copy or printer paper.

10.11 Unique catalogue covers invite closer inspection of what's inside. *Courtesy of Saks Fifth Avenue.*

Outdoor Advertising

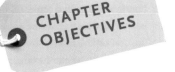

CHAPTER OBJECTIVES

After you have completed this chapter, you will be able to discuss:

★ The history of outdoor advertising and how it has evolved into today's media offering.

★ How the outdoor advertising formats in use today compare to those of other print and broadcast media in terms of importance to the retailer's promotional budget.

★ How the Outdoor Advertising Association of America assists advertisers with their promotional objectives.

★ The purpose of the Traffic Audit Bureau in regard to verifying the circulation of outdoor advertising displays.

★ Some of the traditional formats of billboards used to attract pedestrian and vehicular traffic.

★ Why digital billboards are more effective than their traditional counterparts.

★ Backlit transparencies and their effectiveness for motivating shoppers to buy.

★ How shopping bags have been transformed into promotional pieces rather than serving only utilitarian purposes.

★ The advantages and disadvantages of outdoor advertising.

Outdoor advertising is the oldest advertising medium. It evolved from ancient carvings in stone, bronze, and wood. More than 5,000 years ago, in ancient Egypt, hieroglyphic messages were used to direct travelers to the places they were seeking. About 2,500 years later, Egyptian merchants used stone to etch messages about their wares.

Much later, when paper was first developed and printing presses were built, the outdoor poster became a prominent fixture. By the fifteenth century, the outdoor poster was an accepted means of advertising in European countries. Four hundred years later, the billboard was transformed into a medium that featured artistic designs as well as messages. Artists of significant renown tried their hands at the outdoor medium, and the likes of Daumier, Manet, and Toulouse-Lautrec created masterpieces of poster artwork.

In the United States in the late nineteenth century, many companies began to lease wooden boards on which they posted their advertising messages, or *bills,* as they were called, hence the name *billboard.* From that time on, commercial enterprises have recognized the worth of the outdoor advertisements and have since used them to display their messages.

Today, strolling down the street, driving through both urban and suburban areas, standing on corners, or waiting for public transportation invariably exposes the individual to a variety of outdoor advertisements. High above the buildings in major cities, Gap stores and other merchants use billboards to promote their company's offerings, and at bus stops, Banana Republic is calling attention to its brand. Even shopping bags, once considered simply functional and disposable, have become an important vehicle for retailer advertising.

Although **outdoor advertising** provides retailers with many benefits, its use in terms of a merchant's overall advertising budget pales by comparison to

11.1 Outdoor posters are found on primary and secondary arteries. *newscom.*

11.2 Bleeds give posters an artistic feeling. *Hernis.fr/Superstock RF.*

Eight-Sheet Posters

With measurements of 6 feet by 12 inches, **8-sheet posters**, or junior panels, as they are called by the industry, are primarily used in urban and suburban areas, on city streets, and commuter railroad stations. As is the case with the larger variety of outdoor advertisements, they are usually changed every 30 days. Production techniques are also the same as for 30-sheet posters.

Painted Bulletins

The largest of the traditional outdoor advertisements is the **painted bulletin**. Typically, it measures 14 feet by 48 feet, giving the advertiser 672 square feet of space in which to present a message.

There are two types of painted advertisements: the **rotary bulletin** and the **permanent bulletin**. The rotary bulletin may be dismantled and then reassembled at different locations. The rotational periods generally range from 60 to 90 days. By using this format, the advertiser can communicate the message in a variety of locations within the desired trading area, as in the case of the retailer with branch stores. During the typical 1-year life of a painted message, it can be seen by the vast majority of those to whom it would have appeal. The permanent bulletin remains in one location. It is usually placed in a heavily traveled area and has the potential to reach a large number of people in the marketplace. A retailer, for example, who wishes to lead a driver to the store's location might use this format.

The painted bulletin is generally purchased on a one-unit basis, unlike posters, which are produced in quantities. The designs range from the traditional to three-dimensional, many with moveable parts. Many are even extended past the regular size limits by adding top, bottom, and side extensions. The extensions must conform to the regulations established for the locations in which they will be displayed.

The painted bulletins may be hand-painted indoors or on location, or produced using computer software and specially designed printers, or using silk-screening or lithography processes.

Video Mobile Billboards

One of the more recent innovations is the use of **video mobile billboards**, especially on the sides of trucks and vans that travel the streets of major cities. Advertisers can show their messages to a wide variety of audiences, and these ads may be regularly changed as needed with a minimum of effort. Video mobile billboards are an especially good tool for retailers who want to advertise their products and where they can be purchased.

Segway Advertising

The Segway, a unique means of transportation seen in many malls and on main shopping streets, has become a vehicle for advertising purposes. These two-wheeled electric vehicles that most often transport security staff throughout an area such as a shopping mall have been adapted to feature advertisements on their front panels. **Segway advertising** is especially useful for merchants located in the malls that use them and on busy thoroughfares to feature stores within that area.

Digital Billboards

In places such as outdoor arenas, sports venues, and roadsides, **digital billboards**, according to the OAAA, are one of the fastest-growing advertising concepts. The messages typically change every 8 to 10 seconds, so they are likely to hold the viewer's attention longer than a standard sign or billboard. More and more retailers are using digital billboards to promote their stores (Figure 11.3).

Transportation Shelter Panels

Many cities and municipalities use shelter protections to shield riders waiting for buses and trains. The walls of these semi-enclosed structures often feature traditional posters and backlit transparencies (discussed later in the chapter) of area retailers (Figure 11.4). Because they spend as much as 20 minutes on average in these shelters, the waiting crowd is more than likely to read the ads mounted in **transportation shelter panels**.

Exterior Transit Panels

Some retailers, such as Gap and Banana Republic, use the roofs of taxis to advertise their names, merchandise, store locations, and institutional messages. Regularly seen on taxi tops in major urban centers, **exterior transit panels** are an effective way to reach both residents of and visitors to targeted areas (Figure 11.5).

11.4 Those waiting to board a train or bus are sure to read these types of ads. *Creative by www.Alexdaledesign.co.uk.*

11.5 Shoppers are often tempted to visit the stores that advertise using these exterior panels. *Ellen Diamond.*

The panels are similar to traditional billboards in terms of production and contractual arrangements for the spaces they occupy. One major difference between the typical billboard and the rooftop panel is that the latter must be carefully designed to quickly capture the attention of passersby because the image quickly fades from sight. This is accomplished with the use of eye-catching color combinations, limited copy that can be rapidly understood, fonts that are easy to read, and simple design. Too busy an advertisement in this venue is ineffective.

Bus sides allow for horizontal, elongated ads that can be seen by passengers waiting to board the bus, by pedestrians, and by passing motorists (Figure 11.6).

In addition to the sides of these moving vehicles, their backs (and the backs of taxicabs as well) are used as advertising space. Automobile drivers and passengers can easily see the ads featured on **bus tails**. Because tail ads are often seen for a longer period of time than the side-panel ads (e.g., by motorists behind the bus or taxi), the messages and artwork can be more complex. A combination of good artwork and descriptive copy can encourage consumers to seek out the retailer.

Car Cards

Buses and subway cars often feature interior panels used to display advertisements. Typically, **car cards** line the spaces over the windows and are usually 11 inches tall and up to 48 inches wide. At the front and rear of public transportation vehicles, there are areas for advertisements of varying sizes, depending on the holders or frames installed.

Whereas the message on the outside of a bus must be conveyed in a matter of seconds because the vehicle is moving away from the observer, the interior transit advertisement may be studied for as long as the passenger is en route to his or her destination. Commuters often spend as much as 40 minutes or more on the bus or subway, and some of that time is spent reading the car card advertisements. Car cards can serve as a form of repeat advertising; many commuters ride the bus or train twice a day, 5 days a week, on their way to and from work, so they are repeatedly exposed to the ads. Many passengers read or listen to music during the commute, but they usually examine the transit ads as well, particularly if the car is too crowded to politely open a newspaper. The extended viewing time for interior transit ads makes them ideal for advertisers who have a lot of information to include in their ad.

WANT THE CAR? CHECK OUT
WWW.BARNEYS.COM

BARNEYS
NEW YORK

PEACE & LOVE

11.8 Shopping bags are "walking" advertisements for retailers. *Courtesy of Barneys.*

reused on every shopping trip. These are especially appealing to retailers and shoppers who want to support the green movement.

Whatever materials are used, shopping bags may be customized to fit any retailer's needs at prices that are relatively low, especially when the advertising advantage is considered.

Advantages and Disadvantages of Outdoor Advertising

Given that outdoor advertising is so cost effective, its advantages are considered by many industry professionals to be as positive as the considerably

higher-priced media. The advantages include the following:

1. Unlike other media that require close attention to hear or see the details of the message, the outdoor ad is generally absorbed in seconds and does not require taking time to understand its concept.

2. Hundreds of thousands of people can, in the course of a day, see a billboard when passing on a major highway, making it an excellent producer for potential sales, especially in local markets where it is placed.

3. Unlike television and radio, which can be turned off, bypassed with the use of recording technology, or ignored as in the case of newspapers and magazines, the outdoor

billboard or sign is generally noticed, even if that is not the intention of the viewer.

4. The cost of producing a billboard or other poster and the cost of the rental space for showing it are relatively inexpensive.

5. With its continuous placement, it is likely that the same people will see the billboard again and again, giving it the advantage of frequency.

6. When coupled with other media ads, outdoor advertising is an inexpensive adjunct.

7. With exciting color and creative imagery, outdoor advertising has the ability to capture immediate attention.

On the negative side, there are the following considerations:

1. Opponents of outdoor advertising contend that it causes blight on the highways and may be the cause of accidents.

2. Outdoor advertising is usually effective only when simple messaging is used, because the ads are often seen by automobile drivers who pass them by in a second or two.

3. The effectiveness of outdoor advertising requires a long-term commitment by the advertiser.

Summary of Key Points

◆ Outdoor advertising dates back more than 5,000 years, making it the oldest form of promotion. Throughout the ages, it has stayed relevant to advertisers, offering changes due to innovative technology.

◆ Through the establishment of such organizations as the Outdoor Advertising Association of America, the Out-of-Home Video Advertising Bureau, and the Traffic Audit

Bureau, outdoor advertising's image has improved, as has its importance to users of this medium.

◆ There are numerous types of outdoor billboard advertising, which include the traditional offerings such as 30-sheet posters, bleeds, 8-sheet posters, and painted bulletins, as well as the newer video mobile billboards, Segway installations, and full-motion TV screens.

◆ A recent innovation in the measurement of billboard watchers has made circulation figures more reliable (as discussed in Media Insight 11.2).

◆ Digital billboards are one of the fastest-growing additions to the advertising scene because they generate excitement for the observer and provide images and messages that change every 8 to 10 seconds.

◆ The backlit transparency has transformed the traditional outdoor sign that offers limited viewing time because of its ineffectiveness during the night into one that has 24-hour visibility.

◆ Shopping bags have been transformed from utilitarian sacks into containers that also provide advertising for retailers by using their signatures or logos on the bags' surfaces.

◆ A significant advantage to the use of outdoor advertising is that it can reach as many as hundreds of thousands of people in 1 day, making it very cost effective.

For Discussion

1. Describe the early characteristics of outdoor advertising and contrast them with today's outdoor advertising.

2. What are some of the key criticisms of billboard advertising as demonstrated by

Terms of the Trade

30-sheet posters

8-sheet posters

backlit transparency

blanking paper

bleed

bus sides

bus tails

car cards

digital billboards

exterior transit panels

Highway Beautification Act

light box

outdoor advertising

out-of-home advertising industry

painted bulletin

permanent bulletin

recycled paper

rotary bulletin

Segway advertising

transportation shelter panels

video mobile billboards

watchdog organizations

many public-interest groups? Which piece of federal legislation contributed to curtailment of its use?

3. What are some of the key points in the code of ethics established by the Outdoor Advertising Association of America?

4. List and describe three traditional billboard categories and how they differ from each other.

5. Discuss the technology reviewed in Media Insight 11.2, and explain why it has improved the credibility of the medium.

6. What advantage does the digital billboard have that the traditional type does not?

7. How are bus sides and tails being used by retailers in their advertising plans?

8. How has the use of the backlit transparency improved as an advertising tool compared to nonbacklit transparencies?

9. In what way have movie theaters entered the advertising arena?

10. What are two disadvantages to the use of outdoor ads in the form of highway billboards?

Exercises and Projects

1. Visit any major downtown areas, arenas, sports venues, or any other places where digital billboards are being used to analyze their content and effectiveness. Retail-oriented billboards would be preferred, but for the purpose of analysis of the format, any other subject or message is acceptable. To have a point of reference, three such installations should be photographed. When this has been accomplished, complete the following table and present your findings to the class using the photographs.

Advertiser	Type of Artwork	Message	Change Frequency

2. Position yourself at a busy downtown intersection for the purpose of discovering and recording outdoor advertisements on bus sides and tails and on taxicab roofs. Photograph five different ads. Mount each photo to a sheet of paper, and prepare a written report discussing the names of the advertisers, the artwork and messages employed, the vehicles that featured the ads, the approximate time each ad was able to be seen, and so on.

Web Site Exploration for In-Depth Analysis

Out-of-Home Video Advertising Bureau
http://www.ovab.org
   A complete overview of what the Out-of-Home Video Advertising Bureau does for the outdoor industry, including research sources for in-depth analysis, the latest news and events, and so on is presented on this site. This is an excellent site for those interested in broad outdoor advertising research.

Business.com/
http://www.business.com/directory/
   This site offers a number of different portals where the researcher may find helpful information on such areas as outdoor advertising agencies in the United States and beyond, digital billboard advertising, targeted advertising solutions, and more.

PART FOUR

CREATING THE ADVERTISING

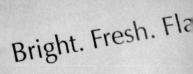

Print Media

CHAPTER OBJECTIVES

After you have completed this chapter, you will be able to discuss:

★ How the roles of the copywriter and art director interface to bring an ad to fruition.

★ What resources are available to the art director for the purposes of choosing advertising illustrations.

★ The role of the layout artist in the formation of the print advertisement.

★ Many of the points that should be considered when producing a headline.

★ The definition of a halftone and how it differs from photographs.

★ The different principles of design and how each contributes to an advertisement's structure.

★ Why white space is so vital to the overall composition of the print advertisement.

★ The different dimensions of color and why even the laypeople interested in advertising should understand them.

★ What is meant by *color harmonies* and the differences in each.

★ Some of the psychological aspects of color and how they affect advertising.

★ The traditional stages of development in layout preparation of a print ad.

★ The differences between rotogravure and screen printing.

★ The terms *point* and *pica* as they are used in advertisement measurement.

★ How the four-color process is achieved for color ads.

After the preliminary research, including analysis of the target markets, has been completed, the planning and budgeting strategies have been thoroughly investigated, and the different media have been considered for use in the advertising program, it is time to create and produce the advertisements. This phase, before the actual ads are seen by the consumer, is a painstaking one that requires considerable concentration.

Looking through the pages of the print media reveals the many different approaches advertisers use to catch the eyes of the potential purchasers of their merchandise. The competition to capture viewers' attention is fierce among the countless retail advertisements that appear in newspapers and magazines, direct-mail brochures and flyers, outdoor installations and transit offerings, and those featured on retail Web sites and social networking sites, so the importance of eye appeal cannot be overstated. Ads must be carefully created to follow the principles of design: they must have balance, emphasis, proportion, contrast, harmony, and sequence.

People purchase the newspaper, which accounts for most of retailers' print advertising, primarily for the news, columns, editorials, and other regular features, which adds another level of competition for attention. Ads must be exceptionally eye-catching if the reader is to grant them more than a cursory glance. With this in mind, the creative team must always be prepared with devices such as attention-getting headlines, imaginative artwork, and other bold attention grabbers that will motivate the reader to take a longer look. Remembering that the life of the newspaper is often limited to the time of the daily commute, the chore for the creative team is a formidable challenge.

The magazine, although longer-lived than the newspaper, nonetheless offers its own challenges to the creative forces. The considerable expense of magazine advertising warrants careful planning in terms of advertising content. Because magazines are often kept for long periods and are often passed on to other readers, their messages must remain fresh and exciting for long periods of time.

Direct-mail brochures and flyers, outdoor ads, and transit pieces also demand creativity and professionalism to ensure the attention of the consumers.

The manner in which the creative team's effort is transformed into the printed page is extremely important. Today's technology requires a wealth of mechanical know-how in order to make the transition from concept to print in a timely, high-quality, and cost-effective manner. Everyone concerned with the creative and production phase must be sufficiently knowledgeable to bring the print ad to fruition. In retailing, where time is of the essence in product or promotional advertising, all the participants in the process must work together to ensure that the ad, when designed, will arrive at the publication in time for it to meet the deadline for ad placement.

Creating the Print Advertisement

Creating a print advertisement is usually a group effort. A growing number of major retailers are opting for outside resources to create their advertising campaigns, but whether an in-house department or an outside agency handles the advertising, there is generally one individual charged with making certain the retailer's criteria are met. If it is an advertising agency, an **account executive** oversees the projects.

The information pertinent to an ad is supplied by a retail executive whose sole responsibility may be advertising or by someone such as a buyer or merchandise manager who has firsthand knowledge of the products or promotions on which the ad centers. For institutional advertisements, the information generally comes from the public relations person or department or from a store department, such as customer services, that formulates a pattern of goodwill. It is imperative that those responsible for the ad's creation are armed with all of the pertinent information

necessary to make the advertisement meaningful. Often, an **advertising request form** (Figure 12.1) containing information such as merchandise description, prices, promotional concepts, and so forth is sent to the in-house advertising manager or agency account manager so that he or she has a complete understanding of the important points to be stressed in the advertisement.

In small retail operations, where costs are a major concern, one person, generally a freelancer, is hired to write the copy, provide the artwork, and produce the layout. Of course, some small merchants choose to develop their own ads. In such cases, it is imperative that they understand the key elements of ad creation. In Media Insight 12.1, an industry professional addresses some of the considerations in creating print advertisements.

In large retail organizations that have an in-house advertising department or that hire an ad agency, the tasks are usually divided among three individuals: the copywriter, the art director, and the layout artist.

The Copywriter

The **copywriter** uses the information regarding the nature of the ad (usually provided on the advertising request form) to develop a story that will translate all of the information into an ad that will motivate the reader to examine it and ultimately act on its message. If the advertisement is composed solely of a written message, there is no need for communication with the art director. Except for closeout or promotional advertisements, in which the written word often suffices, the copywriter works in conjunction with the art director so that their work can be dovetailed to produce the best possible ad. They may have one or more brainstorming sessions, depending on the nature of the ads and whether it is a onetime production or a full campaign. In either case, working in tandem helps them produce the most meaningful and productive ads.

The Art Director

The **art director** is responsible for selecting the artwork most appropriate for the advertisements. The art may be original drawings, photographs taken specifically for the project, **in-stock photography**, **clip art**, or stock drawings. Many fashion

ADVERTISING REQUEST

THIS FORM WILL NOT BE ACCEPTED UNLESS INFORMATION IS COMPLETE

CIRCLE ONE   Z   DI   X

DEPT. NO.

	DATE	SIZE		DATE	SIZE
☐ TIMES			☐ COLONIE		
☐ NEWS			☐ AMSTERDAM NEWS		
☐ POST			☐ SUFFOLK SUN		
☐ L.I.P.			☐ OTHER (LIST)		
☐ NEWSDAY			☐		
☐ WEST. GRP.			☐		
☐ N. H. REG.			☐		

MERCHANDISE FOR NEW ART WORK IS DUE IN 15th FL. LOAN ROOM WHEN PINK SHEET IS DUE

EXCEPTION: Ready-to-wear merchandise is due directly after weekly Merchandise Review Meeting. Bulk merchandise should be available on the floor for movement to studio, or for sketching, when called for. Merchandise in LOAN ROOM? ☐ Yes ☐ No

Do not request New Art Work BEFORE checking file FOR OLD ART.

No. of Illus.	Illustrations to be featured. Points to be emphasized
No. of New	
No. of Old	Date and medium in which old art ran last (attach proof)

OTHER MEDIA ☐ MAGAZINE   NAME _____ ISSUE _____   ☐ SALE BOOKLET   ☐ OTHER DIRECT MAIL   ☐ RADIO   ☐ TV

MAIL ORDERS Yes ☐ ☐ No   PHONE ORDERS Yes ☐ ☐ No   COUPON Yes ☐ ☐ No

TOTAL AMT. OF MDSE. AT RETAIL $ _____   NO. OF UNITS _____   DAY SELLING IS TO BEGIN _____   NUMBER OF DAYS ON SALE _____

ON SALE AT: (CIRCLE) ALL STORES - H. S. - R. F. - HUNT. - B. S. - JAM. - W. P. - PARK. - FLAT. - NEW HAV. - QUEENS - COLONIE - NEW ROCHELLE - SM. HAV.

ABOUT THE MERCHANDISE: (NOTE: Please complete the following IN DETAIL.)

	ITEM	STYLE NO.	CURR. RETAIL	ADV. PRICE	QUOTE PHRASE & PRICE*	SIZES	COLORS
1.							
2.							
3.							
4.							
5.							
6.							

MOST IMPORTANT SELLING POINTS (from customer's view) AND SUPERIORITY TO COMPETITIVE ITEMS. (Use other side if necessary.)

IMPORTANT: PINK SHEETS WILL NOT BE ACCEPTED UNLESS THE FOLLOWING INFORMATION IS PROVIDED.

1. TEXTILE FIBER PRODUCTS
List all information on the product label. If available, a fiber identification tag may be stapled in place.

2. NON TEXTILE PRODUCTS
Copy from label or tag all information relative to composition of parts of product including finishes.

3. ELECTRICAL ITEMS
Copy all name plate ratings including volts, amps, watts, horsepower, BTU, CFM, etc. Indicate if UL approved.

THIS IS A ☐ SALE   LAST PREVIOUS DATE _____   LAST PREVIOUS PRICE _____

☐ CLEARANCE   ☐ SPECIAL PURCHASE   ☐ MFG'S CLOSE-OUT   ☐ OTHER

INFORMATION ON COMPARATIVE PHRASES: (Note: Complete in detail as applicable.)

1. ☐ "REGULARLY" - means temporary reduction. Refers to price immediately before sale and price to which merchandise will return following sale.
   (a) period during which merchandise was selling on floor at regular price _____
   (b) approximate number of units _____ Is this the normal selling rate? _____
   (c) Is stock to be augmented with merchandise which is not identical? _____

2. ☐ "ORIGINALLY" - means first price during the recent course of business. (Recent course of business is current selling season for seasonal merchandise such as apparel and sporting goods, etc. and not more than 12 months for non-seasonal merchandise such as furniture, appliances, etc.).
   (a) period during which merchandise was selling on floor at original price _____
   (b) approximate number of units _____ Is this the normal selling rate? _____
   (c) Is stock to be augmented with merchandise which is not identical? _____

3. ☐ "COMPARABLE VALUE" - merchandise of equal grade and quality in all material respects.
   OR
   ☐ "VALUE" - identical merchandise selling in other stores.
   Indicate stores at which merchandise is likely to be found. _____
   If in Macy's stock, indicate style # and price. _____

BUYER OR ASST. BUYER   MDSE. ADM. OR V.P.   COMP. OFFICE REPRESENTATIVE

PART 1 ADVERTISING DEPT. COPY

12.1 Advertising request forms are completed before an ad is placed. *Courtesy of Macy's.*

retailers, in particular, opt for specially crafted artwork that sets them apart from their competition. The ultimate choice often depends on the company's advertising budget. If the advertising project is a campaign, the art theme is generally carried throughout the program.

The Layout Artist

The task of the **layout artist** (Figure 12.2) is the ultimate placement or positioning of the work provided by the copywriter and art director. He or she prepares a preliminary layout encompassing all of the components of the advertisement, such as the

Creating the Best Print Ads

Michele Pariza Wacek

Want to create print ads that get results? The following are three keys to get you started.

1. Write for the eye.

Print ads are visual. Therefore, craft ads with the eye in mind.

Eyes are kind of picky, though. So, here's a checklist of what eyes like and don't like:

• A catchy headline that encourages them to read more.

• Art, such as photos, illustrations, clip art, shapes, etc. Eyes like art. When you create the ad, create words *and* the visual at the same time. Words and visuals should work together.

• Designed in an interesting, intriguing, attention-getting manner. Eyes like that. Remember, graphic designers are your friends. If you don't have training in graphic design, I strongly urge you to hire a graphic designer to create your ad. The results will be well worth it.

• White space (blank space in the ad). Eyes like white space. Eyes don't like print ads stuffed with words and/or art. Those ads look way too difficult to read and comprehend, [so] eyes will skip over those ads and find other open, clean ads to look at. (And if they do, you might as well have never bought the ad in the first place.)

2. Write for the busy eye.

Nobody is reading a newspaper because they want to see your ad. (Okay, your mother is the exception.) People are reading the paper because they want information. Reading your ad is an afterthought, [so] they aren't going to spend a whole heck of a lot of time on it.

A common mistake is asking print ads to do too much. To be successful, print ads must:

• Capture the attention of your potential customers,

• Encourage those potential customers to remember what you want them to do,

• Then persuade them to actually do it.

That's a lot to ask for one little print ad.

Print ads should have one message and one message only. The more "extras" about your business you start throwing into the ad, the more convoluted the ad is going to become, and the less likely your potential customers will act upon your ad.

Now at this point you may be thinking, "Okay. We need one message. That message should be to get my potential customers to buy something, hire my services, donate money, become a volunteer, etc. Right?"

Well . . .

For one thing, that's a pretty big leap for your potential customers. Getting potential customers to buy without first developing a relationship with them is, again, asking an awful lot for one little print ad. You might be better off inviting potential customers to take one small step in the buying process. For instance, stopping in the store for a free gift, logging on to your Web site to enter a contest, putting their names on your mailing list,

trying a demo version of your product, etc. Let them get to know you.

3. Keep your target market in mind.

Your message should be focused on your customers' needs, not your own. Getting customers to buy your products and services is *your* need. How your products or services solve your customers' problems is *their* needs. See the difference?

That's why so many retail stores have sales. They're effective because they're solving a need (saving customers money). But saving money is not the only need. There are many others.

You should also think about ways to add value without bargaining on price (this position can backfire). Contests, free gifts, free reports, free food—stuff like that. Think outside the box. And use that value as a way to set yourself apart.

Creativity Exercises— Learn by example

One of the best ways to learn how to craft successful print ads is to study what's out there.

• Get out a newspaper or a magazine and open it. See where your eyes go. What ads attract your eyes? What ads drive them away?

• Which ads have headlines that intrigue you? Graphics that capture your attention? Copy that encourages you to find out more? Why?

• Now look at ads that do nothing for you. Why don't you like them? Are they too cluttered? Too difficult to understand? Have a headline that makes you yawn?

Sometimes you can learn as much, if not more, from bad examples as you can from good ones.

Copyright 2006 Michele Pariza Wacek.

headline, subheadline, message, illustrations, and so forth, all of which are fully discussed later in the chapter. After the layout has been examined by the parties responsible for the final representation, and any changes have been made to alter the ad, the finished layout is ready for production.

Components of a Print Advertisement

Both the copy and the artwork have different elements that must be addressed before they are assembled into an advertisement. For the copy, the headline and subheadline, as well as the body of the message, must be developed. Generally, each of these elements is used in an ad, but this is not always a requirement. In a retailer's fashion ad, for example, where a famous designer's unique creation is featured, there may be no need for copy as a motivational device. The use of the designer's signature or logo might be sufficient to attract the reader's attention. The decision is usually left to the creative team. Typically, however, the following elements compose the retail advertisement.

Copy

The written portion of the ad, or **copy**, must be carefully developed to catch the attention of the reader and present a message or story about the nature of the presentation and the action that the readers might take to avail themselves of the offer. First and foremost, it is the headline that must be carefully crafted to catch the reader's eye.

THE HEADLINE

This attention-getting device usually makes the reader stop and determine whether to read further. If the **headline** does not generate immediate interest, the remainder of the ad probably will not be examined. There is no specific direction

12.2 The layout artist prepares the ad's layout.
© LWA-JDC/Corbis.

or foolproof formula that goes into the creation of a good headline. The professional understands the tried-and-true rules of headline writing and applies them to every situation. For retailers with little experience in creating advertisements or with limited budgets that preclude hiring a professional, there are some points that should be considered when writing the headline:

1. *Keep it simple:* Simplicity is the key to an eye-catching headline. Unless the situation is unique, the words should be restricted to no more than ten words. A recent ad campaign from Saks Fifth Avenue uses "Want It!" as its simple headline.

2. *Use a benefit:* Headlines such as "Famous Designer Collection Offered at Rock-Bottom Prices" or "Furnish Your Home Today with No Payments for One Year" clearly invite further inspection of the ad.

3. *Avoid generalities:* Unless it is clearly appealing to a specific market or audience, the headline will not attract attention.

4. *Target an audience:* The headline should be addressed to a market segment such as teenagers, seniors, and so forth, to encourage that group to read the body of the ad.

5. *Use the right font and type size:* The headline must be easily read. It must not use fonts that are difficult to comprehend quickly. Although Old English is an artistic style, it is often too flowery for a headline. The size is also imperative. It must be sufficiently large and bold to capture the reader's attention.

6. *Provoke curiosity:* Readers are often motivated to read the body of the ad if the headline makes them curious. In fashion advertising, for example, a headline that says "Guess Which Famous Couturier Will Appear in Person Today?" will attract fashion devotees.

7. *Focus on a specific brand or label:* Headlines such as "Rockport Is All About Ease" and "Introducing Ralph Lauren Purple Label" use the brand name to attract attention.

THE SUBHEADLINE

A headline alone is sometimes insufficient to convince the reader to read on. Although it might gain the reader's eye, it may need a subhead to further develop the intent of the ad before using body copy to complete the message.

Subheadlines are set in smaller types sizes and usually different fonts than the ad's headline. They are usually longer than the headline and provide a little more information to engage the reader's interest in the body of the ad. It is important for the headline and the subhead to demonstrate some relationship. An example of this combination was featured in a Dillard's promotional ad that used copy alone rather than a combination of copy and artwork. The headline in large, bold type read:

Save an extra 40% off

The subheadline followed:

That's a savings of up to 82%

The intent was to catch the eye with the discount and then underscore its overall savings with the subheadline (Figure 12.3).

SLOGANS

In some advertisements, retailers use the same **slogan** again and again so that it becomes embedded in the consumer's mind and increases memorability of the company. For many years, Bloomingdale's has used the slogan *It's Like No Other Store In The World*, Macy's uses *The Magic of Macy's*, and Lord & Taylor uses *Shop Smart at Lord & Taylor* (Figure 12.4). Although slogans are difficult to create because a powerful and catchy message must be packed into just a few words, successful slogans create widespread name recognition for the advertisers.

LOGOS

The use of **logos** or symbols has long been a tradition in product and retail marketing. Think of a Ralph Lauren T-shirt with the polo pony emblazoned on it. The reversed overlapping C's in Chanel ads, the LV in Louis Vuitton advertising, the

RALPH LAUREN

The Ultimate Experience
Madison Avenue at 72nd Street

12.3 Subheadlines help get the reader to read the rest of an ad. *Courtesy of Ralph Lauren.*

12.4 Slogans often increase memorability for the consumer. *Courtesy of Lord & Taylor.*

HOLIDAY SHOPPING GIVING YOU A HEADACHE?
TAKE TWO (OR MORE) OF THESE.

GIFTS UNDER $75
lordandtaylor.com

SHOP SMART AT *Lord & Taylor*

VISIT OUR FLAGSHIP STORE ON FIFTH AVENUE AT 39TH STREET

stylized crown for Rolex ads, and the YSL used in Yves St. Laurent designs and promotions are just some of the logos used for recognition purposes. Despite the attention given to the logo and its development, some industry insiders wonder if it is a thing of the past. In Media Insight 12.2, a case for its death is offered.

THE BODY COPY

With the headline and subheadline in place, the copywriter has the task of writing a message encompassing the point of the ad. These words are used to amplify the message and, it is hoped, motivate the reader to take action. The depth of the **body copy** varies among advertisements. Its

You May Love the Logo, But It's a Dying Breed

Martin Lindtrom

"Make it bigger!" an executive screamed as I desperately sought a sign-off on an ad for a major fashion brand. It wasn't the first time this situation had come up. In fact, it seemed like every meeting ended up in discussions about the placement and size of the logo. It was as if, over time, the logo had become the holy grail of branding; the rest was more or less an add-on. Don't believe we live in a logo-obsessed world? Just pay a quick visit to Times Square.

As we are exposed to millions of messages in our lifetimes, does the logo retain its magic? Or are we caught up in a format that once worked but is out of date?

The Centers for Disease Control and Prevention estimates that 20 percent of all adults in the United States—about 45 million people—smoke cigarettes. That's despite the fact that we all know it's unhealthful and that in many places it's almost impossible to light up indoors. Most cigarette advertising was banned decades ago in many countries. Yet Marlboro, for one, is high on Interbrand's 2008 list of the best global brands.

Faced with limited media in which they can brandish their logos, tobacco companies still have managed to craft clever brand strategies. Marlboro's solid sponsorship of Europe's Formula One racing has made the brand's red Ferrari cars iconic. Could it be that cigarette cravings can be triggered by images, such as those red Ferraris, that are tied to a brand of cigarette but not explicitly linked to smoking? Does a smoker need to read the word *Marlboro* to feel compelled to tear open a pack?

The answer can be found in a small region in the brain called the nucleus accumbens—the craving spot, which controls our pleasures and addictions. It is a lie detector. You may claim to be unaffected by tobacco ads, but your nucleus accumbens will reveal the truth.

One of Britain's leading scientists, Oxford's Gemma Calvert, and I set out to find out what really goes on in the subconscious mind when it is exposed to cigarette-advertising imagery. The subjects of our neuro-marketing study were smokers, former smokers, and people considering smoking. All were asked to refrain from smoking for 2 hours before the test, to ensure that their nicotine levels would be equal.

First, they were shown subliminal images that had no overt connection to cigarette brands—a red Ferrari, a cowboy on horseback, a camel in the desert. Next, they were shown explicit images such as the Marlboro Man and Joe Camel, the Marlboro and Camel logos, and branded packs of cigarettes. In both cases, we used MRI to look for activity in the nucleus accumbens. We wanted to find out if the subliminal images would generate cravings similar to those generated by the logos and the clearly marked Marlboro and Camel packs.

The Results

To no one's surprise, the MRI scans revealed pronounced responses in the craving region of volunteers' brains when they viewed the cigarette packs. But when the smokers were exposed to the nonexplicit images—Western-style scenery, etc.—there was almost immediate activity in the exact same region. In fact, the only consistent difference was that the subliminal images prompted more activity in the subjects' primary visual cortexes—as might be expected, given the more complex task of processing those images. There was a similar response among former smokers (but no response among people who had never smoked before).

More fascinating still, when Dr. Calvert compared the responses to the two different types of images, she found even more activity in the reward and craving center when subjects viewed the subliminal images than when they viewed the over images. In other words, the logo-free images associated with cigarettes triggered more cravings among smokers than the logos themselves or the images of cigarette packs, a result that was consistent for both Camel and Marlboro smokers.

What does this mean in practical terms? When the contour Coca-Cola bottle was invented in 1915, the original brief was to develop a bottle so distinct that if you dropped it on the floor and it smashed into dozens of pieces of glass, you'd still be able to recognize the brand. Move on from the logo and begin to develop "smashable" components—color, shape, sound, smell—indirect signals that tell a story about the brand without the logo. Such components engage the consumer in figuring out who's behind the message and, most importantly, speak to the subconscious mind. You won't find a logo on the front of an iPod, yet its iconic look is enough for you to know what brand it is. The same is true for a McDonald's roof, a blue Tiffany box, and a Marlboro cowboy. The logo isn't dead yet, but I would bet its days are numbered.

Source: Martin Lindstrom. "You May Love the Logo, But It's a Dying Breed." Advertising Age, December 1, 2008.

volume depends on the nature of the ad. Retailers of fashion merchandise often opt for fewer words and let the artwork tell the story. When the body copy warrants written emphasis, it usually concentrates on selling points or features and benefits to the purchaser, reassurances such as ease in making returns, delivery options, and so forth.

It is important to present the retailer's case in as few words as possible. Lengthy explanations, if not essential to the offer, should be avoided. Wordy messages, especially in newspaper ads that must compete with pages and pages of reading material, may seem too daunting for busy consumers to read.

Illustrations

Unless the advertisement is promotionally oriented, artwork is essential to an ad and is often the element that captures readers' attention. The use of photographs, halftones, and drawings enhance any written message. The art director in an in-house department or an advertising agency is responsible for the type of graphics or illustrations that will best capture the reader's attention, but few create their own artwork. Specialists—artists, photographers, graphics artists, stylists—are employed by the retailer or hired on a freelance basis to create the visuals for the ads. These professionals have the expertise to create ads with the look and feel—sophisticated or casual, fancy or simple, serious or fun—that best meets the advertiser's needs (Figure 12.5).

The Layout

As individual elements, the headlines, subheadlines, slogans, body copy, and illustrations do not make an entire advertisement. They must be arranged in some organization or format that makes the eye move from one component to the next until the reader has focused attention on its entirety. The arranger of a symphonic performance knows how to use the instruments in the orchestra in an effective manner to generate excitement; the layout artist does the same with the elements that are made available to him or her. Judgments must be made in terms of how to properly place the pieces to produce the best eye-appealing advertisement that will motivate the reader to act in a positive manner. Sound layout design involves understanding design principles and how **white space**, or negative space, interacts with the advertisement's elements.

PRINCIPLES OF DESIGN

In preparing the layout, it is necessary for the **principles of design** to be incorporated in the plan. They are **balance**, **emphasis**, **proportion**, **contrast**, **harmony**, and **sequence** (Figure 12.6).

- *Balance:* Balance involves the eye's impression of equal weight distribution. To test for balance, an imaginary line is drawn down the advertisement's center, and a comparison is made to determine if both sides "weigh" the same. One side need not be a mirror image of the other to be balanced but should provide an impression that it is similar. There are two types of balance used by layout designers: **symmetrical balance** and **asymmetrical balance**. Symmetrically balanced advertisements use a formal approach in which each side of the ad is identical to the other. This is a safe way to achieve balance, but it often produces an unimaginative look. On the other hand, asymmetrically balanced layouts are informal and generally more exciting. The balance is achieved by using different elements on either side of the advertisement's center that, when properly placed, give the impression of equal weight. Asymmetrical balance is more difficult to achieve and requires more sophisticated placement to be successful.

- *Emphasis:* One element of the ad should be selected as the **focal point** to which the eye is drawn. The focal point may be the headline, photograph, drawing, logo, symbol, or anything else that is considered vital to the advertisement's success. If each element is similar in size, stature, and importance, emphasis is lost.

- *Proportion:* The size of the elements should fit the space of the advertisement. An oversized headline in a limited amount of space not only leaves little room for the remainder of the message and the artwork but also gives the advertisement a disproportionate appearance.

- *Contrast:* To bring interest to the layout, a variety of sizes, shapes, and tones should be used. Different fonts or typefaces, of which there are hundreds, can be used to achieve

contrast, as can both dark and light tones. Variation of color also provides contrast. If a word or sentence in the body copy is *italicized* when all of the others are roman, the contrast draws the eye and emphasizes the word or sentence.

◆ *Harmony:* Although contrast is important to achieve interest, the elements of the advertisement must fit together in some harmonious relationship. That is, an advertisement designed to give the impression of traditional fashion should make certain that the photography and type style are suited for each other. It is much the same as the apparel designer who makes certain that the garment's trimmings enhance the silhouette. Without attention to this principle,

CHANGE
IS THE
ONLY
CONSTANT

CHANEL
Sandal, 895.00.
Shoe Salon.
Sunglasses, 535.00.
Clutch, 1,295.00 each.
Necklace, 1,705.00.
Choker, 725.00.
Designer Handbags.

Neiman Marcus

the layout might appear confusing to the observer.

◆ *Sequence:* When elements are placed in an orderly fashion, the eye will move from one element to the next until all have been examined. The best sequencing involves getting the eye to focus from left to right and from top to bottom. This is achieved by drawing attention first to the advertisement's most important element, and from there getting attention to move across and down.

WHITE SPACE

To emphasize the artwork and copy of the advertisement, it is essential to avoid **clutter**, which is achieved by leaving space around them. Without attention to this detail, the art and copy will run into each other, making the ad visually unappealing and difficult to read. The amount of white space, or negative space, used is an arbitrary decision. Too little will cause clutter, and too much might result in a fragmented advertisement (Figure 12.7).

White space often runs to the outside edges of an ad, giving the ad a larger, more open appearance than if it were framed by a border. The open effect can also be achieved using bleeds, where the advertisement's image runs all the way to its outside edges. Layout designers use positive and negative space to achieve the effects that best serve the purpose of the advertisement.

12.6 *(opposite)* A good layout uses the principles of design. *Courtesy of Neiman Marcus.*

12.7 The use of white space relieves the ad of clutter. *Courtesy of Tiffany & Co.*

give voice
TO YOUR HEART

For cherished family
For dearest friends
For your one and only
Something from out of the blue,
To be treasured always

A. Petals key of diamonds set in platinum, 2 ¼" long, $6,500.
B. Platinum chain, 16" long, sold separately, $325. Longer lengths available.
Front cover: Fleur de lis key of diamonds set in platinum, 1 ½" long, $2,650.
Platinum chain, 16" long, $325. Longer lengths available.

800 843 3269 | TIFFANY.COM

Color: Enhancing the Advertisement

Color is used to draw attention to and set the mood for an advertisement. Although it is sparingly used in newspapers, it is an essential ingredient in most magazine advertising. Black and white sometimes produces a meaningful message to readers, but color ads generally gain the most attention.

Understanding the use of color and its power as a marketing tool is essential for those involved in advertising design to produce the most eye-appealing ads. Professionals are equipped to make the most appropriate use of color, but those with less formal training must also understand the dimensions of color, the harmonies that are used, the terminology, and the psychology of color. Retailers such as merchandisers and buyers who often have input in advertising decision making and entrepreneurs who participate in advertising approval, though they do not create the ads, must be sufficiently color savvy to make educated assessments of the ads that have been created for them.

THE DIMENSIONS OF COLOR

A basic understanding of the color terminology used by advertising professionals is essential for anyone involved in evaluating color advertisements (Figure 12.8). Following are some of the terms used to describe the dimensions of color:

- *Hue:* **Hue** is the name of the color. Yellow, red, and blue are known as the **primary colors** from which all other colors are produced. Sometimes, these pure colors do not fulfill the requirements of an advertisement. In such cases, variations are used to achieve the requirements set forth by the creative advertising team. Mixing the pure colors results in these variations. Orange, for example, is a **secondary color** produced by mixing red and yellow.

- *Value:* The lightness or darkness of a hue is its **value**. White is added to a hue to lighten the color, resulting in a **tint**. Black is added to produce what is technically known as a **shade**. These additions change only the values, not the colors. Differ-

ent values offer the advertising designer a wealth of options to make the ad more visually appealing.

- *Intensity:* The saturation or purity of a color is known as its **intensity**, or the brightness or dullness of the color. Intensity may be varied by adding middle gray to the dye or adding the complement (discussed shortly) of the color. Colors in their purest states are most brilliant and might be too "alive" for the ad, thus requiring the use of a less intense or duller hue.

COLOR HARMONIES

A **color harmony** is a scheme or arrangement that is easily accomplished by following specific rules based on a **color wheel** (Figure 12.9). The color wheel helps the user to understand the relationships of colors and apply them by using their location on the wheel. It is an excellent concept that allows even those not knowledgeable about color to understand its do's and don'ts.

Some of the color harmonies used in advertisements include the following attributes.

- *Monochromatic:* The **monochromatic color scheme** arrangement uses only one hue. Initially, this might not seem very stimulating, but its proper use has potential visual elegance. Using tints and shades of one hue, then highlighting it with such neutrals as black and white, not technically colors, the designer can achieve an advertisement that immediately attracts the eye of the reader.

- *Analogous:* Colors that are next to each other on the color wheel may be used in combination to form the **analogous color scheme**. This arrangement gives the advertiser greater freedom, unlike the limitations set forth in the monochromatic arrangement. As with the monochromatic scheme, neutrals, along with tints and shades, provide more variety.

- *Complementary:* When color selection in advertising builds on two colors that are directly opposite each other on the

12.8 *(opposite)* **Proper color use is essential to good advertising.** *Courtesy of Burberry.*

BURBERRY.COM

BURBERRY
PRORSUM

the stage of converting the image into film. The process is known in the industry as **computer to plate (CTP)**.

OFFSET LITHOGRAPHY

This process, which is the most widely used by the newspaper industry, requires that the image to be printed is etched on thin aluminum plates that are wrapped around cylinders. The inked plate image then comes into contact with a rubber blanket on a second cylinder, which then transfers the image to the paper on yet another cylinder.

ROTOGRAVURE

The process of rotogravure provides excellent color quality, which makes it the perfect process for printing Sunday newspaper supplements, catalogues, and magazines. The printing is achieved by means of tiny inkwells. Suction is used to pull the ink from the wells and onto the paper. It is extremely cost efficient for printing runs greater than 100,000 pieces; smaller runs generally rely on offset lithography.

SCREEN PRINTING

When limited production runs are needed, as in the case of posters, screen printing is often the choice. Screen printing involves using a silk or synthetic screen stretched tightly on a frame, onto which a "film" or stencil is adhered. The design is cut from the film to create a stencil, and only those areas that are cut away allow the color to penetrate. Inks are then spread over the screen by using a squeegee and pushed through the stencil, printing only the unprotected surface. Each color in the advertisement requires a separate screen. If, for example, the ad features four colors, four screens must be prepared and run separately to complete the piece.

Typography

For a print advertisement to maximize its potential as an attention-getter, it must be composed of type that not only delivers but also enhances the message. A mood can be created, an image can be achieved, and readability can be maximized with the proper typeface. There are hundreds of different styles of type, from simple to ornate, as well as a wealth of sizes.

12.12 Publications provide vital information for potential advertisers to examine before making an advertising decision. *Courtesy Condé Nast Publications.*

TYPE SELECTION

The typographer's first step is to select the **typeface** that will best serve the advertisement. Two commonly used typefaces are sans serif and old Roman. Each typeface offers a basic set of letters (both uppercase and lowercase), numerals, and punctuation characters called a **font**. When two or more series of typefaces feature variations on one design, they are part of a **type family**. Figure 12.13 features some of the most commonly used advertising typefaces, and Figure 12.14 shows variations of the same fonts. In choosing the appropriate typeface for an advertisement, it is essential that it reflect the image of the ad, is easy to read quickly (especially when the ad appears in newspapers, which have a short life), is a combination of uppercase and lowercase letters (which are easier to read than all capitals), and is the right size to be easily read as well as to work in balance with the rest of the ad.

TYPE MEASUREMENT

Typographers use a standard measurement system to mark the copy being prepared for typesetting. The units are measured in points and picas.

- A **point** is the unit for measuring the height of the type. There are 72 points to the inch. Thus, 72-point type is 1 inch high; 36-point type, 1/2 inch; 18-point type, 1/8 inch, and so on. Type may be set at any point; however, anything less than 6 points is too small to read. The space between the lines of type, known as **leading**, is also measured in points. Typically, a few points are used to separate the body copy in an advertisement. Figure 12.14 features the various sizes of type of the same typeface.

- A **pica** is the unit for measuring the width of the type. There are 6 picas to the inch, so, for example, 48 picas is 8 inches.

After the decisions regarding type measurement are made, the next production stage centers on typesetting. The process is most often accomplished using a computer.

Artwork

Most retail product advertising makes extensive use of artwork in conjunction with the written message. Photographs, transparencies, or drawings must be transformed into a **photoengraving**

Advertising Production Association of Los Angeles (APALA)

The Advertising Production Association of Los Angeles (APALA) is a nonprofit association of advertising professionals in such fields as graphics communication, print production, advertising production, and digital production. Founded in 1945, it serves southern California with a significant number of forums that educate its membership with the latest innovations, advances, and directions in advertising production. It provides an environment in which industry professionals can come together to exchange information with their peers to improve their contributions to the field as well as to the companies for which they work. As a bona fide nonprofit association, the group is governed by bylaws and an elected board of directors.

To provide its membership with continuous new information regarding print production, in addition to its forums APALA holds regular monthly meetings, annual vendor showcases that feature the latest in technological equipment and software, career-enhancing workshops, achievement awards to honor industry professionals, and a monthly newsletter, both in print and on its Web site. Also offered on its Web site are opportunities for membership networking and access to industry leaders.

Some of the workshops offered by industry experts through APALA include Print Production Checkup and Makeover, focusing on career checkups and professional makeovers; The Role of Print in the New Media Mix, assessing the various avenues of communication available; and Social Networking Demystified, a crash course on this communication tool.

APALA's mission is to promote the interests of those in the field and to provide opportunities of both a personal and professional nature.

armchair ARABELLA, Carlo Giorgetti e Massimo Scolari 2010 | www.giorgetti.eu | illustration by David Downton @ Serlin Associates

Arabella

GIORGETTI®

MILANO VIA MONTENAPOLEONE 18 | DEN HAAG | NEW YORK | KÖLN

GIORGETTI NY 440 Lexington Avenue, Suite 504 NY, NY 10016 tel 212 989 3200 showroom ny@giorgetti-usa.com www.giorgetti-usa.com to find a dealer in your area please call 888 836 2100

necessary to ensure that the desired colors have been achieved. Traditional proofing that requires close examination by a professional's eye is still used, but **digital proofing** has become the method of choice by many advertising production companies. In either case, the ad cannot go to press until proofing is done and color corrections, if necessary, are made.

Proofing can result in many revisions. When color perfection is of the essence, as it is in fashion advertising, in particular, the process may require many revisions.

Paper Selection

After the layout is approved, the copy is written, the artwork is selected, the typeface in the appropriate sizes is chosen, and all of the elements are arranged in a format expected to bring positive results for the advertiser, the final stage is to choose the paper grade most appropriate for the advertisement. Paper or stock selection is not always an option for the advertiser and thus must be left to the publication. Newspapers, for example, are printed on **newsprint**, and magazines generally use glossy, coated stock. For direct mail, transportation shelter displays, car cards, and so on, the choice of paper is left to the advertiser. Some of the more commonly used papers include **offset paper**, used primarily for letterpress printing; **cover paper**, a heavy stock sometimes used for covers on booklets; **text paper**, when textures are required for booklets and brochures; and **bond**, when high-quality personalized announcements are needed for communication with special customers.

Summary of Key Points

- To draw attention to the newspaper and magazine advertisement among so many competing ads, it is essential for the creative team to be prepared with imaginative headlines, exciting artwork, and a carefully planned layout.

- The three major professionals in the production of advertisements are the copywriter, the art director, and the layout artist.

- The headline, often the portion of the ad that captures the reader's attention, must be simple, suggest some benefit, avoid generalities, target an audience, use the right font and type size, and provoke curiosity to motivate action.

- In the preparation of an ad, each of the design principles must be addressed and applied so that the best possible advertisement will be produced by the creative team.

- The use of color is imperative in publications such as magazines and must be created in harmonies or schemes that most often follow the rules based on the color wheel.

- The psychology of color should be understood so that color can be used in ads to evoke the desired response.

- Layout preparation in print advertising often follows a traditional approach, which includes the use of thumbnails, roughs, and comprehensives or mechanicals.

- Offset lithography, rotogravure, screen, and digital printing are most often used in the production of a print ad.

- It is essential for a retailer to understand the specifications and requirements of ad placement in order to make meaningful production decisions.

- Type selection and measurement are essential to the production of every print advertisement.

For Discussion

1. What sources does the art director turn to for artwork other than original art to be used in advertising?

2. Why is the headline so important in print ads, and what are some of the points that must be considered before one is written by the copywriter?

Broadcast Media

CHAPTER OBJECTIVES

After you have completed this chapter, you will be able to:

★ List and discuss the various stages of the preproduction of television commercials.

★ Describe the important points a scriptwriter of television commercials usually addresses in the final script.

★ Identify the numerous trade associations and unions in the television industry.

★ Explain the different production techniques used by those involved in the actual production process of making a television commercial.

★ Discuss some of the processes used in transitioning from the production to postproduction stage until the final cut has been achieved.

★ Explain why client approval is needed after a commercial has been considered to be a finished product by the team that produced it.

★ Discuss why the production of a radio advertisement is easier to accomplish than that of a television commercial.

★ Explain how a client can select a "voice" for a radio commercial without actually interviewing prospective candidates.

Although television continues to be an excellent medium for a wealth of different types of advertising, as discussed in Chapter 9, "Television and Radio," its use pales by comparison to newspaper, magazine, and direct-mail advertising. However, it is used a great deal by promotion-oriented merchants such as Men's Wearhouse and Jos. A. Bank. They also make considerable use of radio advertising because it requires a relatively modest investment; can be quickly designed, often without the use of an ad agency; and plays a practical role especially for local retailers who want to get their messages across to the consumer.

Merchants who use television have significant advertising budgets and are willing to participate in what is often a long and tedious endeavor. Radio production is not nearly as difficult to develop and, therefore, is often the choice of the retailer who uses it to make last-minute offers to the listener, wants to add "voice" to its ad programming, and has previously achieved a return on investment that warrants its use.

When color and movement is warranted by retailers, television, with all of its often complicated components, answers the need. From the inception of the idea to writing the script, to the actual "shoots," along with production and postproduction editing, television provides action unattainable from the other media. When visualization is unimportant, but speaking the story using words that foster imaginative insights is imperative, radio advertising fits the bill.

The various stages of creative development and production are explored in this chapter.

Many of the preproduction tasks can be helped along by tapping the expertise of trade associations and unions that specialize in one or more of them. Advertising agencies and many television production companies have their own rosters of groups they use for production purposes, but others, such as retailers who decide to produce their own commercials, need to make their own contacts. Table 13.1 lists some of these organizations.

PRODUCTION OF THE COMMERCIAL

The technical aspects of production are essential to a television commercial's success. Professionals are needed to operate recording and sound equipment, to oversee lighting and set assembly, to direct the cast, and to edit the video. Their expertise in techniques such as **mood lighting**, **dissolves** (the manner in which the different scenes are transitioned from one to the other),

fades (slow change into a black screen) and **cuts**, **zooming** in and out (transitions from long shot to close-up and the reverse), special effects, use of recorded music, and so on, will ensure the best overall production.

In addition to new footage, many commercials employ stock footage, which can be purchased from a supply house for far less than the cost of shooting new video. The stock footage is dovetailed with the new footage during the editing process. With the vast selection of stock footage available—anything from falling stars to fireworks, from dolphins cavorting in the waves to night traffic streaming across a bridge—even a tight budget will not limit the imagination and creativity necessary for an exciting commercial.

"It's a wrap" when the shoot is completed, and the next step is postproduction.

TABLE 13.1

Trade Associations/Unions

ORGANIZATION	LOCATION	CONTACT NUMBER
Association of Location Scouts and Managers	New York	212-807-0399
American Federation of TV and Radio Artists	New York	212-532-0800
Association of Independent Commercial Producers	New York	212-929-3000
Association of Independent Creative Editors	New York	212-665-2679
Casting Society of America	New York	212-868-1260
Make-up Artists & Hair Stylists	New York	212-627-0660
New York Production Alliance	New York	917-848-2553
Radio and Television Broadcast Engineers	New York	212-354-6770
Script Supervisors/Continuity & Allied Production Specialists Guild	North Hollywood	818-509-7871
Set Decorators Society of America	North Hollywood	818-255-2425
Society of Camera Operators	Toluca, CA	818-382-7070
Theatrical Wardrobe	New York	212-957-3500

POSTPRODUCTION

After the footage has been shot, the final stage is to edit it into a **final cut** that combines all of the components of the production. For a 30-second commercial, it is not unusual to require a few hours of actual shooting. Scenes are shot again and again until the one that will make the final cut has been recorded. The following are some of the components of postproduction.

◆ *Editing* involves assembling all of the elements that go into the production of the television commercial: graphics, music, voiceover, filmed sequences, still shots, and so forth (Figure 13.4).

◆ *Graphics* include not only art and photographs but also opening titles and other text presented as written messages rather than spoken lines. During postproduction,

the **graphics** are placed in the appropriate positions.

◆ *Music*, prerecorded to highlight the action, is then added to accompany the footage. Some commercials use original music specially composed and orchestrated for the production; others use portions of music published for general use. Unpublished music is also readily available at modest cost.

◆ The *voiceover* must be perfectly inserted at the exact time the footage it describes comes on the screen. This synchronization is extremely important to the quality of the commercial. Viewers are distracted by out-of-synch voice and video and may miss the main point of the commercial.

◆ *Special effects*, such as zooming and fades, are added to make the piece more artistic.

13.4 Editing involves assembling all of the elements that go into a TV production. *Erik Freeland/Corbis.*

13.6 The studio must be carefully selected to produce a clear message.
Benjamin Antony Mann/Sodapix/Corbis.

for radio commercials are often very good sources for demos. For live commercials, the script is often read by the station disk jockey, news broadcaster, or perhaps station manager. Live commercials must be delivered by excellent readers because there are no retakes as in the case of the prerecorded commercials.

◆ *Music and sound effects* are generally essential to enhance the spoken words and set the mood of the piece. Because radio is purely an audio medium, the music and sound effects must be carefully selected to make a lasting impression that is pleasing to the ears. These elements must be selected as the script is being written so

that they can be dovetailed with the words to provide an effect that stands out in the mind of the listener.

◆ *Studio* selection is particularly important, unless the message is delivered live. The facility must have a good sound engineer, equipment that will faithfully record the commercial, a music library with a wealth of music options when the music hasn't been specially composed for the project, soundproofing that will eliminate any noise interference, and sufficient space for others, such as ad executives, clients, and scriptwriters, so that last-minute adjustments can be made (Figure 13.6).

- *Commercial length* should be determined so that the finished product will meet the time requirements of the client and the station on which it will be aired. The actual time can be measured by reading the commercial at least one time before it is recorded. A good reader is able to pace the timing so that it will not be shorter or longer than needed to fill the time slot. Typically, commercials are 30 to 60 seconds long, allowing enough time for all of the pertinent information to be delivered. Media Insight 13.1 addresses how much time a radio commercial should take in order to be effective.

- *Frequency of airing* the commercial should be carefully determined by the client and ad agency, if one is used. In the absence of an agency, the radio station can guide the advertiser regarding the number of airings necessary to make an impact on the targeted market. As a rule, commercials that are aired only once offer little value in creating business for the retailer; even once a week is insufficient for positive results. The best chance for success is to run the commercial multiple times in one day and for as many days as the message remains timely and as the budget allows.

- *Audience targeting* requires care in determining which stations, programming, and time slots will provide the best listening audience. This information is available from ad agencies. If this is a go-it-alone project, the client should listen to the stations in the broadcast area in order to make informed decisions about reaching the desired audience.

PRODUCTION

Radio commercials are far less complex than television commercials to produce. At the recording studio, the sound engineer takes sound levels to ensure perfect recording, the actor or actors read the script, the director stands by to make adjustments, and so forth. After it is satisfactorily recorded (which generally involves several takes), the soundtrack is edited during postproduction.

POSTPRODUCTION

Postproduction is less complicated for radio than for television because there are no visuals involved. Essentially, the recorded soundtrack is augmented with the appropriate music and sound effects to make it fit the mood or tone of the commercial. Synchronization between voice and music/sound effects is critical to producing a quality radio commercial. Using the right music, at the right volume, with the best of the recited message can make all the difference in the success of the commercial.

Client Approval

Before the commercial is aired, the client and all of those responsible for the project must review it. If errors are identified, they are corrected, and the commercial must be reviewed again before the client signs off for final approval. The commercial is then duplicated and delivered to the stations on which it will run.

Summary of Key Points

- The use of broadcast media, although extremely important in advertising, pales in comparison to the use of other media for the retailing community.

- The creation of a television commercial is divided into three stages: preproduction, production, and postproduction. Each is essential to realizing the goals of the project.

- The preproduction stage of development for a television advertisement is extremely important to both the client and producer because it involves budgeting, generating concepts and ideas, determining the amount of time the finished product should run, scriptwriting, storyboard creation, casting, selecting location sites, and choosing wardrobe.

- In the production of a television commercial, the project generally involves a number of different participants who belong to various trade associations and unions.

Special Events

In today's retail environment, where competition is at an all-time high, exceptional efforts are required on the part of each merchant to ensure profitability. Every year seems to bring new challenges to this arena, making it difficult for even the marquee retailers to maintain themselves as industry leaders. In especially depressed times, such as those that began with the recession in 2008 and continued with the collapse of many standard-bearers in the business and banking communities, consumer spending plunged to levels not known since the Great Depression. Economic strife, of course, adversely affects the retail industry, making it extremely difficult to maintain projected sales levels and satisfy clienteles who once seemed to effortlessly purchase anything they desired.

To meet the competitive challenges in the troublesome times as well as when prosperity allows for significant consumer spending, one of the ways in which retailers, both large and small, distinguish themselves is by sponsoring **special events** to attract consumer attention and ultimately result in increased sales. Merchants use special events in their stores to increase shopper traffic, and they are also using some of these motivational devices for their Web sites and catalogues and as offerings on social-networking sites.

Whether it is an anniversary sale, an in-store celebrity appearance, a fashion clinic hosted by a famous designer, a product demonstration, or anything that is atypical of the company's regular merchandising practices, these events, if properly promoted, generally catch the attention of the consumer and often translate into purchases.

In retailing, special events are often held between Thanksgiving and Christmas, but they can be used at any time of the year to boost sales.

THE 83RD ANNUAL

MACY'S
THANKSGIVING DAY PARADE

SEE IT LIVE IN NEW YORK CITY OR ON NBC · 9AM TO NOON, THURSDAY, NOVEMBER 26, 2009

Experience the wonder, magic and excitement
of Macy's Thanksgiving Day Parade®!

All the world loves a parade! Be a part of this beloved holiday tradition featuring
giant balloons, marching bands, magnificent floats, and your favorite celebrities.

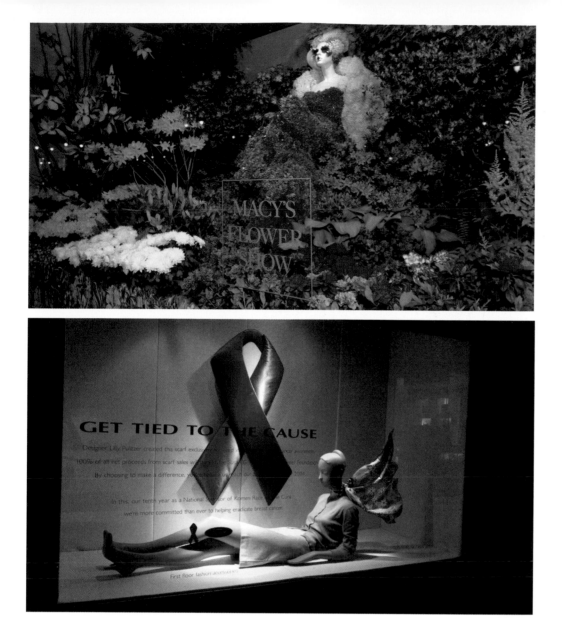

14.2 *(top)* The annual flower show has become a Macy's institution. *Jennifer Greylock/ AP Images.*

14.3 *(bottom)* Charitable activities are part of many a retail store's special events programs. *Jennifer Greylock/ AP Images.*

Following are examples of the many different events to aid charities:

- Saks Fifth Avenue's Key to the Cure is an annual weekend event that began in 1999 to fight women's cancer. With the assistance of celebrities from the design world, stage, screen, and television, the event raises approximately $250,000 each year. The recipients of the funds are such organizations as the Breast Cancer Research Foundation, Cleveland Clinic, Boston's Dana-Farber Cancer Institute, and others. Saks donates 2 percent of a weekend's sales receipts from all of its regular stores, Off-Fifth outlets, and its Web site.

- Bloomingdale's, in its New York City flagship store, features an annual spring and summer fashion show to raise funds for the New York University Child Study

Center, the nation's leading organization for research, prevention, and treatment of child and adolescent psychiatric and learning disorders. With well-known celebrities participating in the event, the company raises about $100,000 each year.

- Nordstrom helped raise over $100,000 by allowing people a sneak peek at its store opening in Cherry Hill, New Jersey. This onetime event had more than 1,200 people who paid $100 each on hand for the event that benefited The Links, Inc., the Philadelphia Museum of Art, and Symphony in C.

CELEBRITY BOOK SIGNINGS

Booksellers such as Barnes & Noble bring shoppers to their stores through **celebrity book signings**, featuring authors who speak, answer questions, and sign autographs (Figure 14.4).

Fans have been known to line up for hours to meet the authors and get signed copies of their books. Celebrity authors such as Magic Johnson, Phil Mickelson, Suzanne Somers, Anne Murray, and others make the rounds of stores throughout the country to sell their books, benefitting the retailer with many more visitors than usual.

FOOD DEMONSTRATIONS AND WINE TASTING

Many supermarket chains, such as Fresh Market, and warehouse clubs, such as Costco, regularly hold events that feature food preparation and sampling and wine tasting from different vineyards. On any given day, Costco has numerous food stations featuring different types of products that are sold on the premises lining the sell-

ing floors. Similarly, wine tasting has become a special event that draws people into supermarkets and specialty wine stores. In both of these venues, customer traffic usually increases, as does the sale of the products that are demonstrated.

COSMETIC DEMONSTRATIONS

Cosmetics retailers sometimes increase sales through the **demonstration** of their products (Figure 14.5). Professional makeup artists are hired to offer free makeovers using the featured cosmetics to interested shoppers. Curious onlookers stop to watch the transformation of the participant from "plain" to "striking" in a matter of approximately 30 minutes. Not only the participant but also the onlookers are often motivated to purchase the products.

14.4 Celebrity book signings bring large crowds to the store. *Peter Kramer/AP Images.*

PERSONAL APPEARANCES

By advertising the in-store **personal appearance** of an entertainer, athlete, designer, or other famous personality, the store is sure to motivate visits from people who admire the celebrity (Figure 14.6). Guests commonly sign autographs, speak on a particular topic, promote a new collection, and so forth. The goal is to increase store traffic and thereby generate sales. Gina Brooke, makeup artist for Madonna, visited Barneys in its New York City Madison Avenue flagship store and drew enormous crowds that generated cosmetic sales. Others have included Justin Timberlake at Saks Fifth Avenue, Mary Kate and Ashley Olsen at Barneys, David Beckham at Selfridges in London, and Lady Gaga at HMV Oxford Street, also in London.

FASHION SHOWS

Long the darling of the special event roster, the fashion show continues to be one of the offerings used by retailers to introduce new collections, raise funds for charities and other worthy causes, highlight seasonal offerings, promote a new designer, and so forth (Figure 14.7). Its long-standing purpose is to bring shoppers to the store. Most fashion merchants produce many shows throughout the year.

The major retailers have in-house experts to create the show's concept, gather the merchandise for showing, and perform all of the activities necessary for success, but the smaller merchant often must handle the production himself or herself. Media Insight 14.1 covers a few points that can help make a fashion show more effective. Although the article is directed toward clothing designers and boutiques, its suggestions may be used by any retail operation.

14.5 Cosmetics demonstrations often draw big crowds and help sell the products. *Hiro Masuike/The* New York Times/*Redux.*

14.6 Personal appearances account for large crowds. *Wireimage/ Getty Images.*

Fashion Show Formats There are usually three types of shows that retailers use for special events: the runway show, the fashion parade, and the trunk show. Each serves a different purpose.

- The **runway show** is the most commonly used format and involves a raised runway on which models move from one end to the other so that viewers can closely inspect the styles being presented. Typically, at these events the spectators are seated on either side of the runway. The presentation might be formally arranged to include scenery, live or recorded music, dramatic lighting, and commentary. Today, however, scenery is not typically used in these productions; the fashions being modeled are the center of interest. The models used in these productions range from professionals who command significant sums for their

appearances to in-house employees. When the show is more informal and cost saving is a factor, the latter suffices. In some cases, retailers have been known to use students from nearby educational institutions as a means of cutting expenses.

- The **fashion parade** is a less-formal presentation where models merely parade through the store's restaurant or selling floors wearing the clothing and accessories that are for sale (Figure 14.8). Models are often seen carrying small signs indicating the price of the outfit, the designer's or manufacturer's name, and the location in the store where the outfit might be more closely inspected and purchased. In the restaurant setting, models often stop at tables to answer questions about the garments they are wearing. Most often, the fashion parade is used to

14.7 Fashion shows
help sell merchandise.
Courtesy of Nordstrom.

feature merchandise that will stand out from the outfits worn by the shoppers. Furs and evening apparel, for example, are the perfect choices for the sales floor fashion parade.

◆ The **trunk show** is a concept that manufacturers and designers use to show their collections (Figure 14.9). The merchandise is brought to the stores in containers or trunks (thus the name) and featured for a day or two. Customers are invited through special invitations or advertisements to come to the store to see the collection. It is the hope that the abundance of the merchandise in these collections will spark the interest of the attendees. A company representative or designer usually covers the event and mingles with the shoppers to answer questions about the lines and sometimes offer adjustments in the individual

pieces to suit the special needs of the store's customer. Sometimes models are used to display the garments and to walk through the department that is featuring the show. Not only do trunk shows give individuals the opportunity to see an entire collection in addition to what the retailer usually stocks but they also provide an arena for those who are fascinated with the celebrity designers who come to the store.

Fashion Show Arenas When the retailer chooses to feature a major runway show for fund-raising or to bring attention to an up-and-coming designer, the event takes place in a location other than the store. For some of these events, theaters are rented, which provides a more formal setting and allows for larger audiences than on-premises sites usually permit. Because theaters are already fitted with sound systems, professional lighting,

14.9 Trunk shows often bring designer enthusiasts to the store. *WWD/Condé Nast/ Corbis.*

a stage, and permanent seating, the production of the event is easier. Other fashion arenas include specially erected tents in the retailer's parking area, the main promenades of shopping malls, museums that might benefit from the production, prominent restaurants, and ballrooms.

Elements of a Fashion Show For the show to deliver a successful return on its investment, whether its purpose is to sell merchandise or raise funds for charity, it must incorporate a number of elements. The elements vary from show to show, depending on its size and budget.

◆ The merchandise is central to the success of any fashion show. Whether it is a designer collection or a moderately priced assemblage of merchandise, the items selected must be appropriate for the invited guests. Fashion-forward merchandise is incorrect for an audience of middle-income, traditionally dressed individuals; likewise, a collection of mundane designs will not motivate high-fashion enthusiasts to purchase. The number of outfits should be limited to between 20 and 75, which can be modeled within 30 minutes. Although 30 minutes is considered to be the right amount of time to hold the audience's interest, sometimes a special collection calls for a longer presentation.

◆ Models are one of the more important elements in a fashion show of any classification (Figure 14.10). The best models are those who have the right physical proportions to carry the clothes as well as a unique appearance that further enhances what is being featured. It might be unique facial features or a manner of distinctive walking that will create excitement and show the clothes to their best advantage. Of course, budget constraints often preclude the use of professional models, thus requiring recruitment from other sources, such as colleges, members of a charity that is being favored with the proceeds of the show, or company employees who have the right physical characteristics for modeling. Those with professional experience do not require time-consuming rehearsals, whereas the others generally need professional coaching to do a satisfactory job.

◆ Facilities that satisfy the needs of the production, as discussed earlier, are essential.

◆ Lighting must be appropriate to transform the chosen arena into a perfect setting for a fashion show. Spotlights should be used to highlight the models as they traverse the runway so that each outfit can be easily seen by the audience.

◆ Music, either prerecorded or performed by a live band, guitarist, or pianist, should provide the right tempo to accompany the models' walk down the runway.

◆ Behind-the-scenes participants such as the show's director, stage manager, commentator (if one is used), dressing room attendants, and any others should be carefully selected to make certain that the show is a success.

FAMOUS CHEF PRESENTATIONS

A special event that usually provides significant attendance uses chefs from well-known restaurants to cook their specialties in the store (Figure 14.11). These shows take place either in the store's special events area, if it has one, or directly on the selling floor of the cookware department.

CORPORATE EVENTS

Retailers can host corporate get-togethers at their premises, providing a place where a company's professionals can gather and mingle with coworkers. One very successful endeavor of this nature is Saks Fifth Avenue's Corporate Outreach Program, which has been ongoing at its flagship store in New York City since January 2007. Companies such as Continental Airlines, Deloitte and Touche, and JPMorgan Chase have held corporate events at the store. Saks says that these events have translated into significant sales.

FASHION FORUMS

Merchants who specialize in fashion merchandise often feature special events, or **fashion forums**, that focus on the upcoming trends and other fashion agendas. A store's fashion director, fashion journalists, fashion forecasters, and other notables in the field appear at the store and lend their expertise to fashion devotees.

14.10 The models are an integral part of a show's success. *WWD/Condé Nast.*

14.11 Famous chefs draw large crowds to stores. *Jamie McCarthy/ Getty Images.*

14.12 Sampling is a way
to introduce shoppers to
a company's products.
*Harry Choi/TongRo/
Corbis.*

Bloomingdale's

This world-famous upscale department store, now part of the Macy's Inc. organization, has made partnering with other companies a regular part of its special events program. In its New York City flagship store and other units in the company, Bloomingdale's offers a variety of joint ventures that serve its own needs, such as selling merchandise and participating in social programs, as well as the needs of its partners who have similar goals.

Some of the more recent special events partnerships that have significantly increased store traffic and attracted attention from the press include the following:

◆ Partnering with the AIDS research group amFAR in conjunction with fashion designer Kenneth Cole for a series of AIDS awareness events has raised significant sums for the research organization. In addition to the monies raised, Bloomingdale's contributed $75,000 to amFAR.

◆ Turner Classic Movies and Bloomingdale's partnered to present "Lights, Camera, Fashion," which helped celebrate the fashions of Hollywood's leading men and women. Thirty-six stores in 18 markets participated to bring, according to the Bloomingdale's Web site, "Hollywood's influential fashion to stores across the nation."

◆ Together with Young Indie Films, Bloomingdale's launched an extensive film-themed marketing campaign. The project used emerging filmmakers to shoot and produce 4-minute films on location in New York City over the course of 15 days, each of which had subtle references to brands and featured actors in Bloomingdale's apparel.

◆ In a joint venture with Echo, a scarf manufacturer, Bloomingdale's used a panel of experts to provide tips on the art of scarf tying. Using vintage styles and current products, experts demonstrated how a wardrobe can be updated with a scarf.

◆ *GQ* partnered with Bloomingdale's to present an exclusive suiting event, inviting men to an incentive-based shopping experience. Those who attended were treated to cocktails, hors d'oeuvres, shoe shines, and manicures. With purchases of $2,000 or more, customers received a $500 discount as well as a gift bag valued at $500, filled with electronics, a featured liquor, accessories, skin care, and men's fragrances.

◆ Bloomingdale's partnered with Get Married, the only multichanneled wedding resource, for a pre-wedding special event. Celebrity appearances, gifts, participation in two contests, a gift bag, and more were all part of the event. Vendor participants offered the brides the latest tips and trends in product selection and wedding planning.

◆ Levi's, *GQ*, and the CFDA (Council of Fashion Designers in America) each shared in a joint venture with Bloomingdale's to introduce a limited edition of a new jeans design created by designer Robert Geller. This event gave a great deal of publicity to each of the participants.

This is only a partial list of the cosponsored events that Bloomingdale's participates in each year. These cosponsored events are a mainstay in its special events program.

SPECIAL SHOPPING NIGHTS

Many fashion retailers present special nights aimed at **fashionistas** and **shopaholics** who come to their stores to be treated to a host of activities that include meeting celebrities, learning about haute couture, mingling with designers, listening to special musical performances, and so forth. Macy's, Bloomingdale's, Saks Fifth Avenue, and other leading fashion emporiums regularly attract large crowds to these events.

PARTNERING EVENTS

Often, two or more businesses join forces to produce special events that serve their individual needs. For example, a fashion designer and a retailer might both benefit from a fashion show featuring the designer's garments that are sold at the retailer's store. Or a research organization and a retailer might join forces to raise awareness for the research and bring shoppers to the store. Not only are both partners' needs fulfilled but joint sponsorship often results in sharing the costs of production. These **partnering events** have been especially successful for Bloomingdale's, the subject of Focus 14.2.

Merchandise Promotions

Although the institutional technique is a subtle way for retailers to gain business, most retailers also participate in a number of events designed to quickly sell specific merchandise. The events are generally geared to the disposal of unwanted merchandise.

LIMITED-PERIOD SALES

Many merchants offer discounts on some or all of their merchandise for limited time periods when sales have slowed. It might be for a single day, 3 days, or sometimes even for a few hours during a shopping day. Because these are time-limited offerings, they attract shoppers who might wait for sales to make their purchases.

SENIOR DAY SALES

Periodically, some retailers offer discounts to their senior customers. Belk, for example, offers a 15 percent discount on merchandise purchases for individuals who are 55 or older. The sale takes place on one or two of the slower selling days of the week to encourage traffic in the store.

PRIVATE SALES

Many merchants use the **private sale** as a special event to reward customers for their loyalty (Figure 14.13). Customers are given special prices for their past patronage, whereas walk-in customers are excluded from receiving the discounts. Brooks Brothers, in its regular stores and outlets, periodically features such an event called "Friends and Family." It notifies regular customers of special sales that offer a minimum of a 25 percent discount on purchases for a limited time period. Invitations are sent via standard mail or e-mail. Other merchants use variations on this format to reward their clienteles with special savings for past patronage.

TRADITIONAL SALES

At the conclusion of a regular selling period, it is a common practice for retailers to eliminate their unsold inventories at reduced prices, especially if the merchandise is fashion-oriented or seasonal and thus might not have future appeal. These events might come immediately after Christmas, after the Fourth of July, or anytime the merchant feels he or she must dispose of unwanted inventories. The trend now is for these **traditional sales** to be held earlier than they used to be, a result of the economic downturn affecting consumer spending. Before the economic downturn, new merchandise was held for a later date. With the earlier promotion consumers are motivated to spend earlier than usual.

In addition to being concerned primarily with merchandise disposal, retailers also use traditional markdown periods to bring a new group of shoppers to the store who otherwise might not be able to afford the original prices. Many retailers are appealing to two customer bases in their stores. Saks Fifth Avenue, Bloomingdale's, Neiman Marcus, and other stores that appeal to the more affluent shoppers fill their stores with other market segments when they advertise broad markdowns. When second and third markdowns are necessary and prices again fall, still other groups become interested in purchasing.

GIMMICK SALES

Some retail organizations employ **gimmick sales** to attract attention. The ultimate reward for the shopper is often a price reduction, and the methods of motivating shoppers to buy are sometimes unique. These include such events as "Assistant Buyer Days" or "Manager Days," which attribute special prices to the unique merchandise acquired by these individuals. Shoppers who are

FRIENDS & FAMILY

WEDNESDAY, MAY 5 – MONDAY, MAY 10, 2010

Enjoy a special 25%* savings
on all your purchases.

Offer valid in all U.S. and Canadian Retail,
Brooks Brothers Country Club,
"346" Brooks Brothers, Factory and Airport stores,
online at **BrooksBrothers.com** or by phone.*

To redeem in stores, please present this invite
at time of purchase. For online and phone orders,
please use code **friend99** to redeem savings.

Brooks Brothers

BrooksBrothers.com/friends   800.274.1815

14.13 Private sales to regular customers usually result in increased sales. *Courtesy Brooks Brothers.*

unaware that stores generally do not rely on these employees for merchandise acquisition are often motivated to head to the stores or the Internet to take advantage of the unusual offering.

Frequency of Special Event Presentations

Running the gamut from the occasional presentation to the long-running spectacular, special events are the brainchildren of publicists, special promotion directors, event planners, and other industry experts. Their frequency often depends on what's happening at any given time in the trading area of the retailer. Vignettes of theatrical productions often serve as the basis for an event and are generally held only once when the vehicle is at its peak publicity potential. At the other extreme are the events such as the Macy's Thanksgiving Day Parade, which has captivated audiences for many years and is considered to kick off the holiday shopping season.

Most major department stores, the leaders in special events presentations, fill their calendars month after month with offerings intended to capture the attention of regular clients as well as potential customers. The purpose is to increase store traffic and, of course, sales. Looking at any major department store's planned events immediately reveals that planned store events bring shoppers to the stores and the potential for increased sales. This concept is very popular with shoppers and productive in terms of sales for the organization.

Summary of Key Points

◆ Retailers of all sizes and merchandise classifications offer a variety of special events to meet competitive challenges, increase shopper traffic, increase sales, and foster their images as socially responsible businesses.

◆ The responsibility for the production and direction of special events varies from company to company. Most major organizations have a promotional department charged with producing the event, whereas at the small store operation, it is usually the owner who develops and implements the event.

◆ Special events fall into two categories: institutional offerings and merchandise promotions. The former encompasses a wealth of different formats intended to promote goodwill, build a positive image, and increase sales. The latter is used primarily to sell merchandise as quickly as possible.

◆ Some companies such as Macy's have had such success with special events that the events have become long-running spectaculars.

◆ Charitable events are always present in the retailer's promotional bag of tricks. They not only result in increased sales but also present the retail establishment as a socially responsible business.

◆ Fashion shows have been a mainstay of fashion-oriented retail operations for many years. They generally take the form of runway shows, informal fashion parades, or trunk shows. Each requires a different amount of organization, with the runway show most often the most demanding in terms of preparation.

◆ Often, retailers partner with outside organizations such as design companies and manufacturers, charitable foundations, and others in their special events offerings. This arrangement helps to cut the expense of running the special event while at the same time promoting another's cause or purpose.

◆ Merchandise promotions are special events designed to quickly dispose of unwanted merchandise. They run the gamut from traditional sales to limited-time sales promotions.

For Discussion

1. What are some of the reasons retailers of all merchandise classifications use special events as part of their promotional plans?

2. Who usually has the responsibility for the development and implementation of special events in both the large and small retail operations?

3. In addition to helping generate sales, why do retailers sponsor institutional special events for current customers as well as prospective customers?

4. What are the three major types of fashion show presentations that retailers use to stimulate business, and how do they differ from one another?

5. List and discuss the different elements used in the production of a runway fashion show.

6. What is meant by the term *partnering event* as it relates to retailing, and why do so many merchants use this strategy to promote business?

7. Discuss the different merchandise promotions that retailers use to dispose of merchandise and how they differ from each other.

8. In addition to the regularly produced special events that take place year after year in retailing, what else motivates the merchant to offer onetime special events?

- A description of the event

- Components of the event

- How it was publicized

2. In addition to preparing the chart, collect samples of print ads that were used to call attention to the event. Using the information and ads that were collected, prepare a presentation for the class.

3. Contact five different charities to learn about their partnering endeavors with retailers to promote their causes. Prepare a list of events they have used in the past that helped them raise awareness and funds for their charity. With the information gathered, prepare a table featuring the following:

- The name of the charity

- The partner for the event

- The nature of the event

- How the event was promoted

Exercises and Projects

1. Choose a major retail organization and study its commitment to the use of special events. Through direct contact with the operation's publicity, promotion, or special events department, investigate its special events program for a period of 1 month. Choose a month when seasonal events are most likely to be planned (Christmas, Valentine's Day, back to school). Using the store's calendar of events, develop a chart that features:

- The company name

- The name of the special event

Web Site Exploration for In-Depth Analysis

Friends & Foundations of California Libraries—Event Planning Tips
http://www.librarysupport.net/librarylovers/eventips.html
This is an excellent article about event planning. It offers a complete overview of the aspects of planning a special event.

Entrepreneur.com
http://www.entrepreneur.com/startingabusiness/businessideas/startupkits/37892.html
A wonderful, complete overview of all of the aspects that must be addressed for those wishing to start a special events business.

Visual Merchandising

CHAPTER OBJECTIVES

After you have completed this chapter, you should be able to discuss:

★ The factors that affect different approaches used in the planning and development of visual programs.

★ The personnel who develop the concepts used in visual merchandising.

★ The centralized visual merchandising concept whereby all visual presentations for every store are planned at company headquarters.

★ The use of interior settings to promote merchandise that individual departments wish to emphasize.

★ The components of a display, including mannequins, props, lighting, signage, and graphics.

★ The variety of themes used for visual presentations, such as seasonal settings, holidays, creative undertakings, and institutional events.

If the retailers' advertising efforts and special events offerings have sufficiently stimulated consumers to visit their stores, the next step is to provide visual excitement that will greet shoppers at the entrance to the selling floor and to offer additional visuals throughout the store to motivate consumers to take a closer look at the merchandise offered for sale. In today's retail arena, where the product mix is similar among competitors—and in some cases just about the same—visual presentation can give the retailer a competitive edge.

A case in point is the **visual merchandising** effort that has transformed Crate & Barrel from just another home furnishings store into a magical environment that immediately stimulates the shopper to take a better look at the products that stock the shelves. Glassware, tableware, serving utensils, and other items are so magnificently displayed that the ordinary becomes extraordinary. The wide selection of items is not unlike the merchandise seen in most shops, but visual merchandising expertise has made them seem more appealing.

Being able to create displays that stop shoppers in their tracks and compel them to look is no simple matter. Whether it is an upscale fashion emporium such as Saks Fifth Avenue or a mass merchandiser like Target, the visual merchandising direction must be carefully developed. In the case of major retail operations, the task is left to professionally trained staff members who carry out the visual programs. Small entrepreneurs who might operate a boutique or specialty store often hire freelancers to handle visual displays. Others perform the display tasks themselves— and do so quite successfully if they understand and apply the principles of visual displays. It is a waste of precious window and interior display space if the visual presentations do not motivate closer inspection of the merchandise.

Some major retailers have established visual direction that immediately conveys a signature or look. Lord & Taylor, for example, has captured the attention of onlookers with its imaginative Christmas windows, which have become theatrical attractions. Every year around Thanksgiving, Lord & Taylor window presentations make use of animation that raises display to new heights. Visitors to its New York City flagship store eagerly await each year's window display with great anticipation and excitement. With different themes each year, these visual offerings may help motivate people, after they have finished marveling at the windows, to enter the store to purchase their holiday needs (Figure 15.1).

Planning and Developing the Visual Program

Retailers use a host of different approaches in carrying out their visual merchandising programs. Factors such as size of the organization, number of in-house professionals, number and location of the branches or units, and budgetary constraints usually dictate which approach best suits their visual merchandising needs. In the case of budgets, especially when retailers are facing an economic downturn, it becomes necessary for visual merchandisers to achieve high levels of display excitement without spending fortunes to do so. Media Insight 15.1 explores ways to create display excitement on a budget.

Build Visual Impact on a Budget

Faith Bartrug

Props and decoratives are the starting point for displays that surprise, delight, and sell. And they're far cheaper than, say, an entire store renovation. Some strategies to make the most of your visuals [follow]:

• *Make visual techniques the new props.* Inventively hanging, folding, and layering a category of product can become the signature decor element. Denim apparel stores are on the cutting edge of this trend. Levi's hung denim in rows from the ceiling for a "wow" factor that also adds texture. Barneys built a large-scale bear out of denim, and Diesel recently created an entire window display with denim in different folded poses. There are new ways to layer denim on tables—hang it from rods, clip it with anchor bolts, roll it like towels into cubbies . . . all demonstrating the use of visual technique as the "prop" to romance the product. Using the visual creative process freshens the store and can become a signature differentiator for a retailer.

• *Integrate props and decoratives with graphics to craft a work of art.* One example that caught my eye was Adidas's wall display.

Different decorative picture frames—some with graphics, some with monitors—combine to form its logo. Another approach would be using a wall appliqué with a silhouette of a girl who is extending a 3-D hand form to display accessories. Installations like these are the results of teamwork between the visual merchandisers and graphic designers. They demonstrate that display is a creative outlet.

• *Think "eclectic," not monotone.* Mix nostalgic and artful props and decoratives with everyday objects to create something unexpected. Feel-good storytelling can focus on generations past. So use recycled and vintage objects to connect emotionally with customers. Urban Outfitters displayed sneakers hung on a string and quilts (with retro plaid patterns) stapled on shelves to line them. Barneys formed razor blades into patterns around the jewelry. Diesel featured notebook paper filled with doodles as the backdrop to watches. Juicy Couture displayed shoes and socks on tarnished silver trays, and Forever 21 and FACE Stockholm both have used vintage head forms.

• *Play with multifunctional elements.* In this economy,

props, decoratives, and mannequins need to multitask. More and more retailers are reusing props and repurposing them from season to season. I design families of props in which every element has a dual purpose. A tray can flip over to become a riser, and bustforms can hold graphics as well as apparel. This saves retailers time and money. But the key is to make sure that they are being refreshed and that the new uses create the essence of change in the space.

Visual merchandising with props tells a story around the product that should educate the customers and do the job of a salesperson. This, in turn, requires less labor and increases ROI [return on investment].

Source: Faith Bartrug. "Build Visual Impact on a Budget." VMSD Magazine, May 2009.

In-House Visual Departments

Full-line and specialized department stores such as Macy's, Saks Fifth Avenue, Nordstrom, Bloomingdale's, Neiman Marcus, and Lord & Taylor use an **in-house visual department** to plan and execute all of the window and interior visual presentations for the flagships and branches. The teams are headed by a **director of visual merchandising**, who presents the overall plan to the staff, sets target dates for the visual promotions, implements the promotion, and coordinates the efforts with other managerial personnel such as buyers and merchandisers. The director is completely in charge of every aspect of the store's visual merchandising commitments. Coordination with and cooperation from the buyers and merchandisers are necessary to make certain the products to be visually promoted arrive on time from the vendors. Equally important is interfacing with the advertising department to make certain that any ad campaigns will be sufficiently and accurately reflected in the store's window and interior displays.

The visual director compiles a **window calendar**, listing the dates set for the displays, the merchandise that will be used, and any special requirements of the displays. An accurate picture of all of the items to be displayed, the windows they will occupy, installation dates, and any ad tie-ins for the presentation are included in the window calendar. In this way, everyone on the in-house visual team knows precisely what elements are needed for successful displays (Figure 15.2).

Those in charge must also oversee the installations in branch stores. In these outlying units, a visual manager, aided by one or two assistants, implements the plans developed by the flagship's visual director, making certain that displays similar to those in the main store have been faithfully reproduced. Periodically, visual directors visit the branches to evaluate how faithfully his or her direction has been followed.

Centralized Visual Merchandising

Multiunit chains dominate the retail field. It is not unusual for a chain organization to number 1,000 or more units. Companies such as The Gap Stores Inc., Eddie Bauer, Limited Brands (including The Limited and Victoria's Secret), and Williams-Sonoma do not have visual merchandis-ers in each store but instead make use of managers and assistants to install visual presentations that have been developed for them in corporate or other centralized facilities. Others, such as Crate & Barrel, use a combination of a **centralized visual merchandising** and in-store **trimmers**. The centralized visual plan is an extension of the organization's overall philosophy. Just as the merchandise is centrally purchased by buyers at corporate headquarters and the policies are centrally developed by top management, the concept of visual merchandising is also centrally planned.

To carry out the visual merchandising vision in these companies, chains generally follow a routine that uses **model windows** and interiors to design their presentations. They then photograph the models and transmit the pictures to the various stores for reproduction. In addition to these photographs, drawings and written directions are sent to help the installers complete the job. These detailed directions and visual materials are necessary for the faithful reproduction of the displays because those doing the installations are not professionally trained visual merchandisers.

Some of the chains prepare a **display presentation kit** that, in addition to the detailed directions and illustrations, includes graphic presentations depicting exactly where each item should be placed, signage that should be used, props, and price tags.

Freelance Arrangements

For merchants who do not have the advantage of in-house visual teams to develop and execute presentations, **freelancers** who specialize in merchandise display are available. Some charge an hourly fee for time and for the props and materials they use in their client's windows and interiors. Others charge a flat fee per trim, and others contract for a certain number of "changes" throughout the year.

Just as artists have different painting styles, visual merchandisers and trimmers have their own distinctive styles and approaches. Before a freelancer is hired, his or her work is usually assessed to make certain that both the client and the installer agree on the terms. Most freelancers prepare **photographic portfolios** that feature examples of

UPDATED WINDOW SCHEDULE					
WINDOWS 15 & 14 38TH ST CORNER	WINDOWS 13, 12, 8, 7 5TH AVENUE	WINDOWS 7D, 6D, 5D, 4D DREICER BLDG 5TH AVENUE	WINDOWS 11 & 9 FRONT ENTRANCE 5TH AVENUE	SMALL WINDOWS & SHADOW BOXES	SUNDAY ADS IN CONJUNCTION WITH WINDOWS
INSTALL TUESDAY	INSTALL TUESDAY	INSTALL WEDNESDAY	INSTALL THURSDAY		
JULY 30 Continued	**JULY 30** Continued	**JULY 31** incl. Windows 7, 8 DKNY Color TBC	**AUGUST 1** Continued		**AUGUST 4**
AUGUST 6 A-Line	**AUGUST 6** A-Line Lime/Purple with mailer	**AUGUST 7** Continued	**AUGUST 8** Yeohlee Purple Velvet 2 figures		**AUGUST 11** Nautica NYT 5 × 21
AUGUST 13 Continued	**AUGUST 13** Continued	**AUGUST 14** Nautica Women's	**AUGUST 15** Continued		**AUGUST 18** Polo Jeans NYT 5 × 21
AUGUST 20 Lauren Ralph Lauren	**AUGUST 20** Lauren Ralph Lauren	**AUGUST 21** Continued	**AUGUST 22** Polo Jeans Men's/Women's		**AUGUST 25** Lauren by Ralph Lauren NYT 12 × 21

their work. Some even produce video presentations that are distributed to prospective clients. Others merely present lists of stores that use their services so that the new prospects can view their work firsthand and talk with other clients. After a freelancer is chosen, a **freelance contract** should be drawn, indicating the exact details of the agreement. In this way, both sides understand what display outcome is expected.

Do-It-Yourself Installers

Although today's retail establishments are most often major operations such as department stores and specialty chains, dotted throughout the country are numerous small stores that serve the special needs of certain consumer groups. Boutiques, for example, continue to appeal to

upscale fashion enthusiasts, small specialty food merchants sell gourmet foods to food lovers, and single-unit limited-line stores specialize in one product to appeal to a particular group. These entities generally do not use the services of freelancers but instead rely on their own instincts to create window and interior displays. Although their visual merchandising talents are not usually professionally obtained, some have sufficient knowledge about design to install displays that serve their purposes.

No matter who has the visual responsibility in a retail organization, it is essential to learn about the latest innovations in the display world, what products are available to use in attention-getting presentations, which resources provide unusual

15.2 Window calendars feature the assignment of window space. Courtesy of Lord & Taylor.

VMSD

Originally published as *Display World Magazine* in 1922, VMSD *(Visual Merchandising and Store Design)* magazine is the preeminent publication devoted to visual merchandising. It is considered the bible for department store and chain organization display professionals, merchants who want to learn about industry initiatives, freelancers, and anyone interested in matters of visual merchandising. Each month, the magazine, owned by ST Publications, features news and events that concern retail display, visual designs that merit recognition for their uniqueness, strategies to improve sales through visual presentation, and new products including mannequins, signage, props, lighting, and anything that goes into making visual presentations better.

In addition to an editorial commentary in each month's edition, the magazine concentrates on special features of interest to those in the visual display profession. Here is a glimpse of its editorial calendar for a publishing year:

- Each January the buyer's guide issue addresses everything current that vendors have available for the retail clientele.

- Each April focuses on lighting trends and different fixtures and illumination products used for windows and store interiors.

- The May issues look at mannequin trends and the different types of mannequins that are new to the marketplace.

- June reviews in-store digital media that can be used by merchants of every size and classification.

- October focuses on green initiatives.

- Each December features the best of the year in each retail category.

props, and so forth. The simplest way to keep abreast of the industry's latest offerings, ideas, suggestions, and other important display information is to read *Visual Merchandising and Store Design (VMSD)* magazine, the subject of Focus 15.1.

Visual Merchandising Settings

There are two distinct areas of the retailer's premises that are used to feature the merchandise that is available for sale: the store's windows and interior spaces. The window display is meant to entice shoppers to enter the merchant's premises. When the curious shoppers have been drawn inside the store, the interiors must provide further motivation and entice shoppers to purchase.

Windows

Many different types of store windows are found in today's retailing arena. They range from the traditional, large, formal windows that flank the flagship store entrances to the smaller **shadow boxes** used to highlight small items. In between, there are other windows, including **corner windows**, **open-back windows**, **islands**, **arcades**, **circular windows**, **vitrines** (pedestals topped with small glass cases), and **windowless windows**, which are used in many malls. Each type of window offers the visual merchandiser a different challenge: some are easier to trim than others, and some make the task a formidable one.

Although the traditional large windows are mainstays of central shopping district flagship stores, their presence is not generally evident in the branches of these same retail giants. With the vast majority of these units occupying mall space, where rental costs are always upwardly spiraling, such window configurations take too much space from the overall square footage of the store to justify their presence. Instead, these giant windows that serve as the settings for imaginative show-stopper displays now are often large panes of glass through which shoppers may look into the stores. The "open-back," or *windowless window* as it is sometimes called, uses little in formal display, but enough to invite shoppers into the store.

Interior Settings

A walk through any retail operation reveals a wealth of potential display settings in which merchandise might be featured. They include platforms strategically placed near elevators or escalator landings, on display counters such as those used extensively in the cosmetics stations on the main floors of all department stores, free-standing vitrines, tops of merchandise fixtures that hold hanging garments, and risers that are often situated at the store's entrances. When less window space is available in a store, these interior spaces are essential to highlight the store's more appealing merchandise.

Designating specific designs for interior locations is simpler than for windows because interior displays are usually located in the selling departments and feature the merchandise unique to those departments. In these interior spaces, visual merchandising is often the responsibility of both the visual department and the managers of each section of the store. Installations that require new backgrounds and props are done by the visual team, which also places the merchandise. After the initial display is completed, subsequent changes using the same backgrounds are usually done by department personnel who, for example, make mannequin and other merchandise changes as needed.

When management decides to bring new life to a merchandise classification, some stores combine both their window and interior spaces to broaden the appeal of this merchandise. Such was the case when Saks Fifth Avenue committed itself to create new interest for its shoe collections. As discussed in Media Insight 15.2, the company took on every retailer's challenge: "compelling that prospective customer on the sidewalk to stop, look, enter, and buy."

Display Components

Just as the advertising print media relies on certain elements such as headlines, subheads, body copy, and artwork to make the presentation most appealing to the eye, so visual merchandising and display rely on a variety of components. These elements vary according to the settings in which they are featured, the merchandise, the nature of the presentation, the signage, and so forth. Some require an abundance of props, whereas others might require only a mannequin on which an ensemble is featured.

Mannequins

One of the more important components used in fashion windows is the mannequin (Figure 15.3). It is generally the mainstay of window displays and is generally its **focal point**. Often, two or more mannequins are used in a display to carry a central theme.

Choosing the right mannequin to create visual excitement and promote the store's image requires careful thought. There are many mannequins to choose from. In addition to traditional human-form mannequins, designers can choose from among **stylized mannequins**. These include **ethnic mannequins** to appeal to multicultural clientele, **futuristic forms**, inexpensive **representational forms**, and **trimmer-constructed mannequins**, which are created by visual merchandisers and offer limitless variations at modest cost.

As is the case with other products, mannequins are available from a variety of resources around the world. Although each source serves a particular need for the visual merchandiser, only one, the subject of Focus 15.2, is considered the preeminent designer and manufacturer.

In addition to the full-size model, trimmers use other forms to serve their purposes. These include women's **torsos** or three-fourths forms for swimsuits; male **suit forms**, which are more popular than full mannequins for suit displays; **blouse forms**; and a variety of hands, hosiery legs, and shoe forms.

Props

Set decoration, done correctly, establishes a mood or theme for a visual presentation. Sometimes sparseness best emphasizes a product, but more often, props are used to enhance the merchandise. **Props** are available from a variety of sources, usually from prop manufacturers. A creative designer can turn the most unlikely pieces—an

15.3 Mannequins enhance the themes of many displays.
Fairchild Publications, Inc.

Shoes on Eight

Saks' big, grand footwear floor is a must-see in New York

Saks Fifth Avenue generated an enormous public relations blitz to announce its renovated shoe department on the eighth floor of its New York flagship. The message to the world—in newspapers, magazines, TV and radio articles and ads—was: "10022-Shoe, a department so big, it needs its own ZIP code."

But every retailer knows the ultimate challenge is on the street—compelling that prospective customer on the sidewalk to stop, look, enter, and buy. And Saks met this challenge in a customarily creative way. The grand announcement of "10022-Shoe" (the "ZIP code") was splashed across the store's Fifth Avenue windows in September, as Tim Wisgerhof, Saks' senior creative director, visual merchandising, practically reinvented the display and presentation of shoes. Each of the six full-size feature windows on Fifth Avenue was divided into 12 parts and each one of those parts was made to look like a 41-cent U.S. postage stamp

featuring a celebration of shoes, including all the major brands: Jimmy Choo, Prada, Roger Vivier, Miu Miu, Stuart Weitzman and the rest.

Inside the store, a shoe sculpture on the main floor, designed by John Jefferys of Exhibitology Inc. (the Brooklyn, NY, fabricator), grabs attention. It's based on an original line drawing of a shoe commissioned by Saks from Canadian graphic artist Marian Bantjes. There's also an express "10022" elevator directly to the eighth floor.

Outside the elevator doors on 8 is what Karen Oleson of design firm Hambrecht Oleson calls the necessary wow factor. A 70-foot-long murano-glass sculpture, consisting of 2500 hand-blown glass bubbles, winds its way through the center of the 20,000-square-foot selling space.

William Herbst, Saks' senior vp, construction, design, planning and visual, says one of the goals was motivating customers to travel through the department from front to back without the use of high interior walls. The outer perimeter walls gently undulate to define specific brand statements, encouraging customer

meandering from one designer area into the next.

The low walls and broad vistas invite the customer into a sweeping salon environment with maximum merchandise exposure. An array of textures and materials, including limestone, white Carrera marble, and wood, creates a stage for the broad selection. Venetian plaster, mirrors, and illuminated satin draperies embellish the walls. Jewel tones are interspersed as a common thread in an otherwise neutral palette, appearing in upholstered furniture and strategically placed ovals in the flooring pattern that subtly direct the customer through the selling space. There's also an eclectic mix of furniture, from a modern Saarinen table to vintage found items and custom workhorse fixtures.

The message is the merchandise, elevated by signature shoe risers designed by Karen Parver, Saks' visual director of stores. Mosaics grace the inside of the few interspersed vitrines, which are the only recesses in the department; everything else protrudes outward toward the customer. Frosted glass panels emblazoned with the "DNA"

logo pattern (the new signature SFA logo divided into 64 parts) create varying planes and depths that frame and contain suspended metal and glass shelving. Curved banquettes trimmed in gray mohair become intimate enclaves where customers interact with one another.

Moving shoes to the eighth floor increased the department's selling space by 35 percent and doubled the available stock area. Exploring the science of the stock room, the design team put functionality first by providing movable shelving behind the sales counters. Additionally, discretely located computer stations—or "client telling stations"—were placed on the selling floor, allowing sales associates to access customer profiles, purchase history, and stock level information.

Once you get past the marketing blitz and amazing windows, after all, this is the business of selling shoes. And Saks now has its biggest platform yet for doing so.

Source: Eric Feigenbaum, "Shoes on Eight." VMSD *Magazine, November 2007.*

---

antique gumball machine, a feather boa, a spill of colorful stones—into artistic displays.

DISPLAY HOUSE PROPS

A variety of props are readily available from producers who construct just about anything the installer needs for an effective visual presentation. Suppliers are located in many major cities throughout the country and especially in places

such as New York City, Chicago, Los Angeles, Miami, and San Francisco. In addition to displaying their props in showrooms, the manufacturers gather at trade shows featuring every conceivable type of prop a display designer might need. One of the most important expositions is GlobalShop, where visual merchandisers can find ready-made props and can also have pieces custom-made for their presentations. The display expositions are

15.5 Found objects make unusual, cost-effective props. *John Aquino/WWD/ Condé Nast/Corbis.*

are available in **low-voltage bulbs** that effectively illuminate while reducing energy costs.

- **Halogen lighting** is extensively used by visual merchandisers because of the dramatic, intense rays it throws. Halogen light is unlike any other. It is ideal for enhancing a focal point in a display or providing a general wall "wash." Halogen bulbs also have a longer life, about double that of an incandescent bulb.

- **Neon** has some use in visual merchandising. Once primarily used to identify the name of the store on its façade, visual merchandisers use it in interior displays to call attention to a particular department or merchandise collection. Advantages of neon, or cold cathode, its technical name, are that it can be easily shaped to any form, can be produced in vivid colors, is virtually maintenance free, and costs little to operate.

LIGHT FIXTURES

There are many types of fixtures that may be used to provide the proper illumination for windows and interior displays. Each offers special advantages and must be chosen with these in mind. The two major types are described as follows.

- *Recessed lighting* has the advantage of providing light in an unobtrusive manner. Cans or containers are recessed into ceilings and can hold a variety of bulbs, including incandescents, fluorescents, and halogens. They are used for overall, general illumination as well as for spotlighting when the recessed fixtures feature swivel rods.

- *Track lighting* is functional fixturing that allows the lights to be adjusted to target specific areas. The tracks come in many lengths and house a variety of cans to fit any display style or store image. If positioned properly, these containers can effectively wash complete walls or highlight display focal points (Figure 15.6).

15.6 Track lighting allows light adjustments. *Frank and Helena/ cultura/Corbis.*

Signage

Signage in a display is the component that tells a story. The different types of signs may be used to identify the name of the designer whose collection is being featured, the theme that is being depicted, special promotional offerings, and so forth. These are presented in many forms, including **banners** made of paper or plastic; fabric; **fixture-contained signage** to identify the products displayed on a rack; and **pennants** made of felt, paper, or other materials for emphasis about the merchandise offering.

Graphics

One of the cost-saving components used in many retail window and interior displays is **graphics**. Many merchants such as Gap and Abercrombie & Fitch use many of these pictorial devices as the centerpieces of their visual presentations. Today's technical advances in photography and printing afford the retailer a multitude of images from which to choose with minimal effort and cost (Figure 15.7).

Graphics are available from a variety of resources. These include **original photography** available from in-house photographers or freelancers, **stock photography** from stock houses that have thousands of images on hand at nominal prices, and photos from **stock agencies** that supply photographs of every size, shape, and classification. The range of graphics, apart from the traditional, that are available today includes the following:

- ◆ **Backlit transparencies** employ an image in a light box that brings life to the graphic. They are used in abundance on selling floors to highlight specific merchandise.

- ◆ **Prismatic displays** provide motion to the graphic. The display unit somewhat parallels the venetian blind; it is made up of slats that automatically turn and change the image.

Also imperative to the effectiveness of displays are the design principles and use of color. As emphasized in the chapters on media, these must also be considered when planning and executing a visual presentation.

Themes and Settings for Window and Interior Displays

Just as set designs for the theater and movie screen enhance the story, visual displays enhance the merchandise or message intended for the consumer. The display is often the attention-getter that turns the shopper's head and makes further inspection necessary.

If a visual merchandising team has done its job satisfactorily, a particular image of the store becomes apparent in a display. This image might be captured through the simplicity of a single mannequin in a window surrounded by a minimalistic setting, by a variety of products augmented with signage to convey a promotional image, or by many other approaches.

Although most professional visual merchandisers have the ability to create and deliver displays of distinction, they are often limited by the store's budget. Especially during economic downturns when budgets are strained, the "all-out" presentation must be curtailed and ingenuity must take over. No matter which theme is being used to impart a display message—and there are many—the settings must be sufficiently exciting to be motivational devices that encourage purchasing.

The themes designed for windows and interiors range from the typical seasonal and holiday offerings to the more creative presentations that rely on the imagination of the visual merchandiser to develop.

Seasonal Displays

Standard among the many types of visual presentations that stores use as part of their display calendars are those that introduce each season of the year. They occupy window and interior spaces long before the shopper is expected to purchase. This early time frame is necessary to introduce the latest fashions and styles in the hope that onlookers will remember what is being featured and will either buy early or come back for later shopping sprees. The customary time for the trimming of fall windows, for example, is in June when the current summer merchandise goes on

15.7 Graphics are excellent, inexpensive display props. *Andrew H. Walker/ Getty Images.*

sale. In the fashion-forward emporiums, May might show a smattering of what's to come in the fall in "teaser" windows (Figure 15.8).

Within each of the seasonal display periods, different promotions take place. Back-to-school, a major selling theme for many retail establishments, coincides with the introduction of fall merchandise. Retailers with children, preteen, teenage, and college-bound clienteles mix the general fall themes with presentations of these merchandise classifications. Similarly, later in the fall season, Christmas is the major emphasis in retail displays because as much as 75 percent of retailers' annual business occurs during this season.

Each season's display environments must be designed using themes and settings that will not only enhance the merchandise offerings but also be sufficiently exciting to motivate the consumer to purchase. The merchandise may be central to the success of any product display, but it must be presented in themes that are imaginative and different from all that which the competition is featuring in their windows and interiors.

Holidays

Christmas is unquestionably the major holiday of the year for the majority of the retailing world, but other holidays play a vital role in the years' total volume. Visit any fragrance department the week before Mother's Day and you will witness a special frenzy and an abundance of merchandise available. The selling period for each holiday varies, as does the number of departments served by the holiday displays. Valentine's Day promotions require just a few days before the actual event, whereas Christmas lasts from Thanksgiving to the actual holiday (Figure 15.9).

In addition to the blockbuster holiday presentations such as Christmas, Valentine's Day, and Mother's Day, other holidays also play prominent roles.

- *Presidents' week* has become an essential part of many retailer display efforts. From the very upscale fashion establishments to those that concentrate on mid- to lower price points, this period has become a time for major clearance events to take place. Beginning in the 1960s, when a

15.8 Seasonal displays are typical of the themes that retailers use in their visual presentations. *Courtesy of Tiffany & Co.*

few merchants opened their doors for a final cleanup of winter merchandise, the practice caught fire. It became established as a time when visual merchandisers put on their promotional hats to create displays that would clean house of unwanted goods. With comparatively low budgets, the emphasis is generally on signage and graphics, each relatively inexpensive to produce, that couples the sales message with a smattering of institutional themes that depict the holiday.

◆ *Easter*, unlike Christmas in retailing (when merchants pull out all the stops to motivate consumer spending), is a holiday that is usually coupled with spring displays. Except for a few merchandise classifications, such as children's wear, which gets the major share

of visual presentation, this holiday period is not a major theme for visual merchandisers.

◆ *Columbus Day*, like Presidents' week, is a time for major price reductions. Special sales usually revolve around coat inventories, a somewhat traditional event for merchants. Themes that honor Columbus are popular, but with little money budgeted for this occasion, the major display components are signage and graphics.

Creative Themes

The ingenuity of the visual team is often at its best when it is called upon to develop concepts that do not fall within the traditional display categories. The theme may be based on a special event, a newsworthy topic, or the recognition

15.9 Holidays are excellent for visual themes.
Karne Vano for The Pottery Barn.

of a successful theatrical achievement. For the Christmas 2007 major window presentations, Barneys New York, the upscale fashion emporium, chose the green movement as its theme. Departing from the usual Christmas ornamentation and fanfare, the visual team created distinctive displays in their main windows that captured the attention not only of the passersby but also of the editorial press, which gave recognition to the displays in newspaper columns and television newscasts (Figure 15.10).

Institutional Themes

An **institutional theme** is often used to capture the moment for retailers. Its message or theme is generally subtler than other concepts, but its impact on the consumer is often beneficial to the store's image. Using themes such as charitable events, salutes to theater companies, and the celebration of a particular social event are typical of these displays. The horrific event that shook the world on September 11, 2001, took center stage as an institutional theme that year and for months

afterward. Just about every major retailer in the United States featured a patriotic window display with the American flag as its centerpiece. Each display spoke of patriotism and concentrated on that theme rather than on those that promoted sales.

Executing the Visual Presentation

It is imperative for the visual merchandiser to master the theories, design fundamentals, mannequin use, color selection, copy preparation, and so forth, but it is equally important that he or she is competent assembling the components into a good presentation.

The installation of a display requires an approach that is carefully planned and executed and that focuses attention on every detail (Figure 15.11). For the unseasoned display installer, it is beneficial to prepare a written outline that addresses

15.10 The environment is an excellent subject for a creative display. *Tina Finebarg/ AP Images.*

all of the parts of a display. For the professional trimmer, this detailed plan is unnecessary because he or she has the experience necessary for the perfect execution. However, when a centralized visual merchandising plan is used, as previously discussed, every detail must be noted so that those following the plan will properly install it. A basic set of rules that address the various stages of developing and installing a visual presentation follow.

Merchandise Selection and Preparation

Unless the institutional theme is used in a visual presentation, the merchandise, first and foremost, is the main ingredient. The selection of items to be displayed varies among organizations. In large department stores, as well as in centralized operations such as chains, for example, the divisional merchandise manager or buyer chooses the display merchandise. At the small, independent specialty store or boutique, the pro-

prietor usually has the final say. In any case, the merchandise must be timely, have positive eye appeal, and have the ability to make a statement.

To maintain merchandise control and to understand the reasons for the display selections, large retailers use **merchandise loan forms** that require information such as key selling points, the dates of merchandise availability, prices, and so forth. These completed forms accompany the merchandise to the visual department so that the data can be used in creating the best possible display. After the display has been dismantled, the merchandise is returned, along with the form, and the department from which it was borrowed confirms its receipt.

Props and Materials Assemblage

When the theme of the display has been decided, specific props and materials must be assembled for the installation. Such items are either purchased

15.11 The execution of a perfect display requires attention to many details.
Tina Finebarg/ AP Images.

new or reused from previous displays. Reusing existing props may require refurbishment or at least a fresh coat of paint. For major presentations, such as those used in Christmas windows and interiors, new in-house construction is sometimes used, or purchases from outside resources are often the answer. These displays are planned months in advance of the installation so that the props and materials will be on hand when needed.

Preparation of the Display Space

Too often, the space in which the display design is to be presented is sorely neglected. It might have stains on the window flooring, cracks in the walls, fingerprints on the glass windows or counters, stray pins on the floor of the window, or burned-out lights, each of which can seriously detract from the presentation's overall effectiveness. To avoid these common mistakes, some merchants use a **window and display case checklist** to make certain that everything has been carefully scrutinized before the installation proceeds.

Selection of Mannequins and Display Forms

When apparel ensembles are featured in windows and interiors, full-size mannequins are the best way to show them. It enables the shopper to immediately appreciate the garment's silhouette and determine if it is appropriate for his or her needs. The selection of the particular model to use depends on what the merchant has available. Most major retail operations have a large display warehouse where mannequins are stored and can select from them the models that fit the particular focus of the display. Of course, smaller operations have little choice but to use what is on hand.

In smaller windows, such as showcases, the life-size mannequin is out of the question. Instead, other forms such as three-quarter torsos are used to display the products.

Lighting Preparation

Usually, the last step of the installation of a display is lighting. Not only must each light fixture be examined for burned-out bulbs, but portable spotlights should be assembled in the right number to adequately illuminate the presentation. The variety of bulbs available to today's trimming staff is sig-

nificant and, therefore, requires careful consideration before the appropriate ones are selected.

With many passersby of store windows even when the shop is closed, there is a need to keep the lights on until most of the potential lookers are no longer available. A **display time clock** can be used to automatically turn the lights on and off at preset times. If lights are left on continuously, little purpose is served when shoppers are no longer passing by the displays, and the energy costs will escalate.

Installation of the Display

The trim follows after all of the other elements are addressed. The installation usually follows these steps:

1. The space is prepared, making certain it is in the best shape possible for an effective display.

2. The props are placed and anchored to make certain ambient movement does not cause them to lose their positioning.

3. If mannequins are used, they are strategically placed amid the props and then dressed with the preselected merchandise. The dressed mannequins should be fitted with the appropriate accessories as well, and it is imperative that any visible "hang-tags" be removed so as not to detract from the display.

4. If forms other than mannequins are used, they should be positioned in the appropriate places.

5. Spotlights should be focused on the areas that the displays wish to highlight.

6. Signage and price tags, if used, should be inserted.

7. The floors in a window installation should be examined to make certain they are free of damage or litter. Many trimmers use **display socks** over their shoes to eliminate the possibility of staining the floor covering.

8. The entire display should be examined to make certain its appearance is exactly as intended.

Summary of Key Points

◆ The planning and development of a retailer's visual program depends on the size of the organization, the number of units in the company, and its budget.

◆ Retailers have a number of different options to follow in planning their visual presentations, such as maintaining an in-house staff, using a centralized system, hiring freelancers to carry out the tasks, and creating the displays by themselves.

◆ Visual merchandising settings are limited to windows and interior spaces. Each offers numerous variations on the spaces, with windows providing such options as large formal windows, shadow boxes, islands, arcades, and windowless windows, and interiors using just about any high-traffic area in the store, such as elevator landings and store entrances.

◆ The components of a visual presentation include mannequins, props, lighting, signage, and graphics. Each has a variety of options for the trimmer to choose from to present an eye-appealing display.

◆ Visual merchandisers with limited budgets can create effective displays using discarded props that can easily be restored with a fresh coat of paint or by borrowing merchandise, such as musical instruments, settees, ladders, and so forth, from other merchants.

◆ Lighting is an essential ingredient in visual merchandising because it can be used to illuminate the display's focal point. With numerous choices, the visual presenter has to carefully choose lighting that best showcases the display.

◆ The use of graphics in visual presentations has become very popular because of the ease with which they can be acquired, the wide selection available, and the comparatively low costs.

Terms of the Trade

arcades
backlit transparencies
banners
blouse forms
centralized visual merchandising
circular windows
corner windows
director of visual merchandising
display presentation kit
display socks
display time clock
ethnic mannequins
fixture-contained signage
floodlights
fluorescents
focal point
found objects
freelance contract
freelancers
futuristic forms
graphics
halogen lighting
incandescents
in-house visual department
institutional theme
islands

low-voltage bulbs
merchandise loan form
model windows
neon
open-back windows
original photography
pennants
photographic portfolios
prismatic displays
props
representational forms
shadow boxes
spotlights
stock agencies
stock photography
stylized mannequins
suit forms
torsos
trimmer-constructed mannequins
trimmers
visual merchandising
vitrines
window and display case
    checklist
window calendar
windowless windows

♦ Any number of themes are used in trimming distinctive window displays, including seasonal motifs, holiday events, and institutional types, such as those that commemorate social, historical, and charitable events.

8. How do institutional themes differ from the traditional promotional themes that merchants use in their visual merchandising programs?

9. What are some of the steps used in execution of a visual presentation?

For Discussion

1. Describe some of the different approaches that visual merchandisers use to carry out the programs in retail operations.

2. Why do many chain organizations use centralized visual merchandising in their display programs, and how are these actions accomplished?

3. If a retailer is too small to have an in-house display team or staff that uses centralized visual merchandising, how can he or she accomplish effective window and interior displays?

4. Discuss the vast array of mannequins available to the retailer and why care should be exercised in choosing those that should be used in displays.

5. In addition to the props available from display houses, what are some of the other resources that visual merchandisers use to obtain them?

6. List and explain the differences among the various types of light sources used to illuminate window and interior visual presentations.

7. Why have graphics become so important in visual merchandising, and from what types of resources are they available?

Exercises and Projects

1. Make arrangements with three different retailers for the purpose of learning how they plan and develop the visual merchandising programs in their companies. Make certain you contact a department store, a unit of a chain operation, and a small store to determine how each one's approach is different from the others. Prepare a presentation before the class regarding the uniqueness of each operation's visual merchandising program.

2. Scout the downtown central shopping districts, malls, and local shopping areas to identify the different types of store windows being used to display merchandise. Prepare a table of five different types and how they differ from each other. In addition to logging the information, take photographs of each type and affix the photos to the table you constructed.

Web Site Exploration for In-Depth Analysis

Visual Merchandising and Store Design
http://www.vmsd.com

   Visual Merchandising and Store Design is the trade periodical most widely read by professionals in the field. It offers a variety of topics each month that address innovative and distinctive subject matter.

National Association of Display Industry (NADI)
http://www.nadi-global.com

   The National Association of Display Industry (NADI) is the largest trade organization for the visual merchandising industry. Its Web site offers a wealth of information that is continuously updated.

Public Relations: Promoting *and* Advancing *the* Retailer's Image

CHAPTER OBJECTIVES

After you have completed this chapter, you should be able to discuss:

★ The meaning of public relations and how it differs from publicity.

★ Different arrangements that retailers use in their quest for effective public relations.

★ Some of the tools that public relations teams use to gain favorable publicity for their clients.

★ Several of the activities in which retailers engage to promote their company images.

★ Some of the fundamental principles associated with success in terms of placement for the print, broadcast, and Internet media.

★ Why public relations professionals should avoid granting an "exclusive" to a media outlet for publicity purposes.

★ The importance of the follow-up with the editorial press after a press release makes their publications.

★ How the awareness of public relations is advanced to those in the profession.

The retailer's reputation and its very existence most often depends on the image the retailer projects to its regular clientele and prospective shoppers. Building and maintaining a solid reputation is not an easy task, given the complexity of the retailing arena and the many interactions the merchant has with the public every day.

To put its best foot forward, the retailer often turns to a **public relations specialist** to handle the all-encompassing challenges that come from doing business with the public. Satisfying the retailer's needs requires intensive day-to-day efforts focused on promoting its products, crafting stories that enhance the company's image, developing tactics to improve the retailer's position in relation to the competition, and more. The public relations department or outside firm must be able to tell a great story and spread the word about the company.

The most widely accepted definition of **public relations (PR)** is the one formally adopted by the Public Relations Society of America in 1982: "Public relations helps an organization and its publics adapt mutually to each other." The term *publics* encompasses many different groups, such as employees, customers, and local communities. As a function of management, the role of public relations is to analyze public opinion that might impact the company; counsel all levels of management in regard to policy making, including such issues as dealing with problems, social responsibilities of the organization, and communication efforts; and plan a wide variety of other efforts necessary to gain favor with its targeted publics.

Although PR professionals are generally engaged in highlighting the retailer's positive attributes, they are sometimes called upon to right the wrongs that may have occurred in the everyday operation of the merchant's business. If, for example, a retailer has received bad press because of a misleading or misconstrued advertisement, action must be taken to

TABLE 16.1 — 2008 Twenty Leading Independent PR Firms

RANK	FIRM	LOCATION	NET FEES	EMPLOYEES
1	Edelman	New York	449,231,193	2,997
2	Waggener Edstrom	Bellevue, WA	119,670,000	843
3	APCO Worldwide	Washington, DC	112,400,000	569
4	Ruder Finn Group	New York	96,112,000	545
5	Text 100 International	San Francisco	63,000,000	540
6	Qorvis Communications	Washington, DC	34,919,065	96
7	Schwartz Communications	Waltham, MA	31,049,817	199
8	ICR	Westport, CT	26,202,272	98
9	Dan Klores Communications	New York	22,400,000	120
10	Taylor	New York	20,205,000	105
11	Gibbs & Soell	New York	19,258,660	101
12	WeissComm Partners	San Francisco	18,981,000	86
13	Padilla Speer Beardsley	Minneapolis	15,952,172	102
14	Peppercom	New York	13,548,322	75
15	Allison & Partners	San Francisco	13,082,100	81
16	Capstrat	Raleigh, NC	12,500,000	77
17	French/West/Vaughn	Raleigh, NC	12,497,377	83
18	Shift Communications	Brighton, MA	12,233,693	100
19	RF/Binder Partners	New York	12,220,000	74
20	CRT/Tanaka	Richmond, VA	12,087,881	64

Source: www.odwyerpr.com.

Freelancers

Many in-house and PR agencies use **freelance PR professionals** to augment their permanent staffs. Freelancers are self-employed individuals who offer their services for one-time projects. They are remunerated in a number of different ways. Some are paid an hourly rate, with the average fee of about $150 per hour. If the project is to last for a day or more, the going rate is typically from $300 to $1,000 per day. Still others use auction Web sites where those in need of PR assistance bid for the individual's services. Two of the more widely used auction sites are www.IFreelance.com and www.Guru.com.

No matter who has the responsibility for public relations in an organization, there are certain steps that should be taken to achieve positive results. In Media Insight 16.2, the author provides some surefire approaches to designing a program that delivers the right punch.

Edelman

Founded in 1952 by Daniel J. Edelman, its present-day founder and chairman, Edelman has made the leap from a small PR firm to the largest in the world. Based in New York, with offices across the globe, it employs more people and grosses more money than any other PR firm. At the beginning of 2009, it employed almost four times as many employees as the next leading independent PR firm and had net fees that were also four times that of the next important player in the field.

As expressed in Edelman's welcome statement, "We are on a mission: to make public relations the lead discipline in the communications mix, because only public relations has the immediacy and transparency to build credibility and trust." The company continues to build relationships with clients in numerous industries, one of which is retailing, by enlisting "average people, friends and families, everyday employees, as well as recognized experts—to build brands from the bottom up." All of this is accomplished through the traditional methods of disseminating information, such as editorials, word-of-mouth, experiential marketing, and the newest formats that include bloggers, social networking, and online conversationalists who passionately communicate their feelings about specific categories and topics.

Unique in its methodology, Edelman has its own proprietary planning tools that enable its clients to expand their programs and improve their share of target markets. Among these tools are:

◆ *Life Moment Mapping:* "A process that analyzes how brands can best connect with various behavior-changing life moments in order to create meaningful dialogue and increase share of relationship with target consumers throughout their lives."

◆ *Consumer Tribes:* "Profiles of different consumer demographics to understand what influences their behavior and buying decisions."

◆ The *"Chocolate Fudge Cake"* layered editorial planning approach: "Helps extend the reach of media placements by building volume, scale, and dimension."

Edelman's mission continues to be "to provide public relations counsel and strategic communications services that enable our clients to build strong relationships and influence attitudes and behaviors in a complex world."

Source: Information from www.edelman.com.

Why PR Packs a Punch

Robert A. Kelly

Done right, it delivers the key, target audience behaviors you know you must have to achieve your organizational objectives.

I refer to perceptions of your organization and resulting behaviors such as:

• customers making repeat purchases;

• prospects starting to do business with you;

• employees really valuing their jobs;

• suppliers doing all possible to expand your relationship;

• community leaders strengthening bonds with you;

• businesses seeking beneficial joint ventures;

• unions bargaining more frequently in good faith; and

• legislators and political leaders viewing you as an important member of the business community.

Yes, public relations indeed packs a punch, but only when it's based on a solid foundation. Namely, its fundamental premise. People act on their own perception of the facts before them, which leads to predictable behaviors. When we create, change, or reinforce that opinion by reaching, persuading, and moving to desired action those people whose behaviors affect the organization, the public relations mission is accomplished.

And, notice, please, the implication is that when managers start looking for a return on their public relations investment these days, many will want to see the kind of key stakeholder behavior change that leads directly to achieving their objectives.

Does your public relations program pack such a punch?

It can if you commit to action steps like these.

The previous list of key audiences is a good one, but only you can create the ideal list of the most important external "publics" whose behaviors affect your organization the most.

Then, prioritize them as to impacts on your enterprise, and let's work on the target audience at the top of the list. By the way, the test for listing an audience asks "Does its behavior affect my operation in any way?" If it does, list it.

Do you know for a fact how this audience perceives your organization? Why take chances? Interact with audience members and ask many questions. What do they think of your enterprise? Do you notice negativity in their responses? How about rumors, misconceptions, inaccuracies?

With responses to such questions in hand, you're ready to set down your public relations goal. In other words, the specific perception problem and thus behavior change you want. For instance, kill that rumor as soon as possible, straighten out that misconception or untruthful belief, or correct that inaccuracy.

So, what do you do with that public relations goal? Not much without a strategy. But with the right one, you are quite likely to achieve your goal. Happily, when dealing with opinion and perception challenges, you have just three from which to choose: create perception/opinion where there may be none, change existing perception, or reinforce it. The strategy you choose will complement your new public relations goal.

Now comes the hard work, creating just the right message for transmittal to your target audience. It must lay out the truth clearly and creditably, so consider it carefully. The features of a successful corrective message are clarity, believability, persuasiveness, and a compelling presentation. Remember, the message aims to alter existing perception.

Presumably, you will not follow the lead of the artillery commander who told his men, "Point your cannons in any direction and fire when you feel like it!" Rather your "beasts of burden," your communications tactics, will carry your message directly to the right eyes and ears among members of your target audience.

The list of such tactics is a long one and includes everything from speeches, newspaper/radio interviews, and press releases to op-eds, brochures, e-mails, and many, many others.

It won't be long before you are looking for signs that your public relations program is working. And this can best be achieved by a new round of perception monitoring out there among members of your key target audience. Same questions as the first go-around, but now you're looking for responses indicating that perception has been altered in your direction.

Things not moving fast enough? Broaden the variety of communications tactics you use and their frequencies. And take a hard look at the facts undergirding your message.

Together, these steps will create a public relations effort that packs the punch you really want.

Source: Robert A. Kelly. "Why PR Packs a Punch." www. prcommentary.com.

Components of Public Relations

Public relations is a multifaceted concept. It is often confused with **publicity**, but the two are different. Publicity is just one part of public relations, albeit generally the most important part, especially for the retail industry. The PR firm Cuclis PR sums it up this way: "The goal of public relations is to mold opinion. The saying 'perception is reality' speaks to the need for public relations. Public relations works to protect an organization's or individual's reputation. Effective PR strengthens credibility, enhances image, develops goodwill, and influences behavior. Speeches, special events, newsletters, annual reports, and news releases are examples of PR."*

Although public relations involves activities such as lobbying on behalf of the client, counseling every level of management within an organization regarding policy decision making, developing relationships within an organization to foster employee effectiveness, and so forth, it is the publicity component that receives most of the PR department's efforts. Some of those publicity efforts that have retail-oriented implications are discussed next.

Publicity

Commonly confused with advertising, publicity is a different marketing tool that businesses use to get their messages out to the public. The major difference is that advertising is paid for and publicity is free, often making it more credible in the eyes of the public. *Free* may be the operative word that many use to describe publicity, but it should be noted that a significant amount of money is often spent to gain publicity. In the retail arena, for example, Macy's is the recipient of free publicity from the print and broadcast media with its Thanksgiving Day Parade; however, it has spent millions on the production of the event. Thus, although the press attention to these events actually costs nothing, many dollars are spent to warrant the favorable publicity.

Gaining favorable publicity is no easy task. The competitive nature of retailing and the vast

number of companies that compose its playing field make it an everyday challenge for those in retailing to translate events and happenings into stories that will capture the attention of the media. The PR professionals use a variety of tools to regularly gain access to the media.

PRESS RELEASES

One of the tried and true ways in which to communicate a company's image and promotional endeavors is with the **press release**, which today is usually distributed by e-mail. A press release is generally a one- or two-page document describing a newsworthy item about which the retailer wants to inform the consumer. Day after day, PR professionals prepare the releases in the hope that the media will find them worthy of mention in print or on the air. The key to a retailer's message being accepted for publicity purposes by the media is the newsworthiness of the action. For retailers, any of the following might pique the interests of editors:

- *Opening a new unit* is often of interest to those who cover retailing news. Openings are generally given publicity if the unit is a departure from the retailer's usual method of operation. When Bloomingdale's opened its Soho store with a specialty store concept, in New York City, and later did the same for its Chicago store as a home furnishings' freestanding unit in the landmark Medina Temple, it garnered significant free publicity.

- *Global expansion* usually interests the editorial press. When Ralph Lauren entered the Russian retail arena with two shops, the press gave it invaluable publicity.

- *Charitable events* are often reported by newspapers and on radio and television. When major fund-raisers such as those that benefit the Susan G. Komen for the Cure foundation, a major cancer fund-raising organization, are partnered with other companies, free publicity is often achieved.

- *Exclusive celebrity collections* often make headline news. When Kohl's signed its agreement with Lauren Conrad, author, fashion designer, and television personality, and when Target captured an exclusive deal

---

*From www.cuclispr.com.

Neiman Marcus. For example, Neiman Marcus honored the top ten women of Collin County, Texas, in 2009, honoring them for their contributions to the community and local nonprofit organizations. Not only were the recipients recognized for their efforts but Neiman Marcus received invaluable free publicity from the Star Community Newspapers group that serves the area.

Of course, not all PR work is concerned with promoting goodwill projects. When a crisis occurs, PR personnel must respond quickly to dispel any negative publicity that might affect the future of the company.

Employee Relations

The success of the retailer depends not only on satisfactory merchandising but also on the quality of its employees at every level of the organization. The PR team is often charged with presenting information in its releases that attracts the best possible staff. They also use devices such as internal newsletters to help maintain an engaged workforce.

Sponsorships

Another job of the PR departments in retail operations is to sponsor events to raise money and/or awareness. There are countless venues for **sponsorship**: Toys For Tots, the USA Swim Team, blood drives, and the Society for Prevention of Cruelty to Animals (SPCA), to name just a few. Some businesses sponsor a onetime event, and others sponsor their favorite cause (or causes) on a regular basis. Similar to other PR activities, sponsorships receive free publicity from the media that ultimately results in increased business for the sponsoring companies (Figure 16.3).

Getting Public Relations Messages Placed

The volume of press releases and other PR efforts sometimes makes it hard for one release to stand out among the others and grab a busy editor's attention. What might seem a newsworthy occurrence to those who design and implement the various PR tools may not strike those in the media as important to its readership or broadcast audience.

To gain as much press space as possible, it is important to establish a good relationship with those who hold the power of the pen. Contacts in the editorial world must be developed over time. When a PR professional proves himself or herself reliable and gains the trust of the media, his or her releases are more likely to be read and valued. Therefore, choosing a reputable PR agency is extremely important to ensure the retailer-client's messages reach the right media.

Some of the fundamental principles associated with successfully placing information in the print, broadcast, and Internet media follow.

The Print Media

Newspapers and magazines both fall into two categories: consumer publications and business publications. Business publications are further broken down into consumer and trade publications. PR agents must understand the differences among them and know which of them best serve their client's needs; they must also understand the publications' purposes and interests in order to send the right information to the right publication—and avoid inundating a busy editor with information he or she cannot use. By responsibly submitting appropriate press information—*before* the closing deadlines—PR agents can develop a positive relationship with the editors.

PUBLICATION SELECTION

Every newspaper and magazine is targeted toward a specific market. The *New York Times*, for example, appeals to more affluent readers than any of the other dailies and features columns that would be of interest to this group. Its pages are filled with retail advertisements, most of them fashion-oriented, and it publishes a Style section on Sundays, so it seems quite natural that the *Times* will contribute space to cover newsworthy events of the retail industry (Figures 16.4a and b). Of course, other newspapers target population segments that also warrant publicity pieces. The *Daily News*, another New York publication, targets a less affluent reader and therefore receives much promotional retail advertising. It, too, will publish publicity pieces about promotionally oriented stores.

Magazines are also directed toward specific interest groups, and their retail advertisements reflect

Macy's is a proud national sponsor of

Go Red For Women®

Our Hearts. Our Choice. Choose to Speak Up! **learn more**

the campaign

Go Red For Women is the American Heart Association's nationwide movement that celebrates the energy, passion and power of women to band together and wipe out heart disease, the #1 killer of American women and men. The color red and the red dress have become linked with the ability all women have to improve their heart health and live stronger, longer lives. Since 2004, Macy's customers and employees have contributed more than $21 million to the Go Red For Women movement. It's time to take charge and give your heart the love it deserves!

- take fashion to heart and <u>buy the INC International Concepts Red Dress</u>
- watch the Go Red For Women <u>public service announcement</u>
- check out the Go Red For Women <u>TV commercial</u>
- join Go Red For Women! <u>sign up now</u>
- <u>take heart health to heart</u>
- <u>make a donation</u> to the American Heart Association
- tell us how you Speak Up against heart disease <u>in person</u> or <u>online</u>
- for more info & to join Go Red For Women, check out <u>GoRedForWomen.org</u> or en espanol <u>GoRedCorazon.org</u>

Geoffrey Beene is proud to honor Macy's national sponsorship and support the American Heart Association's Go Red For Women movement with a $100,000 contribution.

---

their readership. The seasoned PR professional must examine every conceivable publication with potential for publicity before going to its editorial staff to gain coverage.

In addition to consumer-oriented newspapers and magazines, trade periodicals are excellent places to gain recognition of the retail industry. Such matters as management hires, innovative merchandising initiatives, and so forth are of interest to the readership. In particular, *Women's Wear Daily*, *Visual Merchandising and Store Design*, *Advertising Age*, and *Stores* magazines are excellent publications for PR people who represent retailers to approach for their publicity efforts.

DEADLINE AWARENESS

To make certain that a story will be inserted in the desired edition of the publication, it is necessary to know the deadline by which a story must be delivered in order to be considered. Although the dailies are available up to press time for the latest news story, the columns or articles that might feature retail events often require more lead time

16.3 Sponsorships provide positive publicity for retailers. *Courtesy of Macy's.*

Happy Campers Command Stage in Macy's Parade

Young performers from Stagedoor Manor, a Catskill theater camp, have their final rehearsal in Manhattan before participating in the Macy's Thanksgiving Day Parade.

RUTH FREMSON/THE NEW YORK TIMES

By PATRICK HEALY

Everything was fine with Macy's Santa-sleigh float until the elves showed up.

It was 8 a.m. on Thanksgiving Day, and 15 young children — mostly of Macy's employees — were decked out in red-and-green elf costumes on Central Park West, where the floats were queued for the annual Macy's parade. Also on hand were 20 teenage actors with Stagedoor Manor, a Cats-

kills theater camp, who had spent four days in rehearsal to ride the float and perform in the parade for the first time.

The curveball of elves having dibs to the Santa float might have ruffled your average adolescent eager to have a star turn in a nationally televised parade. But Stagedoor kids are legendary pros. They handled the surprise with poise and humor as they rechoreographed their number to create

enough room on the float for the elves, who ended up peppering the actors with questions about how to break into show business.

"This is what live theater is all about, these last-minute changes," said Aaron Albert, 17, who has spent the last six summers at Stagedoor Manor, as he stood atop the float.

"Adjusting a performance is the fun of the experience, but also the terror of it," continued Mr. Al-

bert, who flew in from Los Angeles, where he is a cast member in Disney XD's new musical comedy show "I'm in the Band." "As long as no one falls off the float or throws up, it'll be a success."

No one fell off and no one got sick. (A golf cart did bump into the float and bruised two young women walking beside it.) And at the end of the parade route, just before NBC's coverage wound

Continued on Page 5

16.4a

16.4a and b The Style section often provides positive press for fashion retailers. *Courtesy of the* New York Times.

and earlier deadlines. The Sunday editions, made up of numerous sections, often carry a different deadline schedule. Magazine deadlines, because of the more complicated publishing procedures, are considerably earlier than newspaper deadlines. The easiest way to find out the actual deadline dates is to call the publisher.

THE EXCLUSIVITY FACTOR

From a PR standpoint, promising an exclusive story is usually a professional faux pas and is unlikely to help get the story published. If the story is newsworthy, all of the targeted media will be interested in it. Also, the relationship with media

resources that were "scooped" might be damaged. Stories of special interest are best served by making press or media kits and releases and allowing the media editors to do their jobs, deciding whether or not to publish them.

THE FOLLOW-UP

Getting the message printed is certainly a credit to the publicist. To improve the chances of achieving subsequent publicity recognition and space, it is imperative that a positive relationship is developed with the press. After an article is written, a cordial and complimentary note of appreciation is appropriate.

392 PART FIVE: PROMOTIONAL TOOLS USED BY RETAILERS

PHOTOGRAPHS BY RUTH FREMSON/THE NEW YORK TIMES

Above, foreground from left, Andrew Kotzen, Chris Murphy and Sara Frost of Stagedoor Manor in the Macy's parade. Below, Amanda Yuan, left, A. J. Achinger and Avery Adams in rehearsal.

Happy Campers Command Stage in the Macy's Parade

From First Arts Page

down, the 20 Stagedoor performers — along with 47 other cast mates from camp who greeted the float there — pulled off their two-minute-plus song-and-dance number, "Santa Claus Is Coming to Town," and joined other dancers for Macy's "I Believe" closing anthem.

"Our actors were thrilled, we were thrilled, and I think Macy's was thrilled," said Cindy Samuelson, the producer and owner of the 34-year-old camp, which normally operates only in the summer. "So much went into this first professional outing of ours in New York City since the '70s: I'm so thrilled, and relieved."

Ms. Samuelson approached Macy's about performing in the parade after watching it last Thanksgiving and thinking that her young actors would be a good fit. Her parents, Elsie and Carl Samuelson, who founded the camp, were longtime fans of the

parade, and Stagedoor actors have been known for years for their high caliber: Zach Braff, Jennifer Jason Leigh and Natalie Portman are among the many working alumni.

The camp — which was the setting and inspiration for the 2003 movie called, appropriately, "Camp" — made DVDs of Stagedoor summertime productions for Macy's to consider. Stagedoor produces 15 shows every three weeks, for a total of 45 each summer.

In September, Stagedoor was given the go-ahead for the parade, and invited 67 of its campers (from 22 states and three countries) to come to New York to rehearse and perform. Stagedoor charged each actor $200, which covered only part of the expenses, with the camp picking up the rest.

The rehearsal days in a Midtown Manhattan studio were long, but the young actors were in good spirits during a break on

the afternoon before Thanksgiving. The choreography for "Santa Claus Is Coming to Town" had changed because it had been running long: a hip-hop-style dance

number was excised and a greater emphasis was put on smiling dancers doing more traditional jazzy moves.

"We basically learned two dif-

ferent numbers in four days, but that's not so tough compared to what we do at camp, where we put on major shows in just a few weeks," said Abby Lett, 16, who is from Dallas and has spent five summers at Stagedoor. (Stagedoor fare is hardly kids' stuff: last summer the camp did "Sweeney Todd" and six other Stephen Sondheim shows in a single weekend.)

The routine itself was like a number out of the television show "Glee," which was wildly popular among the teenagers. Two adorably sad-faced tweens were told, "You better not pout" by another actor to start off the number, which ultimately included dozens of performers dancing, singing, twirling, dipping and hoisting one another aloft, as well as one boy doing a perfectly executed series of back handsprings.

At the rehearsal and on Thanksgiving morning, several of the actors repeated one another in expressing gratitude for

being included in the parade, a memory they said — in the sincere and un-self-conscious way of many actors — that they would cherish for the rest of their lives.

"As much as it's taught me how to perform, Stagedoor's mainly given me a place that I can really call home," said B. J. Myers, 15,

---

Young performers have a debut in a Thanksgiving spectacle.

---

who is from Atlanta and has spent two summers at camp. "When I'm out in the real world, I feel very out of place. Everyone out there is the same. No one is really as different as we are. Camp gives us a place to be who we are, who we were born as."

16.4b

The Broadcast Media

Although television and radio are sometimes interested in covering retail-oriented events, airtime is often extremely limited. National and local news of a general nature get preference, with the **soft news** often used as filler.

SELECTION OF THE OUTLET

There are two different types of programs that provide publicity for the airwaves: news broadcasts and **broadcast magazines**. The news broadcast is the standard type that covers timely news reports. Interspersed between the hard news items are stories that might include something related to retailing. The broadcast magazines such as *20/20* that cover a few stories in detail once a week might occasionally give coverage to a retailer if its story is unique. With the popularity of 24-hour news on cable television, stories related to the retail industry might get coverage.

When the item is simple and maximum exposure is the goal, news releases are best sent to every news director in the hopes that a spot will be assigned to a story. If the event is of a special nature, such as the annual Macy's Thanksgiving Day Parade, and extended time is necessary for maximum publicity, only the most appropriate of the television or radio shows should be contacted.

DEADLINES

Deadlines for broadcast are important to understand. An important story in a newspaper or broadcast medium can be inserted right up until press time, and often while another topic is being explored, and breaking news bulletins are sometimes used for grave matters. For retailing stories, however, the piece is often taped in advance and carefully edited to fill a specific time slot. Unless it is of vital importance to the viewing and listening audience, the piece will be considered only if there is sufficient time to produce the segment.

INTERVIEWS

Radio and television are natural choices for interviews. Stations are always eager to allocate time to individuals who might have something newsworthy to say. Even though retailing might not be a universally intriguing topic, interesting interviewees often attract an audience. If the individual is a colorful character in terms of appearance or communication, he or she might be a good choice

for the station. If the personality is a designer who has just signed an unusual exclusivity agreement, the story might get aired, or if an in-store appearance of a celebrity would seem of interest, it might pique the interest of the media outlets.

THE FOLLOW-UP

As in the case of the print media, letters of appreciation are always in order after the segment has been used. The key to continued exposure is to develop a relationship with the individuals in charge of programming.

Internet Blogs

When Internet users conduct searches of any topic, they are inundated with **blogs** that offer personal opinions on the subjects being researched. There are bloggers who deal with a wide array of subjects, and retailing is one of them. Setting up a blog is simple, and countless numbers of individuals with opinions to express have taken to this route to share their thoughts about any topic. The Web site www.retailblogmarketing.com notes that according to the search engine service Technorati, by the end of 2008, 184 million people on the Internet had started their own blog and 346 million people were blog readers.

Blogs have become the rage in the promotion and publicity of just about any merchandise classification. Blogging has changed the way many consumers get their product information and has significantly influenced purchasing. Bloggers, both experts and laypeople, have become authoritative figures in spreading information. Many people in the PR business agree that those who do not use the blog as a means of spreading their messages are missing out on motivating large segments of the population to buy their products.

Some of the highly favored retail-oriented blogs, according to www.about.com, include Retail Contrarian, Retail Design Diva, Retaildoc, Rick Segel's Blog, and Specialty Retail Expert.

E-mail

People with e-mail accounts are regularly bombarded with messages from a host of retailers wanting to publicize information about their organizations and offerings. Whatever the occasion—a special in-store celebrity appearance, an anniversary sale, the arrival of a new collection,

Public Relations Society of America

The world's largest organization for the publications community is PRSA, the Public Relations Society of America, which was founded in 1947. Representing professionals all over the country and in every PR discipline, it provides a wealth of knowledge to those involved in the profession as well as to students wanting to enter the field. Its size can best be judged by its membership, which includes a community of more than 21,000 PR and communications professionals from every corner of the country. In terms of college and university affiliations, the PRSA has as members more than 10,000 students who are part of a subsidiary group, the Public Relations Student Society of America.

Among its many services, the PRSA provides professional development for industry participants, sets the standards that will result in excellence in performance, promulgates ethical practices, and provides numerous other services from which members may choose to better their performances. Of paramount importance to its membership are the following:

◆ It enables members to participate in networking with other professionals in the field. This benefit enables everyone to interface with other members to share in specific knowledge and expertise at regularly held niche conferences.

◆ It sponsors events such as *Silver Anvil Evening,* in which awards for individual accomplishment and achievement are bestowed.

◆ It promotes continuous learning, which benefits members through professional development programs and industry conferences that feature outstanding leaders in the industry.

◆ It offers two important publications that help keep those in the field abreast of important issues. *Public Relations Tactics*, a monthly newspaper, features trends, news, and how-to information designed to help professionals improve their performance. *Public Relations Strategist*, a quarterly journal, offers fresh perspectives and new concepts to bring performance to the highest level.

Rounding out its offerings to the membership are the *Voices of Public Relations* ongoing podcasts, which feature dialogues with PR practitioners and blogs of PR professionals.

Source: Information from www.prsa.org.

an exclusive designer collaboration—e-mail provides a way for a publicist to extol the virtues of the operation without incurring significant expense. E-mails can be artistically designed using photographs and other images, although sometimes a simple, straightforward letter works best. Whatever the format, more and more retailers are using e-mail along with other PR devices to get their names in the minds of consumers.

Terms of the Trade

backgrounders

blogs

broadcast magazines

deadlines

For Immediate Release

freelance PR professionals

independent PR firms

in-house PR department

media kit

networking

podcasts

press kit

press release

public relations (PR)

public relations specialist

publicity

soft news

sponsorship

Advancing Public Relations

For the field of public relations to continue to serve the needs of the retail community as well as other institutions, it is essential that those in the profession understand the principles and practices that contribute to its success. PR professionals can stay abreast of developments and changes in the field through membership in trade associations and through publications that offer invaluable pertinent information, ideas, and suggestions that will impact performance.

The Public Relations Society of America (PRSA), the subject of Focus 16.2, is one such organization that advances the profession.

Summary of Key Points

◆ Although highlighting the retailer's positives is a major task of a PR professional, he or she is sometimes called upon to dispel any negative bad press that the company has received.

◆ The vast majority of retailers and other organizations use independent PR firms to handle their PR needs because outside firms offer objectivity and new ideas and they can be hired on an as-needed basis.

◆ Freelancers are alternatives to in-house and outside PR organizations; their services are also available on an as-needed basis and at hourly or daily rates that are usually below that of the PR organizations.

◆ The most important role played by a PR company or in-house department is to gain favorable publicity for the company through means such as press releases, media kits, and sponsorships.

◆ To get as much favorable press coverage as is possible, it is necessary to establish a good relationship with media sources.

◆ No matter which media outlet is used for publicity purposes, it is essential to follow up the placement with the people who made the publicity possible.

◆ The awareness of the latest approaches used in public relations is best achieved through membership in PR trade associations and by faithfully reading the publications that cover the field.

For Discussion

1. Although the terms *public relations* and *publicity* are often used interchangeably, why is it a mistake to do so?

2. In addition to fostering a retailer's positive image in the press, why is it necessary for PR professionals to be adept at crisis management?

3. What advantages and disadvantages are there in the use of in-house PR departments?

4. What advantages are there for the retailer to use an independent PR firm instead of an in-house operation?

5. Describe some of the events that retailers use to gain favorable publicity for their companies.

6. What is the different between a press release and a press kit?

7. Describe some of the components of media kits that merchants use to spread the word regarding an upcoming special event.

8. What are some of the types of sponsorships that retailers use in the pursuit of favorable publicity?

9. Discuss some of the fundamental principles associated with success in terms of placement of information with the print and broadcast media.

10. Why are Internet blogs so important to gain publicity?

Exercises and Projects

1. Pretend you are a freelance PR professional who has been hired by a small retailer to publicize a fashion show it is holding to benefit an organization that contributes money for cancer research. Using the following, prepare a press release for transmittal to the editorial press in the retailer's trading area:

   ◆ Your choice of charity that focuses on cancer research (available through an Internet search).

   ◆ A fictitious independent retailer (women's, juniors, or teen clothing).

   ◆ Your choice of fashion show presentation (see Chapter 15 for guidelines).

   ◆ Date: (choose a date).

   ◆ Time: (choose a time).

   ◆ Place for presentation: local auditorium (create a name).

   ◆ Mention that proceeds from the event will benefit the charity.

   ◆ Mention that light refreshments will be served after the show.

   ◆ Cost of admission: $20 (check made out to the charity).

   ◆ Any other relevant information of your choice.

2. Your PR firm has been contacted by a major retailer such as Macy's or Bloomingdale's for the purpose of preparing a media kit that will help promote its upcoming special event honoring a famous apparel designer. Prepare the kit, addressing the following:

   ◆ The name of a designer of your choice

   ◆ The tools you would use to promote the event

   ◆ The name of the store that will sponsor the event

   ◆ The dates, time, place, and other pertinent information about the special event

Web Site Exploration for In-Depth Analysis

Public Relations Society of America
http://www.prsa.org
   This major PR organization provides in-depth information and a broad range of services to its members in public relations.

O'Dwyer's Public Relations News
http://www.odwyerpr.com
   This site provides breaking news about public relations and offers advice on constructing a job search of the industry.

PART SIX

PUTTING IT TOGETHER

Dovetailing *the* Advertising *and* Promotional Tools

CHAPTER OBJECTIVES

After you have completed this chapter, you should be able to discuss:

★ The different steps in an advertising campaign.

★ How a small retailer may promote a special event without using a public relations firm to develop the presentation.

★ How a special promotion can benefit both the retailer and a charitable organization.

★ The planning strategy a small merchant should use to ensure the success of a special promotion.

★ Some of the promotional tools that small retailers can use in planning a special event without incurring considerable expense.

★ How free publicity may be achieved for a special event.

★ How refreshments could be used for an event without incurring any expense for the retailer.

As we learned in the preceding chapters, retail advertising and promotion takes many shapes and forms. Each offers a specific avenue for the merchant to reach patrons as well as prospective customers. Advertising and promotional activities are necessary to succeed in the ever-growing competitive retail environment.

Using only one advertising and promotional device is often insufficient to achieve success. A one-day sale and an in-store celebrity appearance, for example, require different approaches to advertising and promotion. The complexity of the event dictates which advertising venue and how many of them might best ensure success.

Professional retailers, especially major organizations, are familiar with how to maximize their advertising strategies. Most use in-house public relations staffs or independent agencies to guide their promotional efforts. Smaller retail operations generally do not have either the budget or the need for professional public relations experts. Instead, they sometimes contract a **freelance consultant** to handle the chores, and for very small retail ventures such as boutiques, many practice **do-it-yourself promotional planning** in the quest for efficient advertising and promotion.

In this concluding chapter, attention focuses on the different steps that retailers use in their advertising and promotional campaigns and how a small merchant develops such a campaign that encompasses the components necessary to translate an idea or concept into one that is as professional as those achieved by larger merchants, but without the expense.

Using some of the typical components that retailers and other businesses use in developing complete campaigns, Fairfax Gallery embarked upon a promotional campaign to capture the attention of the consumers in its trading area.

This material is drawn from a case study of a real public relations effort through a partnership among a small retailer, an artist, and the Juvenile Diabetes Research Foundation (JDRF).

Before the actual study is explored, it is essential to offer some of the typical considerations that should be addressed before embarking on a specific advertising and promotional campaign. Different projects require different attention, but the following are some of those considerations that all retailers should address before the campaign begins and after it has been completed.

Advertising Campaigns— A General Approach

Proper planning is essential before any campaign gets under way. First and foremost, it must be determined if the effort is to be strictly an ad campaign or one that also involves promotional links. If the campaign solely concentrates on advertising by running a series of ads linked together on specific media with a common theme aimed at a specific market, it is known as an *advertising campaign*. If, however, there are other promotional tools such as special events and visual merchandising incorporated in the undertaking, it will be expanded to an *advertising and promotional campaign*. In retailing, this latter approach is often used. Some of the essentials of such campaigns are discussed next.

Establishing the Campaign's Objectives

Throughout a retail operation's existence, there are numerous endeavors that are used to increase its position in the field. These include improving customer recognition, expanding the existing operation, introducing private label collections, and so forth. When the campaign's goal is established, it should be clearly stated for management to examine and to use later to measure the campaign's success.

Defining the Scope of the Market

The size and scope of the market for which the campaign is directed must be clearly defined.

If there is more than one segment, each might warrant a different format. For example, if one market is targeted to Hispanics, it might call for copy in Spanish.

Budgeting

When determining the size and scope of the campaign, it is necessary to set a budget allocation for the project. The costs should be divided among the various media necessary to complete the campaign and the different promotional tools, if any, that might round out the undertaking. Even the major retailers are cost-conscious.

Anticipated Outcomes

It is extremely important to set goals for the campaign. They may be merely overall sales figures, numbers of transactions, and so forth. In this way, when the final evaluation of the project is reviewed, it will be easy to see if the anticipated goals were reached.

Advertising Media Selection

With all of the media available to the retailer, it is important to earmark those media that have the most potential for a successful campaign. Newspapers have long been a retail advertising mainstay, but newer outlets such as the Internet and social networks might also be considered.

Promotional Devices

In addition to the ad campaign, many merchants use a variety of promotional tools, including special events such as fashion shows, to complete their campaigns. These tools should be carefully chosen and used to maximize consumer response.

Advertising and Promotional Design

After the media has been selected and the promotional tools have been chosen for the campaign, it is important for the design of the undertaking to be considered. Artwork, copy, agency participation, and so forth must be addressed to make certain that all of the elements of the campaign have been fully addressed.

Advertising Placement

At this point, the ads must be sent to the media that has been selected. The ads may be placed by agencies or by the retailers themselves. Care must be exercised to make certain that the ads reach the media in a timely manner so that they can be examined before the actual placement occurs. This will prevent any misunderstandings or errors that could mar the outcome of the campaign.

Evaluating the Outcome

It is essential to determine whether the campaign has sufficiently produced the anticipated outcomes. This may be accomplished in-house or by a marketing research firm. In either case, it is important to learn if the right approaches were used or if some adjustments should be made for future campaigns.

The following is an example of how a small retailer can use a campaign to improve recognition and increase sales.

The Case of a Promotion for a Small Merchant

Fairfax Gallery, a small chain of art galleries with two units, is typical of most small retail chain organizations. The owner oversees the entire operation, which employs a manager for each shop and six other employees who handle sales, frame making, delivery, and so on.

In addition to selling original artwork directly to consumers, the galleries regularly feature special events to promote the works of individual artists. It is for this type of endeavor that Fairfax Gallery undertakes a full-scale promotional campaign to ensure success. Being a small retail operation, it has neither in-house staff nor an outside PR firm to oversee its promotional activities. Instead, with the knowledge of promotional planning the proprietor has accumulated through his years in business, his relationship with the local media, and the aid of a freelancer, many special events have resulted in significant sales as well as positive image building for the company.

Focus 17.1 provides insight into the operation of the Fairfax Gallery.

In the event about to be discussed in detail, the gallery owner Jack Slaughter; signature artist

Fairfax Gallery

In 1994, fresh out of college, Jack Slaughter attempted to fulfill his dream of becoming a retail entrepreneur. While he was in college, he supported himself by working in a frame shop and learned how to make frames for pieces of art. With the technical knowledge he accumulated from that endeavor and the knowledge he gained from taking business courses, he decided to open a frame shop of his own.

After graduation, he rented a small shop in his hometown in an upscale area that was inhabited by people who were interested in art. Opening The Framing Establishment was his first step toward his ultimate goal of becoming an art dealer. His reputation grew from word-of-mouth advertising, and eventually he was able to hire another individual to help him with his framing orders. After 3 years, he decided to purchase a small building in the area that would give him more space for his expanding venture. The move was a good one that resulted in his becoming the premier framer in the market.

In business for 5 years, Slaughter decided to try his hand at selling art. The shop was transformed into a gallery with the framing portion moved upstairs. The profits from the framing enabled him to promote the art. Slaughter represented local "emerging" artists and was able to get a small return on his art investment.

The turning point that led to his opening a second gallery and becoming recognized as a force in the Jacksonville, Florida, art world was his chance meeting with Ellen Diamond, an art professional who had just moved to the area from New York. After seeing her work, he decided she was the artist he would promote, a decision that helped him become a mainstay for interior designers who purchased art for their clients.

With two galleries, each serving upscale markets, he focused his efforts on Diamond's works and fulfilled his dream of entrepreneurship.

Source: Personal interview.

Ellen Diamond; Diamond's husband, who had previous experience with publicity; a representative of JDRF, the beneficiary of the proceeds expected to be realized from the event; and a freelance professional all played a role in its planning.

Planning Strategy

Several months before the special event took place, the group of individuals met to explore the manner in which it would go forward. Ellen Diamond, the artist to be highlighted in the promotion, has gained recognition for her garden and landscape paintings, which were inspired by her travels both in the United States and abroad. Given her recognition by critics and collectors, the group decided that a one-woman show would be best to underscore her talent and bring attention to the gallery. They named the upcoming presentation Courtyards and Gardens.

After carefully examining a list of events that would take place within the 6-month period under consideration for the show, and to make certain that the opening night would not have competition from any other events scheduled for that time in the gallery's trading area, a date was chosen.

This initial meeting, the first of several, addressed such areas as the number of original pieces of art that would be needed for the show, promotional tools that would be used to publicize the event, the specific roles of those involved in the planning, the budget, and so forth. Each participant was given his or her assignment to bring the promotion to fruition. The gallery chosen for the event was the larger of the two that Fairfax operates.

Promotional Tools

The group knew that a number of different promotional tools would be needed to guarantee a successful turnout. They determined that their budget would allow for print advertising, an outdoor banner for the gallery announcing the exhibit, the purchase of a mailing list to augment the gallery's and the JDRF's existing lists, the design and printing of posters, and re-freshments to be served. Of utmost importance in the planning was the manner in which **free publicity** would be achieved from the editorial community.

Advertising

With limited money for advertising, it was agreed that a full-page ad was warranted in one of the city's major arts and business publications. Available at numerous locations throughout the city and by subscription, *Arbus* magazine (Focus 17.2) was selected as the publication most likely to reach the surrounding art community and prospective purchasers of art.

The advertisement occupied the **inside back cover** of *Arbus*, one of the locations considered most beneficial to advertising, and featured a headline that spelled out the artist's name across the top of the ad, a subheadline that presented the exhibit's title, the dates of the run, a mention of the artist's reception, the gallery name and location, and mention of the Juvenile Diabetes Research Foundation as recipient of a portion of the proceeds. Figure 17.1 is a copy of the *Arbus* ad.

In addition to the magazine advertisement, a smaller piece was placed in the *Ponte Vedra Recorder*, a local newspaper received by an affluent community within reach of the gallery. The group agreed the exposure through this newspaper warranted the nominal cost of the ad.

The broadcast media was considered as an adjunct to newspapers and magazines. The group decided, however, that a television commercial was beyond budget and radio was the wrong venue for a visually oriented project.

What did appeal to the group was direct-mail advertising. An eye-catching mailer would warrant the expense involved in its design and the costs of mailing the pieces. The freelancer involved in the campaign had the professional training to create a direct-mail brochure. The expense of producing the brochure was considered nominal for the sales results and publicity it was expected to produce for the gallery and the artist. The mailing was sent to the gallery's own list, the JDRF's list, and selected ZIP codes purchased from a **list house**. Figure 17.2 shows the direct-mail piece.

The brochure was mailed 10 days before the exhibit opened to allow sufficient time for it to reach the targeted audience. Using **PRSRT first class mail**, which requires a permit from the U.S. Postal Service and that the mailing be presorted according to mailing routes, provided a reduced mailing rate. It also allowed for undeliverable pieces to be returned so that the names and addresses of those households could be removed from future mailings.

Another method that was used to attract people to the exhibit was e-mail. The JDRF had an extensive list of e-mail addresses of those who had patronized some of the fund-raising events in the past and would probably be interested in the organization's newest effort to raise money. Its list, coupled with the one Fairfax Gallery had accumulated, was used for a blast campaign to augment the other advertising activities.

The final advertising component used in the campaign was a poster. Five hundred pieces were printed and distributed to various places in the surrounding communities. They were displayed in libraries, schools and colleges, store windows and doorways, and other such places to attract passersby. A copy of the poster is featured in Figure 17.3.

Visual Merchandising

For those motivated by the advertising campaign to visit the gallery and for the pedestrian and vehicular traffic that typically pass the gallery, visual merchandising was considered next. The main window would feature the painting that was used in the magazine ad and poster. The smaller windows would feature other paintings in the collection. A large banner, pictured in Figure 17.4, would hang on a prominent wall outside the gallery to attract the passersby.

Inside the gallery, the paintings were hung according to what each painting depicted, giving order to the presentation. Lighting was the essential element that brought attention to each piece.

Refreshments

At the rear of the gallery, in the third exhibit room, there was a bar replete with wine, beer, soft drinks, and an assortment of finger food. The

Arbus

Arbus, the magazine that would eventually become the definitive outlet for north Florida's arts and business community, was first published in 1993 in Jacksonville, Florida. The brainchild of its publisher, Cinda Sherman, it has steadily gained recognition from the community it serves. Published seven times annually, *Arbus* reaches a large audience through subscription and availability at outlets throughout Jacksonville and many surrounding areas.

Originally a one-woman operation, the magazine now features numerous contributing writers and photographers. Regular features include coverage of the social events of the community, an arts and events calendar, art perspectives, art-oriented articles, highlights of women in business, and articles that deal with the current art and business communities.

Arbus has become the vehicle in which businesses and art galleries regularly advertise. The pages of each issue are replete with stories that are beautifully enhanced by exceptionally artistic layouts designed by professionals. The cover of each issue is carefully designed to bring attention to the magazine and generally focuses on an art-related event in its trading area.

Other publications have had difficulty in maintaining a loyal readership and some have ceased operation, but *Arbus* continues to serve the art and business community with its award-winning format.

ELLEN DIAMOND

COURTYARDS & GARDENS

APRIL 4-19, 2008
Artist's Reception: Friday, April 4, 5:30-8pm

⨍ fairfax gallery

4216 HERSCHEL ST., JACKSONVILLE, FL 32210 · WEBSITE: ELLENDIAMOND.COM · 904.384.7724

A portion of the proceeds will be donated to the Juvenile Diabetes Research Foundation

17.1 *(opposite)* Advertising in a local art magazine, *Arbus*, brings attention to a special event. *Arbus*, March/April, 2008. *Courtesy of* Arbus *Magazine.*

17.2 Direct mail brings the special event message right to the consumer. *Courtesy of the Fairfax Gallery.*

17.3 A poster announcing the Courtyard and Gardens event was placed in a variety of locations frequented by art enthusiasts. *Courtesy of the Fairfax Gallery.*

positioning of the refreshment center was important so that visitors had to walk past the entire
exhibit to enjoy the refreshments. In this way, every
piece of artwork received attention from the guests.

The beverages and finger food were donated by
local businesses. This arrangement is typical of
events with a charity component. Both the event
planners and the sponsors benefit from this arrangement: the planners for budgetary reasons
and the sponsors from the positive exposure.

Publicity

The success of any retail special event often
depends on the exposure it gets from the media.

Alongside the paid-for advertising, free publicity
from the editorial press is an invaluable contribu-
tion to the event. Consumers realize that advertising is a form of promotion and that its content
is sometimes biased in terms of the way the
advertiser tells the story. Publicity, on the other
hand, a "free" promotional benefit, is considered
to be less biased than advertising.

Achieving a substantial amount of publicity
from the media is accomplished by using a
seasoned public relations professional. It is often
accomplished with the use of **press releases**,
as discussed in Chapter 16, "Public Relations:
Promoting and Advancing the Retailer's Image."
The press release that was used for this event is
featured in Figure 17.5.

17.4 A banner with
recurring special
events theme is used
to attract passersby.
*Courtesy of the Fairfax
Gallery.*

ELLEN DIAMOND: Courtyards and Gardens
April 4-19

A new exhibit by one of Florida's most renowned artists, Ellen Diamond, will be presented at the Fairfax Gallery in Avondale for two weeks beginning with a **grand opening on April 4 from 5:30 to 8:00 PM**. Her contemporary impression painting style will be seen in a variety of works that capture the essence of exciting courtyards and gardens both in the United States and abroad. Inspired by visits to magnificent gardens and courtyards in foreign lands such as Paris, Giverny, the Cote D-Azur, Provence, Tuscany, and Mexico, domestic areas such as Napa Valley and Charleston, as well as Jacksonville and Ponte Vedra Beach have inspired her to create this magnificent collection.

The recipient of many awards, her reputation has gained her national and international recognition and is found in private as well as corporate collections.

In addition to providing a "feast for the eyes", the exhibit will also benefit the Juvenile Diabetes Research Foundation with a donation of a portion of the proceeds.

Ellen Diamond will be at the Fairfax Gallery in Avondale on Friday, April 4 beginning at 5:30 PM to answer any questions you might have about her style of painting, inspirations, background, and training.

17.5 A press release announces the impending special event to the media. *Courtesy of the Fairfax Gallery.*

arbus

NORTH FLORIDA'S ARTS & BUSINESS MAGAZINE
MARCH/APRIL 2008

THE ART OF WATER GARDENS · WOMEN IN BUSINESS · JACKSONVILLE JAZZ FESTIVAL

17.6 The *Arbus* magazine cover gives
the event a great deal of free publicity.
Arbus, March/April, 2008.
Courtesy of Arbus *Magazine.*

17.7 Unusually large coverage of this special event gave a significant amount of free publicity to the retailer and the artist, as seen by the eight-page artist profile featured in *Arbus*. *Arbus*, March/April, 2008.
Courtesy of Arbus *Magazine*.

Spring Blossoms

ARTIST PROFILE:

ELLEN DIAMOND'S
LIGHTNESS OF BEING

BY JANET HERRICK

If you stare at an Ellen Diamond painting long enough you see more than just the layers of her training, you see the layers of her train of thought. Composition is everything to her when creating a work of art. Her post-impressionistic brushwork and sensibilities, and her love of light and color give vibrancy to her work, but it's her composition that anchors it. In her latest collection of work, Courtyards and Gardens, Diamond paints more than a history of the physical, she creates spaces infused with a sense of possibility.

DELPHINIUMS IN THE COUNTRYSIDE

TWO FAR LEFT: SAN MIGUEL COURTYARD; THE IRIS PATH; GARDEN STEPS

The main characters of Diamond's paintings are not people, but the components of place itself in the absence of people. In essence, space and place are both actor and stage. The mood of light, texture of architecture, characteristics of flora, and deep perspective of the pathway pulls the viewer in. To her, courtyards and gardens are the ultimate place of possibility. These are places with stories to tell, if one just listens closely enough. They are spaces where people meet to laugh and love, mourn and heal, reflect and grow. Diamond explains that, in Europe, courtyards and gardens were as essential to a home's layout as the kitchen or bedroom. "But in the U.S.," she says, "these types of spaces are harder to find unless you go to a city with a long European influence. Savannah and Charleston are examples of two such places."

Therefore, when she visits areas like these, both in Europe and the U.S., she becomes a shutterbug, shooting roll after roll of film to collect as much visual information as she can. When she returns to her studio, she goes through all her images, again and again, looking for the one thing from each image that speaks to her. "Look at that wall," she says as she riffles through an enormous shoebox of photos taken from one city alone. "Look at those roof tops. Ah! Look at those windows! Look at those geraniums! There is so much to choose from. I love putting all of these individual parts together to create a new space." Color is just as important as composition to Diamond, and is integral to her identity as an artist. "My passion is to take a simple subject and interpret it into something that is exciting in color. With...color as my favorite ingredient, I attack each canvas with gestural brushstrokes and a spontaneity that achieves a contemporary impressionist style."

Diamond's studio is walled with hundreds of art books that she regularly thumbs through for insight. "I've recently been studying Bonnard paintings that emphasize intense vertical lines on tall narrow canvases, not just in the painting, but the shape of the canvas itself. Again, I am not so much looking at how he painted his pieces, but how he crafted his compositions. I challenge myself when I take on such a perspective."

LUNCH IN A TUSCAN GARDEN

71

CHARLESTON COURTYARD

BENCH AT THE CUMMER GARDENS

A FRIENDSHIP BLOOMS IN FAIRFAX.

Diamond's unique vision of space and color was the seed of her early relationship with Jack Slaughter, owner of Fairfax Gallery in Avondale and Ponte Vedra. Says Slaughter, "About ten years ago, when Ellen first came to my gallery in Avondale to show me some of her work, I immediately knew that this was to become a lasting relationship. For many years, artists came to me to represent them; some were talented, others just didn't have it. Seeing Ellen's paintings was a different experience. Her magnificent canvases took my breath away, and have been doing so since our first meeting."

Diamond was thrilled to find that Slaughter really understood her processes, and the relationship between them took root and quickly grew, as did her fan base. "My clientele is, at once, in love with her paintings," explains Slaughter, "whether they capture the local landscapes, or the vistas of Provence and Tuscany, which she regularly visits each summer to paint in plein air. So many of the collectors of her work wait in anticipation for her to return from abroad to see what she has produced. They have learned that with each trip there will be bountiful canvases to please their senses. Her shoreline subjects of North Florida, sunflower fields and markets in Provence, seascapes on the Côte D'Azure, fields in Tuscany, and the St. Johns waterways have become favorites in my galleries and ultimately in private and corporate collections."

BRINGING INSPIRATION HOME.

Diamond has taken the cue from the power of courtyards that she has so admired and created her own delicious

BENCH AT THE CUMMER GARDENS

PALM VALLEY GARDENS

private botanical space at her home in Ponte Vedra. An undulating stone path leads from the back patio to terraced bedding and potted flowers, and settles on the central focal point—a cascading waterfall. "I love the sound of the water," says Diamond, as she closes her eyes and soaks in the sound. "It can soothe me the way nothing else can." The view of her garden from her second story art studio, bordered by the marshes of Guana River State Park just beyond, is breathtaking. "Listen hard enough on a quiet day," she says, "and you can hear the Atlantic Ocean breaking in the distance." It's the kind of space that begs to be painted. And like her paintings, the composition of her garden anchors the space where color and light play upon each other to entice the senses. "Yes," she says, "I am so very happy not to have to travel far for inspiration. I treasure this space."

The Zen quality of her home allows Diamond to immerse herself in her work, and she continues to build her collection of courtyard and garden images for her two-week show at the Fairfax Gallery in Avondale beginning April 4.

Says Slaughter, "Her latest effort of capturing the brilliance of courtyards and gardens, both here and abroad, promises to bring accolades from collectors and critics alike. Seeing a preview of some of the latest collection in her studio has reminded me of her uncanny ability to interpret what she has seen into breathtaking paintings."

GIVING ART FROM THE HEART.

The Courtyards and Gardens show has inspired Diamond in many ways and on many levels. "Painting has been my way of communicating with art lovers," she says. "Inspired by an overwhelming response to my work,

I continue to be motivated by the wonderful reception of my pieces. Just give me a canvas, and a handful of paints and brushes, and I will spend each day bringing joy to my life."

But there is another element about the show that is driving Diamond: it is her love for her grandson, Michael Litt.

"Michael was diagnosed with juvenile diabetes at age thirteen, but he's got a great spirit, and he's also had tremendous support. Now he is a senior at Stanton College Prep High School, he's captain of the basketball team and he's a great academic student. In honor of him, I am donating a portion of the funds raised from the Courtyards and Gardens show to the Juvenile Diabetes Research Fund." Diamond is not new to this type of generosity: she is widely known and well respected for her support of many fine organizations to whom she has donated work. As both her artwork and deeds show, Ellen Diamond's strong inner core anchors her in joy, and allows her work to express her buoyant lightness of being.

Courtyards and Gardens, April 4 to 18, 2008. Fairfax Gallery, 4216 Herschel Street, Jacksonville, 384-7724.

BUQUET FROM THE GARDEN

Another way publicity is achieved by the retail community is by developing positive relationships with the press. A positive rapport with the media often provides access to those who write and deliver favorable publicity pieces.

Jack Slaughter and the publisher of *Arbus* magazine had developed a longtime relationship that often brought about positive publicity for the events he presented. In the Fairfax Gallery special event, this relationship helped to garner significant publicity for Ellen Diamond's Courtyard and Gardens exhibition.

Also important in the amount of page space devoted to publicizing the exhibition was the publisher's enthusiasm for the work of the artist. The two circumstances led to a significant amount of publicity for the special event. Finally, the fact that this event benefited a charity ensured that this exhibition was perceived as a socially responsible activity for its readership.

Publicity in the *Arbus* issue that preceded the opening of Courtyards and Gardens was achieved in three separate spaces of the publication.

Magazine Cover

A coup for the event was achieved when *Arbus* decided to feature four panels of art from the Courtyards and Gardens event on its cover. The four pieces of art from the collection, placed in an eye-appealing fashion, graced the March/April cover of the magazine, shown in Figure 17.6. It not only served the magazine well but also gave the upcoming event considerable exposure.

Artist Profile

An unusually large profile of the artist was featured in *Arbus*. A story based on an interview with Ellen Diamond filled eight pages. Accompanying the article were numerous full-color depictions of the works of art that were featured in the exhibition. The article with all of the artwork is featured in Figure 17.7.

Art Perspective

A two-paragraph summary of the exhibit was featured in the "Art Perspectives" section of the magazine. This provided yet another level of publicity for the Courtyards and Gardens special event.

Culmination of the Promotion

When the day finally arrived for the Courtyards and Gardens special event to occur, all of the planning proved to be beneficial to the gallery, the featured artist, and the JDRF. Large crowds were attracted to the gallery for the opening and for the 2-week period that followed. Not only did it give favorable publicity to Fairfax Gallery and Ellen Diamond, but each was rewarded by significant sales. The JDRF benefited from a portion of the proceeds and raised public awareness of juvenile diabetes.

Summary of Key Points

◆ The steps in running a campaign are essential to follow so that it will benefit the retail organization, no matter how large or small.

◆ Small retailers wanting to promote a special event may do so without using a public relations firm by either using a freelancer or by using the do-it-yourself approach.

◆ When planning a special promotion, it is essential to arrange a planning strategy before any advertising or publicity is pursued.

◆ A successful special promotion is generally assured if there is significant advertising for the event and some publicity is achieved from the editorial press.

◆ The expenses of running a special promotion may be offset by the retailer if he or she partners with another entity.

◆ Publicity comes from the use of press releases and the continued positive relationship with the media.

For Discussion

1. How does the small retail operation differ from its large counterparts in terms of achieving public relations?

2. How did the proprietor of the Fairfax Gallery tackle the problem of promoting the gallery's special event without the use of an outside PR firm?

3. With very limited funds for advertising, why did Fairfax choose *Arbus* magazine to promote Courtyards and Gardens?

4. In addition to doing its own promotion for the special event, what other approach was used to gain publicity?

5. Why was a banner used to announce the special event?

6. How did Fairfax Gallery provide refreshments for the event without incurring any expense of its own?

7. What was the reason for the unusual amount of free publicity space that *Arbus* provided to publicize the Courtyards and Gardens event?

8. What were the three forms of publicity that Fairfax received from *Arbus* magazine?

Exercises and Projects

1. Using the Fairfax event Courtyards and Gardens as a guide, select an event (a fashion show, a charity luncheon, etc.) that a small store might choose to promote itself and its merchandise, keeping in mind that the use of an outside PR firm is too costly. List and describe the various steps, in terms of advertising and promotion, that might ensure free publicity for the event.

2. Prepare a press release for the media to publicize a special promotion (of your choosing) for a small store operation. The release must include all of the pertinent information to make it appeal to the market served by the merchant. Assign a title to the event, and complete a document that should grab the attention of the editorial press.

Terms of the Trade

do-it-yourself promotional planning

free publicity

freelance consultant

inside back cover

list house

press releases

PRSRT first class mail

Index

Nielsen Media Research, 83, 204, 212, 213, 264
Nielson Online, 162
Noncompeting companies, 136
Nonethnic population, 83
Nonprofits, partnering with, 120
Nordstrom (retailer), 40, 106, 115, 291, 335
Nouveau riche, 66
NPD Group (market research firm), 347
NutriSystem, Inc., 117–19
N.W. Ayer & Son (ad agency), 7

O, The Oprah Magazine, 198, 199
Obama, Barack, 20, 46, 80, 91, 122
Objective-and-task method, 108–9
Occupation, purchase decisions and, 61
Office of Consumer Protection (Pinellas County, Florida), 37
Offset lithography, 300, 302
Offset paper, 307
Off-the-card rates, 192
Omnicom Group (holding company), 131, 132
One-second commercial, 313
Online editions (newspapers), 84, 91, 156
Online focus groups, 74
Online radio services, 217–18, 220, 227
Online utilization, 238–39
    See also Internet
On-screen movie theater ads, 272
Open-back windows, 360
Original photography, 369
Orlando, Tony, 117, 118
Osmond, Marie, 117, 118
Outdoor advertising, 13, 259–77
    advantages and disadvantages of, 274–75
    backlit transparencies, 93, 272, 273
    digital billboards, 264–65, 268
    8-sheet posters, 268
    ethnic minorities and, 93
    exterior transit panels, 268, 271–72
    formats for, 263–72
    government regulation of, 263
    industry associations, 260–63
    painted bulletins, 268
    shopping bags, 259, 273–74
    30-sheet posters, 265
    Traffic Audit Bureau and, 263
Outdoor Advertising Association of America (OAAA), 262, 263
Out-of-home advertising industry, 263
Out-of-Home Video Advertising Bureau (OVAB), 260, 265

Packaged Facts (research firm), 80
Package pricing, radio, 224, 225
Painted bulletins, 268
Palmer, Volney B., 130
Pantone Color Institute, 297
Paper selection, 307
Partnering, 120
    special events, 349, 350
Patagonia, Inc., 17, 42, 44, 247, 249
Patronage motives, for buying, 72
Payne, Neil, 24
Pennants, 369
Percentage-of-sales method, 108, 111
Per column inch, 168

Performance-based fees, 138
Permanent bulletin, 268
Personal appearances, 337, 338
    See also Celebrity appearances
Personal communication, 222
Pew Internet and American Life Project, 97, 234
Photoengraving, 303
Photographic portfolios, 358–59
Photography
    digital, 304
    halftones, 304–5
    in-stock, 282, 369
    original, 369
Physiological needs, 70, 71
Pica (type measurement), 169, 170, 303
Pink sheet, 196
Planning strategies, 11
    advertising, 116–22
    integrated marketing communications, 103–5
    newspaper ads, 174
    See also Budgeting strategies
Playbill magazine, 186
Podcasts, 395
Point-of-purchase advertising, 14, 127
Point-of-sales signage, 127
Point (type measure), 303
Pollack, David, 235
Population concentration
    ethnic groups, 84
    purchasing behavior and, 60–61
    See also Demographic analysis
Pop-under advertisements, 239
Pop-up advertisements, 239
Portable people meter (PPM), 226
Position preference, 192
Position rates, newspaper, 170–71
Postproduction
    radio ads, 323
    TV ads, 319
Pottery Barn (retailer), 252, 253
PR. *See* Public relations
Prandoni, Paolo, 264
Preferred position rates, 170–71
Preprinted inserts, 160, 167
    See also Inserts
Preproduction
    radio advertising, 320–23
    TV advertising, 312–18
President's week displays, 136, 370–71
Press kits, 389
Press releases, 387–89, 409–10
Prestige products, 71, 194
    See also Luxury goods
Price points, 105
    magazine, 179
Pricing
    eBay, 239
    radio air time, 224
    television ads, 312
    See also under Cost; Budgeting strategies
Primary colors, 294
Principles of design, 290–91, 293
Print advertisements, 7, 234, 281–309
    artwork, 282–83, 290, 303–7
    color in, 294–99
    components of, 285–301

cost comparison, 160
creation of, 282–85
creativity in, 281–82, 284
layout artist for, 283–85
layout preparation, 300–301
logos, 286, 288, 289
paper selection for, 307
producing, 300–307
    See also Magazine advertisements; Newspaper advertisements
Printers Ink Model Law of 1911, 21, 23
Printing processes, 300, 302–3
    four-color, 160, 167, 305
Print media, public relations and, 390–93
    See also Magazines; Newspapers
Prismatic displays, 369
Private brands, 7, 15–16, 106–8
Private sales, 350, 351
PRIZM (Potential Rating Index ZIP Code Market), 61
Product advertising, 14, 109
    in magazines, 194
    in newspapers, 163
Product demonstrations, 336–37
Production, radio ads, 323
Production costs, 212
    See also under Cost
Product placement, 23
Profitability, 14, 16–17
Project billing, 138
Promotional advertising, 7, 109
    in newspapers, 119, 163–64
    special promotions, 9
    top ad agencies in, 133
Promotional campaign, 401, 403–11
    direct-mail brochure, 404–5, 407
    planning strategy, 404
    poster, 405, 408
    tools for, 404–5
Promotional devices, 402
Promotional direction, 14
Promotional planning, 401
Proofing, 305, 307
Proportion, 290
Props, for visual displays, 357, 361, 363–65, 373–74
PRSRT (presort) first class mail, 405
Psychographic segmentation, 64–66
Psychology, of color, 297–99
Publicity, 387, 388, 404, 409–11
Public relations (PR), 41, 142, 379–97
    broadcast media and, 394
    community relations and, 389–90
    components of, 387–90
    crisis communications plan, 381–83
    deadlines for, 391–92, 394
    getting messages placed, 390–96
    image and, 379
    independent firms, 380, 382–83
    in-house departments, 380
    press releases, 387–89, 409–10
    responsibility for effective, 380–86
    sponsorships, 390, 391
Public Relations Society of America (PRSA), 395, 396
Public relations specialist, 379
Puffery (exaggerated claims), 32, 242
Purchasing power, 83
    See also Buying